AF632411

LIBRARY USE AND USER RESEARCH
(With Twenty Case Studies)

By the Same Author

1. Information Behaviour of Scientists and Engineers: A Case Study of Indian Space Technologists (1995)

About the Author

Dr. M.S. Sridhar is a post-graduate in mathematics and business management and a doctorate in library and information science. He is in the profession for last three decades. For last 23 years he is heading the Library and Documentation Division of ISRO Satellite Centre, Bangalore. Earlier he has worked in the Libraries of National Aeronautical Laboratory (Bangalore), Indian Institute of Management (Bangalore) and University of Mysore. Dr. Sridhar has published 42 research papers in professional journals, presented over 20 papers in conferences and seminars, delivered a number of professional lectures and published three books entitled *User Research: A Review of Information Behaviour Studies in Science and Technology; Problems of Collection Development in Special Libraries* and *Information Behaviour of Scientists and Engineers.*

LIBRARY USE AND USER RESEARCH

(With Twenty Case Studies)

M.S. SRIDHAR
M.Sc., M.Lib.Sc., MBA, Ph.D.
Head, Library and Documentation
ISRO Satellite Centre, Bangalore

CONCEPT PUBLISHING COMPANY, NEW DELHI-110059

All rights reserved. No part of this work may be reproduced, stored in a retrieval system, or transmitted in any form or by any means, electronic, mechanical, photocopying, recording or otherwise, without the prior written permission of the copyright owner and the publisher.

ISBN 81-7022-969-3

First Published 2002

© M.S. **Sridhar** (*b.* 1949)

Published and Printed by
Ashok Kumar Mittal
Concept Publishing Company
A/15-16, Commercial Block, Mohan Garden
NEW DELHI-110 059 (India)

Phones: 5351460, 5351794
Fax: 091-11-5357103
Email: publishing@conceptpub.com

Dedicated
to
My Wife
Late S. Suvarna

PREFACE

User studies and user research have been very systematised in UK, USA and other countries over the last three decades. India is catching up with the west in this regard and the present book comprising twenty user studies is a notable contribution.

Dr. M.S. Sridhar, Head, Library and Documentation Division of Indian Space Research Organisation Satellite Centre, Bangalore has over a period of more than ten years carried out these studies with Space Scientists as his clientele and brought to bear their typical needs, use of library collection and the nature of their interactions with the library, their information and communication behaviour as well as their information seeking and gathering behaviour. The findings have been quite beneficial in enhancing the effectiveness of the library/information services. The author has examined in great depth the same set of user population over a decade which considerably helps all those interested in having an insight into the behaviour patterns of the users as they interact with the library. It is a significant contribution indeed. The value of the findings is enhanced by the use of combination of latest tools and techniques of investigation, which is another prominent feature of the case studies.

The first three chapters, viz., 'Understanding the User', 'A Review of Use and User Studies in Science and Technology', and 'Background about the Case Studies' could be considered as the introductory chapters to the actual case studies presented in the next seven chapters. With the increase in use of communication and information technologies in the libraries/information centres, there is the live danger of taking the user for granted. The author, thus, rightly brings home in the first chapter the need for and the ways in which the user could be understood. This is followed by a comprehensive review of the literature on use and user studies in Science and Technology. The next chapter gives the users, here the Space Scientists and Technologists and the library/information environment in which they live and interact.

Chapters 4 to 10 directly deal with twenty case studies which the author carried out over a period of ten years. Case Study 01 focuses on 'Patterns of user visit and in-house use' of ISAC library/information centre. The inferences drawn although appear to be simple carry greater importance. Case Study 02 deals with the user behaviour within the library and his interactions with the facilities and services provided. As the author points out there is dearth of such studies which helps in planning the physical layouts, relevance and utility of various services, etc.

Chapter 5 under the heading 'user requirement' presents 2 case studies. What are the real needs of scientists and technologists in a given environment has been a baffling question. Case Study 03 is a bold venture in this direction. The nature and type of information required by the space scientists and technologists have been identified and grouped under eleven heads and their frequency assessed. S&T news and basic S&T information get the top ranks among the needs.

The next Case Study 04 entitled 'Customer characteristics as criteria for market-segmentation' explores the possible correlation of information requirements of space scientists and technologists with their individual characteristics as users. Characteristics such as status, educational qualifications, subject specialisation, nature of work, experience, professional activities and achievements have been considered and their impact on information requirements examined based on field data which is indeed commendable and valuable contribution to user research.

Chapter 6 deals with user-participation in collection development which is another area where user studies have made notable contribution. In a special library, user participation in building a relevant collection which meets the complex and changing needs of the clientele assumes greater importance. The Case Study 05 brings home the low user-participation and the reasons thereof. The suggestions given by the users for procurement of books need serious consideration. Case Study 06 shows clearly that book procurement delay acts as a demotivator in user participation.

The next chapter 7 focuses on the live and current issues in special libraries. In all there are five case studies in this chapter, viz., 'Lent out use of library collection', 'Use of technical reports and standards', 'Subject and longitudinal use of books', 'Use and cost benefit analysis of current journals' and 'Non-use and non-users of libraries'.

Case Study 07 dealing with lent out use of library collection brings home higher use of books followed by reports and then standards. More importantly it brings out the limitations of use study. In the words of Sridhar, "If a use study is not properly designed with adequate reliability and validity", results can cause serious distortions and lead to disastrous decisions.

Case Study 08 compares the relative use of reports and standards. NASA and ESA reports are used heavily. Another finding, viz., 78 per cent of reports are not issued out even once and nearly 9 per cent of reports accounted for about 74 per cent of total use, is revealing. However, this study has helped ISAC library to know the nature of non-used reports and also how use is related to different issuing agencies, other criteria of a report.

Do the specialists have preference in the use of subject book? Which books are preferred? Is the use of subject books consistent over a period of time? Answers to such queries have been sought in the Case Study 09. 'The average use per book increases more uniformly, steadily and steeply in the case of use over year of acquisition than it does in the case of use distribution over age of book' is a revealing finding.

In the next Case Study 10, the author strives to caution user researchers on the application of the technique of cost benefit analysis (CBA) to decide the subscription policy of current journals. CBA may not provide a totally satisfactory solution to decide about the retention or rejection of a current journal. This technique, he points out, must be used in conjunction with intuitive judgment.

Non-use of library resources is a common phenomenon. But this is against the basic tenets of library/information science. Why readers do not use adequately the variety of information resources so thoughtfully (perhaps) collected by library professionals? Which resources are there? What personal characteristics promote/hinder use/non-use of resources? Such are the issues that worry a serious librarian. The author takes up these issues in the Case Study 11 entitled 'Non-use and Non-users of libraries'. The survey points out that there is a need to identify the characteristics of the non-users and their specific needs. Status, academic/ professional qualifications, nature of work performed are the characteristics positively related to the use/non-use relationship. Again promotion of academic/professional activities turns the non-users as users of libraries.

In chapter 8, three case studies are presented relating to 'User interactions with library'. Routine and ordinary user interactions like document reservation pattern, behaviour of users while consulting a card catalogue have been well studied and useful implications drawn. The Case Study 12 on document reservation brings out meaningful implications of document reservation pattern for designing a better lending system and collection development policy. The Case Study 13 on card catalogue points out that in ISAC library the classified catalogue is least used while the subject catalogue is heavily used. One important implication drawn here is that there is need to change the arrangement of charged slips from the accession number of the documents to their call numbers or report numbers.

The Case Study 14 is a unique one. Very few such studies have been done in India. Here, the author has painstakingly developed 'library-use index' and 'library-interaction index' which he defines elaborately and their relationship with the personal characteristics of users like status, qualifications, nature of work and specialisation studied. These indices serve as rational devices in understanding information-behaviour of scientists and technologists. They also assist in making rational assessment and effectiveness of ISAC library. More such studies in different work environment would be helpful.

The next set of 5 studies in Chapter 9 have been grouped under the heading, 'Information and Communication Behaviour'—an area which is heavily being investigated in the recent years. Case Study 15 attempts to study 'collaboration' in publishing among scientists and technologists of ISAC. There appears to be an inverse relationship between productivity of papers and the number of authors per paper. Further, it points out low productivity and high collaboration and co-authorship pattern among space technologists. Reasons for low productivity of papers have been traced. The study has also identified two large intersecting communication groups with 65 per cent of authors contributing 94 per cent of the papers.

When a particular author cites the work/works of another author/ authors, it indicates he considers the published work worth reporting and worthy of consideration by other researchers. Thus, citation patterns throw light on the communication behaviour among Science and Technology workers. Case Study 16 dwells on this issue. Ninety per cent of the space technologists communicate through conference papers and journals. In decreasing order of the sources cited are journals, books, technical reports and lastly, the conference papers. Another unusual finding is that for the space scientists and technologists, Indian journals and foreign and international conferences serve more as publishing outlets than sources for citing. Self-citation in very high. Indian journals claim a profile of "high publishing and low citing" as far as space S&T workers are concerned. Not all the journals highly used for publishing papers are highly cited and *vice versa*. It is gratifying to observe that all highly used journals for publishing papers and highly cited journals are available in the ISAC library. As expected, all highly cited journals are of foreign origin. However, 3 out of 8 highly used journals for publishing papers are of Indian origin.

Use, citation and publishing in journals is a cyclical process. But is there any correlation among these processes? The next Case Study 17, tries to find an answer to this query. Subject to certain limitations, it is found that there is slight positive correlation between publishing in and citing from a journal. However, use of journals is found to be independent of publishing and citing.

Case Study 18 deals with an interesting topic where very less research work is reported. Is there a difference between men and women scientists/technologists as far as information gathering and information communication are concerned? From the data gathered and analysed, it is found that women space technologists did not differ significantly from men in many aspects. The data bring home that women were more information conscious and active than men as far as seeking information from formal sources of information and contacting inter-personal sources of information within the organisation are concerned. However, women had difficulty in accessing inter-personal sources of information outside their organisation.

It is now well accepted that informal communication and inter-personal communication among scientists/technologists within an organisation act as important sources for information-gathering and dissemination. The author, in Case Study 19, has attempted a detailed analysis of communication behaviour of S&T personnel in ISAC. The study brings the variety of purposes for which S&T personnel seek informal communication and points how the library could play a significant role in such matters. A case is made to provide better formal services to these engineers who have been denied access to intensive informal communication networks. Another significant application the study brings out is that high information potentials, communication stars, technological gatekeepers and 'linking pins' need to be provided with extra formal information services so that they act as disseminating agents for formal information system. How true! Where our scientific and technical libraries stand in this regard?

The last Case Study 20 in chapter 10 reports about the ISB of Indian Space Technologists in relation to their personal characteristics like status, qualifications, nature of work, specialisation, experience, professional activities and achievements based 'performance' source of the outstanding findings of this localised study are worthy of consideration: (1) Information-services for increasing productivity and enhancing work performance, self-progress, departmental promotions, continuing education do differ very much from one another; (2) Current awareness services need to be provided to the scientists/technologists at their workspots; (3) Similarly, there is a necessity to provide information-services of the 'primary library' on a regular basis right at the place where the space technologists work; (4) A large part of the work-related information needed by the space technologists can be met from a well organised, comprehensive and internally-generated information sources like technical reports, conference papers etc. As such information cannot be provided to all, surrogates of such documents should be made available with a note about their location, etc.; (5) There is an urgent need to have a centralised data bank of trade literature; (6) There is a need for intermediary information specialists; (7) Encouraging and giving due credit for publishing activity is more likely to result in an increased use of literature more frequently and systematically.

Dr. M.S. Sridhar has taken pains to present based on actual case studies of Indian space technologists on a vide variety of issues delineating their implications for enhancing the effectiveness of an information system. Many of the findings are true for many of our other scientific/technical libraries. Citation of past studies and extensive literature used and suggestions made for further user research speak of his dedication and commitment to the information profession. This document serves well the students, the teachers, the library/information professionals as well as all those interested in enhancing the effectiveness of the scientific/technical libraries and information centres.

Prof. H.A. KHAN

Mysore
April 30, 2001

PREAMBLE

It is often said that many libraries in this country and elsewhere are established without systematic efforts to study the requirements of users. The process of understanding users is neither simple nor one time activity. Even after establishing a library with stated or assumed objectives, there is a constant and greater need to understand its customers, their interactions with library and their communication and information behaviour. Such activities, based on feedback, do help to rectify the fallacies in the design. A systematic evaluation of the library and its services is possible and become meaningful only when such studies are carried out. With this objective, many case studies have been carried out about the Indian space technologists who are the primary users of ISRO Satellite Centre Library. Here is a collection of twenty such case studies. Though each one appears to be independent, ISRO Satellite Centre Library and its users are at the helm of all these studies and they are integrated to give a holistic view of information behaviour of Indian Space Technologists. Most of them have already been reported in diverse set of professional journals and conferences.

The first chapter sets background about use and user studies. The second chapter reviews related past studies. The third chapter provides background for all case studies to follow. Chapters 4 to 10 group these twenty case studies in a logical and topical way. These case studies were developed independently as well as by-products of a main study of information seeking behaviour of Indian space technologists and hence some repetitions in introductory parts and data became inevitable. The results presented in these studies, especially those written before completion of main study, are tentative. Case studies are open for constructive criticism and valuable suggestions from all concerned.

I wish to express my sincere gratitude to Prof. H.A. Khan, Retired from Department of Library and Information Science, University of Mysore, Mysore (who was also the official guide for the research project), for his valuable guidance, suggestions and patient hearings and thought provoking discussions during a number of sittings over six years or so and also for his kind favour of a preface to the book.

I remain grateful to Dr. P.S. Goel, Director, ISRO Satellite Centre for kind permission to publish the book. My heartfelt thanks are due to my seniors and many friends and colleagues at ISAC whose encouragement and active participation and support have made these case studies possible.

I owe a lot to referees and editors of the journals in which these case studies are originally reported. I acknowledge their encouragement in my professional endeavour.

Lastly, I wish to thank M/s Concept Publishing Company, New Delhi for having undertaken the responsibility of publishing the book.

Bangalore M.S. SRIDHAR
August 21, 2001

CONTENTS

LIST OF TABLES

LIST OF FIGURES

LIST OF ACRONYMS AND ABBREVIATIONS USED

AIAA — American Institute of Aeronautics and Astronoutics

AMCP — Army Material Command Pamphlet (USA)

ANSI — American National Standards Institution

BARC — Bhabha Atomic Research Centre (India)

BASR — Bureau of Applied Social Research (Columbia University)

BRTT — British Reports, Translations and Thesis

BSI — British Standards Institution

CBA — Cost Benefit Analysis

CBRI — Central Building Research Projects

CEA — Cost Effectiveness Analysis

COSPAR — Committee on Space Research (International)

CRUS — Centre for Research on User Studies (University of Sheffield)

CRUSK — Centre for Research on Utilization of Scientific Knowledge

DOS — Department of Space (India)

ESA — European Space Agency

ESRO — European Space Research Organisation

GEC — General Electric Company (U.K.)

GFW — Society for Space Research (West Germany)

GRA&I — Government Reports, Announcements & Indexes

GSFC — Goddard Space Flight Centre (USA)

HIP — High Information Potential

IASLIC — Indian Association of Special Libraries and Information Centres

IEEE — Institute of Electrical and Electronics Engineers

ISAC — ISRO Satellite Centre

ISB — Information Seeking Behaviour

ISI — Indian Standards Institution

ISRO — Indian Space Research Organisation

ISSP — Indian Scientific Satellite Project

IST — Indian Space Technologists

JPL — Jet Propulsion Laboratory (USA)

JPRS — Joint Publications Research Service (USA)

JSS	—	Joint Services specification (Ministry of Defence, India)
KGI	—	Kiruna Geophysical Institute (Sweden)
LIP	—	Law Information Potential
MIL	—	Military Standard (USA)
MSFC	—	George C Marshal Space Flight Centre (USA)
NAL	—	National Aeronautical Laboratory (India)
NASA	—	National Aeronautics and Space Administration (US)
NOAA	—	National Oceanic and Atmospheric Administration (USA)
NRC	—	National Research Council (USA)
NTIS	—	National Technical Information Service (USA)
PB	—	Publication Board (USA)
PRL	—	Physical Research Laboratory (India)
RAC	—	Reliability Analysis Centre (Rome Air Development Centre, USA)
RADC	—	Rome Air Development Centre (USA)
RAE	—	Royal Aircraft Establishment (UK)
SCI	—	Science Citation Index
STAR	—	Scientific & Technical Aerospace Reports
TAC	—	Technology Application Centre (The University of New Mexico, USA)
TDP	—	Technology Development Programs
TIFR	—	Tata Institute of Fundamental Research (India)
UDC	—	Universal Decimal Classification
WFEO	—	World Federation of Engineering Organisations

1

UNDERSTANDING THE USER
Why, What and How?

User studies are quite familiar to everyone. Familiarity often leads to complacency and which in turn can cause retardation in further research. There is so much said about user studies that it becomes embarrassing to tell anything about the topic. An attempt is made here to present the significance and scope of user studies as well as the methods and techniques together with a step by step procedure for conducting sound user studies in a simple and brief way.

User studies, use studies, information-need studies, information transfer studies, communication behaviour studies, information dissemination and utilisation studies, user-research, etc., are all closely related and often not precisely defined. The terminology depends much on the approach and the angle from which one sees. There are several overlapping facets included in these studies. As such scope of user studies is enormous. User component will have bearing on almost all aspects of library and information system. For the purpose of this presentation let us assume that all such research inquiries about users (including non-users as well as potential users) with a view to understand their characteristic features, needs, preferences, practices, opinions, attitudes, behaviour, evaluations, etc., with respect to library and information services that are offered or likely to be or need to be offered. The ultimate aim is to help designing, altering, evaluating and improving efficiency and effectiveness of library and information systems and their products/services in meeting their predetermined goals. It may be noted here that use (and non-use) as well as user (and non-user) are with respect to information as well as services, collection, and whole library/information system.

It is also necessary to note the limitations of use and user studies. Use studies may not reveal the spill over effects of use, indirect use of a library and many fruitful interactions of users with library. Further, use of a library and its utility to users are often quite different. A library may be used but it may not be useful; another may be useful but may not be used; a third may be neither useful nor used and ideal is one which is both used and useful.

For understanding the user, many approaches (or models) have been used as conceptual frameworks. For example, constructivist model (Dervin) views information as something constructed by the user and says that individuals constantly strive to make sense of themselves and their environment through continual adjustments. Another cognitive model (Belkin) emphasises the cognitive activity in individual user and explore the problem state and how information is sought and matched to solve the problem. Another model (Taylor) seeks to understand how specific environment including physical setting, nature of information and nature and characteristics of problems affect information seeking by users. Yet another (Kuhlthau) identifies stages of research where intervention on the part of information professionals can help users both identify and resolve their information needs.

Need for Use and User Studies

'Use' is the key purpose and 'User' is the key and dynamic component of any library and information system. Customer oriented approach, design and evaluation are the founding pillars of any enterprise. As such use and user studies including non-use and non-user studies are required to be carried out as long as library and information systems are required and existing. Here, the use includes 'non-use' and user includes potential user, non-user, under-privileged, un-served, under-served and deprived users. A non-user could be an involuntary non-user who do not have a library to use or voluntary (wilful) non-user. A voluntary non-user is one who has access to a library and lives in an information rich society and yet suffers from information malnutrition (Sridhar, 1994).

User studies are a must at the time of designing a system or service. The efficient and effective operation of a library system or service also calls for periodic user studies. The effectiveness of a library and information system depends on the extent to which the system characteristics correspond with the users and in how much the potential users are willing and able to make use of it. System designers, planners and managers of library and information systems have to properly consider the role of human factors and their effect on acceptance and utilisation of information. Relating the system or product/service being designed to the perceived needs of those for whom it is intended as well as to guide the operation of the system by the knowledge about the user and to justify the existence of the system are essential. User studies can also stem from the efforts of evaluation of a system or service.

A systematic user study can also reveal some unanticipated data about the dynamic component of user. It may also promote a new course of action hitherto not considered and hence helps efficient and effective operation of the library and information system. Further, as no system has the luxury of unlimited resources and funds, user studies are required to check whether intended goals are served by the system, if not, to alter the priorities and programmes so as to ensure judicious allocation of limited resources. User studies are also required not only to determine and confirm the general patterns of use of libraries but also to identify departures from the norms (in specific cases), even if it is only in small areas. User studies help improve public relations of a library with its users and explain what librarians have found out by more indirect means. User studies, like market research, provide effective ground for marketing service products of libraries. In nutshell, user studies is an area of continuous librarian-education about users than user-education about library and understanding users is a must.

What to Understand about Users

Though existing records, MIS and other indirect data can provide knowledge about use and users of a library, for many of above tasks direct contact with users is necessary. By observing or questioning users, a systematic user study helps to discover (i) characteristics; (ii) information requirements (needs); (iii) behaviour, attitudes, opinions, priorities, preferences, and evaluations of users.

Characteristics of Users

No user-community of an information system is fully homogeneous. Though a majority of the users of a system would come together for a particular purpose and are comparable by one or two criteria, they are divided among themselves by many individual characteristics. As noted earlier, the knowledge of the population being served by an information system is an essential requirement for providing useful services. Just like understanding the user is half the battle in providing information-services, knowing the structure and composition of the user-community in terms of various characteristics by which they can be compared and contrasted is half the task in understanding the users.

The characteristics of users are innumerable and there are several ways of grouping them. Apart from identifying many characteristics of users as recipients of information the institutional environment and work activity (job) have major impact on information users. The three clusters of factors which affect user's utilisation of information are psychological factors, effectiveness of available services and characteristics of the user and his environment.

User-studies look for similarities and differences among the users in terms of their backgrounds like status, age, experience, education, specialisation, field of research, discipline, etc. When the analysis is at the organisation level (as against individual level) they look for differences in nature of organisations, and at the same time users were also grouped as theoreticians or fundamental research workers, experimentalists or applied research workers, technologists, technicians, practitioners, etc.

Most of the studies have adopted the individual as the unit of analysis. However, occasionally analyses have been carried out at group, unit or organisation levels treating the organisation as a composite entity and drawing typical representatives. At this level, variations within the organisation are ignored and the nature, type and size of the organization become variables.

In user studies with the individual as the unit of analysis, it is possible, and easy, to list many characteristics of individuals. Unless the relevance and the context of a user-characteristic are clearly established, it is likely that the results will be conflicting. "To attempt to isolate each environmental element seems hopeless, but awareness of the variety of environments may lead to potentially useful hypotheses" (Krikelas, 1983, p. 11). The number of systems to which each user belongs and the variety of roles he has to play are important in understanding the information-transfer process.

User-characteristics could be internal or external to the individual. They may also be classified as sociological, demographic, psychological, personality (work-related), organisational, professional, etc. Some specific characteristics of interest in user studies are age, experience, gender, educational level, performance, productivity, creativity, motivation, emotional stability, temperaments, interests, personal idiosyncrasies, productivity, communication, citation and other activities, nature of work or function, various roles, responsibilities, and status of users have also to be understood in user studies.

User Requirements

The deliberate use the term 'requirements' rather than the 'needs', 'wants' and 'demands' is because it represents all the three concepts. The information-requirements refer to a lookout for a sort of relevance of information to a given user and to his areas of concern, interest, and likes. In the process it is to know the amount of irrelevant information he is prepared to tolerate. Relevance is not a simple property inherent in information, but varies with content, format, context, the variety of uses of information as well as user himself. "The selection and reception of the information will depend upon the individual's conception of his own needs; one man's information is another man's noise . . ." (McGarry, 1975, p. 58).

It is extremely complex, varied and difficult to measure information-need. While discussing the issue of information-needs, a natural assumption is to consider the needs as perceived by the users. But some are of the view that there is a need to create information-needs among users if they do not exist and that information-seekers may be ignorant of the information that would be useful to them.

Information-needs are affected by many factors. Range and knowledge of information-sources/facilities available, varieties of uses to which information will be put, the background, motivation, professional orientation, discipline, type and area of work and other individual-characteristics of the user, the social, political and economic system as well as the consequences of information-use. Due to this contingency nature, generalised one-time conclusions about information-needs of users is impracticable. Of all the factors influencing or determining the user-needs, two factors which may not always be congruent, are the corporate objectives of the organisation where the user is employed, and the needs of the individual user.

Studies relating to 'information-needs' categorise needs as 'perceived needs' and 'actual or idealised needs', 'immediate needs' and 'deferred needs', 'continuous needs' and 'discrete needs', 'regular' and 'irregular needs'. Further, information needs could be unexpressed or expressed/articulated, felt or unfelt, dormant or deliquescent. In addition, information-needs of users can be expressed in terms of time (i.e., urgency), content and amount or quantity of information. Accordingly, information-needs have been classified as needs for single fact or exhaustive information. up-to-date, historical or current information, technical or business information. However, information-needs are frequently determined in terms of kind of message, i.e., nature and type of information, the types of document embodiments of information needed and the purpose of use. Very few studies have investigated and focused on the need for substance or nature of material in terms of characteristics of texts.

Some of the significant classifications, based on the nature and type of information sought by users, are personal, technical and task-related information, current, specific and exhaustive information, theoretical information, experimental results, data, methods and procedure information, educational information, methodical or how-to-do-it information and task-related information. In addition, it is also possible to determine the amount or level of information required in core *versus* peripheral areas of interest of users as well as the non-technical information required, information requirements in new fields *versus* old fields. The profession and organisation oriented, work-related information-needs are the main information-needs with which user studies are concerned apart from day-to-day personal needs, life-long learning or educational needs, and needs about the governing rules of the society around user.

Behaviour, Attitude, Priorities, Preferences, Opinions and Evaluations of Users

Behaviour is a broad concept. It involves attitudes and character traits of individuals as well as environmental determinants. Behaviour is considered to be a compromise and a result of multiple forces to which individuals are subjected to. Attitude itself is a latent state of readiness to respond in particular ways. They are normally dormant most of the time but they represent what we are prepared to do. In other words, attitude is a tendency to act or react in a certain manner when confronted with certain stimuli. Attitudes are expressed in speech or behaviour when object is perceived. Like other components of behaviour, attitude is an abstraction and hence it is difficult to directly measure attitude. One has to infer attitude from overt behaviour. Attitudes are often related to feelings and emotions.

An individual's enduring persistent response pattern across a variety of situations is called personality. It comprises of relatively stable patterns of action, i.e., traits, dispositional tendencies, motivations, attitudes and beliefs, which are combined into an integrated self-structure. 'Trait' is used to classify and describe certain persistent and fundamental human characteristics, both learned and original. In the increasingly enduring and deepening order we find beliefs followed by attitudes, values and personality in individuals.

There are many ways of looking at user behaviour in libraries and in relation to seeking, gathering, using and communicating information. For example, one may attempt to study motives and purposes of seeking information, nature and type of information required, ways and means of acquiring information, sources of bibliographic (reference) information used, delegation of information-gathering work, time spent on information-gathering activities, dependence on sources of information, tolerable delay in supplying information, satisfaction about existing sources of information, informal communication network and the communication behaviour, inter-personal information sharing, use of library and user interactions with the library, etc.

Research Procedure for Conducting User Studies

The unhappy relationship between research and practice in librarianship has often been aired by many experts as they are not mutually nourishing each other. Same is the case with relationship between research in librarianship and other related fields of inquiry. The need for looking at research, practice and education for librarianship as an integrated learning system has to be emphasised for development of librarianship as an academic discipline and achievement of excellence in professional practice. "Unless appropriate and sufficient research is conducted, the library community will not be able to transform itself but will be absorbed by other groups that will take over the information function in society" (Maguire, 1986, p. 3).

Having seen the importance and vast scope of user studies as well as the need for integrated approach to research in librarianship, let us see the scope of methods and techniques of user studies. Sound methods and techniques used in research serve as a barometer to measure the quality of research in that field. Tested methodology is very much required for research to enable researcher to objectively navigate through his research, to put him back in the right track in case he deviates from the path and to help him to achieve the objectives of his research without wasting his efforts.

User studies are basically concerned with people, their attitude, priorities, preferences and behaviours. Hence the methods and techniques used by social researchers particularly behaviour scientists and psychologists are quite relevant for user studies. It is neither feasible nor desirable to discuss in this presentation, the entire research methodology required for user studies. Some methods and techniques of research predominantly used or required to be used for sound user studies will be highlighted with certain limitations and problems, if any. Lastly, the terms 'method' and 'technique' are often almost interchangeably used. Methods and techniques are those used in performing research operations. While 'technique' refers to behaviour and instruments used in research operations, 'method' refers to behaviour and instruments used in selecting and constructing technique (i.e., methods are more general). On the other hand, research methodology is a science of studying how research is done scientifically. In other words, research methodology is a way to systematically solve the research problem by logically adopting various steps. Interestingly, research itself is a search for new knowledge through objective, systematic and scientific method of finding solution to a problem.

Following are the main steps for conducting user studies:

(i) Selection and formulation of research problem and working hypothesis.
(ii) Literature survey.
(iii) Overall design or planning the strategy of the study.
(iv) Sampling and sampling strategy or plan.
(v) Data collection.
(vi) Measurement and scaling techniques.
(vii) Pilot study.
(viii) Processing and analysis of data.
(ix) Testing of hypotheses.
(x) Interpretation, generalisation and realisation of objectives.
(xi) Preparation, writing, presentation and dissemination of research results.

The above steps are not exhaustive, nor mutually exclusive but represent a series of closely related, continuously overlapping and interdependent non-linear actions.

Before discussing the process of user research as a step-by-step procedure, it may be desirable to briefly note the assumptions and qualities of good research. Good research relies on empirical evidence, utilises relevant concepts, presupposes ethical neutrality, is committed to only objective considerations, makes widely known the methodology for critical scrutiny and testing through replication, aims at probabilistic predictions as well as formulating most general axioms or scientific theories and most importantly encourages rigorous, impersonal mode of procedure dictated by the demands of logic and objective procedure. In other words, good research is systematic, logical, empirical and replicable. The scientific method employed ensures clearly defined purpose, explicit procedure which can be continued, open design leading to objective results, frankness (even reports flaws), adequate analysis of data with appropriate methods, validity and reliability of data, conclusion confined to those justified by data and confidence, reputation, experience, honesty and integrity of researcher.

Selection and Formulation of Research Problem and Working Hypothesis

It is very important to note that research problem should not be borrowed. Every researcher has to find his own problem. Experts, guide, experience and literature (to know gaps) are only aids for selection and formulation of a research problem. One should try to ask right question in an unbiased, unattached and objective way without 'mother complex'. It is necessary to be uncommitted and have more than one problem to ponder and interact before final selection and settlement.

Avoid superficial, obvious, overdone and controversial subject as well as too narrow or too vague problems. The problem should not only suit researcher interest, competence and ability but also be novel, significant and useful to practitioners. Utility of expected findings be given adequate importance. Lastly, it is better to carry out a preliminary or feasibility study to check availability of required data and cooperation of people.

Having selected the problem it is necessary to formulate the research problem and develop working hypothesis, if necessary and possible. The steps involved in this process are:

(i) Stating problem in a general way.
(ii) Understanding the nature of the problem.
(iii) Survey of available literature and past studies.
(iv) Developing ideas through discussion (experience survey).
(v) Rephrasing the problem with clear objective and/or hypothesis, title, terms and concepts, assumptions and postulates, significance and value of the study, suitability of the problem in terms of ability, time, money, data, etc., scope and limitations in terms of time and space coordinates, unit of analysis and environmental conditions.

Literature Survey

Literature survey is not a stage in the process of research but starts at the time of selection of a problem and ends, probably, after publishing and dissemination of results of research. As a continuous activity literature survey should ensure avoiding duplication of research, integration of new findings to the literature/knowledge of the discipline, prioritising research activities and incremental growth of theories.

Planning the Strategy or Overall Design of the Study

Research design is a tentative outline of proposed research work. If research is a journey with definite points of departure and arrival, then the design of it must project and predict in between sequences of activities like target, geography, resources, means, plan, synopsis, time schedule and final plan to share the experience with others.

Proper research design provides firm foundation and allows smooth and efficient sailing of project yielding maximum information and reliability of results, helps organising one's ideas, gives chance to foresee flaws and inadequacies, incorporates by learning from others critical comments and evaluations. Like a successful journey research broadens researcher's mind, gives fascinating and exciting experience, insight into work around, provides opportunity to meet people, gives fun and rewards, but often research is also tedious and monotonous.

Design is a decision-making process. Research design, as strategy, has to be comprehensive, flexible, appropriate, efficient, and economical. It is easy to suggest a problem but difficult to make a good research design. Each research work is unique and demands unique research design and unique combination of data collection methods. A good research design is half the battle. The process involves a series of steps including identification and delimiting of variables. There will always be a trade off of resources, cost, time and reliability of results with fruits expected of the study. If the design is for an experimental study which is proof oriented and requires substantial resources in terms of efforts and costs the results are likely to be more decisive. On the other hand, if the design is for an exploratory study which is often insight-oriented with flexibility and is relatively cheaper and smaller, it may not lead to any definite conclusions. In research design one has to choose appropriate combinations of methods and techniques based on objectives, implications of results, environmental factors, resources, kind of data required, etc. What goes on in the design is creating the conceptual structure and blue print for collection, measurement and analysis of data. In other words, decisions regarding what, where, when, how much, by what means concerning research are made in the design.

Broadly, there are three types of research designs. They are: (i) formulatory and exploratory design, (ii) descriptive and diagnostic design, and (iii) experimental design or hypothesis testing. Discussion of these designs is outside the scope of this presentation. However, it is very important to note that librarianship in general and user studies in particular have rarely adopted experimental design which has several advantages over the other designs. In designing a user study one has to be doubly cautious about the relation between two variables as well as differences between cause and effect.

Sampling and Sampling Strategy or Plan

Sampling is one of the important steps in user studies which is often overlooked by stating that some random or non-random sample design has been adopted. Development of proper sampling frame and a definite plan for obtaining a sample from the sampling frame based on random sample design (rather than non-random design) is necessary. A good sampling design should be economically viable, able to control systematic bias, lead to optimum size of sample but small sampling error, enable results be applied to the universe in general with a reasonable level of confidence (i.e., reliability) and the resulting sample should be adequate, truly representative and similar to population.

In practice many researchers overlook the appropriate probability random design for choosing sample and determination of sample size. Non-probability sampling like convenience sampling and purposive sampling should not be thought of unless it is for a qualitative research. Right type of simple or complex random design has to be chosen for sampling. The sample size depends on nature of units, population and study, number of variables, groups and sub-groups to be studied, intended depth of analysis, precision and reliability of results required, level of expected non-response, size of questionnaire and population and available resources. It should be noted that the size of sample is more important than the proportion of the population represented by sample. There are well established statistical techniques to determine the sample size.

Data Collection

There is a wide array of methods and techniques for data collection as far as user studies are concerned. Judicious selection of one or more methods (preferably a combination of methods) with trade off amongst factors like suitability to problem, available resources, competence of researcher, kind of data required to be produced and the level of precision required is necessary. It is often said that the common sense is the chief requisite and experience the chief teacher in deciding on data collection method.

Use existing (secondary) data already collected by some one else for general or different purpose with sufficient scrutiny about their reliability, suitability and adequacy. Often historical method, bibliometric studies, use studies, meta analysis, content analysis, etc. depend on secondary data. For primary data, which is more important and reliable than secondary data, one has to resort to standard methods like observation, interview, questionnaire, interview schedule, panel study, mechanical devices, projective techniques, sociometry, depth interview, etc. In such cases researcher collects original (primary) data afresh by either experimenting, examining and observing the subjects and records or by asking or questioning orally or in writing the concerned people like subjects (users), experts and others who know subjects.

While asking people, problems may emanate either from those who answer (respondents) because of awareness, irrationally, inadmissibility, self-incrimination and politeness or from those asking because of very presence and disclosure of identity and background of research and/or respondents or from the ways of asking/questioning people like the language and tone of questions, length of questionnaire, time required to answer the question, ambiguities, embarrassing question, illogical sequence, leading questions, loaded word or phrase, in-built coercion, unspoken assumptions, etc. In addition, non-response, disinterestedness, carelessness, prejudices, prestige bias, ignorance, misunderstanding, hallo effect and response sets on the part of respondents are other problems to be taken care in questioning people. There are many practical hints like coding, provision for neither agree nor disagree type of responses, avoiding double negatives, hypothetical and double (complex) questions, etc.

There are other more appropriate methods of data collection for user studies like panel studies including diaries, report of summary of activities, solution development records, projective techniques (including word projectio.ı tests, pictorial and play techniques), snowball techniques, network analysis and use of mechanical devices like eye cameras, audio meters, random alarm mechanism, etc. which are almost never used in library research in India. Methods like critical incidence technique, longitudinal design, etc. are more like normative principles which are very useful in data collection by any of the above methods.

Lastly, case studies and evaluative studies are two important ways of carrying out user studies, discussion about them is beyond the scope of this presentation.

Measurement and Scaling Techniques

Another important aspect often overlooked in library research in India is measurement and scaling of data collection instruments. Sound measurement must be precise, unambiguous, free from errors, valid, reliable and practicable. As mentioned earlier errors may crop up from respondent, situation, measurer or instrument. To test the soundness of the measuring instrument, the validity of the tool (in terms of content validity, criterion-related validity and construct validity), reliability (in terms of stability and equivalence) and practicality (i.e., economy, convenience and interpretability) have to be examined. Appropriate scaling techniques have to be used in case of measuring attitude, behaviour and personality and other qualitative and abstract concepts. Scaling is a method which changes attributes (a series of qualitative facts) into variables (a quantitative series). In other words, scaling is a procedure for assignment of numbers or symbols to (i.e., quantitative measures of) subjective abstract concepts (or property of objects). There are scaling techniques like rating scales and ranking scales, scale construction approach like consensus, item analysis, cumulative scale and factor analysis approaches and already developed scales like differential, summated, cumulative and factor scales which are rarely heard in librarianship.

Pilot Study

Like trial of a dress maker, it is desirable to try out methods and techniques chosen for main data collection in a pilot study, which helps in estimating time required, detecting flaws, weaknesses and ambiguities, using pre-formulated questions and/or responses (instead of open end question), knowing in advance the kind of data likely to result, the kind of analysis required, expertise available for analysis, computer facility required, estimating the resources required and finally gaining access to and cooperation of respondents.

Processing and Analysis of Data

The processing and analysis of data collected is an important step in user studies. Often researchers either under process or over-interpret the data. The processing and analysis of qualitative data differ substantially from that of quantitative data except where scaling techniques are used to convert qualitative data into quantitative data. Qualitative data involves subjectivity, feel and flavour of the situation and hence consumes more time and efforts for collection as well as processing. As it is not amenable for statistical manipulation, extrapolation of findings is difficult. Qualitative data calls for sensitive interpretation and creative presentation.

Levels of measurement (i.e., nominal, ordinal, interval and ratio) determine the kind of statistical technique to be used for processing data. The processing involves editing, coding, classification and tabulation of data in order to achieve data reduction and presentation. The analysis of data (both descriptive and inferential or statistical) involve exploratory analysis, computation of certain indexes or measurers, searching for certain patterns of relationships and trends, estimating values of unknown parameters, testing of hypothesis for inferences, and graphical presentation.

Appropriate statistical techniques depending on number and type of variables have to be employed for processing and analysis. It is very important to understand the merits and limitations of various bivariate and multivariate measures as well as differences among measures of association, correlation, and cause and effect. Important techniques like chi-square test, co-efficients of regression, multiple and partial correlations, index numbers, time series analysis, ANOVA, ANOCOVA, discriminate analysis, factor analysis and cluster analysis are largely untouched in Indian library research including user studies.

Testing of Hypothesis

As mentioned earlier, it is very unfortunate that research in librarianship has very rarely resorted to experimental design and testing of hypothesis. A hypothesis as a tentative hunch explains the situation under observation so as to design the study to prove or disprove it. What a researcher is looking for is a working or positive hypothesis. It is very difficult, laborious and time consuming to make adequate discriminations in the complex interplay of facts without hypothesis. It gives definite point and direction to the study, prevents blind search and indiscriminate gathering of data and helps to delimit the field of inquiry. Absence of a clear theoretical framework and lack of ability to logically utilise it and failure to be acquainted with the available research techniques are the main reasons for not resorting to formulation and testing of hypothesis. It is also equally important that the researcher should not start out to prove or disprove hypothesis nor try to defend his hypothesis.

A good and usable hypothesis should be precise, simple but not obvious, conceptually clear, have empirical referents, specific and limited in scope, consistent with most known facts, state relationship between variables and related to available techniques and body of theory. A statistical hypothesis is a predictive statement (usually put in the form of a null hypothesis and an alternate hypothesis) capable of being tested by scientific methods and that relates an independent variable to some dependent variables. What a researcher bets in advance of his experiment that the results will agree with his theory and cannot be accounted for by the chance variation involved in sampling is hypothesis testing. In other words, hypothesis testing is a procedure which enables researcher to decide whether to accept or reject hypothesis.

There are many concepts like Type-I and Type-II errors, one-tailed and two-tailed tests, significance test, important parametric tests like Z-test, t-test, F-test and non-parametric tests like Kolmogorov-Smirnov one sample test, Runs test for randomness, sign tests, Fisher-Irwin test, McNemer test, median tests, Chi-square test, Wilcoxin-Mann-Whitney U-test, Wilcoxin matched pair or signed rank test, Kruskal-Wallis or H-test, Kendall's co-efficient of concordance etc. most of which are yet to be employed in library research. What is surprising is that user research is market research in librarianship but user research has not even adopted a fraction of methodology adopted in market research.

Interpretation, Drawing Inferences, Generalisation and Realisation of Objectives

Immediately followed by processing and analysis of data, interpreting the results and drawing inferences have to be carried out. In this crucial step, the complex task/theme is divided into sub-themes and arranged in a logical order. The activities involved are explaining summarised data through tables, charts and diagrams, identifying extreme cases and tendencies, drawing inferences with conditions, if any, enumerating qualitative and extraneous data in support of inferences and tendencies, comparing the results with theory and results of earlier studies, summarising and generalising the findings/results, realisation of objectives, discussion of implications of results and findings and suggesting topics for further research.

The purpose of interpretation is to draw inferences from data, expounding relationships and processes underlying the findings, searching for broader meaning of research findings, understanding and explaining what has been observed in the study, providing theoretical conceptions to serve as a guide for further research, for better appreciation of findings and make others to understand the real significance of findings, to understand the abstract principles that work beneath finding, linking the results with that of others, arriving at generalisation after repeated testing of hypothesis, to take decisions based on implications of results, to predict concrete world of events and to maintain continuity of research.

Interpretation is an art and requires great skill and dexterity. It is necessary to make optimum use of data and techniques and avoid over, under, mis-, wrong/incorrect and out of the context interpretations. One should be impartial and have patience and proper perspective and look for relevance and generalisation and not false or broader generalisations. While interpreting research findings one has to take care of representativeness of data, nature of questions, type of responses, handling 'don't know' type of responses, ways of representing data (percentage, mean, standard deviation, chi-square and hypothesis test, correlation co-efficients, etc.) and elaboration of results. Proper care should be taken to avoid spurious explanations and study the deviant cases thoroughly before interpretation.

Preparation, Writing, Presentation and Dissemination of Research Results

Communication is utmost important in research and naturally in user studies. Research as a means to an end/change depends substantially on effective communication. Communication both within methods, tools and techniques like questionnaires as well as two-way communication both with participants/respondents and those who sponsor the research have to be clear. Communication should take place throughout the research work. Excellent research is wasteful if not communicated appropriately. Communication is, like sharing the experience of journey, an obligation of research to those who participated, cooperated and interested in it. Dissemination of research results ensures integrating it with the existing body of knowledge and avoiding duplication of work, others to learn from one's mistakes, anybody to replicate the study, bring in improvements to methodology and clears doubts and suspicion, if any, in the minds of people.

Communication of research has to be necessarily written and widely published in addition to oral presentation, if possible. As far as substance of the report is concerned adhering to the objectives, knowing the audience, starting with sentence outline rather than topical outline, use of right language and time as well as uniform style and making it short and attractive in appearance are very important. As far as formats and aids of writing research report are concerned, use of headings, sub-headings, quotations, footnotes, exhibits, etc., as well as standard procedure regarding preliminaries, main text and end parts of the report are explained in many written sources. Care should also be taken regarding uniformity in presenting appendices, bibliography, glossary, index as well as typing instructions and proof reading of the text.

Conclusion

Even though there is a subtle dichotomy in the use of methods and purposes of user studies, most of the user studies are imitative than imaginative, exploratory rather than experimental and descriptive rather than decisive. Majority of them have adopted survey and case study methods rather than controlled or quasi-controlled experimental methods (with questionnaire technique rather than observation technique for pseudo-objective and quantitative research rather than objective and qualitative research with the dubious purpose of generalisation of findings beyond the population concerned). They often dealt with more of 'what' than 'why'. In other words, the basic research aspect of why the user behaves as does is rarely attempted. As a result the numbers and opinions have become predominant in user studies. Unfortunately what majority users say has become the ultimate truth forgetting the fact that what a user say is not always what he needs or does.

Asking people (through questionnaire, interview, discussion or diaries), observing users and their activities, content analysis (of records), semi-controlled experiments on subjects and a host of indirect methods could be employed more fruitfully in understanding users. While choosing appropriate methods, choice has to be made between qualitative and quantitative approach, survey/case study and experimental method, cross-sectional design and longitudinal experimental design, depending on problem, available resources, competence of the staff and the kind of data desired. In the process of collecting data, number of problems like non-response, disinterestedness and carelessness, bias, prejudices, ignorance, misunderstanding, 'hallo effect' and response sets of respondents have to be faced and suitably resolved.

The general picture of the findings like 'average user of an average library' is less useful to practical situations. Use of holistic qualitative methods are badly needed in this area of research. Over-concentration on how users obtain information rather than what they want, why they want it and what they do with it as well as on formal communications (documents) than informal (interpersonal) communications are increasingly making the results more useful to sociologists of science than information professionals.

In the same instance, user studies have totally ignored the study of non-users as they either keep themselves away and mum or pretend and say as users. It is extremely difficult to conduct a non-user study and hence the number of non-user studies are too few compared to large number of user studies reported. There are no systematic attempts to study non-users, under-privileged, unserved, under-served and deprived users and their problems of information malnutrition. Non-user studies require costly and refined methods and techniques (Sridhar, 1994). The ratio of actual users to potential users of a library by itself is a rough measure of the impact of the library and its market penetration capability. At the same time we need to be cautious about limitations of user studies and note that often use of a library by its users and its utility to its users are quite different.

There are many methods and techniques of social research particularly those used in psychology and sociology which need to be tried for user studies. For example, the projective techniques and multiple complementary methods of data collection (triangulation techniques) would be more appropriate to user studies than traditional questionnaires.

Irrespective of excellent methods and techniques adopted, the findings of most of the user studies (and even so in respect of findings of many social research) are often subjected to cynicism and criticism if they are of extreme in nature, i.e., either too simple, common, obvious and expected or totally unbelievable/unexpected. To combat such criticisms, one has to have foolproof research design, hard and reliable data with systematic and accurate analysis and interpretation. Further, user studies demand a mixture of common sense and technical expertise.

2

A REVIEW OF USE AND USER STUDIES IN SCIENCE AND TECHNOLOGY

Information is an amorphous concept, less susceptible to a precise definition. Yet, everyone has to deal with it in many ways throughout one's life. "Indeed, information has been described as the fifth need of man ranking after air, water, food and shelter" (Kemp, 1976, p. 101). Information-collection, transfer and use are all-pervasive and universal activities in all walks of life. Knowledge[1] in general and information in particular become more meaningful and 'explode' into power only when it is transferred and communicated. In other words, information is activised by communication. Information and communication are equally important in the efficient and effective management of any enterprise. They have definite relations with performance of R&D organisations and industries as well. The purpose of transfer and communication of information is 'use'. Without the intention on the part of the ultimate receiver or beneficiary of information to use it, the whole exercise of transfer and communication becomes futile and information transferred becomes redundant. On the other hand, seeking and communicating information are two sides of the same coin from the viewpoint of individuals concerned. Both have the same purpose: use. Information which has no use is no information. Thus the central thread of the whole range of activities relating to information-transfer and communication is 'use'. Hence the emphasis on 'use' and user-orientation to communication and information—whether from a formally designed and operated information-system or from an informal source. A wide range of research works centred around 'use' and user of information called 'use and user-studies' have cropped up in the last four decades.

The user is the key person in any information-system. All the luxuries of information-revolution and problems of information-explosion are centred round the user and his convenience. Understanding the user is half the battle in providing information-services. As such, understanding 'user' is an important and a continuous activity. 'Know thy customer' is the cardinal rule of any business enterprise. Accordingly, extensive market research, customer-behaviour studies and demand forecasting are carried out in business. A formal information centre or library is yet to pick up these activities in the same spirit.

There appears to be a lopsided emphasis in library and information field on user-education than on understanding the user. This is largely due to the systems designed and implemented, which are unfriendly, complex and not concerned with the perceived needs of users. What is more important is intensive librarian-education about users than mere education of users of the existing system (Thompson, 1982, p. 11). Accurate and up-to-date knowledge about users and their information-behaviour is one of the essential ingredients for designing an information-system. The need is for user-driven design than technology-driven design and more research on human variables of information-system than technology and system variables (Atherton, 1975, p. 672). Unfortunately, the emphasis in the profession has been on imparting technical skills than information skills. The effectiveness of library and information-system depends on the extent to which the system-characteristics correspond with the user and on how much the potential user is willing and able to make use of it.

System designers, planners and managers have, by and large, failed to properly consider the role of human factors and their effect on acceptance and utilisation of information (Mick, 1980, p. 21). Oldman (1976, p. 1) reviewing the research in librarianship says "A particular style of systems analysis has dominated library management research both in this country [U.K.] and in the United States in the last decade. The starting point for this research has been the library system. A more important starting point is the *target* for information—the individuals who constitute the 'receiving' community". "It is well recognised that the user has been given inadequate consideration from almost any point of view in most information-supplying systems existing today. . .". Landau and others (1975, p. 422) further say ". . . in a great majority of cases, the user is neither understood nor studied nor, in some cases, even identified until after the system is already evolved or in a completely operational state. Some have characterised this as an 'upside-down system design".[2]

Research in library and information science is more meaningful if the findings increase the efficiency and effectiveness of information flow. To do this the emphasis should shift from system or service-oriented research to user-oriented research. Like in business, efforts should be put in primarily to relate product or system design to the perceived needs of those for whom the product or system is intended and the system operation should be guided by the knowledge about the user (Cronin, 1981, p. 37). Finally, selling or promoting the information-services and user-education should only take a secondary position subject to the condition that the system design is based on a proper understanding of the user.

For various reasons, the literature on user-research has necessarily been voluminous. Yet, findings are disproportionately smaller. Ignoring extensive data, repetitive as well as fragmented presentations, the literature does not appear to be so voluminous. The behaviour-related research in information-storage and retrieval is not great—either absolutely or relatively. Very little is known about user's preferences which can be used with confidence in the design of a new information-retrieval system. Due to its contingency nature very few studies can be considered to be relevant for a given user-population.

Markee (1972, p. 119) stresses the need for user-research in the parent organisation and says that "a review of the library literature reveals that the amount of library research being done by the librarian at his institution is not in proportion to his professional responsibilities". He answers the question as to where the research should originate by saying that the "library research should begin and continue right in the parent institution". This bottom-upward approach can only provide a solid foundation for national information systems of developed and developing countries.

Even though considerable research has been done in the area of user-studies in developed and information rich countries, especially U.S.A., Britain, Western and Eastern European countries, practically nothing substantial is done in less developed countries in general and India in particular. Not even a single major user-study in any of the areas of science and technology has been done in the country. Even the major national information system designs were not preceded by systematic, reliable and comprehensive user-studies. As such many present systems are surviving under 'symmetry of ignorance' (Kunz *et al.*, 1977, pp. 67-68), mathematical induction of convenient good or bad things, subjective considerations and idiosyncrasies of people involved in planning information systems. Other systems are thriving under dubious reasons of avoiding the duplication of research and resultant economic benefit arising out of information systems but the hidden apparent reasons of an information systems, as Myers (1970, p. 26) says, could be treating information system as a prestige centre or a form of fringe benefit to employees or a paid up insurance to serve an unanticipated need or to sublimate the feeling that one does not read or a centralised way of budgetary control over expenditure on documents.

USER-RESEARCH IN GENERAL

The studies named variedly as 'user-studies', 'information-need studies', 'use-studies', 'information-transfer studies', 'communication-behaviour studies', 'information-behaviour studies', 'dissemination and utilisation studies' are closely related, and often not precisely defined. Menzel (1966, p. 43) tried to delineate these studies and said "when approached from the point of view of the scientist or technologist, these are studies of scientists' communication-behaviour. When approached from the point of view of any communication medium, they are use-studies. When approached from the point of view of the science communication system, they are studies in the flow of information among scientists and technologists". Hence the terminology depends much on the approach and the angle from which one sees.

It may be noted that significant contributions to this area of research have been made by psychologists, sociologists, behavioural scientists and others in addition to library and information science personnel. As a result, the literature is scattered across many disciplines and varied collections have to be scanned for location of literature. Further, there is a very wide variation in the scope of user-studies. These studies touch upon many peripheral areas such as bibliometric studies, use-studies and citation studies. There is no consistency in the use of terms and concepts in user-research. Loose and interchangeable use of terms have made it difficult to compare findings of various studies. As a result, user-research is continuing without much consolidation.

Though it is very difficult to make an accurate estimate of the total number of user-studies/bibliographic items of literature on user-research, there are several estimates made by experts. Kunz and others (1977, p. 10) have estimated more than 2000 bibliographic items as of 1977, Crawford (1978, p. 61) found some 1000 papers in 1979 and Stibic in 1980 (1980, p. 17) estimated that there are about 1000 papers dealing with the problems of information needs and habits. The growth rate is estimated as some 30 studies a year. Krikelas (1983, p. 5) says "simply from the point of view of mass, user-studies probably form the largest single body of research literature in librarianship". User-studies in science and technology alone are considered numerous. Depending on the definition of user study, while the estimate of Line (1968, p. 10) varied between 400 and 600 studies, Brittain's (1970, p. 13) estimate varied from 400 to 800. Distrust of previous findings and the conviction that scientists in a particular environment are unique in their information-seeking behaviour are two reasons for so many user-studies (Paisley, 1965). Many of these studies are largely repetitive without much cumulation of knowledge about users and a single study often leads to multiple bibliographic items with varying degrees of duplication of data and information. User-studies are basically behavioural and social research oriented studies essentially involving extensive data and descriptive literature and their scope is very vast. Hence, depending on purpose, scope and quality criteria of the reviewer, estimates of the number of user-studies have varied widely.[3]

Geographically and historically, USA has taken a lead in empirical user-research followed by UK and other European countries (Kunz *et al.*, 1977, p. 10). Studies on information needs and uses were rigorous in USA during 1960s, but the early 1970s also saw a remarkable array of concerted efforts in other nations, particularly UK, Canada, The Netherlands, Russia and East Germany to study the information needs and uses of scientists and technologists (Lin and Garvey, 1972, p. 5). One can call 1960s and 1970s respectively as the renaissance of user-studies in USA and UK. Other countries in general, developing and under-developed countries in particular, do not have much to claim even today in this area of research (Lipetz, 1970; Crane, 1971).

CONCEPTUAL FRAMEWORK AND THEORETICAL BACKGROUND FOR USER-RESEARCH

One of the widely accepted conceptual frameworks for user-research is that suggested by Paisley (1968). He places the information-user at the centre of ten systems, namely cultural system, political system, membership group, reference group, 'invisible college', formal organisation, work team, one's head/mind, legal and economic system and a formal information system each forming concentric circles around the user. Except one's own head or mind, all other systems are external to the individual and they form his environment. However, one should not forget the complex interactions involving one's own head/mind in terms of personal attitudes and accumulated experience with one's present role, function, task and all other environmental systems. It is these complex interactions which lead to individual information-behaviour. This conceptual framework, however, is in congruence with the functionalist theory/view of scientific growth propounded by Merton (1957) especially the fact that science exists as a sub-system within a larger social system. Yet, some hold the view that scientists live in two worlds, scientific world and a separate 'outside' world (Garvey, 1979, p. 3). From this it appears that each one of the systems proposed by Paisely are not only task-dependent and situational, but also exert influence on the user to a varying degree.

The factors/variables which affect information-transfer process and user-behaviour are innumerable and any empirical study has to make its own assumptions to simplify the situation (Oldman, 1976, p. 34). Otherwise, one would be lost in the jungle.[4] A model of information-seeking activities of scientist and his research group presented by Orr (1970) provides a fairly exhaustive list of factors that affect the scientist's information-seeking behaviour. He asserts that any particular type of communication-behaviour must be assessed in relation to all other communication-behaviours.

In the past, there was no agreement about the scope of information-seeking behaviour as well as user-studies. 'Seeking' is used interchangeably with 'gathering' and 'using' information. The terms 'communication-behaviour' and 'information-transfer/flow' are used almost synonymously with information-seeking behaviour. However, a thin line of demarcation can be drawn. Information-seeking behaviour studies confine to the point of view of user as receiver of message or information. The communication behaviour studies primarily emphasise user as producer and/or sender of message or information. Hence as a person communicating information, user plays the role of source of information or a creator of a source of information. Thus, the user often plays multiple roles such as receiver, creator and sender of message in information and communication-behaviour studies. The third broadly related area is the information transfer/flow studies where the whole process is looked at from a systemic view without much slant to either receiver or sender of information. Wersig (1970, 1973) as well as Wersig and Windel (1981) discussed the systematisation of user-research and divides it into four areas emphasising user as channel for communication, as information receiver, as data sources and as information sender. Thus user assumes the role of a channel and a source too. Kunz and others (1977, p. 66) also identify how the distinction between 'users' and 'sources' of information is vanishing and both become 'partners' participating in the networks of knowledge generation and transfer.

In the process of seeking information what mainly takes place is an effort to match a cognitive need of user with a source of information and seeking supply of information to satisfy the need. This process naturally involves many phases and factors. First, the need could be unclear and uncertain.

Secondly, user could be biased, subjective, conservative, habituated and having his own styles and idiosyncrasies.[5] Further, apathy towards a new service or system[6] is not unusual and in one case researchers were reluctant towards new services (even though they desired) and did not even directly examine the service attributing it to lack of time (Trueswell *et al.*, 1965; Van Cott and Kincade, 1967).

Havelock and others (1969, p. 4.10) observe that "... individuals who are consistently exposed to innovations which fail or innovations which produce only minimal success may develop a general resistance to the acceptance of innovations". It appears like an inverse of 'success breeds success theory' and 'Matthew effect'.[7] They conclude "... that individuals are just not very simple; they continue to elude the social scientists' attempts to place them in neat categories which would provide the base for clear theoretical statements" (p. 4.11). As such, the individual's initiative plays an important role to recognise a need for information, to seek and search information and to use it irrespective of availability of services (Wilkin, 1981, p. 4.30). However, this does not underestimate the importance of availability of information facility/ service for one to seek and use. In fact, availability or existence of needed information is one of the necessary conditions, next only to the need and the initiative to use. Then comes the sufficient conditions that the available facility/service should not only be accessible to the user but also easy to use. Above all, the user should perceive that the source or facility is useful for the need concerned. The perceived utility of a source is based on both the quantity and quality of information expected from it. Ignorance about a piece of useful information either due to the apathy of the user or due to failures. Of information system when realised leads to alter the composition of monitor, reserve and supply of information in a cost efficient way to yield a relatively satisfactory information supply provided the ignorance is neither too small to worry about nor too large to be remediable (Wilson, 1977, p. 74). In the process of adaptation of altered system the cost in terms of time and efforts is optimised and sources that adapt to needs of user are preferred to sources which require the user to adapt himself. In other words, personal information-gathering is often purposive, adaptive, habitual and economical (Wilson, 1977, p. 80). The lack of awareness on the part of the user about existing information-systems could also be a factor for its non-use in addition to convenience, responsiveness and ability to conduct dialogue with the system (Ackoff *et al.*, 1976, p. 143).

Atherton (1977, p. 7) summarises these factors involved in seeking and using information in the following words: "The working habits of the individual needing information, the importance placed on getting it, the facilities available for seeking it, the knowledge about the facilities, the judgment of their value, the estimate of the probability of getting what is wanted—all of these factors may affect information-seeking behaviour. Unless a person who wants information is fairly sure of getting it without much trouble, he is apt to do without it if it is not essential. Relying on memory, skirting around the issue or making do with incomplete or vague information from a colleague are not unusual behaviour traits. There is, however, a small group of users who actively seek information spending effort and resources to acquire pertinent information and these users in fact are the most progressive in economic activity". Scientists and engineers are more likely to invest or reinvest efforts and resources for reinventing than to derive it from the research or development work of someone else, especially someone they don't know, in a different organisation and in a different discipline (Havelock *et al.*, 1969, pp. 8-16). They may even estimate that generation of new knowledge will be cheaper than an expensive and possibly fruitless search (Paisley, 1968, pp. 19-20).

The complex trio concepts, viz., accessibility, 'ease of use' and perceived utility of a channel are extensively investigated by Allen and Gerstberger (1967, 1968). The concept 'ease of use' which is akin to 'law of least effort', Mooer's law[8] and 'why bother theory of information usage' (Cooper, 1978) appears to be the supreme criterion in use of a source of information (Rosenberg, 1966, p. 19). Moor (1972) has developed a model incorporating seven dimensions as measurable components of the concept 'ease of use' of an information system. The dimensions are—movement required (out of the user's personal work area), time delay, interaction, interface structure, required location of use, permanence (nature of information provided) and response filter. The model was empirically tested from the data from R&D personnel and concluded that these dimensions do serve as a model for identifying behaviour.

A REVIEW OF SELECTED INDIAN USER-STUDIES

It has to be stated regretfully that, so far, no single comprehensive user-study has been reported in the country relating to scientific/technological institutions. Many piecemeal research works of varying qualities have possibly been done and only some of them have been published. Even with a liberal yardstick about the soundness of methodologies adopted, comprehensive and adequate samples studied and rigorous analysis of the data, one cannot find enough empirical studies covering many types of users and many aspects of information-behaviour. One striking feature of the Indian literature on user-research is that there are a large number of so-called theoretical and review types of papers repeatedly stressing the need for user-studies, quoting the findings of the studies of either USA or UK, suggesting further research in the area and, unfortunately, without any data or observations of their own. An equally good number of other studies appear to be of an ephemeral nature and of peripheral interest to user-research. Another feature is that there is an over-emphasis on bibliometric studies in general and citation studies in particular. But the utility of such studies in understanding the users is limited. Besides, there are a number of master's degree theses, submitted to various library schools, of highly limited scope and utility (obviously due to limitations of resources, expertise and time). But only a few of such studies are known outside the library schools concerned.

In the last five years, hardly 4.69 per cent of the published articles dealt with user-studies (Amba and Raghavan, 1985, p. 133) and among the ongoing doctoral research just one study each is on communication and use/user-study (Kumar, 1983). A large majority of over 25 papers published so far in the *Library Science with a Slant to Documentation* under information-user-studies series as well as those published elsewhere under similar names do not directly deal with information-behaviour aspects. A recent special issue of *ILA Bulletin* (Vol. 22, No. 3-4, October 1986, March 1987) on users' approach to information which carried nine papers on the topic is not an exception. Ironically, the second IASLIC seminar (1965) dealt with 'users and library and information service', but not even a single paper presented in the seminar carried any hard survey data worth comparing with the user-studies of that time in USA and UK. Even a seminar on "the role of the libraries in communication process and information flow" (Singh, 1980) saw hardly any primary data under its themes of 'communication', 'information flow' and 'the librarian/information scientist as a communicator'. All the presentations were of theoretical and casual nature with no specific orientation to communication and information-flow process.

It is not unexpected that Ranganathan (1970) gave a framework and foundation for user-behaviour studies in India when he discussed the psychology and the nature of work of users. Among the theoretical and review-type publications, Gopinath (1984) gave a bird's eye-view of latest trends in information-sources, information-transfer and communication as well as a review of significant studies of information-seeking behaviour (n.d.). He has also analysed the nature of work of product design engineers and the process of product design (presumably a mass produced consumer product) to identify the decision-making situations leading to a need for a particular type of information-services in industry (Gopinath, 1980). Here the need for product-related information is discussed from the angle of maker of the product rather than the user of the product. Rajagopalan and Rajan (1984) presenting an account of programmes and activities on user-studies in India with emphasis on success and shortfalls, try to deduce, from the five laws of library science propounded by Ranganathan, a conceptual framework for user- and use-studies. This paper is supposed to be a stock taking of Indian user-studies, user-education programmes and use-promotion studies. The authors claim that there exists a fairly good body of literature reporting user-studies at the level of individual libraries (p. 4). However no single major or minor user-study has been cited in support of it. Hence it is difficult to judge on the scope and nature of the studies they hint at. In a recent review of information-requirements and information-gathering habits of scientists, Satyanarayana (1985) draws heavily from the findings of studies done elsewhere to categorise users in general, assess their information needs, sources and use of information and attempts to draw his own conclusions. Gupta (1981) reviews literature about type, sources and channels of information used in three stages of technology-transfer, namely, idea-generation, problem-solving and implementation and diffusion. Krishan Kumar (1982) stresses the need for user-studies and development of expertise within the country and also presents a programme for determining information-needs of health science users. Saha (1970) presents yet another theoretical paper quoting observations and findings of stalwarts like Bernal and Line without any data or conclusion of his own. He stresses the need for the development of a sound methodology and research into factors determining information-use pattern and categorisation of users. Unfortunately he goes on to make guess-type observations such as ". . . the user-studies in a mission-oriented library and information service are much less complex as the user population is less divergent in nature and relatively known" (p. 5) which is far from the truth.

As regards studies reported with some statistical data, way back in 1964 the Scientific Information Bureau (Rao, 1966) of Defence Science Laboratory, Delhi made a too simple a pilot-survey about information activities in 21 R&D laboratories/establishments of the Ministry of Defence. Though the survey produced simple data about available information facilities, publishing pattern and broad communication activities, this is probably the first and one of the very few attempts of user surveys at the national level by a government agency. Rao (p. 4) found in this survey that the optimum size of an R&D laboratory for maximum production of papers is 250 persons and laboratories other than equipment intensive laboratories showed greater output in terms of research papers.

Srinivasan (1970) stressed the need for more economical methods of user studies in developing countries and advocated indirect studies such as citation studies, analysis of records of user requests, inter-library loan and other observations ignoring the fact that reliability of research findings cannot be fully sacrificed for economic considerations. Srinivasan himself restricts to reporting elementary statistics of citations (not even percentages are worked out), translations, inter-library loan requests of scientists of Central Building Research Institute (CBRI), Roorkee.

Pruthi and Nagpaul (1978, 1979) investigated the communication patterns in two research projects (with 40 and 5 persons) of a national laboratory through profiles, two sets of questionnaires and structured interviews with a longitudinal approach to examine the relationship of communication-patterns to individual's status, educational level and social relations, to identify technological gatekeepers, to study the role of formal and informal communications in problem-solving and idea-generation. Though the study is on a specific aspect of communication with limited sample, this is worth considering for the sake of good design and data collection methods. Pruthi and Nagpaul (1978, p. 55) found predominantly internalised communication activity[9] within the project teams of R&D scientists and little inflow or outflow of information to other groups. The outside-the-organisation contacts were predominant in smaller projects than bigger projects and the 'gatekeeper-construct' gets diluted with the increase in team size. They (p. 56) also found significant effect of work relationship on communication.

B.N. Singh (1981) in his analysis of 1971 citations from articles and comments appearing in two engineering-oriented Indian journals coupled with a questionnaire survey of 55 research engineers and engineering faculty (with 42 responses) at three technology institutes tried to assess the information-needs of engineering scientists in India. The limited sample as confessed by the author and the limitations of citation analysis cause aspersions on the reliability of the results of this study. For an example, an observation that electronics, telecommunication and industrial engineers cite to the maximum from other disciplines (Singh, 1981, p. 183) is highly vague as an equally strong interdisciplinary need for information is expected in many other disciplines too. Surprisingly, he did not find any influence of status of the scholars on their information needs (Singh, 1981, p. 182). He found that current reading materials provided a little over one-fifth of the references to the researchers of his sample. But surprisingly, as many as 70 per cent of the references were found by chance by the respondents of this study (Singh, 1981, p. 172).

It may be desirable to summarise here the publishing and citing patterns of Indian scientists and engineers. The rank order of document-forms cited by Indian scientists and engineers do not differ very much from others (Sridhar, 1985, p. 261; Srinivasan, 1970; Shalini and Chudamani, 1978, p. 103; Singh, 1981, p. 179). But, generally, Indian authors had oriented locally for publishing and cited heavily from foreign sources. Conferences are found more as opportunities for disseminating and transferring information than as sources for citations. Lastly, the Indian authors have more self-citations than others. There is a slight positive correlation between publishing in and citing from a journal. However, the use of a journal is found independent of publishing and citing (Sridhar, 1990).

Sridhar (1987, 1995) using multiple and complementary investigation methods ('weekly summary of information related activities', questionnaire, interview, observation, analysis of records, semi-controlled experiments, and other indirect methods) has carried out a broad-base-line (almost census) study of information-seeking behaviour of the Indian space technologists of a single organisation and tried to relate various aspects of information-seeking behaviour to their characteristics like status, experience, nature of work, qualifications, specialisation and professional activities and achievements. This is a broad-based (yet focused) study with innovative variety of techniques and extensive hard data. This study had many in-built case studies in it.

In a case study of in-house use of library documents and seat occupancy, the space technologists were found to visit the library more during departmental reviews for promotion. The distribution of user-visit data over a typical day was bimodal, roughly symmetric and the same was cyclical over a typical week with maximum during mid of a working week (Sridhar, 1982). Like use of library documents, the reservations made by the space technologists for lent-out documents followed skewed distribution and year of acquisition of a document had a stronger effect on its chances of getting more reservations than year of publication (Sridhar, 1983). In another study, it was found that less than one-fourth of the space technologists have had participated in collection development of the library (Sridhar, 1983). Yet another case study showed non-use of classified catalogue, heavy use of subject catalogue and a roughly symmetric bimodal distribution of card catalogue consultation over a typical day by the space technologists. Further, card catalogues are consulted most of the time either to locate a document on the shelf or to interact with the circulation counter than for literature search (Sridhar, 1986).

In a subsequent analysis Sridhar (1987) found no significant differences between men and women space technologists in time spent in information-gathering, including the relative time spent and dependence on formal and informal sources of information, intra-organisational communication, use of bibliographic references, degree of delegation of information-gathering work and use of library documents. However, women tended to have fewer inter-organisational contacts, more consultations with colleagues for references and more interactions with the primary library than men. Women space technologists did not differ from men in making borrowed use of library documents but differed significantly in in-house use and interactions with the library.

A few other studies which carried some statistical data are that of Nagarajan (1970) on information needs of technocrats in industries, Krishan Kumar (1968) about teachers and research scholars of the Department of Chemistry of the University of Delhi, Bhavani (1982) on publishing pattern of 125 physicists and chemists and Kanaka Rekha (1984) on communication-behaviour of Indian food technologists.

Interestingly, it is the academicians and students of library and information science who have conducted some surveys and gathered hard field data. In addition to Bhavani (1982) and Kanaka Rekha (1984) cited above, Kailash Chandra Garg and Ashok Kumar (1984) surveyed 150 scientists for their information-gathering habits in three unspecified

R&D laboratories of Delhi through questionnaire with 50 per cent response. Not only was the sample inadequate (physics, chemistry and mathematics were represented by 46, 11 and 18 respondents respectively), but also the response-sample characteristics were not analysed. Garg and Ashok Kumar (1984, p. 71) found that time spent (on information gathering) is independent of specialisation, qualification and rank of user-scientists.

Again, pointing out the non-availability of comprehensive user-studies and the studies relating to information needs of users in India, S.N. Singh (1979) reviewed the project works of four of his master's degree students at Banaras Hindu University mainly based on citation analysis, observation, questionnaire and interview techniques and concluded that no single method is foolproof. In fact, however poor they may be (obviously due to the limitations under which they are carried out), it is only the students of library and information science who have gathered some field data within the limited resources and time. Unfortunately, a large chunk of them go unnoticed as they are neither fully bibliographically controlled nor the findings of a majority of them are published.

STUDIES ON USE OF LIBRARY COLLECTIONS BY SCIENTISTS, ENGINEERS AND TECHNICIANS

A use study has to necessarily keep a set of defined population of user. in the background. It is also necessary to understand other related concepts and terms like need, want, demand and requirement before commencement of any use study.

'Need' is a more abstract and difficult-to-define concept. Both Ford (1980) and Krikelas (1983, p. 6) define 'information need' as an awareness or recognition of not knowing or existence of uncertainty. The draft definitions of 'need', 'want', 'demand', 'use' and 'requirement' in relation to information proposed by Brittain (1971) and supported by Line (1974, p. 87) are quite adequate for the purpose.

Need is what an individual *ought* to have, for his work, his research, his education, his recreation, etc. A need may or may not be identified as want.

The interesting and most practical aspect is that ". . . needs arise out of the roles an individual fills in social life. So far as specialised information system is concerned, the most relevant of these roles is 'work role', that is, the set of activities, responsibilities, etc., of an individual, usually in some organisational setting in pursuit of earnings and other satisfactions" (Wilson, 1981, p. 9).

Want is what an individual *would like* to have, whether or not the want is actually translated into a demand on the library. Individuals may need an item they do not want, or want an item they do not need. A want, like a need, is a potential demand.

Demand is what an individual asks for; more precisely, a request for an item of information which is believed to be wanted. Individuals may demand information they do not need, and certainly need or want information they do not demand. Demand is partly dependent on expectation, which in turn depends partly on existing provision of library or information-service. A demand is a potential use.

Use is what an individual actually *uses*. A use may be a satisfied demand, or it may be the result of browsing or a chance. Individuals can only use what is available. Use is, therefore, heavily dependent on provision and availability of library and information-service. A 'use' usually represents a need of some kind. But 'need' is independent of 'use'. Uses can be partial indicators of demands, demands of wants, and wants of need. Identification becomes progressively more difficult from the 'hard' use to the often nebulous and unstated need.

The term 'user' includes actual as well as potential users and even non-users. The concept of 'use' is often defined as the extraction of content from a message to meet a need. The operational definition of 'Use' for collecting data about the use of the library documents could be stated as physical selection and the act of leafing through pages of document as far as in-house use is concerned (Kent *et al.*, 1979, p. 61) and for circulation or loaned use, each record of having lent-out or renewed is considered as one externally circulated use of a document.

Requirement is a useful bridging term; it can mean what is *needed* what is *wanted*, or what is *demanded*, and can, therefore, be usefully employed to cover all three categories. But the term 'requirement' is closer to the term 'need'. Many studies of 'needs' have in fact been studies of 'requirements'.

There have been many use-studies of library collections and majority of use-studies have analysed what is used, frequency of use, lifetime and obsolescence rate of material used etc., with varied objectives. They were also thought of as demand-studies. Studies of user-interactions with libraries did not receive enough attention in the past. Many indirect studies like bibliometric and citation studies have also attempted to study and determine use of library collections by scientists, engineers and technicians, but owing to their in-built limitations and non-local scope their utility and even reliability are limited. The critical incident data of specific demands made on typical libraries should reveal behavioural trends, and indicate their underlying motivation better than a theoretical and qualitative investigation (Slater and Fisher, 1969, p. 1).

At the outset, it should be made clear that the use of a document or library does not imply its utility or usefulness. Nor does a high or intensive user-interaction with the library necessarily imply that the user is an intensive user of the library or a highly library-dependent user. "An information-system may be used, then, but not be useful; it may also be useful, but not used. It may even be neither useful nor used. It is ideal if it is both used and useful" (Kochen, 1976, p. 150).

Depending on the intensity of use, the users are classified as 'High Information-Potential' (HIP) and 'Low Information-Potential' (LIP). LIPs are further divided into (i) the NOSTALGIC, who would like to keep informed but never have time, (ii) the BEREAVED, who think it is now too late to update themselves, and (iii) the LOST SOULS, the confirmed non-users (Shuchman, 1981, p. 1). Secondly, the number of users who have need of information far exceed those who actually use information (Atherton, 1977, p. 7). At the same time, it should also be noted that the services of libraries are not restricted to those actually use them, but reach others via actual users due to 'spill-over effect' (Wilson, 1977, p. 83). As a matter of fact the LOST SOULS (among engineers) might be heavy users of information in different forms (Shuchman, 1981, p. 23). Thirdly, the "... concern with users should not be equated with an objective of maximising use (sales)" (Oldman, 1976, p. 37). Lastly, it is not yet established that the use of libraries has any definite influence on anything else (Ford, 1977, p. 101).

Use of Library Collections: Some Findings

One of the ways of exploring use and user studies is to study the actual incidents of use of information and documents. By and large, the use of library collection is a 'minority event', i.e., a very small segment of rightful members really use collection of their 'primary library'. Like insurance, for a majority of the users the library appears to be a necessary adjunct to the regular work without much direct consequence attributable to the existence of the library. However, its absence is normally felt by some marginal users too. The studies of Shuchman, Scott, Gilmore and others, Slater and Fisher and that of 'The Social Survey' have very much shown this aspect. For an example, 'the social survey', in its survey of UK electrical industrialists found that in case of those firms which had a library less than half of them used it and 18 per cent of the respondents said that they did not use libraries of any kind (Scott, 1960, p. 36). Similarly, in the case of Slater and Fisher's survey (1969, p. 21) the ratio of potential-users of library to total membership was 26.3 per cent for industrial firms and 22.6 per cent for government establishments. Surprisingly the same was as high as 69 per cent in an Indian study (Sridhar, 1985, pp. 31-32). A study of science library at MIT (Bush *et al.*, 1956, p. 94) showed that the ratio of visits to enrollment as 0.37 and Shuchman (1981, p. 30) found technical libraries serving only a small proportion of the engineers. When the use of library documents is examined we find that still smaller segment of users use library documents typically following the 80/20 rule.

Just as inter-personal communication follows the inverse square law, the amount of use of a library is also inversely related to the square of the distance between the library and the functional group to which a user belongs (Frohman, 1969). Yet the psychological distance may be more important than physical distance (Line, 1974, p. 48).

Among all types of documents, 'use of journals' has been studied by many with different methodologies. It was found in these studies that a major portion of the reading of the scientists, engineers and technologists is in journals (Shaw, 1971, pp. 23-24, 32-35 and 81-82). In journal-reading behaviour, "issues" like how many journal, a user regularly reads, how much time he spends on journal reading, the place of reading journals and the factors which affect journal reading have also been investigated. Though the findings are almost unanimous that a user can cope up with his field by reading few journals, the average number of journals actually read varied widely. In Menzel's study (Columbia University, 1958, p. 135), three most important journals accounted for 0.49 fraction of articles read by research scientists. Two surveys of Case Institute of Technology (1960, p. 12) showed that ten mostly read journals accounted for 55.1 per cent and 49.8 per cent of the chemists' journal reading time respectively. Many studies have confirmed that an average scientist/engineer/technologist reads 5 to 15 journals while normally a scientist reads more journals than an engineer or a technologist (Scott, 1959, p. 113; Martyn, 1964, p. 20; Bernal, 1948; Martin, 1962, p. 98; Wood and Hamilton, 1967; Graleswka-Vickery, 1976, p. 274; Hanson, 1964, p. 65; Ford, 1977, p. 32). The use of books and other documents of library have very widely varied from library to library, from subject to subject, and no generalised conclusion except 80/20 rule cited above can be made as far as user-behaviour is concerned.

Correlation of Use of Library Collections with User-Characteristics: Some Findings

The correlation of use of library documents with user-characteristics has not always shown consistent results. Interestingly, a person who saw more journals tended to be active in many ways like attending more meetings and conferences, actively engaged in the work and having better qualifications (Scott, 1959, p. 28).

First of all, the use of library documents is found to vary with the type of organisation and users. Those employed in government establishments and industries have made relatively less use of library (and journals) than those employed in academic and non-profit organisations (Slater and Fisher, 1969, p. 15; Meadows and O'Connor, 1969). The analysis of use of library in science subjects *versus* engineering/technology is found to be fairly close to that of scientist *versus* engineer/technologists pattern, i.e., scientists particularly those in research made more use of libraries than engineers and others (Case Institute of Technology, 1960, p. 21). Surprisingly, the average number of documents consulted by scientists (3.9) was lower than that of engineers, but the used to useful documents ratio was more favourable for scientists. The pressure of time bothered engineers slightly more than it did scientists, but slightly less than it did non-technical personnel. Technicians were found to be underprivileged group in the information-complex (Slater and Fisher, 1969, pp. 17-18 and 50).

The use of library documents (and journals) was found to be linearly and positively related to age and experience of users as per studies of Scott (1966, p. 28), Lipetz (1970), Fearn and Melton (1969). However, beyond the age of 45 years and 10 years of experience the use was found to decline. But the opposite (i.e., negative relation) was found in studies like that of Bath University Library (1971), Barkey (1966) and Ford (1977, p. 93). Women space technologists did not differ from men in making borrowed use of library documents but differed significantly in in-house use and interactions with the library (Sridhar, 1987). Again the use of the library was found to be positively related to the level of education of the users (Scott, 1966, p. 16; Lipetz, 1970; Fearn and Melton, 1969).

Creativity, performance, excellence in work and publication activities are also found to be positively related to use of libraries (Lufkin and Miller, 1966, p. 180; Case Institute of Technology, 1960, p. 21). However, a recent study found no strong relation between use of libraries and academic performance of users (Hiscock, 1986). In addition, high status scientists and engineers tended to use more of library materials and subscribe to more journals (Shaw, 1971, pp. 17, 20, 48-49) and managers and supervisors, particularly those in research and production areas, tended to read more journals than others (Scott, 1960, p. 28).

User-Interactions with Library: Some Findings

Like 'use of library', user-interactions with the library is also a phenomenon of a minority of users. In fact, both the use of library and the user-interactions with the library are highly interdependent and related. However, there is not much research work done about user-interactions with the library. What is available in literature are fragmentary stray attempts to study some interactions of users with libraries. This may be partly due to the time-consuming observation technique to be followed for the purpose. For the same reason many use-studies also did not venture to consider the in-house use of library documents.

A user visits the library for many purposes. Interestingly, Slater and Fisher (1969, p. 29) found that 38 per cent of their respondents visited their libraries for work space (11% exclusively for work space). Even in the study of science library at MIT (Bush *et al.*, 1956, p. 88) a considerable number of persons used the library only as a study hall to make use of their own material. On the contrary, Scott (1959, p. 113) found that 59 per cent of the respondents claimed to do most of their journal reading at home followed by 27 per cent at place of work, 2 per cent during journey on train, 3 per cent in a library, 1 per cent in other places and 2 per cent of the respondents did no reading of technical journals. In a study of in-house use of library documents and seat occupancy, the space technologists were found to visit the library more during departmental reviews for promotion. The distribution of user-visit data over a typical day was bimodal, roughly symmetric and the same was cyclical over a typical week with maximum during mid of a working week (Sridhar, 1982). Like use of library documents, the reservations made by the space technologists for lent-out documents followed skewed distribution and year of acquisition of a document had a stronger effect on its chances of getting more reservations than year of publication (Sridhar, 1983). In another study, it was found that less than one-fourth of the space technologists have had participated in collection development of the library (Sridhar, 1983). Yet another case study showed non-use of classified catalogue, heavy use of subject catalogue and a roughly symmetric bimodal distribution of card catalogue consultation over a typical day by the space technologists. Further, card catalogues are consulted most of the time either to locate a document on the shelf or to interact with the circulation counter than for literature search (Sridhar, 1986). A rational summary of enormous data of use of the library collection and interactions with the library by Indian space technologists is done by way of developing suitable indexes of library-use and user-interactions with library (Sridhar, 1988).

There are no comparable results of earlier research about specific aspects of user-behaviour within library as far as scientists, engineers and technicians are concerned. Most of the findings of user movement/traffic, card catalogue-consultation, in-house use, length of stay, seat occupancy, etc., are that of academic or public library users. Apart from science library at MIT mentioned above, Pings and Anderson's (1965) study of user movement/flow pattern, the study made by the University of Cambridge Library Management Research Unit (1975) about seat occupancy, and Campbell and Shlechter's (1979) study of library design influences on user-behaviour are some of the studies in this direction.

USE OF INFORMATION BY ENGINEER-PRACTITIONERS

Information and communication are all-pervasive human activities. Every one of us (including the present act of the author and the reader) most of the time of our work and life deal with information. The domain of information for any individual can be broadly grouped as:

(i) Professional and work-related information;
(ii) Information for academic or educational attainment;
(iii) Recreational and cultural information;
(iv) Business, economic, social and general information.

These groups are neither mutually exclusive nor exhaustive. It is difficult to clearly identify the boundaries of above types of information. One's professional information could be another's business information. Of course, one's information could also be another's noise and *vice versa*.

The Process of Seeking, Collecting and Using Information

A typical user might come in contact with a source of information in any of the following ways:

(i) Regular browsing of sources of information to identify relevant information to match stored 'needs' and expected future needs and collect information to meet them;
(ii) Known item searches for sources already known for repeated use for a new purpose;
(iii) Specific information/subject search;
(iv) Accidental acquisition of information.

What takes place in the process of seeking, collecting and using information by an individual in a specific subject search is mainly an effort to match his or her requirements with suitable sources of information and seek supply of information to satisfy the need in a cost-efficient way. Some of the factors which determine the degree of success of this process are:

(i) The clarity, certainty and strength of the *need*;
(ii) The initiative, objectivity, habits, styles and idiosyncrasies of the individual (*user*);
(iii) Availability/existence, physical proximity, accessibility, ease of use, degree of interpretedness and perceived utility of the source.

How the process is subjected to the cost-efficient approach can be explained as follows. Unless a person who wants information is fairly sure of getting it without much trouble, he is apt to do without it if it is not essential. In other words, users will utilise an information-service only when doing so costs them less than not using it [Mooers, 1960, p. (iii)]. Relying on memory, skirting around the issue or making do with incomplete or vague information from colleague are some alternatives. Errors in matching process and ignorance about a source of information may lead to alter the composition of monitor, reserve and supply of information in a cost efficient way to yield a relatively satisfactory information supply provided the ignorance is neither too small to worry about nor too large to be remediable. In the process, because of problems of 'access to excess' one might even feel that generating new knowledge is cheaper than an expensive and possible fruitless search. Further, sources which are adaptive to the needs are preferred by users.

The demand for library or information service, its nature and magnitude depend on the perceived need as well as the perception of opportunity to do something to meet that need and vary according to a variety of stimulating or inhibiting factors. The strength of the need or importance of a requirement in conjunction with the perception of probable efforts determines whether or not user pursues his search and if pursued how far he pursues. Further urgency of a requirement will determine when a search is pursued and it may vary over time.

Information needed to solve a problem may not exist and hence cannot be retrieved. One may not even know that the information does not exist unless one performs a search for it. The information existing may be wrong. Above all, information cannot be retrieved even if exists unless it is first identified. Finding the specific information could be difficult, tedious, frustrating and time consuming. There is no ideal centralised worldwide data book which can instantaneously provide desired information. One may have to use sub-optimal means and methods. Knowing the system itself may be complex task and assistance of a specialist required. Policies of libraries, logistics, classified nature of information, language, etc., may necessitate patience and persistence.

Among the factors mentioned above, the accessibility and ease of use are considered to be stronger than the perceived utility, quality and amount of information expected from a source. An irrationality or a curious filtering process is that engineers use channels (sources) in proportion to accessibility and ease of use, but they accept ideas from those channels in proportion to technical quality (Gerstberger and Allen, 1968; Rosenberg, 1970).

The Engineer-Practitioner

An engineer as a practitioner has unique ways of seeking, gathering and communicating work-related information and he differs substantially from others like scientists, researchers and academicians. The differences in needs and demands for information are more strong related to the kind of employment and type of organisation than the discipline. 'Practice' is concerned with the production of goods to consumers or provision of services to clients. It is distinct from 'research' or 'science' which normally focuses on the generation of new knowledge either for knowledge sake or for practice as well as for 'consumption', i.e., the private utilisation of goods and services. Practitioner might also generate new knowledge and consume goods and services from other areas of practice. In other words, 'research' and 'consumption' are incidental to practitioners.

Some of the distinct characteristics of engineer-practitioners relevant to the study of use of information are:

(i) Working in crises mode or under considerable pressure to get on with the job or to meet tight schedules.

(ii) Not necessarily under pressure to make heavy use of new professional information.

(iii) Older knowledge and skills are valued because these allow a person to avoid delays associated with searching for and validating new knowledge.

(iv) Initiate actions and make decisions within a context of imperfect or incomplete knowledge and search for 'satisfactory' solutions rather than 'best' solutions.

(v) The need to combat professional obsolescence by some form of lifelong education is recognised by only leading members.

(vi) Communication patterns are constrained due to confidential nature of areas of work.

(vii) Contribution to professional knowledge is considered as incidental and by-product of their activities. Continuous integration of new ideas within existing practice is not encouraged.

(viii) Isolation from other members of profession and little contact outside their immediate group.

(ix) Affected by controls of standards, codes of practice, procedures, regulations and legislation.

(x) Wide variation (Heterogeneity in the organisation of work. For example, managers draw heavily on variety of information of local interest in brief and development engineers work in project mode and get involved in long prototype testing phase. Often they close their minds to new information/ideas which cause deviations and/or delays to project).

The above characteristics of engineer-practitioners have a lot of bearing on their use and communication of information. Other general characteristics in common as well as in contrast to characteristics of scientists are discussed in the succeeding section.

The Engineer *Vs.* the Scientist as Information User

Whenever engineer as information user is thought of, a comparison of engineer's pattern of using information with that of scientist comes to fore front. Extensive studies on information-behaviour of the engineer *versus* scientist have repeatedly shown and confirmed that engineers are 'papyrophobic'[10] (as against 'papyrocentric' nature of scientists), predominantly oral and informal communication-oriented, 'localite'[11] with group allegiance (as against 'cosmopolite' nature of scientists) and mostly compelled to choose projects with less autonomy. The main motivation of engineer-practitioner is to produce things or bring good things to life as against the motivation to publish in case of scientists. Engineers work in close association with co-workers, likely to have greater internal communication and look upon 'technological gatekeepers'[12] within the organisation for information (Morquis and Allen, 1966). Engineers draw most of their information (63%) from in-house sources (Rosenbloom and Wolek, 1967).

Wilkin (1981) refused the general finding (or belief!) that engineers read less than other professionals stating that the complex relationship between engineers and their sources of information is still not well understood and findings were often interpreted out of contexts.

Engineers and technologists work in industries and in teams (as against scientists working in Universities and R&D institutions). They are less qualified than scientists and operate within a system in which administrative and managerial success is the basis of status and prestige (prestige and status system of scientists is based on scholarly publications and peer recognition). Their main motivation is to produce (as against publishing in case of scientist). Engineers often have higher drives toward achievement and a preference for dealing with objects and processes rather than with people than others (French, 1978, p. 371). Research scientists are in pursuit of truth and knowledge for its own sake. They consider the judgments of their colleagues in science more valid and important than the opinions of the managerial hierarchy and may resist direction and control from non-scientist managers (i.e., clash of 'colleague authority' with 'executive authority'). They are more career-oriented than company. On the other hand, engineers are strongly oriented toward achieving organisation goals, and most aspire to move into the managerial hierarchy. Scientists and engineers are highly critical of management and engineers are even more so than natural scientists (French, 1978, pp. 371-75).

In spite of above alignment of engineers, towards informal sources of information, one cannot lose sight of neat inter-linking and interdependence in use of formal and informal sources of information and the fact that each stimulate the use of the other in many situations and thus act as a mutually supportive, dependent and complementary source of information. Yet the general picture is that scientists are extrovert and depend more on formal sources and engineers are introvert and depend more on informal sources. Within interpersonal sources, scientists contact colleagues outside-the-laboratory more than the engineers do.

Having seen specific characteristics of the engineer-practitioner concerning use of information and how he is contrasted with the scientist, let us note certain common characteristics of both scientists and engineers, particularly creative scientists and engineers.

First of all, the basic needs and drives of creative scientists and engineers are same as that of others. However, they do differ in some important ways. The characteristic that stands out most clearly is their tendency to be much more interested and involved in their work than most other people. The creative process is not a comfortable thing. It involves urge, pressure and some kind of stress application to the person (like labour pain?) leading him to acquire the 'mother complex' about own ideas (egotism or dogmatism?). Further, they tend to have unique set of values which may at times be in loggerhead with immediate goals of the organisation. This tendency is more true with basic or pure researchers than those in applied sciences (French, 1978, p. 371). They are also characterised by broad interest in intellectual activities, reasoning, intelligence, common sense, analytical ability, curiosity, sensitivity to encouragement, divergent thinking, initiative, enthusiasm, excitement, preparedness to undergo hardships, etc. They have education, knowledge and training. Yet self-acquired knowledge and education is most endured. They have exceptionally strong egos and exhibit personal dominance to some extent. Generally, they prefer 'things' to 'people'. They are more open to the irrational in themselves and are great optimists with high degree of self-confidence, which sometimes goes to the point of objectionable arrogance. An important characteristic of creative engineers and scientists for information study is that they tend to accumulate an over abundance of data and information with willingness to ultimately discard. That is why the creative Wilbur Wright said that it is possible to fly without motors, but not without knowledge and skill.

Some Findings and Issues relating to Use of Information by Engineers

The main motivation of an engineer or technologist is to produce something rather than publish and seek peer recognition. But an engineer may seek and use information not only to produce things but for other purposes also. As engineers perform a wide variety of functions, their information requirements are quite varied depending on their respective functions. Firstly, a large portion of time is spent by engineers to know what others have recently done or are doing, to keep up-to-date with the current progress and to give meaning to their own work (the Current approach). The second group is concerned with everyday requirements of specific piece of information, a bit of data, a method, information about apparatus construction, an equation, an explanation of an observation, etc. (Everyday approach). Lastly, the occasional requirement of exhaustive search for information (Exhaustive approach) (Voigt, 1959).

World Federation of Engineering Organisation says that "... the most proper form of information for engineers is the factographic information, analytical-synthetical elaborations and state-of-the-arts" (WFED, 1979, p. 15). The highest ranked type (and nature) of information required by engineers is S&T knowledge for American industrial engineers (82%, Shuchman, 1981, pp. 32-33; 1982, pp. 106-09), everyday information for British mechanical engineers (68.8%), (Wood, 1967, p. 212) and performance-characteristics and specifications (42%) followed by design technique, experimental processes, procedures (13%) for USDOD engineers (Auerbach, 1965, pp. 1-19). To summarise, most of the studies have indicated that roughly one-fifth of the times engineers need a figure or a single simple fact, between a quarter and a third of the times a description of an object, a process, a method or procedure and remaining half of the time general information and ideas from background reading (Hanson, 1964, pp. 67-68).

Three significant sources for innovative ideas or techniques identified are: literature (reading activity), informal discussions with fellow professionals outside-the-organisation and intuition out of own (previous) work (i.e., intra-personal sources). Other less significant sources for innovative ideas are teaching, visiting trade exhibitions, attending courses, conferences and meetings. Interestingly, more aged tended to lean more towards literature and less aged towards informal discussions for innovative ideas (Bernard, *et al.*, 1963/1964, pp. 56-57). Lastly the excessive precision and focus are unwarranted for innovative ideas. A noble laureate (Kelly, 1986, p. 45) says that "... any normally brilliant fellow who allowed himself to be sensitive to creative ideas could by being in the right laboratory at right time, look into some awesomely simple insight. It was just a matter of hanging loose".

Practicing engineers seldom use abstracting and indexing journals. Typically engineers enquire with colleagues rather than searching abstracting and indexing journals for references and go to library shelves rather than card catalogues to choose books. In the process, engineers not only get bibliographic references but also the actual information itself by chance in an unplanned and unintentional way in unfocused browsing and scanning of literature. This is termed as accidental acquisition of information and this may not be a typical way for engineers alone. Such accidental acquisition of information could be increased by a deliberate process of 'peripheration' (normally done as a preparation for inter-personal contact), specialisation in two or more different specialities, having open information-system (as against perfect and closed system), increase in the size of team and identification of largely ill-defined peripheral area of interest.

Engineers delegate the task of information gathering (to junior colleagues and library staff) more than the scientists (Slater and Fisher, 1969, p. 46). The chances of seeking assistance from library staff is higher in case of engineers than scientists, academicians and researchers.

There may not be much differences in the amount of time spent by engineers in information and communication related activities. But some variations in the time spent on information gathering at different stages of a project are noticed. Information gathering is greatest in the initial period of each project, with literature search and outside consultation contributing to the maximum at this stage. The literature search quickly decreases as the project progresses and gets replaced in importance by inter-personal communication (Allen, 1964; Allen and Andmen, 1965; Allen *et al.*, 1966). Regarding the late detection of relevant information the general finding is that engineers and technologists tend to ignore information found late, i.e., after their designs were 'frozen'. Scientists are less preoccupied with time than engineers for information gathering.

Choice of Sources of Information

The choice of a source of information is a matter of judgment. Ideally, information from multiple sources may be more objective than a single source and gathering information and ideas from everywhere to associate them fully with a honeybee mind would be highly rewarding. Engineer-practitioner adopts a more practical, convenient and mostly rational method though not optimal in collecting information. Various factors apart from the task and purpose which affect the choice of a source are already mentioned under 'the process of seeking, collecting and using information'. It is interesting that the engineers do not always turn to information-sources which reward them most. They try to minimise loss than maximise the gain in turning to a particular source, exhibiting a sort of conservative attitude probably due to their objective of doing 'better things' than 'best things' (Gerstberger and Allen, 1968, p. 271). Information which causes delay in the project are often ignored particularly when prototype design is frozen. Yet they first examine the sources having highest probability of success.

In problem solving and decision-making situations, an engineer first, turns most probably to intra-personal reserve supplies such as personal files, one's own head, memory and knowledge (Shuchman, 1981, p. 35; 1982, p. 5; Raitt, 1984, p. 213), failing which or finding it insufficient, next turns to informal channels such as contacting a colleague or delegating it to a colleague, internally generated documents like reports, he then, unless withdraws from the problem or accepts the unsatisfactory situation proceeds to formal information system like a library with or without modifying the nature of the problem. So says Shuchman, "the primary source of engineering information is largely what the engineer keeps in his head . . . or possibly knows where to find in books or catalogues in his office" (1982, p. 5). Since the effects of knowledge and experience are largely involuntary and subconscious, it is felt difficult to make estimate on the nature, size and value of such intra-personal sources of information (Wilson, 1977, p. 61). Despite lower priority accorded to formal sources of information, some of the favourite sources of information to engineers are technical and trade journals, technical reports, standards, patents, suppliers (trade) information (catalogues), data sheets, handbooks, data books and textbooks. The circumstances under which engineers seek information from formal sources are quite interesting. Engineers prefer formal sources of information when they have to (i) minimise risk, (ii) pass on decisions to higher ups, (iii) check authenticity of information from informal sources of information, (iv) fill gaps in information available from informal sources, and (v) overcome difficulty in putting information from informal sources into action.

The limited use of journals by engineers is attributable to the fact that engineers do not encourage the continuous integration of new ideas within existing practice (Wolek, 1969). The prototype model becomes progressively more 'frozen' and decisions irrevocable as the project progresses. They spend 90-95 per cent of a project time in prototype phase compared to limited time (5-10%) spent on systems-definition phase and try to build not the 'best' but a 'better' technology than before by focusing on a limited number of alternatives.

A large portion of personal file (or collection) of engineers consists of unsolicited literature (Langrish, 1972) in the form of trade literature/

catalogues, reports, reprints, pre-prints, xerox copies of papers and notes. These 'extracted literature' significantly overlaps with formal sources of information.

Why Engineers Favour Oral, Personal and Informal Sources of Information?

There are many factors which make engineers introvert and seek information from oral, personal and informal sources around them. These can be traced back in the nature of work of engineers and the characteristics of engineer-practitioner discussed earlier. Some of these factors are:

(i) Engineer is mainly concerned with making things work (Wolek 1969).
(ii) Psychological traits that predispose an engineer to solve problems by himself or with the help of colleagues rather than by finding answer in the literature (Anthony *et al.*, 1969).
(iii) Use of relatively (three decades) old basic science inputs for technological innovation (Crane, 1971, pp. 29-30; Price, 1965, pp. 553-68).
(iv) Habituations of engineers with informal sources (Paisley, 1968, pp. 10-11), i.e., past experience and ready accessibility of personal contacts.
(v) Lack of accessible and usable written (formal) sources of information.
(vi) Complexity of information sought (relative to existing knowledge of the seeker).
(vii) Unfamiliarity with information required/sought.
(viii) Time pressure.

Since engineers require more information in the form of descriptions of objects, processes or methods and less of background theoretical reading, they tend to seek information from inter-personal network within the organisations including 'gatekeepers' and outside customers and vendors. Interestingly, enhanced reading activity in an engineer leads him to enhanced inter-personal communication and a positive correlation do exist between oral and written communication activities (Gralewski-Vickery, 1976, p. 277). It was reported in another study (Allen, 1966; 1977) that the high-performing teams made more extensive use of consultants from within the organisation though a 'psychological cost' is involved for an engineer to confess to an internal source of information like colleagues. The social relation among individuals in the organisation often facilitated use of more internal sources.

Further, the practicing engineers, who normally work under the condition of uncertainty and/or anxiety in diverse set of research areas naturally turn first to their colleagues to compare the results with other similar results (Havelock *et al.*, 1969, pp. 4-12), to get a tailor made solution synthesised to support a finding (Ackoff *et al.*, 1976, p. 148) as a source of confidence and reassurance, to get details concerning procedures or experiments, to cut short the lag in publication-time (Hall, 1972, p. 14), to have expert assistance in locating diverse set of published material (Crane, 1971, p. 30), to communicate interpersonally the complex messages (Wolek, 1970) and to fill the gap between supply of and demand for information (Kunz *et al.*, 1977, p. 9).

There is a 'rich' period of preparatory activity preceding the actual exchange of information in informal discussions which necessitates intermittent use of written and other formal sources of information by engineers. The preparatory activity consists of: (i) 'piggy backing', i.e., storing the information-need with the hope of an accidental encounter with the required information, (ii) 'friendly consultations' with the intention of making friends known about one's interests, and (iii) 'professional peripheration' to get sufficient background and understanding to enable him to approach a competent person (Wolek, 1972).

Informal Communication of Engineers

It is obvious from the results of past studies that the below-ground network of informal incidental communication is vital for practicing engineers. Informal communication becomes 'life blood' for engineers work for various reasons. Some of them are:

- (i) Oral communication is most effective mode in crises and when time is pressing.
- (ii) Words are supplemented by gestures and tone of voice.
- (iii) Ease of perception and mutual evaluation.
- (iv) Immediate to and fro feedback.
- (v) Precision of interaction is much higher.
- (vi) Statements are less guarded and more revealing.
- (vii) Invaluable during the process of gaining experience.

(viii) Important way of learning about new methods and equipment, the characteristics of which are difficult to convey in writing.
(ix) A way of receiving feedback about own ideas and theories.
(x) Conversation with a person aids the assessment of his quality.

There have been many suggestions about fostering and facilitating informal communication within the organisation as well as with outside-the-organisation. According to Menzel, frequency and usefulness of informal communication can be increased by formal arrangements such as seminars, colloquia, common lunches, coffee hours, journal and discussion clubs, proper spatial arrangements and time schedules and appropriate composition of staff taking into consideration age, status, size and organisation of teams, interests among colleagues, presence of some men who have access to fellow professionals elsewhere and those who can attract visitors from elsewhere. The communication with 'outside-the-organisation' can be enhanced by facilitating meetings, conferences, official visits, correspondence and many subsidiary positions and secondary affiliations such as membership of committees, journal editorial boards, visiting lecturerships, etc. (Columbia University, 1958, pp. 167-72). Lickert (1959, p. 194) through his 'linking pin' concept has advocated appropriate formal organisation structure so that atleast one member of every organisation unit should also be a member of the organisational unit immediately higher in the organisational hierarchy, i.e., a sort of overlapping groups in the organisational structure. Pelz and Andrews (1976, p. 53) found that frequent contacts with many colleagues is more beneficial than frequent contact with just a few colleagues and contact with many colleagues both inside and outside one's own group is better than having many colleagues in one place and a just few in other places. Proper architectural layout of the organisation and spatial location of persons in congruence with organisation structure, liberal tours, travels, long distance telephone and other facilities as well as job mobility facilitate informal communication.

Interpersonal communication is a vast area and it has strong roots in social sciences, particularly psychology.

The Engineer-Practitioner as Information User: A Summary

Let us summarise the information gathering patterns of engineers based on past research, particularly the nature of information required, accidental acquisition of information, delegation of information gathering task, use and dependence on information sources—formal, documentary, informal, intra- and inter-personal sources of information and late detection of information. Information-needs of engineers differ widely from those of scientists and other R&D workers. The differences in needs and demands for information are more strongly related to the kind of employment and type of organisation than the discipline.

The accidental or chance or unplanned acquisition of pertinent information occurring in the case of some engineers might have been caused by the process of 'peripheration' as a preparation for inter-personal contact, specialising in two or more quite different specialities, having open information-system as against perfect and closed system, increase in the size of the team and identification of a central core area and a largely ill-defined peripheral area of interest by engineers. In other words apparently irrelevant or non-specific information also plays an important role in the process of problem-solving by engineers. Generally, engineers were found to delegate their information gathering task to others more than scientists.

The factors which decide the choice of a source of information by an engineer apart from task and purpose of seeking information, are physical proximity, accessibility, perceived quality and utility, 'ease of use' and previous experience about the source or acquaintance with the source. These factors are very much interrelated. It is found that accessibility and 'ease of use' are stronger factors than perceived quality and the amount of information expected to yield by a source. An irrationality (i.e., a curious filtering process) is that engineers use channels in proportion to accessibility and 'ease of use', but they accept ideas from those channels in proportion to technical quality (Gerstberger and Allen, 1968; Rosenberg, 1970).

Both formal and informal sources of information are used to meet the information-needs of engineers. Certain needs are associated with certain sources, usage of which varies with job function/nature of work discipline, professional focus, organisational affiliation/work environment, education, nationality, user evaluation of the channel, stages of the task, etc. For example, mechanical engineers engaged in research and teaching made greater overall use of literature, and those engaged in practical aspects of engineering like design, testing and maintenance used data sheets, handbooks, BSI documents and trade literature (Wood and Hamilton, 1967). On the other hand, industrial personnel with professional focus tended to seek external personnel communication and journals as compared to internal corporate sources sought by personnel with operational focus (Rosenbloom and Wolek,

1970, pp. 91-92). Defence personnel also turned most of the time to either colleagues or departmental files or personal files for information (Auerbach, 1966, pp. 106-07; 1965, pp. 1-12).

The general picture is that scientists are extrovert and depend more on formal sources and engineers are introvert and depend more on informal sources. Within inter-personal sources scientists contact colleagues outside-the-laboratory more than the engineers do. Such a difference is attributed to the nature of work that engineers are concerned with 'making things work' (Wolek, 1969), the psychological traits that predispose an engineer to solve problems by himself or with the help of colleagues rather than by finding answer in the literature (Anthony *et al.*, 1969), use of relatively (three decades) old basic science inputs for technological innovation (Crane, 1971, pp. 29-30; Price, 1965, pp. 553-68) and training and habituations of engineers in the use of formal information-system (Paisley, 1968, pp. 10-11). Wilkin (1981) refuted the general findings (or belief!) that engineers read less than other professionals stating that the complex relationship between engineers and their sources of information is still not well understood and findings were often interpreted out of contexts.

It is interesting that the engineers do not always turn to information-sources which reward them most. They try to minimise loss than maximising the gain in turning to a particular source, exhibiting a sort of conservation attitude probably due to their objective of doing 'better things' than 'best things' (Gerstberger and Allen, 1968, p. 271).

In a problem-solving, and decision-making situation, an engineer, first, turns most probably to intra-personal reserve supplies such as personal files, one's own head, memory and knowledge (Shuchman, 1981, p. 35; 1982, p. 5; Raitt, 1984, p. 213) (maybe because of factors like accessibility, proximity and ease of use), failing which or finding it insufficient, next turns to informal channels such as contacting a colleague or a ' technological gatekeeper', or delegating it to a colleague, internally-generated documents like reports, he then (unless withdraws from the problem or accepts the unsatisfactory situation) proceeds to formal information system like a library or information centre, with or without modifying the nature of the problem.

The ranking of formal sources of information as needed by engineers has varied widely among different studies. Scientific, technical, professional and trade journals are the single most widely used formal source of information especially for keeping up-to-date by engineers. Though abstracting and indexing journals are valued high, they are relatively less used. Technical reports were found to be next only to technical journals in importance. High-dependence of engineers on suppliers' information or manufacturers' catalogues or trade literature and heavy use of data books and text books are two important aspects of information gathering by engineers.

It is very difficult to say that reading is a superior way of transferring or acquiring information than hearing or other ways of transferring or acquiring information. Informal, oral and inter-personal sources within the organisation are very important sources of information for engineers whether they are direct or indirect (two step/multistage flow), vertical or horizontal in the organisation structure. Great body of information is getting around by a mechanism that can only be termed gossip.

Several reasons were put forth to emphasise the relatively greater role played by informal sources of information in case of engineers. The practitioner-engineers, who normally work under the condition of uncertainty and/or anxiety in diverse set of research areas naturally turn first to their colleagues to compare the results with other similar results (Havelock *et al.*, 1969, pp. 4-12), to get a tailor made solution synthesised to support a finding (Ackoff *et al.*, 1976, p. 148), to have a source of confidence and reassurance, to get details concerning procedures or experiments, to cut short the lag in publication-time (Hall, 1972, p. 14), to have expert assistance in locating diverse set of published material (Crane, 1971, p. 30), to communicate inter-personally the complex messages (Wolek, 1970) and to fill the gap between supply of and demand for information (Kunz *et al.*, 1977, p. 9).

Wolek (1972) found a rich period of preparatory activity preceding the actual exchange of information in informal discussions consisting of: (i) 'piggy backing', i.e., storing the information-need with the hope of an accidental encounter with the required information, (ii) 'friendly consultations' with the intentions of making friends known about one's interests, and (iii) 'professional peripheration' to get sufficient background and understanding to enable him to approach a competent person.

Hence, the primary source of engineering information is largely what the engineer keeps in his head (intra-personal source) or possibly knows where to find in books or catalogues in his office (Shuchman, 1982, p. 5). But the effects of knowledge and experience are largely unconscious, and it is felt difficult to make estimate on the nature, size and value of such intra-personal sources of information (Wilson, 1977, p. 61).

As far as personal collection or personal file of engineers and technologists are concerned, a large proportion of it consists of unsolicited literature (Langrish, 1972) in the form of trade literature/product catalogues, manuals, technical reports, drawings, trade journals, standard specifications, handbooks, reprints, preprints, xerox copies of papers, drafts, quotations, calculations and notes. These 'extracted literature' or 'excerpts from books' or 'dismantled books' significantly overlap with formal sources. The proportion of reports, reprints, preprints and trade literature in personal collection differs significantly with the attributes of an engineer and his area of work. Increasingly, the size, quality, arrangement and indexing of an individual's private library will influence the nature of volume of his skirmishes with any external library or information-service" (Rowley and Turner 1978, pp. 103-04).

Research in the area of late detection of information and tolerable delay in supply of information, reveal that, generally, engineers and technologists have tended to ignore information found late, i.e., after their designs were 'frozen'. The late detection can either indicate conscientiousness or laziness. Engineers who are most likely to detect late information are those who are conscientious in their literature-searching and infrequent users in their haphazard search find more of accidental late discoveries (Skelton, 1973, p. 145). Late discoveries of information might be due to harmless or harmful-costly ignorance. Latter often leads to repentance after late detection.

CONCLUSION

User-research in science and technology area has necessarily occupied a considerable bulk of literature in library and information science with some inconsistencies, less consolidation and relatively less usable findings. There is a dire need for 'meta analysis'[13] of the literature. Most of the user-research has been carried out in USA, UK and other European countries. The developing countries and underdeveloped countries in general and India in particular almost totally lack sound user-research. What is seen in the literature of Indian librarianship is either 'repackaged' information or unpublished surveys made by students of library and information science. No single major user-study in the area of science and technology is done in India. Systematic, continuous, localised and comprehensive user-studies preferably by information-men 'living with the tribe' are very much lacking. Further, the contingency nature of findings of user-research do not allow for borrowing/importing them from developed countries.

The above presentation is only a representative of the type of user-research carried out in the country as far as science and technology information-users are concerned. The review clearly indicates the void in nature of user-research in the country. User-studies have been neglected both at local and national level by planners of S&T information systems. The piecemeal studies have been mostly local studies of a particular aspect of user-behaviour. The majority of even the piecemeal studies are done by academicians and students. Unless sufficient base line studies are done within the country by the information personnel 'living with the tribe', further developments cannot be carried out based only on the findings of studies done in USA or UK.

User-research in general has not paid enough attention to information-behaviour of engineers and technologists as compared to scientists. The lower level engineers or technicians are the most neglected and under-privileged as far as use of information is concerned.

From the review of literature presented, one would conclude that there exists much ado about need for user-research, speculative findings, claims and counter-claims occupied in a large volume of literature with least consolidation and cumulation. The vast scope for further research in terms of different segments of users, different aspects of user-behaviour and attitude with refined methodologies and rigorous analysis of data still remain unexplored. There also appears to be an overemphasis on generalisation of findings of user-research (ignoring finer details of smaller groups of users and their uniqueness) as well as on citation and use-studies.

Refined theoretical frameworks, unambiguous definition of all terms and concepts, interdisciplinary approaches, probe into 'basic' aspect of user research, co-authorship patterns and comparison of citation linkages with co-authorship pattern and informal communication linkages, user-interaction with libraries, problem of 'access to excess', personality traits and psychological dimensions of users, imaginative methodologies, advanced statistical techniques need more attention.

Despite quite a good number of psychologists involved in the study of information behaviour of scientists, engineers and technologists during 1960s and 1970s, there are hardly any true psychological studies of information behaviour of engineers in the strict sense. Most of the studies are either sociological or psycho-sociological (near psychological).

NOTES AND REFERENCES

1. Compared to information, knowledge is believed to be passive and an item of knowledge becomes an item of information only when it undergoes the active process of communication.
2. Brittain (1975, p. 429) says a lip service has been paid to this objective in many user-studies.
3. US Federal Council for Science and Technology (1965) has found that only 58 out of 450 studies identified were based on objective data.
4. Two of the assumptions made recently in Oxford study of pre-clinical and clinical staff of National Health Service of UK are interesting (Brember, 1985, p. 66).
5. In the context of formalisation of informal communication such as 'invisible college' and 'gatekeeper' functions, Cronin observes that "scientists display a remarkable conservation in their information seeking practices" (1982, p. 228).
6. In an interesting account Barber (1961) presented the general resistance of scientists for innovation itself and pointed out elements within science which limit the norm and practice of open mindedness.
7. Merton (1968) first proposed 'Matthew effect which was based on Matthew's Gospel 'For unto every one that hath shall be given, and he shall have abundance; but from him that hath not shall be taken away even that which he hath'.
8. User will utilise an information-service only when doing so costs them less than not using it [Mooers, 1960, p. (ii)].
9. Communication in this study is characterised by its nature, frequency, whether external or internal to the team and time spent on it.
10. The overriding compulsion of scientist to publish (or perish) in the open literature is 'papyrocentric' and the opposite is 'papyrophobic' (Price, 1969).
11. 'Cosmopolite' and 'localite' are sociological concepts based on whether occupational recognition is centred within one's employing organisation or not. (Goldberg *et al.*, 1965, p. 704). Research scientists are more career-oriented than company oriented.
12. 'Communication star' (even, technological gatekeeper') is defined generally as a person who has received or communicated technical information one or more than one standard deviation above the mean level of communication of the group or the mean number of technical choices or the mean number of contacts. The difference between a 'communication star' and a 'technological gatekeeper' is that the communication star appears to play a role in the in-house communication and become a 'gatekeeper' if he also links the laboratory with external environment. On the other hand, an 'isolate' is one who does not communicate with others, is not approached by others, prepares fewer written communications and is significantly less in contact with the outside environment (Allen, 1970).
13. Meta-analysis is a methodology quantitatively cumulating and integrating findings across studies (Gooding and Wagner, 1985, p. 465).

3

BACKGROUND ABOUT THE CASE STUDIES

Use and user studies should necessarily provide adequate background about the organisation, users and the 'primary' library. Lack of sufficient understanding of the context of case studies may lead to misunderstanding of the data and results. The purpose of this chapter is to introduce at once the ISRO Satellite Centre, its library and the 'space technologists', who are the main focus of the case studies to follow in the subsequent chapters. This overview of the library and its users is expected to set ground for proper understanding of the case studies to follow. However, each case study will provide additional information about the background of the study including methodology and limitations.

Space Activities in India

The space research activities started in India in 1963 and the development and application of space technology gained impetus with the formation of the Space Commission and the DOS in 1972. The Space Commission is an advisory and policy-making apex body with responsibilities for framing the policy, formulating budget for DOS and implementing government's policy in matters concerning outer space. The DOS as an executing body has the responsibility for all matters relating to space technology, space applications and space sciences. The ISRO is the primary agency of DOS charged with the responsibility of executing the R&D programmes and schemes of the DOS in accordance with the directives and policies laid down by the space commission and the DOS.

The ISRO Satellite Centre

For the purpose of the studies presented in this collection, users have been exclusively, and fairly exhaustively, drawn from the ISRO Satellite

Centre (ISAC). This enables the investigator to examine in greater detail the background of the users in terms of activities, scope and nature of the organisation. ISAC is one of the four major centres of ISRO located in Bangalore with the responsibility mainly of (1) planning, detailed definition, design, fabrication, testing and integration of all ISRO spacecrafts, (2) development of technology related to satellite mainframe, (3) long-range planning of future Indian satellites. Thus, ISAC is the prime focus of ISRO's satellite programme.

ISAC had its beginnings in the then Indian Soviet Satellite Project (ISSP) (on 1st September 1972) at Bangalore with a small band of specialists. It was also called Indian Scientific Satellite Project (ISSP) and ISRO Satellite Systems Project (ISSP). The first Indian satellite 'Aryabhata' built in this project was launched on 19th April 1975 at Soviet Cosmodrome. Subsequently the project became one of the four full-fledged major centres of ISRO with the present name of ISAC on 3rd November 1976. Since its inception, the centre functioned from hired/temporary premises at Peenya Industrial Estate, Bangalore till it moved to its own premises at Kodihally near Bangalore Airport during May-June 1984.

DOS had a manpower of 15,133 as on 1st April 1985, of which about 66 per cent are technical staff and the rest, the administrative staff. The ISAC's share of manpower is about 12 per cent, i.e., 1834 as on the same date. Nearly 71 per cent of the staff of ISAC are technical (as against 66% in entire DOS), of which 92 per cent are other than Group D employees.[1]

The work at ISAC is divided among various projects and divisions.[2] The projects are organised on inter-division/section and inter-centre basis with identified teams participating in the development tasks at subsystem/system levels of spacecrafts. While the projects are responsible for the execution of specific time-bound tasks, the divisions are entrusted with the responsibility of R&D support required for current and future projects.

In addition to time bound projects, several Technology Development Programmes (TDPs) are undertaken each year by small groups within divisions, each one mainly centred around one or two individuals. The TDPs are low budget and slightly time relaxed R&D projects going side by side with main projects and they act as feeder systems to main satellite projects starting with new concepts and indigenisation of foreign technology.

In addition, technical personnel of ISAC are involved in various supporting technical activities, facilities and services such as environmental test facilities, mechanical fabrication facilities, electronics fabrication facilities, quality assurance, etc.

The term 'space technologists', as used in these studies, refers to scientists, engineers, managers, technocrats, technicians and other technical staff of ISAC excluding group D employees and staff members of library, transport and medical sections.

Nature of Space Technology and Space Technologists

Sketching the nature of space technology, Dhawan (1983, pp. 4-5) says "space flight is primarily a matter of technology rather than science. It is true that the design and development of rockets and spacecraft draw heavily upon the knowledge of many sciences. But this complex combining of technical knowledge from many disciplines to achieve a set task in a very inhospitable environment is essentially an engineering systems job with management techniques which have evolved to deal with the large scale, complex and high risk ventures in which a large number of disciplines, individuals and institutions are inter-linked."

Thus the nature of activities of space technologists is characterised as heterogeneous, high risk, time bound, involving high technology, system analysis/engineering, complex and large scale mission activities. Though the work is often described as R&D, it is less of research and more of development in nature. Hence, it may be more appropriate to classify it somewhere in between R&D and industry. It is a mission-oriented organisation and its scope encompasses a vast variety of heterogeneous subjects. Table 3.1 depicts the composition of the population as at the beginning of these studies.

Further, there exists a considerable staff mobility and turnover, especially in the case of juniors and less experienced staff. This is in addition to mobility due to re-deployment of manpower within ISAC as well as within ISRO. Further, the staff strength of the centre has been on the increase during the study period. Table 3.5. depicting the growth of ISAC Library membership indicates steep increase in staff strength of ISAC. An analysis of membership turnover in ISAC Library during the year July 1982 and June 1983 indicated that there was a 16 per cent increase in membership and about 4 per cent have left ISAC during the year. The total personnel employed at ISAC has doubled in almost five-years period ending 1983 and it is likely to be doubled once again for the next five years.

TABLE 3.1: Specialisation of ISAC Library Users (Space Technologists)

	Specialisation in Highest Qualification	*Population (as of Jan. 82)*		*Response Population*	
		No.	*%*	*No.*	*%*
A	Physics	60	8.3	42	8.3
B	Chemistry	4	0.6	4	0.8
C	Mathematics	(+J) 36	5.0	20	3.9
D	Civil Engineering	3	0.4	3	0.6
E	Mechanical Engineering	233	32.1	137	27.0
F	Aeronautical and Structural Engineering			19	3.7
G	Thermal Engineering			7	1.4
H	Electrical Engineering	16	2.2	17	3.4
I	Electronics	317	43.7	222	43.8
J	Computer Science	(See C)		9	1.8
K	Chemical Engineering/ Technology			1	0.2
L	Material Science			4	0.8
M	Management			9	1.8
N	Others*	57	7.9	13	2.6
	Total	726	100.2	507	100.1

Key: * Others included Metallurgy, Botany, Controls and Dynamics, Statistics, Optics, Atmospheric Science, Electronics—Instrumentation, Photography, Space Dynamics, Keypunching etc.

Note: Eighteen responses invalidated, 7 not answered and 3 errors are not shown in the table.

Space missions need all sorts of hardware from a variety of industries in the country which are directly or indirectly involved in the mission. Space technology has not only acted as one of the catalysts for industrial growth but has also given many spin-offs to industry. About 100 industries have worked with ISRO in supplying materials, equipment and services and about 25 industries have begun using ISRO developed technology for non-space uses. As far as space applications are concerned, many user-agencies such as research organisations, autonomous bodies, government agencies and departments have a close link with ISRO. In this area, team effort from specialists of other agencies is also needed.

Other significant features/characteristics of the space technologists are that they are working in a young organisation and are themselves quite young (the average age is 31 years). The population included 7.6 per cent females. The average experience of the respondents in ISRO, and before joining ISRO, are respectively, 5.9 years and 2.5 years. A large majority of the respondents brought prior experience from industry (41%), R&D organisations (30%) and academic institutions (18%).

Nearly three-fourths (73%) are fairly or fully satisfied with their present jobs. The frequency distribution of performance based on professional activities and achievements (index constructed in a study) showed that about 13 per cent had zero value, 37 per cent scored a low value of 1 to 5, 45 per cent scored 6 to 10 and the rest of 5 per cent a high value of 11 or more.

The index consists of three parts (Table 3.2). The first part includes number of lectures delivered, number of seminars, symposia and conferences attended and number of internal documents/reports prepared in last one year, average number of papers published per year of experience, average number of patents obtained and awards and citations received per year of experience (the latter two with a weightage of 5), number of professional associations, societies, board of studies, editorial committees in which one has a membership and number of professional journals personally subscribed. The second part consists of number of official tours during the last one year and number of committees in which one has membership. The third part consists of number of in-service training received so far and number of part-time studies

TABLE 3.2: Frequency Distribution of Professional Activities and Achievements Index Values

Frequency	*Professional Activities and Achievements Index Value*			
	Part 1	*Part 2*	*Part 3*	*Total Composite Index*
00	63	205	172	26
01	27	43	100	19
02	27	36	22	12
03	28	20	5	9
04	19	21	5	15
05	29	13	1	16
06—10	42	33	0	45
11—15	28	12	0	15
16—20	3	9	0	15
21—30	7	3	0	14
31—40	2	0	0	8
41—50	0	0	0	2
Above 50	0	0	0	1
Total	275	395	305	197

Note: If data is not available for any one of the components, the case is dropped from the frequency distribution of total composite index.

undertaken in last two years. In the development of the above index the final value has been rounded off to nearest integer and if any one of the components is not known the case has been excluded as not known.

Nearly 55 per cent of the population are scientists and engineers by designation and the rest are non-gazetted technical staff. About 12 per cent of the space technologists are technocrats and a little over 5 per cent work exclusively in project management offices and core teams. Over two-thirds (68%) are involved in design, development, fabrication and testing activities and about one-fifth (20.5%) in management, planning and system-analysis work. Large-scale developmental work has necessitated more middle and lower-level and less qualified personnel, particularly in various service sectors. The space technologists show a wide professional diversity in terms of their specialised fields of activities.

The highest educational qualification of the space technologists grouped for both population and response population at the broad level such as undergraduates, diploma holders, graduates, post-graduates and doctorates is shown in Table 3.3. The Table 3.3 shows that about one-fifth of the population consists of undergraduates and another one-fifth diploma holders. Graduates and post-graduates constitute 27 per cent each. The rest of about 5 per cent are doctorates. The significant types of qualifications are: undergraduate certificates like ITI, NAC and NTC (116), diploma in electronics, communication, telecommunication and radio engineering (72); diploma in mechanical engineering (54); degrees like BE (123), B.Sc. (22), B.Tech. (16), ME (45), M.Sc. (63), M.Tech. (64), and Ph.D. (32).

TABLE 3.3: Qualifactions of the Space Technologists

Qualifications	*Population*		*Response Population*	
	No.	*%*	*No.*	*%*
Undergraduates	145	202.	96	18.5
Diploma holders	148	20.7	98	18.9
Graduates	196	27.3	153	29.5
Postgraduates	196	27.3	149	28.7
Doctorates	32	4.5	23	4.4
Total	717	100.0	519	100.0

Note: The table excludes 120 not known cases under population and 16 not answered cases under response population.

Table 3.4 presents the pattern of broad disciplines of the IST like pure sciences, applied sciences/engineering/technology and management based on the specialisation as well as qualifications of the space technologists (doctorates and vocationally trained personnel have been categorised separately in this table). As per Table 3.4, nearly 62 per cent of the population belongs to applied science, Engineering and technology, about 13 per cent to pure science and only 1.3 per cent to management.

TABLE 3.4: Subject to specialisation and Qualifications

Subject	*Population*		*Response Population*	
	No.	*%*	*No.*	*%*
Doctorates	32	4.5	23	4.4
Pure Sciences	85	11.9	66	12.7
Applied Science, Engineering and Technology	443	61.8	326	62.8
Management	9	1.3	7	1.3
Vocationally Trained Undergraduates	145	20.2	96	18.5
Others	3	0.4	1	0.2
Total	717	100.1	519	99.9

Note: Excludes 120 not known cases under population and 16 not answered cases under response population.

By the criterion of subject of specialisation, there are 44 per cent electronics engineers, 27 per cent mechanical engineers, and 8 per cent physicists.

ISRO Satellite Centre (ISAC) Library

It may be more appropriate, at this stage, to know in brief the background and status of the 'primary library'[3] used by the space technologists. The Library of ISAC came into existence in the last quarter of 1972 as a supporting facility to the then ISSP. Later, in 1976 when ISSP became ISAC, the Library attained the status of centre library. The library developed from a small collection of books and a few journals manned by non-professionals. However, the growth was very much accelerated after becoming the centre library and after induction of professional staff in 1978. ISAC library is a special library attached to the mission oriented organisation (i.e., ISAC) and its scope encompasses a vast variety of heterogeneous canonical subjects as mentioned earlier.

Table 3.5 presents the growth pattern of ISAC Library in terms of budget, staff, space, members, collection and services. The steep increase after 1978 in almost all aspects is quite clear. Table 3.6 depicts growth

TABLE 3.5: Growth of ISAC Library Budget, Staff, Space, Members, Collection and Services

Year	Budget (Rs. in lakhs for F.Y.)	Staff			Space		Members	Services*				Collection
		Prof.	Non-Prof.	Total	Plinth area (in sq. ft.)	No. of reading seats		Repro-graphics (in 000's)	Issues (in 000's)	Consul-tations (in 000's)	Total use of documents (in 000's)	
1972	1.02	0	1	1	800	16	NA	NA	NA	NA	NA	212
1973	1.20	0	1	1	800	16	200	NA	NA	NA	NA	1,229
1974	1.53	0	2	2	800	16	263	NA	NA	NA	NA	1,807
1975	1.80	0	2	2	800	16	285	NA	NA	NA	NA	2,328
1976	3.40	0	3	3	800	16	316	NA	NA	NA	NA	3,539
1977	5.20	0	4	4	1,100	16	485	NA	NA	NA	NA	5,005
1978	7.98	3	5	8	2,500	30	633	135	NA	NA	NA	7,274
1979	9.52	4	5	9	2,500	20	692	185	7	NA	7	13,306
1980	13.00	4	6	10	3,000	10	783	233	15	31	46	29,063
1981	20.00	4	6	10	4,000	50	890	260	18	33	51	42,753
1982	22.00	6	5	11	4,000	40	982	300	23	47	70	54,725
1983	28.00	9	8	17	4,000	40	1,160	300	32	64	96	65,563
1984	27.00	10	8	18	8,000	60	1,210	400	25	64	89	79,215
1985	24.60	11	8	19	8,000	50	1,305	505	31	91	122	90,345

Key: NA—not available; *—Other services are enumerated in Chapter 8, Case Study 14; F.Y.—Financial year.

Note: Budget excludes salary, office stationery, fixture, lighting and other utilities, import duties, etc.; Members include only those who have registered themselves and availed library borrower tickets.

TABLE 3.6: Growth of ISAC Library Collection

Year	*Current Periodicals*	*Bound Periodicals*	*Books*	*Reports*	*Standards*	*Micro-forms (Reports)*	*Trade Catalogues*	*Reprints*	*Audio-visual Materials*	*Total**
1972	0	0	212	0	0	0	0	0	0	212
1973	30	0	1,229	0	0	0	0	0	0	1,229
1974	60	0	1,807	0	0	0	0	0	0	1,809
1975	72	54	2,220	54	0	0	0	0	0	2,328
1976	96	405	2,729	405	0	0	0	0	0	3,539
1977	141	604	3761	604	0	36	0	0	0	5,005
1978	208	749	5,740	749	0	36	0	0	0	7,274
1979	337	937	7,639	1,784	518	1,898	304	197	29	13,306
1980	533	1,665	9,040	2,847	1,355	13,425	407	278	46	29,063
1981	575	2,224	9,984	3,369	2,151	24,163	484	316	62	42,753
1982	645	2,780	11,462	4,200	3,065	31,962	698	462	96	54,725
1983	655	3,943	12,748	5,011	3,309	39,022	800	630	100	65,563
1984	631	4,497	14,158	5,947	3,991	48,828	850	840	104	79,215
1985	632	5,670	15,800	6,832	4,645	55,512	890	891	105	90,345

Key: *—The total excludes current periodicals.

of collection in terms of its components such as books, reports, journals, etc. The Library provides most of the routine services of a special library. Many services are quite informal. A large number of short-range reference queries are attended to by the library staff almost daily. The range of the services offered by the library include acquisition, reader assistance, indexing, lending, consultation, inter-library loan, reprographic, micrographic, reference, translation, extension, documentation, current awareness, literature search, reader alert and abstracting services and regular as well as *ad hoc* publications.

NOTES AND REFERENCES

1. Group D is the lowest of the cadre of groups A, B, C and D as per Government of India classification of employees.
2. In October 1984, divisions have been re-designated as groups, and sections as divisions.
3. "The concept of a 'primary library' is based upon the premises that every user should have atleast one library that he can make use of which will put him in touch with the library systems" (Hoadley and Clark, 1972, p. 133).

4

USER-VISIT, MOVEMENT AND LENGTH OF STAY IN LIBRARY

CASE STUDY 01

PATTERNS OF USER-VISIT AND IN-HOUSE USE

Introduction

Normally, libraries keep a register at the entrance of the library for users to record their visit to the library. Like in any other library, in ISAC Library also a good number of users ignore this register. Even though such statistics are useful in knowing library visits of different types of users, peak and lean hours of use, intensity of in-house use, etc., there is no easy and cost-effective way to collect complete data. Keeping this in view, attendance of in-house use of ISAC Library has been recorded at random intervals and analyzed in this study.

Methodology, Sample and Limitations

ISAC Library is housed temporarily in an industrial shed with limited and inadequate reading facilities. There are 20 reading tables and 30 chairs and another 10 chairs with writing pad attachment. Thus, at any time it can accommodate a maximum of 40 users. The total registered members of the library is about 1,000. For the purpose of survey, about 850 technical staff are covered in the study. Library is kept open from 8.00 hours to 17.30 hours on working days and between 9.30 hours to 16.00 hours on holidays except on Sundays and selected public/national holidays.

Attendance of in-house users (i.e., excluding administrative staff of the Centre and those visiting library exclusively to return document or interact with issue counter) of library has been recorded 3-4 times in a working day at an interval of about 2 hours for a total period of two months. The time of recording was continuously advanced by about 15-20 minutes per day. During holidays names of all users who visited library were recorded. Some of the important events which occurred during the period of study (i.e., 16 March 1983 to 17 May 1983) were launching of a satellite built by the centre at one of the other centres of ISRO (which necessitated presence of considerable number of scientists and engineers at the launching centre and other operational areas), part of the reviews for departmental promotion and preparatory time for a forthcoming review of a major project.

In analyzing the data, a simple frequency distribution of sample attendance with maximum, minimum, and average attendance is presented. A time series analysis of the data by moving average method has been made to trace the trend and seasonal variations in attendance in different times of a day, different days of a week and for different weeks and months covered in the study. Also, a comparison is made with overall statistics of user visits and in-house 'use' based on guesstimate records. Membership turnover is also examined to see its contribution in secular irreversible trend in in-house use of library.

The total number of user visits recorded in the study including 5 holidays is 1,721 and it forms nearly 50 per cent of total user visits of guesstimate records. Hence the sample is quite adequate and representative. Nearly, 11,000 in-house 'uses' of various documents in the library during this period is recorded in the guesstimate statistics based on sample recording of number of documents left on reading tables of the library.

Frequency Distribution of Library Attendance

Table 4.1 depicts the frequency distribution of systematic sample library attendance collected during the period from 16 March 1983 to 17 May 1983 along with total number of user visits. By and large, the attendance at a time is mainly conditioned by the available reading facility described above. A maximum attendance of 36 was found once during 16.00-17.30 hours and an attendance of 31 during 11.00-12.00 hours. The minimum attendance of one was found once during 8.00-9.00 hours and once on a holiday. The average attendance works out to 11.6.

Time Series Analysis of the Data

Average as well as moving average attendance at the library at different block hours of the day are presented in Table 4.2.

TABLE 4.1: Frequency Distribution of Library Attendance

No. of Users at a Time	*Frequency of Occurrence*	*Total No. of 'User Visits'*
1	2	2
2	3	6
3	2	6
4	5	20
5	9	45
6	7	42
7	12	84
8	14	112
9	13	117
10	10	100
11	13	143
12	10	120
13	9	117
14	6	84
15	4	60
16	4	64
17	2	34
18	3	54
19	2	38
20	3	60
21-25	8	179
26-30	6	167
31 and above	2	67
Total	149	1,721

TABLE 4.2: Library Attendance at Different Block Hours

Timing	*Attendance*	
	Average	*Moving Average*
8.00- 9.00 Hrs	6.5	9.8
9.00-10.00 Hrs.	13.1	10.4
10.00-11.00 Hrs.	11.6	12.7
11.00-12.00 Hrs.	13.3	11.0
12.00-13.00 Hrs.	8.2	10.9
13.00-14.00 Hrs.	11.1	11.3
14.00-15.00 Hrs.	14.5	11.7
15.00-16.00 Hrs.	9.4	12.2
16.00-17.30 Hrs.	12.7	11.1

As could be seen from Table 4.2, the early morning hours, i.e., between 8.00-9.00 hours have the least attendance of 6.5 and a maximum of 14.5 occurs between 14.00-15.00 hours. It may be noted here that the issue counter is closed between 8.00 and 9.30 hours and on holidays. The next to maximum, i.e., 13.3 occurs between 11.00-12.00 hours. Interestingly, the expectation of higher attendance during the lunch break (12.00-13.30 hours) and tea breaks (10.30-11.00 hrs. and 15.00-15.30 hours) is not supported by the data. However, as per moving average the maximum attendance occurs between 10.00-11.00 hours and 15.00-16.00 hours.

Since the sample attendance is taken at different timings with fixed interval, it fairly represents a continuous data when presented as moving average. The moving average of attendance clearly shows a trend where the attendance gradually increases from early morning till 11.00 hours, falls down at the mid of the day, again increases to reach the maximum at 14.00 hours and falls again at the end of the day. Thus, there are two peak hours for the library. Fig. 4.1 indicates that the moving average of attendance when plotted on graph results in a bimodal, roughly symmetric distribution with two peaks wherein mean and median have almost same value (i.e., 11.2 and 10.9, respectively).

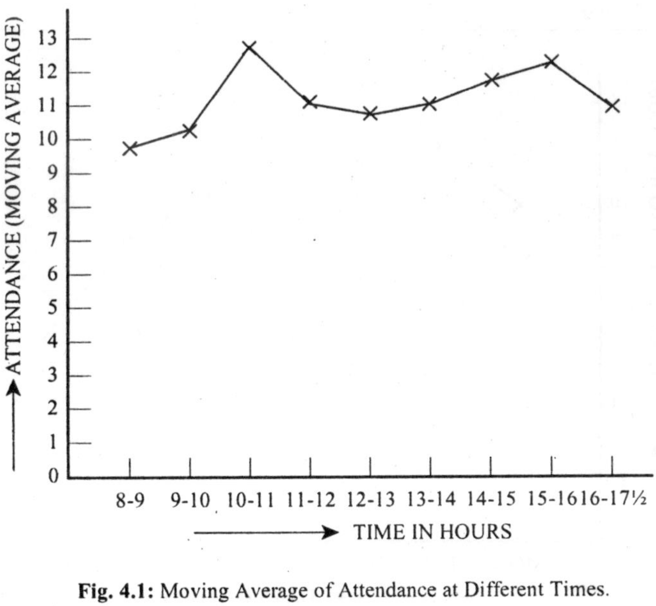

Fig. 4.1: Moving Average of Attendance at Different Times.

The average and moving average of attendance on different days of a week are presented in Table 4.3. It is but natural that holidays get least attendance. The data shows a clear trend of gradual increase in attendance starting from Monday till it reaches maximum in the middle of the week (i.e., Thursday) and again decline slowly at the end of the week. Fig. 4.2 plots the same data to show a rainbow-shaped cyclic variation of library attendance during a week. The diagram represents a rough lepto kurtosis distribution with fairly sharp peak and also a slightly positively skewed distribution.

TABLE 4.3: Average and Moving Average of Attendance on Different Days of the Week and on Holidays

Day of the Week/Holidays	*Attendance*	
	Average	*Moving Average*
Monday	11.0	10.0
Tuesday	10.7	11.6
Wednesday	13.0	11.5
Thursday	10.7	12.0
Friday	12.2	10.4
Saturday	8.4	9.0
Holidays	6.2	—

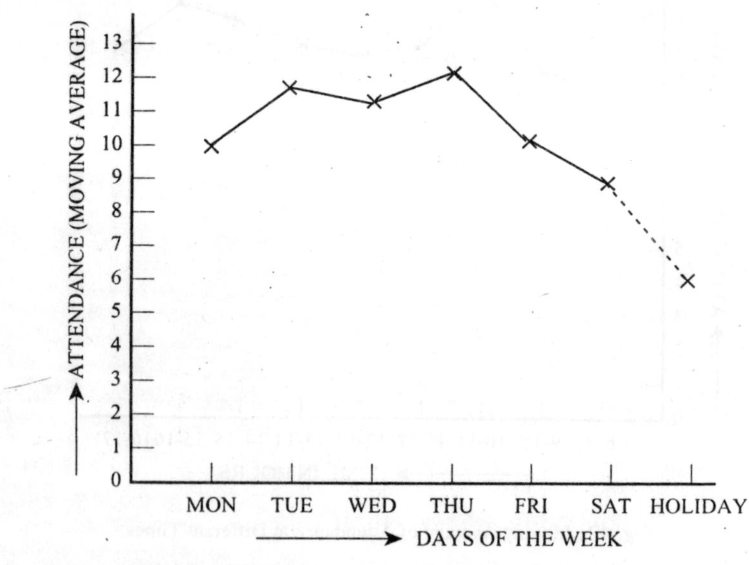

Fig. 4.2: Moving Average of Attendance on Different Days.

Tables 4.4 and 4.5 respectively present the attendance data over weeks and months excluding holiday attendances. Data is inadequate to indicate any cyclic variation. However, it helps to see seasonal variation, if any.

TABLE 4.4: Average and Moving Average Attendance for Different Weeks

Week No.	*Attendance*	
	Average	*Moving Average*
1	14.5	16.3
2	18.1	15.7
3	14.5	14.0
4	9.5	10.9
5	8.7	9.5
6	10.1	9.4
7	9.1	9.5
8	9.4	10.2
9	11.2	10.2
10	10.1	10.7

As could be seen from Table 4.5, maximum attendance at the beginning of the survey comes down from the end of March to the middle of April and shoots up again during beginning of May.

TABLE 4.5: Average Attendance at a Time for Different Months

Month	*Average Attendance*
March	15.4
April	8.7
May	9.5

There are possible reasons attributable to this change. The data substantiates the general belief that during the period of departmental reviews for promotion (i.e., second halfs of March, May, September and December) there will be higher visits to library and greater in-house use of library documents than during any other period. This is obvious from the fact that March has an average attendance of 15.4 whereas April and May have 8.7 and 9.5, respectively. It may also be noted here that more persons appear for departmental review during March and September than in the months of May and December. Secondly, considerable number of users were out of station and also otherwise busy during April for launching of a satellite.

Another important aspect to be taken note of while analyzing the data is library membership turnover. During the period of one year (i.e.,

July 82-June 83), the total membership has increased from 936 to 1,082 with an average monthly addition of 16 and deletion of 4. This accounts for a clear 15.6 per cent annual (or 1.3% monthly) increase in membership. In addition, every month four old members are replaced by four new members who make relatively more visits to library and more in-house use of library documents for acquaintance with the organization and the heterogeneous space technology which is normally not taught as a specialization in the academic institutions. Thus, these factors should have actually made the attendance of successive weeks and months more and hence the variation noticed in April and May compared to March should have been slightly more than what we see now.

Frequency Distribution of User Visits

Table 4.6 depicts how the same data of 1,719 user visits are distributed among 429 (technical) users of the Library.

TABLE 4.6: Frequency Distribution of User Visits

No. of Visits	*No. of Users*	*Total 'User visits'*
1	142	142
2	71	142
3	50	150
4	26	104
5	25	125
6	29	174
7	25	175
8	11	88
9	14	126
10	7	70
11	7	77
12	10	120
13	2	26
14	1	14
15	1	15
16	1	16
17	2	34
18	1	18
19	0	00
20	1	20
24	1	24
25	1	25
34	1	34
Total	429	1,719

The average visit per user is about 4 and the number of visits per user during the survey ranges from 1 to 34. As could be seen from Table 4.6, nearly one-third of the users have made only one visit. On the other hand, 10 intensive users have made, on an average, 20 visits to the library during the sample survey. Further, 368 users (i.e., 85.79% of those visited) have made a total of 1,012 visits (i.e., 58.87% of total visits) and the remaining 61 users (i.e., 14.22%) have made the balance 707 visits (i.e., 41.12%).

A list of 34 users who visited 10 or more times was examined to ascertain any correlation with in-house use and user characteristics. The list does not reveal any clear correlation of in-house use of the library with rank/status of user and user divisions. Thus, the popular belief that the nearness of a division or section to the library plays a positive role in increasing the in-house use of library is not supported by the data. However, slight correlation, if any, is expected when the entire population of 429 users is analyzed in a separate study.

The data in Table 4.6 is reformulated into five groups in Table 4.7 incorporating the remaining 'non-users'. Table 4.7 clearly shows that a small segment of regular users make in-house use of library much more than a large number of total users/members. Since the available reading facility in the library and in-house use are interdependent, it is essential to investigate the reasons for less use or non-use by some members and promote in-house use among infrequent users and non-users.

TABLE 4.7: Intensity of In-house Use

User Type	*Frequency Range*	*Average No. of Visits*	*No. of Users*	*% of Users*	*Total User Visits*	
					No.	*%*
Non-Users	0	0	421	49.53	0	0
Infrequent Users	1—3	1.65	263	30.94	434	25.25
Occasional Users	4—7	5.50	105	12.35	578	33.62
Frequent Users	8—13	9.94	51	6.06	507	29.49
Intensive Users	14—34	20.00	10	1.18	200	11.63
Total	0—34	202	850	100.00	1,719	99.99

Results and Observations

The study reveals that the average attendance at any time is 11.6 and it varies from 1 to 36. The distribution of in-house use of library during a typical day has a bimodal, roughly symmetric distribution with two peaks where the mean and median have almost the same value. The distribution of in-house use over a typical week is cyclic with maximum in the middle of the week and minimum at the beginning and end of the week. The data substantiates the belief that during the season of departmental reviews for promotion, there will be considerable increase in in-house use of library. Secondly, major events/activities of the Centre have caused swift variations in the in-house use of library. The analysis of membership turnover indicates an irreversible trend of nearly 16 per cent increase in membership per year apart from replacement of about 50 existing members by new members in a year.

The average 'user visit' per user during the survey is about 4 and user visits have ranged from 1 to 34 during the survey. Nearly one-third of the users have made only one visit and 10 intensive users have made, on an average, 20 visits during the survey. The study clearly shows that a very small band of users make in-house use of library much more than all others put together.

Following are the further observations made while conducting the survey. It is estimated that on an average five documents are used per visit per user. By and large, in-house use of library is more by new entrants than experienced ones, and by male users than female users. This informal observation of men making more in-house use than women users is disproved on a later case study (Case Study 18). In-house use of library on holidays is more by high-placed scientists and engineers than others. Again, high-placed scientists and engineers use library more during 16.00-17.30 hours of the day than at other times. More non-technical staff of the centre visits library during lunch break. The technical staff from service facilities/sectors have, by and large, made least in-house use of library. Lastly, users from such of the sections/divisions/projects which are near the library have made more use (in-house) of library than others. However, as noted earlier, this is not true in case of intensive users of the library, indicating thereby that strong motivation to seek information is likely to overcome a barrier like distance between the user and the library.

Conclusion

The reading facility at ISAC Library is too inadequate by any standard and this has greatly hampered the in-house use of library. Secondly, the very nature of work of users does not allow them to have regular library hours. In other words, the nature of work of space technologists differs from that of academicians, pure scientists and even R&D workers.

Thirdly, free and fairly adequate reprographic service has enabled many users to carry copies of documents of their interest to their work situations rather than consulting them in the library. Keeping in view all the limitations set out, it may be safely concluded that the in-house use of ISAC Library is quite considerable. A better picture can be had if the data is compared with the data of similar libraries. A separate study is also being carried out to correlate in-house use of library with user characteristics and other variables.

CASE STUDY 02

PATTERNS OF USER MOVEMENT AND LENGTH OF STAY IN THE LIBRARY

Introduction

The user-behaviour within the library in terms of physical interactions with various library services and facilities is an interesting and less explored area in user-research. Such a study has to necessarily exclude the non-users of the population. Like 'use of library', user-interactions with a library is also a phenomenon of a minority of users. In fact, both the use of library and user-interactions with library are highly interdependent and related. However, there is not much work done to study and understand user-interactions with libraries. What is available in literature are fragmentary stray attempts to study some interactions of users with libraries. This may be partly due to the time-consuming observation technique to be followed for the purpose. For the same reason many use-studies also did not venture to consider the in-house use of library documents.

Some past findings about interactions of scientists and engineers with libraries are already presented in Chapter 2.

Interactions of the Space Technologists with their Primary Library[1]

As an extension of a previous study (Sridhar, 1982), a limited sample of the space technologists drawn from the population have been observed for their broad behaviour regarding physical interactions with their 'primary library'.[2] The observations relate to the patterns of library visits, library traffic/user movement, use of various services and facilities (within the library) and length of stay of the users in the library. The

'Primary library' in this study is ISAC Library and it is housed in a centrally located area as part of the main building of the organisation on a plinth area of about 10,000 sq. ft. Approximately one-fourth of the plinth area consists of mezzanine floor. The building was neither designed for the library nor it is adequate to house the library at the time of study.

Pattern of User-Visit to the Library

Based on the data recorded on 24 randomly chosen days during October 1984 and January 1985, it was found that on an average 200 users visit the library (on a working day), of which 55 visited the mezzanine floor of the library where current journals, bound volumes of journals, standards, reprints and product catalogues are housed. It may be noted that sampling is done for selection of days and user visit data was collected for the entire day when selected.

User-Movement/Traffic within the Library

Further, 13 purposeful biased sample of the space technologists (other than those who visited library for a very short time for an issue or return transaction or for indenting or collecting xerox copies) were observed during January 1985 for their movement within the library. In this observation, on an average, a user spent 58 minutes on a visit to the library in 4 to 5 units out of 13 such units within the library. The mapping of users movement indicated that, by and large, the users moved in near critical path avoiding zig-zag movements (except when they deliberately wanted to pay repeated visits to a particular unit). Eight out of the 13 only moved on to mezzanine floor and three of them came down to ground floor for use of books and reports and to make enquiries at the circulation counter. The users have often made more than one entry/interaction/visit to the following units: circulation counter, book stack and reading area for books and reports.

Table 4.8 presents the average user visits to ten service areas (units) within the library together with average length of stay. As could be seen from the table, book stack and circulation counter have accounted for more than half of the total visits (56.8%). Display of new arrivals and reading area for books and reports have been moderately visited by the users. A maximum average time of 27.1 minutes per visit has been spent at the display of new arrivals of journals and current journals followed by 20 minutes in the reading area for books and reports and 16 minutes in the bound journals, standards, reprints and product catalogues unit.

TABLE 4.8: User-Visits to Service Areas within the Library and Length of Stay

Sl. No.	*Service Area*	*Average No. of User-visits per Day*	*Percentage of Total Visits*	*Average Length of Stay (in minutes)*
1.	Circulation counter	170.2	27.7	3.1
2.	Reprographics service	17.3	2.8	
3.	Micrographics unit	3.0	0.5	NA
4.	Card catalogues	32.0	5.2	8.0
5.	Report stack	6.4	1.0	10.0
6.	Book stack	178.8	29.1	12.0
7.	Reading area (books & reports)	67.0	10.9	20.0
8.	Display of new arrivals (books, reports & standards)	82.5	13.4	5.3
9.	Display of new arrivals (journals) and current journals	44.5	7.3	27.1
10.	Bound journals, standards, reprint & product catalogues	12.0	2.0	16.0
	Total	613.7	99.9	

Key: NA—Not available.

Length of Stay of the Space Technologists in the Library

About 30 randomly selected Indian space technologists were observed for their length of stay in the library during December 1984 and January 1985. Counting was done from the time the user stepped into the lib-ary till the time he stepped out. In order to consider serious in-house users, all those who visited either for reprographic service or exclusively to select and borrow documents were excluded. As such no one in the sample had spent less than 20 minutes.

One hundred and eighty minutes was the maximum length of stay by one user, followed by 120 minutes each by two users. The average length of stay of the users based on mean of the ranges is 58 minutes. About 58 per cent of the respondents spent 5-30 minutes per visit in the library in Raitt's (1984, p. 242) study. The number of users and their length of stay in the library based on mean of the ranges are given in Table 4.9. The data in Table 4.9 also indicates that only 7 out of 30 users stayed beyond an hour in the library. In Raitt's study (1984, p. 242), 15 per cent of his respondents spent more than one hour in the library. When this data was plotted on graph, i.e., t, the time in minutes plotted against $N(t)$ the number of users staying longer than t minutes, it resulted in a reverse J shaped curve (Bush *et al.*, 1956).

TABLE 4.9: Number of Users *Vs.* Mean Length of Stay of Users in the Library

Time in Minutes (t)	*No. of Users (N)*	*N(t) (No. of Users Staying Longer than t Minutes)*
30	9	30
45	8	21
60	6	13
75	2	7
90	2	5
120	2	3
180	1	1
Total	30	30

One interesting feature is that the average time spent by the users in journals section is much longer than that spent in books and reports sections despite the fact that fewer users have used journals than books. This partly explains the quantitative under-usage of journals by the Indian Space Technologists. It may be noted that the total number of users in Table 4.10 is shown as 45 (i.e., 15 in excess of sample), as they were common users of both ground floor as well as mezzanine floor service areas during a visit. In other words, almost 50 per cent of those who used books also used journals when they visited the library.

TABLE 4.10: Frequency Distribution of Length of Stay of Users

Time in Minutes	*No. of Users*		
	Ground Floor	*Mezzanine Floor*	*Total*
< 20	4	3	7
20-30	8	0	8
30-40	7	5	12
> 40	5	13	18
Total	24	21	45*

Key: *—Total does not tally to 30 due to 15 users using both the ground floor and the mezzanine floor.

Conclusion

From even a cursory glance at the literature on user-research, it appears that there is a total lack of sound studies of user-interactions with libraries in general and interactions of scientists, engineers, technologists and technicians in particular. A real-time study of physical interactions of users with libraries provide lot of insight for planning physical layouts of libraries, understanding relevance and utility of various services and information-behaviour of users. It is also possible that the existing layout, facilities and services considerably influence user-interactions with a given library. Generally less used and less visited units within a library are more compactly and remotely located causing further reduction in user-visit to those units and hence reduction in use of such services. The profession is far behind in thinking of evolving norms and standards for assessing quantitatively the user-visits, movement and length of stay in libraries.

NOTES AND REFERENCES

1. It may also be noted that, by and large, the users who have made more use of library documents also tend to make more interactions with the library and *vice versa*. Those who made more use of one type of document or more interactions of one type with the library tend to make more use of other types of documents or more interactions of other types. It is the non-users of the library who have remained non-users of almost all the services and facilities of the library tending eventually to become isolated group of non-users. The library-use index of the IST has correlated moderately and positively ($r = 0.53$, $df = 393$, $p < 0.05$) with their library-interaction index (Sridhar, 1988) (See Case Study 14).
2. Just like every library will have a defined set of primary members, every user will have a primary library on which he depends substantially for his information requirements and the primary library enables him to enter the network or system of libraries.

5

USER REQUIREMENTS

CASE STUDY 03

INFORMATION REQUIREMENTS

Introduction

The term 'requirements' is deliberately used instead of 'needs', 'wants' and 'demands' as it represents all the three concepts (Brittain, 1971). Yet the case study in the latter part of the paper is concerned with nature and type of information required/sought by the Indian space technologists (IST). The information-requirements refer to a lookout for a sort of relevance of information to a given user and to his areas of concern and interest, and likes. In the process it is to know the amount of irrelevant information he is prepared to tolerate. Relevance is not a simple property inherent in information, but varies with content, format, context, the variety of uses of information as well as user himself (Cott, 1970). "The selection and reception of the information will depend upon the individual's conception of his own needs; one man's information is another man's noise . . ." (McGarry, 1975, p. 58).

There have been numerous studies as well as reviews about user-needs and requirements, but with little accumulation of body of knowledge. Meaning, scope, levels and types of information-needs have varied very widely. Problems of defining terms and concepts, lack of theoretical frameworks and other problems and issues of an empirical study of information needs and requirements persist (Brittain, 1971, p. 2). The successive reviewers like Menzel, Martyn and Crawford have pointed out (in ARIST, 1966, 1974 and 1978) the extremely complex, varied and difficult-to-measure nature of information-need. Menzel has even preferred to call 'information-needs and uses' as a study of the behaviour and experiences of scientists and technologists. Hatt (1976, pp. 42-43) called them 'user behaviour studies' and Wilson (1981) advocated that the term 'information-needs' should be replaced by 'information-seeking towards the satisfaction of needs'.

While discussing the issue of information-needs, a natural assumption is to consider the needs as perceived by the users. But some are of the view that there is a need to create information-needs among users if they do not exist (Harris, 1985, p. 2) and that information-seekers may be ignorant of the information that would be useful to them (Oldman, 1976, p. 23).

Dervin (1976) has analysed the taxonomy of everyday information-needs of average citizen and proposed a study of six linkages among the following four elements: (1) The individual citizen, (2) Information-needs, (3) Information-sources, (4) Solutions to information-needs. Each one of the linkage represents interaction between two elements. Havelock (1976, p. 211) provided a linkage model/process describing the internal problem-solving cycle within a user who is related to an external resource.

As noted earlier, Information-needs are affected by many factors. Range and knowledge of information-sources/facilities available, varieties of uses to which information will be put, the background, motivation, professional orientation, discipline, type and area of work and other individual-characteristics of the user, the social, political and economic system as well as the consequences of information-use (Cronin, 1981, p. 39; Lin and Garvey, 1972, pp. 8-10). Due to this contingency nature, generalised one-time conclusions about information-needs of users is impracticable. Of all the factors influencing or determining the user-needs, two factors which may not always be congruent, are the corporate objectives of the organisation where the user is employed, and the needs of the individual user.

Typology of Information-Needs

Studies relating to 'information-needs' categorise needs as 'perceived needs' and 'actual or idealised needs', 'immediate needs' and 'deferred needs', 'continuous needs' and 'discrete needs', 'regular' and 'irregular needs'. Further, information-needs could be unexpressed or expressed/ articulated, felt or unfelt, dormant or delitescent. In addition, information-needs of users can be expressed in terms of time (i.e., urgency), content and amount or quantity of information. Accordingly, information-needs have been classified as needs for single facts or exhaustive information, up-to-date, historical or current information, technical or business information. However, information-needs are frequently determined in terms of kind of message, i.e., nature and type of information, the types of document embodiments of information needed and the purpose of use. Many studies have investigated need for channels, but only a few have focused on the need for substance or nature of material in terms of characteristics of texts (Lin and Garvey, 1972, p. 12).

In the past, each study has adopted its own classification based on the nature and type of information sought by users. Some of the significant classifications are personal, technical and task-related information (Ford, 1973, pp. 88-89), current, specific and exhaustive information (Voigt, 1961, p. 4), theoretical information, experimental results, data, methods and procedure information (Columbia University, 1960), educational information, methodical or how-to-do-it information and task-related information (Auerbach Corporation, 1966). Many others like Slater and Fisher (1969), and Hanson (1964) have attempted to determine the amount or level of information required in core *versus* peripheral areas of interest of users. In addition, the non-technical information required, information requirements in new fields *versus* old fields have also been attempted. The profession and organisation-oriented, work-related information-needs are the main information-needs in all these studies apart from day-to-day personal needs, life-long learning or educational needs, and needs about the governing rules of the society around user.

Nature and Type of Information Sought by Scientists and Engineers: Some Past Findings

The findings of different studies on information requirements of scientists, engineers, technologists and technicians roughly indicate that basic S&T information, background information and everyday information on one hand and technical, physical, design and other technical data, facts or figures, product, process, method and equipment information on the other hand have occupied the highest position. For example, need for basic S&T knowledge (82%, Shuchman, 1981, pp. 32-33; 1982, pp. 106-109) by American industrial engineers, everyday information (68.8%, Wood, 1967, p. 212) by British mechanical engineers and background reading coupled with up-to-date information by users of British technical libraries (27% + 19%, Slater and Fisher, 1969, pp. 32-33, 36, 47 and 49) as well as American technical libraries (49%, Rawdin, 1975, pp. 41-42) ranked highest in some studies. On the other hand, performance-characteristics and specifications (42%) followed by design technique, experimental processes, procedures (13%) ranked highest in DOD user-study (Auerbach, 1965, pp. 1-19). A closely similar situation of 33 per cent seeking equipment information, properties of materials, design and performance of plant followed by 11 per cent seeking operating procedures of equipment and plant was found by Cole (1958) and respondents of Herner and Herner (1959) sought process and method information (25.5%), physical, chemical and engineering properties of materials (24.6%), apparatus or equipment information (16.8%), physical and chemical constants (16.4%). A hefty 64 per cent of respondents wanted facts in Raitt's study (1984, pp. 204-208). Thus analysed the World Federation of Engineering Organisations (WFEO, 1979, p. 15): ". . . the most proper form of information for engineers is the factographic information, analytical-synthetical elaborations and state-of-arts".[1] These types of factual data ranked second in the studies of Shuchman, Rawdin, Slater and Fisher. More than two decades ago, Hanson (1964, pp. 67-68) summarised that one-fifth of the times, scientists, engineers, technologists and technicians need figure or a single simple fact, between a quarter and a third of the times a description of an object, a process, a method or procedure and remaining half of the time general information and ideas from background reading.

At the lower end of the need came the business and general information (16%, Shuchman, 1981, 1982), exhaustive information (11%, Rawdin, 1975, pp. 41-42; 18.6%, Wood, 1967, p. 12), ideas, advice and opinion (respectively by 23%, 10% and 8%, Raitt, 1984) and non-technical information (18%, Herner and Herner, 1959).

There were some interesting results about information-requirements of users in core areas as compared to peripheral areas, new areas as compared to developed areas and urgency of demand for information. Slater and Fisher (1969) not only found highest success rates of searches[2] (67%) in core subjects than peripheral subjects (58%) but also found higher demand for information on core subjects in academic libraries and on peripheral problems in other types of libraries. The demand for information on core areas was highest (61%) among scientists and lowest (46%) among engineers and demand for information on peripheral and unfamiliar subjects was highest among engineers compared to skilled workers, technicians, teachers, etc. In support of this, Wood (1967, p. 212) also found that 27.5 per cent of the mechanical engineers needed information outside mechanical engineering. Further, the highest demand for information on practical problems was from engineers (16%) and lowest from scientists (6%) (Slater and Fisher, 1969). Hanson (1964, p. 67) in his analysis of 'acts of library use' found that a-third of use was for information on a specific subject and remainder mainly for browsing or reading current journals. Back (1962, p. 20) speculated that scientists in upcoming and new fields had broader information-needs than those in fairly developed fields. Lastly, by introducing a crude measure of urgency of information-need in the survey, Slater and Fisher (1969) found that 59 per cent of their respondents had some degree of urgency and for 30 per cent time was no object.

Information Requirements of the Indian Space Technologists

The felt and expressed information requirements of the Indian Space Technologists (IST), in respect of nature and type of information, have been ascertained through a questionnaire independently designed and tested for the purpose as part of a larger information behaviour study (Sridhar, 1987, 1995). The response rate in this census survey was 68.5 per cent and the defined population included over 800 scientists, engineers, technicians and technocrats of ISRO Satellite Centre, Bangalore. Data so collected is presented in Table 5.1. It is clear from the Table that the respondents not seeking 'Statistical, economic, business and general information' (J—26.3%), 'Standard and patent specifications and codes of practice' (G—24.1%), 'Computer program and model building information' (F—23.0%) and 'State-of-the-art and review literature' (A—19.4%), are quite considerable. Other types of information as shown in Table 5.1 are required by more than 90 per cent of the respondents.

On the other hand more respondents have highly sought 'Scientific and technical news' (I—47), 'Experimental designs, results and applications' (C—102), 'State-of-the-art and review literature' (A—84) and 'Theoretical background/basic scientific and technical information' (B—84), than other types of information. An interesting feature is that, the state-of-the-art and review literature is not required by 101 respondents while it is highly sought after by 84. The histograms in Fig. 5.1, by showing 'Not required' and 'Rarely required' on one side and the remaining on the other (positive) side, pictorially depict the responses.[3]

As per the weighted mean, the rank order of the nature and type of information required by the IST is as follows:

TABLE 5.1: Nature and Type of Information Required

	Nature and Type of Information	*Not Required (O)*		*Required*						*Mean*	*S.D.*
		No.	*%*	*1*	*2*	*3*	*4*	*Total*			
								No.	*%*		
A.	State-of-the-art and review literature	101	19.4	94	97	144	84	419	80.6	2.03	1.37
B.	Theoretical background/basic scientific and technical information	7	1.3	35	126	280	84	525	98.7	2.75	0.85
C.	Experimental designs, results and applications	29	5.5	59	129	207	102	497	94.5	2.56	1.09
D.	Methods, processes and procedures	46	8.8	69	170	173	65	477	91.2	2.27	1.12
E.	Product, material, equipment and apparatus information	43	8.2	79	195	137	69	480	91.8	2.21	1.11
F.	Computer programs and model building information	120	23.0	147	135	75	45	402	77.0	1.57	1.24
G.	Standard and patent specifications and codes of practice	125	24.1	163	121	77	32	393	75.9	1.47	1.19
H.	Physical, technical and design data	16	3.1	70	178	198	59	505	96.9	2.41	0.96
I.	Scientific and technical news	10	1.9	34	147	192	147	520	98.1	2.82	0.96
J.	Statistical, economic, business and general information	136	26.3	215	122	36	9	382	73.7	1.16	1.20
K.	Others	17	36.2	10	4	9	7	30	63.8	1.55	1.50

Key: O—Not required; 1—Rarely required; 2—Occasionally required; 3—Frequently required; 4—Highly sought-after; S.D.—Standard deviation.

Notes:
1. Three hundred and fifteen have left the open-ended category 'Others' (K) blank.
2. Invalid and not answered responses upto a maximum of 17 in any category are excluded.
3. The mean score for anonymous responses worked out to 1.55, 3.10, 2.30, 2.07, 2.03, 1.14, 1.43, 2.27, 2.57, 0.86 and 0.05 respectively for categories A to K.

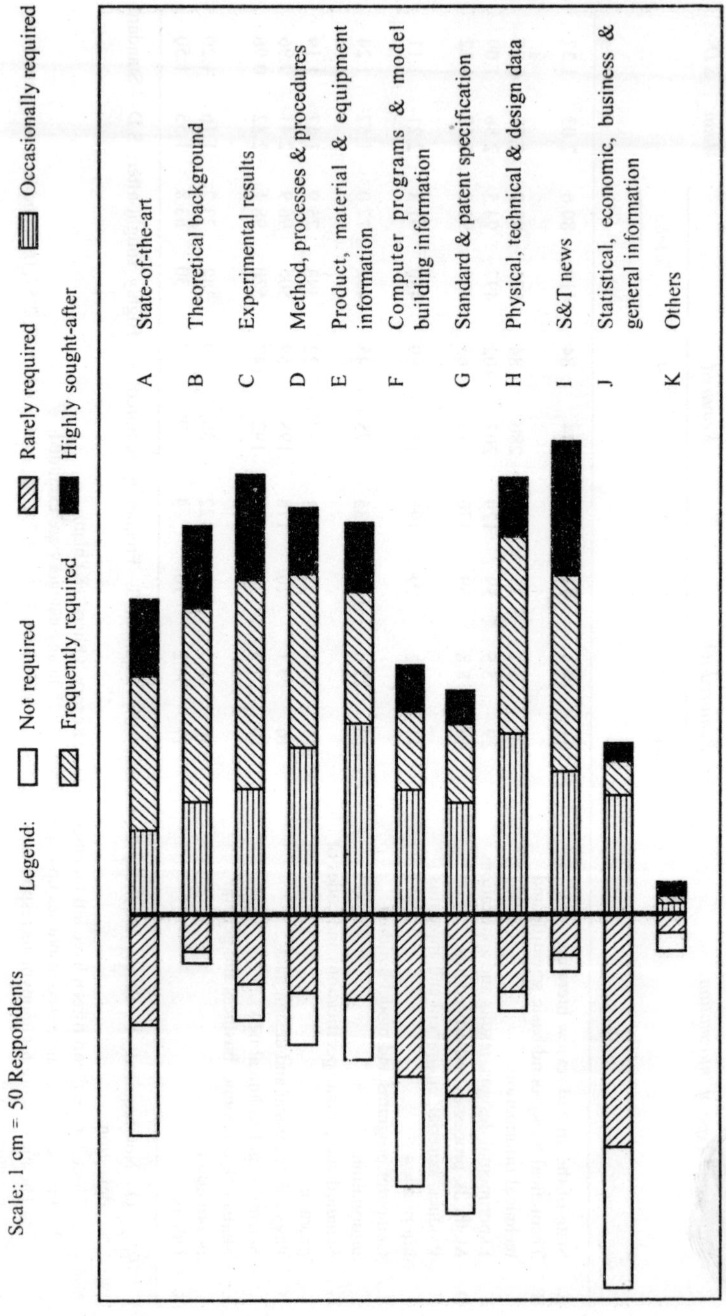

FIG. 5.1: Nature and Type of Information Required.

Rank	*Code*	*Nature and Type of Information*
1	I	Scientific and technical news
2	B	Theoretical background/Basic scientific and technical information
3	C	Experimental designs, results and applications
4	H	Physical, technical and design data
5	D	Methods, processes and procedures[4]
6	E	Product, material, equipment and apparatus information[4]
7	A	State-of-the-art and review literature
8	F	Computer programs and model building information
9	G	Standard and patent specifications and codes of practice
10	J	Statistical, economic, business and general information

Adding/subtracting one standard deviation to/from mean in Table 5.1, one can statistically say that, nearly 68 per cent of respondents have sought 'Scientific and technical news' (I) with the weightage ranging from 1.86 to 3.78; 'Experimental designs, results and applications' (C) with weightage ranging from 1.47 to 3.65; 'Physical, technical and design data' (H) with weightage from 1.45 to 3.37; 'Methods, processes and procedures information' (D) with weightage from 1.15 to 3.39; and 'product, materials, equipment and apparatus information' (E) with weightage ranging from 1.1 to 3.32.

The top ranked need for basic S&T information and S&T news by the space technologists is close to that found by Shuchman (1981, pp. 32-33; 1982, pp. 106-109) about American industrial engineers, Wood (1967, p. 212) about British mechanical engineers, Slater and Fisher (1969, pp. 32-33, 36, 47 and 49) about users of British technical libraries and Rawdin (1975, pp. 41-42) about users of American technical libraries.

The next in the rank order, the space technologists sought experimental designs, facts, data, methods, procedures and product information which again is close to the second ranked type of information in the studies of Shuchman (1981, 1982), Rawdin (1975) and Slater and Fisher (1969). However, this type of information ranked topmost in the studies (of DOD users) by Auerbach (1965, pp. 1-19), Cole (1958), Herner and Herner (1959) and Raitt (1984, pp. 204-208). At the lowest end of the rank the space technologists needed general information (similar to that found by Shuchman, 1981, 1982 and Herner and Herner, 1959), state-of-the art and review literature (similar to that found by

Rawdin, 1975, pp. 41-42 and Wood, 1967, p. 212), model building information and specifications. The above differences appear to be due to differences in structure of the populations studied in DOD user study and by Raitt, the way nature and type of information is grouped and methodology (in case of studies of Cole, Herner and Herner and Slater and Fisher).

Discussions with selected respondents revealed that general information to keep abreast with current developments and specific work related information to solve practical problems are two main types of information required by the space technologists and they seek information only when it is essential. A typical respondent said "I gather information only if utmost needed". However, for information of general interest, they "browse news magazines, technical journals and conference proceedings to keep informed about the latest developments, and use the NASA and ESA reports for futuristic systems planning". They also appear to have moderately strong need for internally generated information and product information. A mission operations person writes that he has greater need to "have full knowledge about every sub-system of satellite" and hence turns mostly to internally generated information. It is interesting to discern from what another respondent has written about how his need for equipment, product and component-related information leads him to seek theoretical background information. He said "when I want some information on any component or equipment I go through the text books to build up the theoretical background and then refer to data and product catalogues and application notes. Then I go through the journals, if necessary". Thus there appears to be an intermittent and intermixed use of different types of information by the IST.

Effect of Change in Nature of Work on Information Requirements

A follow-up discussion held with selected respondents who had substantial change in the nature of work in recent years showed broadly four types of changes in nature of work and their effect on information requirements and information-seeking activities; (i) Changing from operational activity, testing, design and development to supervision and planning has generally increased the need for information. In case of pure R&D works, the original activities continued and for additional responsibilities delegation of information-gathering work became inevitable; (ii) Changing from a specialised area to project work (i.e., from a more specific area to general area) has considerably decreased the need for information except routine information and *vice versa*. Delegation of information-gathering becomes a way of doing work in project, though the need for subject-information is reduced; (iii) Changing from a project work to a facility/service and production sector resulted in further reduction in need for information as the lack of any information did not drastically affect the work in facility/service and production sector. Lack of time and motivation are two major reasons for not seeking information in this area; (iv) Changing from engineering and technology-oriented work to slightly science-oriented work has resulted in increased need for information, particularly, theoretical background and basic S&T information.

Future Information Requirements

A free discussion with selected space technologists about their future information requirements revealed that a large majority (over 60%) do not foresee any significant change in their information requirements in the near future. Even if there is a little change they do not find it difficult to adapt to the circumstances over time. Out of the rest who thought of some changes in their information requirements in future, some expressed their fear at the problem of availability of increased quantity of information than what one could digest (i.e., the problem of 'information overload'). This is not merely because of increased production of information, but because of enlargement of boundary of interest and activities of the organisation. Others thought of the impact of electronics boom and some others explained how the organisation has to intensify its activities, increase its capabilities, reliability, quality and hence risks. The outcome of the discussion is that they are recognising the need for some condensed information services, new media of information and fast serving information agents. A sort of digesting agents as intermediary professionals are likely to come up in the core teams of projects both to cut short delays and face the problem of information-overload.

Conclusion

There is a dire need for proper definition and use of terms in information-requirements studies. The typology of information-needs as well as the way nature and type of information is classified need to be standardised for enabling comparison of similar studies.

Requirements of S&T news and basic S&T information has ranked top to the IST in congruence with the top ranking motives and purposes of the IST like acquiring knowledge about latest developments, self-improvements and keeping update in the field (Sridhar, 1987, 1995). It is pertinent to note that the IST requires simple facts, data, methods and experimental results than state-of-the-art reviews and standard and patent specifications.

Information system design and operation for the IST has to take note of changes in nature of work of the subset of the IST and corresponding changes in the nature and type of information required. Lastly, the futuristic trends of information services and facilities expected by the IST are also to be kept in mind for further planning of information system.

CASE STUDY 04

CUSTOMER-CHARACTERISTICS AS CRITERIA FOR MARKET-SEGMENTATION

Introduction

User-research is the market-research in library and information field. Hence, the market-characteristics or customer-characteristics can be conveniently called user-characteristics for our purposes. Before we discuss various user-characteristics which can be used to segment our market with a case study of Indian space technologists (IST) as users of their 'primary library', let us see the limitations of marketing approach to library and information services. Marketing library services is something new to libraries. At the most promoting of library services is taking place in the profession so far. Libraries which function with the motto of 'free service to all' can hardly claim selling or marketing its services. It is meaningless to market a free service or product. Being paternalistic systems, libraries try to create awareness among users and persuade them to use information, documents and other library services which they think are needed by their users. Under this situation any assessment of 'demand' is dubious. If we really mean selling and marketing of library services, many libraries around us with 'catch-all' and 'do-all' policies may have to be heavily trimmed or stripped down. Users will be shocked to know the exorbitant cost of information and even 'cost per use' of document. So we use the term market to mean the predetermined domain of our customers as per the laid down objectives and not really in the broad sense in which a typical businessman uses it.

No doubt that market-research (user-research) and customer (user) behaviour studies are essential for libraries.

Correlation of Information-Requirements of Scientists and Engineers with User-Characteristics: Some Past Findings

Before some of the results of the past user-research where user-characteristics are related to information-requirements are reviewed it should be made clear that many of these studies are speculative and do not intend to segment their target market but to gain knowledge about behaviour of their customers. The information-needs and requirements have been correlated in the past with discipline (by Singh, Aims, Gray and Perry), nature of employment (by Hanson), nature of work (by Wilson, Gray and Perry), status (by Singh) and experience (by Garvey and others) of users. Unfortunately, the important factors or characteristics which substantially affect user-needs and requirements are not clear and correlation of information needs with many other user characteristics like educational level, performance, etc., have not been dealt with sufficiently in pragmatic studies.

Aims (1965) hypothesised that the information-needs of engineers differ widely from those of physicists and chemists and Gray and Perry (1975, p. 53) speculated that engineers differ widely from those of R&D workers in their information-needs. The differences in needs and demands for information are more strongly related to the kind of employment and type of organisation than the discipline in another study (Hanson, 1964, pp. 69-70). An observation that electronics and telecommunication and industrial engineers cite to the maximum from other disciplines (Singh, 1981, p. 183) is highly vague as an equally strong interdisciplinary need for information is expected in many other disciplines too. Surprisingly, and contrary to others, Raitt (1984, p. 255) has generally confirmed his hypothesis that "... the information needs and communication patterns of scientists and engineers in general are similar and cannot be readily distinguished."

Shuchman (1981) has tried to relate five variables to the nature and type of information sought by American industrial engineers and found that the job activity and type of industry appeared to make the most consistent difference. The occupational role and the nature of work of user is considered to be the most important clue for understanding personal information-gathering behaviour by Wilson (1977, p. 50). As engineers perform a wide variety of functions, their information-needs are quite varied depending on their respective functions. For example, design engineers need numerical data in a compact and easily usable form (Gray and Perry, 1975, p. 55). A recent contrary finding is that the status of the scholars belonging to the research community did not appear to be influencing their information needs (Singh, 1981, p. 182). In another survey, it is found that the least experienced scientists have greater information-needs than the most experienced (Garvey *et al.*, 1975, p. 501).

The above findings are so speculative, theoretical and diverse that generalisation to segment the market based on user-characteristics is made difficult. Yet findings of studies conducted with sound methodology could be taken as basis for segmenting the market.

Correlation of Nature and Type of Information Required by the Indian Space Technologists with User-characteristics

The felt and expressed information requirements of the IST, in respect of nature and type of information, are ascertained through a questionnaire independently designed and tested for the purpose as part of a larger information behaviour study (Sridhar, 1987, 1995). The response rate in this census survey was 68.5 per cent and the defined population of IST included over 800 scientists, engineers, technicians and technocrats of ISRO Satellite Centre, Bangalore. The data so collected has been tested for correlation/association with selected user-characteristics. The results of association/correlation tests of nature and type of information sought with status, qualifications, nature of work, specialisation, experience and professional activities and achievements[5] of the IST are presented in Table 5.2. One may observe statistically significant relation of need for state-of-the-art literature (A), computer programs and model building information (F) and standard and patent specifications (G) with all the above characteristics. The requirement of physical, technical and design data (H) is found to be independent of all the above user-characteristics, except status. Tables 5.3, 5.4, 5.5 and 5.6 respectively present the weighted mean score of nature and type of information sought *versus* status, qualifications, nature of work and specialisation.

Table 5.3 reveals that as the status of a user raises, his requirement for state-of-the-art and review literature (A) ($r_s = 0.95$), experimental results (C) ($r_s = 0.92$), product, material and equipment information (E) ($r_s = 0.98$), computer programs and model building information (F) ($r_s = 0.72$) and physical, technical and design data increases linearly. But the requirement of standard and patent specification (G) ($r_s = -0.72$) decreases linearly as status increases.

TABLE 5.2: Association/Correlation Test Results of Nature and Type of Information Required with (Selected) User-Characteristics

	Nature and Type of Information	*Status*	*Qualifications*	*Nature of Work*	*Specialisation*	*Experience*	*Professional Activities & Achievements Index*
		(r_s) $df = 8$	(χ^2) $df = 16$	(χ^2) $df = 24$	(χ^2) $df = 20$	(r) $df \approx 390$	(r) $df \approx 192$
A	State-of-the-art	0.95*	176.56*	97.86*	83.96*	0.16*	0.42*
B	Theoretical background	0.55	56.20*	29.50	20.11	–0.12*	0.02
C	Experimental results	0.92*	44.35*	27.27	39.51*	0.02	0.09
D	Methods, processes and procedures	0.58	51.20*	45.56*	29.79	–0.03	0.13*
E	Product, material & equipment information	0.98*	27.25*	22.26	43.01*	0.08	0.08
F	Computer programs & model building information	0.72*	83.23*	46.22*	104.30*	–0.21*	0.23*
G	Standard and patent specifications	–0.72*	73.46*	39.36*	67.16*	0.12*	–0.21*
H	Physical, technical and design data	0.72*	13.25	35.79	29.48	0.04	–0.03
I	S&T news	0.43	22.80	21.94	39.98*	0.13*	0.07
J	Statistical economic, business and general information	0.71*	38.30*	41.48*	32.20*	0.05	0.05

Key: *—The association/correlation is statistically significant at 0.05 significance level (p) for a two-tailed test; χ^2—Chi-square; r_s—Spearman rank order correlation coefficient; r—Pearson product moment correlation.

Note: The tabulated values of χ^2 at 0.05 significance level (p) for a two-taield test for 16, 24 and 20 degrees of freedom (df) are 26.296, 36.415 and 31.410 respectively.

TABLE 5.3: Nature and Type of Information Required *Vs.* Status (Mean Score)

	Nature & Type of Information	*Status*										r_s
		A, B, C & D	*E*	*F*	*G*	*H*	*I*	*J*	*K*	*L*	*M & N*	*Total*	
A	State-of-the-art	3.29	3.37	3.06	2.27	1.92	1.44	1.00	0.88	1.21	0.41	2.00	0.9515*
B	Theoretical background	2.81	2.75	2.96	2.74	2.80	2.81	2.82	2.31	2.63	2.11	2.74	0.5515
C	Experimental results	2.76	2.85	2.87	2.60	2.67	2.39	2.44	1.84	2.23	1.82	2.53	0.9152*
D	Methods, processes and procedures	2.05	2.51	2.37	2.25	2.33	2.25	2.32	1.92	2.10	1.60	2.25	0.5758
E	Product, material & equipment information	2.62	2.27	2.54	2.21	2.19	2.04	2.19	2.04	1.93	1.79	2.16	0.9758*
F	Computer programs & model building information	1.52	1.73	1.84	1.65	1.56	1.53	1.55	1.04	0.95	0.47	1.49	0.7212*
G	Standard and patent specifications	0.95	1.38	1.30	1.08	2.14	1.65	1.83	2.04	2.00	2.00	1.52	– 0.7242*
H	Physical, technical and design data	2.38	2.46	2.54	2.45	2.39	2.38	2.43	2.21	2.30	2.44	2.36	0.7227*
I	S&T news	2.95	3.02	2.90	2.61	2.67	2.76	2.82	2.52	2.88	2.89	2.72	0.4303
J	Statistical economic, business and general information	1.29	1.38	1.30	1.04	1.27	1.02	1.27	1.09	1.15	0.65	1.14	0.7121*

Key: r_s—Spearman rank order correlation; *—the critical value of t at 0.05 significance level in a two-tailed t-test for 8 degrees of freedom is 2.306 and the correlations marked * are found valid at 0.05 significance level as their t-value exceed 2.306.

Note: Status A to N are in the descending order of hierarchical rank.

TABLE 5.4: Nature and Type of Information Required *Vs.* Qualifications (Mean Score)

	Nature and Type of Information	*Qualifications*					*Total*	χ^2
		U	*D*	*B*	*M*	*P*		
A	State-of-the-art	0.93	1.21	2.18	2.58	3.52	1.96	176.5601*
B	Theoretical background	2.31	2.88	2.86	2.75	3.35	2.76	56.2022*
C	Experimental results	1.96	2.53	2.75	2.58	2.78	2.52	44.3481*
D	Methods, processes and procedures	1.72	2.40	2.28	2.18	2.96	2.21	51.1971*
E	Product, material & equipment information	1.87	2.27	2.41	2.09	2.35	2.19	27.2499*
F	Computer programs & model building information	0.80	1.38	1.50	1.91	2.43	1.52	83.2269*
G	Standard and patent specifications	2.08	1.91	2.58	1.05	1.17	1.49	73.4616*
H	Physical, technical and design data	2.29	2.62	2.46	2.34	2.43	2.42	13.2545
I	S&T news	2.66	1.13	2.73	2.70	2.91	2.74	22.7967
J	Statistical economic, business and general information	0.88	1.10	1.38	1.16	1.00	1.16	38.2992*

Key: *—The association is statistically significant at $p = 0.05$ as the tabulated value of χ^2 at $p = 0.05$ for 16 degrees of freedom is 26.296;
Qualifications: U—Undergraduate, D—Diploma holder, B—Graduate, M—Post-graduate, P—Doctorate.

Note: The contingency tables on which chi-square test is made are not shown.

TABLE 5.5: Nature and Type of Information Required *Vs.* Specialisation of Users (Mean Score)

	Nature and Type of Information	*Specialisation*						*Total*	χ^2
		A	*C*	*E*	*F*	*H*	*I*		
A	State-of-the-art	2.60	1.74	1.17	2.89	2.06	2.21	1.94	83.9622*
B	Theoretical background	2.98	2.85	2.71	3.11	2.71	2.68	2.74	20.1062
C	Experimental results	2.67	1.74	2.34	2.42	2.71	2.70	2.54	39.5062*
D	Methods, processes and procedures	2.62	2.32	2.07	2.32	2.29	2.18	2.20	29.7875
E	Product, material & equipment information	2.45	1.11	2.23	1.84	2.24	2.26	2.20	43.0080*
F	Computer programs & model building information	2.00	3.10	0.85	2.05	1.53	1.51	1.46	104.3037*
G	Standard and patent specifications	0.93	1.11	2.15	0.95	1.35	1.35	1.52	67.1592*
H	Physical, technical and design data	2.29	1.83	2.53	2.11	2.41	2.49	2.43	29.4793
I	S&T news	3.05	2.65	2.60	2.32	2.94	2.82	2.75	39.9819*
J	Statistical economic, business and general information	1.21	1.22	0.92	0.63	1.24	1.19	1.09	32.1956*

Key: *—Association is statistically significant at $p = 0.05$ as the tabulated χ^2 value at $df = 20$ and $p = 0.05$ is 31.410; *Specialisation* A—Physics, C—mathematics, E—Mechanical Engineering, F—Aeronautical and structural Engineering, H—Electrical Engineering, I—Electronics.

Note: The contingency tables on which chi-square test is made are not shown.

It may be seen in Table 5.4 that the requirement of all types of information except physical, technical and design data (H) and S&T news (I) has varied significantly with the level of qualifications of the space technologists. The relation is not linear in case of any type of information.

Table 5.5 shows that the need for state-of-the-art and review literature (A), methods, processes and procedures (D), computer programs and model building information (F), standard and patent specifications (G) and statistical, economic, business and general information has varied significantly with the nature of work of the IST.

As could be seen from Table 5.5, physicists have sought more of state-of-the-art and review literature (A), experimental results (C), product, material and equipment information (E) and S&T news (I) than other types of information. Compared to others, mathematicians have naturally sought more of computer programs and model building information (F), and mechanical engineers have sought more of standard and patent specifications (G). The requirement of state-of-the-art and review literature (A) and theoretical background (B) is strongest among aeronautical and structural engineers. Electrical engineers require more of experimental results (C) and S&T news (I) than other types of information. Lastly, electronics engineers have also sought more experimental results (C) together with physical, technical and design data (H) than other specialists.[6]

It can also be inferred from the Pearson product moment correlation coefficients (r) in Table 5.2 that higher the experience of the space technologists higher the need for state-of-the-art literature (A) ($r = 0.16$), standard and patent specifications (G) ($r = 0.12$) and S&T news (I) ($r = 0.13$), but lower the need for theoretical background (B) ($r = -0.12$) and computer programs and model building information (F) ($r = -0.21$) and *vice versa*.

The professional activities and achievements of the IST are positively correlated with the need for state-of-the-art literature (A) ($r = 0.42$), methods, processes and procedures information (D) ($r = 0.13$), and computer programs and model building information (F) ($r = 0.23$) but negatively correlated with the need for standard and patent specifications (G) ($r = -0.21$).

The need for the state-of-the-art literature for the IST is, very highly, linearly and positively correlated/associated with status ($r_s = 0.95$), qualifications and nature of work, slightly and positively with experience ($r = 0.16$), moderately and positively with professional activities and achievements ($r = 0.42$). The need for theoretical background is almost linearly and positively related to qualifications of users and slightly and negatively correlated ($r = -0.12$) with length of experience of users. The need for experimental results is very highly and positively correlated ($r_s = 0.92$) with status of users. The qualifications and specialisation of users are also related to the need for experimental results. The degree of requirement of information related to methods, processes and procedures showed a significant relation with qualifications and nature of work and a slight positive correlation ($r = 0.13$) with professional activities and achievements of the users. The need for product, material and equipment information has almost perfectly and positively correlated ($r_s = 0.98$) with status and has a significant relation with qualifications and specialisation of the users. Mathematicians and aeronautical and structural engineers have lesser need and others a higher need for product, material and equipment information which is on line with findings of Shuchman (1981, p. 68). The need for computer programs and model building information has a low negative correlation ($r = -0.21$) with experience, low positive correlation ($r = 0.23$) with professional activities and achievements of users, a high positive rank order correlation ($r_s = 0.73$) with status, a linear relationship with qualifications, curvilinear relationship with nature of work and a significant relationship with specialisation of the IST.[7]

The need for standard and patent specifications is highly and negatively correlated with status ($r_s = -0.72$), slightly and positively with experience ($r = 0.12$), slightly and negatively with professional activities and achievements ($r = -0.21$), and has significant relation with qualifications, nature of work and specialisation of the users. The need for physical, technical and design data is highly and positively correlated ($r_s = 0.72$) only with status of the users. The requirement of S&T news is significantly related to specialisation of the users and slightly and positively correlated ($r = 0.13$) with length of experience of the users. The 'need for statistical, economic, business and general information' is highly and positively correlated ($r_s = 0.71$) with status and significantly related to qualifications, nature of work and specialisation of the users.

From the above discussion and the data in Table 5.6, it is clear that the status of the user has a significant relation with all types of information listed, except S&T news and methods, processes and procedures. Hence, the observation of B.N. Singh (1981, p. 182) that status does not influence the information-needs is disproved in the present study.

Further, the general observation of Garvey and others (1975, p. 501) that the information needs of least experienced are greater than those of

TABLE 5.6: Nature and Type of Information Required *Vs.* Nature of Work (Mean Score)

	Nature & Type of Information	*Nature of Work*							*Total*	χ^2
		A	*B*	*C*	*P*	*D*	*E*	*F*		
A	State-of-the-art	2.83	2.47	2.18	2.32	1.21	1.56	1.85	1.95	97.8563*
B	Theoretical background	2.62	2.84	2.83	3.03	2.58	2.74	2.90	3.24	29.5012
C	Experimental results	2.43	2.44	2.71	2.89	2.40	2.53	2.79	2.52	27.2735
D	Methods, processes and procedures	2.20	2.20	2.29	2.50	2.04	2.31	2.05	2.20	45.5626*
E	Product, material & equipment information	2.45	1.79	2.31	2.41	2.15	2.19	1.89	2.19	22.2593
F	Computer programs & model building information	1.55	1.95	1.69	1.82	1.13	1.38	1.30	1.52	46.2171*
G	Standard and patent specifications	1.36	1.14	1.45	1.39	1.76	1.58	1.74	1.97	39.3603*
H	Physical, technical and design data	2.24	2.16	2.57	2.68	2.43	2.10	2.16	2.41	35.7904
I	S&T news	2.83	2.72	2.74	2.61	2.76	2.62	2.50	2.73	21.9382
J	Statistical economic, business and general information	1.43	1.43	1.16	0.08	0.98	1.26	1.25	1.16	41.4792*

Key: *—The association is statistically significant at $p = 0.05$ as the tabulated value of χ^2 at $p = 0.05$ for 24 degrees of freedom is 36.415, *Nature of Work* A—Management/Supervision, B—Planning/System Analysis, C—Design and Development, P—Both C & D, D—Fabrication and Testing, E—Operational Activity, F—Others.

Note: The contingency tables on which chi-square test is made are not shown.

the most experienced is true, as far as theoretical background/basic S&T information (not S&T news) and computer programs and model building information are concerned. However, the reverse is true as far as state-of-the-art, S&T news and standard and patent specifications are concerned (See Table 5.2 under experience column).

In case of American industrial engineers, Shuchman (1981) has reported that out of the five variables used to evaluate the responses to nature and type of information sought, the job activity and type of industry appeared to be the two that make the most consistent difference. The qualifications (degree) and the date of acquiring the qualifications were not significant variables. As it could be seen from the Table 5.2, the present study does not support the observation of Shuchman. For the Indian space technologists, the status and qualifications made the most consistent difference in (eight of the ten) types of information sought followed by the subject of specialisation (in seven types of information), nature of work and experience (each in five types of information) and professional activities and achievements (in four types of information) and the target market can be conveniently segmented by these user-characteristics.

Conclusion

Being paternalistic systems it is very difficult for libraries to adopt strict marketing approach. Yet it is desirable for them to have extensive market-research (i.e., user-research) and customer (user) behaviour studies in order to make themselves effective to their customers.

Most of the results of past studies on correlating information-requirements to user-characteristics are either speculative or theoretical in nature and are not supported by a rigorous analysis of hard data. The characteristics of users which substantially affect user-requirements are not clearly established. Past studies have not addressed the information-needs and requirements of under-privileged and deprived users and non-users and have also not explored the ways of dissipation of unmet needs (Ford, 1977, p. 20).

It can be concluded from the analysis of the data presented above that the IST as users of their 'primary library' can be segmented by their characteristics such as status, educational qualifications, subject of specialisation, nature of work, experience and professional activities and achievements for planning and providing information services. As the information requirements of each segment within the IST has significantly varied from others the 'primary library' should take note of such segmentation within its target market.

NOTES AND REFERENCES

1. Based on the replies from national members, WFEO (1979, p. 21) identified eight types of data most needed by engineers, i.e., (i) property; (ii) design; (iii) product; (iv) standards, regulations, laws; (v) production and manufacturing procedures; (vi) companies and their marketing products; (vii) market information; and (viii) socio-economic and ecology information.
2. It is possible that respondents ignore failures of searches on areas not really connected with work and hence the actual difference in success rate might be even more.
3. The percentages and other interpretations to the open ended category 'others' (K) have to be viewed with caution. Under responses to 'others', five were explicitly for 'information about educational opportunities in the country and abroad', three about 'management-techniques-related information', and two about 'internal/local procedural information like administrative and accounts procedures', three were closely related to category I, 3 to H, 2 to E and one each to A, C and D. The rest were vague and a conglomeration of more than one category.
4. The requirement of methods, processes and procedure information interrelated moderately and positively ($r = 0.46$) with the requirement of product, material, equipment and apparatus information.
5. An index was developed for each person in the population based on various quantifiable professional activities and achievements like lectures delivered, conferences attended, reports prepared, papers published, patents obtained, awards received, membership in professional bodies, official tours, journals subscribed, committees represented, in-service training received, part-time studies undertaken, etc., in a specified period adjusted to length of experience.
6. However, the need for following types of information varied significantly with the subject of specialisation of the IST. State-of-the-art literature (A), experimental results (C), product, material and equipment information (E), computer programs and model building information (F), standard and patent specifications (G), S&T news (I) and statistical, economic, business and general information (J).
7. Shuchman (1981, pp. 73-74) has reported that "the aerospace engineer is a large user of computer information".

6

USER-PARTICIPATION IN COLLECTION DEVELOPMENT

CASE STUDY 05

USER-PARTICIPATION IN COLLECTION BUILDING

Introduction

Collection development in anticipation of demand is a rule rather than an exception for any special library. On the other hand, every document acquired by a special library should have some relevance to the potential needs of its users. Developing relevant collection in anticipation of demand, depends heavily on active participation of users in terms of timely, adequate and useful suggestions for documents. But direct and overt participation of users in collection building is often limited to a few rightful users of a special library.

The extent of user-participation in collection development at ISAC Library based on specific suggestions/indents of users (during 1982) for books, reports and periodicals is presented here. Such suggestions which were ultimately disapproved by Library Committee represented about 5 per cent of total suggestions and the same are excluded from the study for want of complete and correct data. Similarly, suggestions from Library Committee members are not covered because data regarding such suggestions could not be separated from total documents screened and approved by the Library Committee. However, suggestions from users include those based on regular display of books received on approval basis from suppliers and occasional book exhibitions. In case of periodicals, suggestions received earlier to 1982 (mostly dated back up to 1978) are also included as they are one time suggestions. It may be noted here that in addition, the Library has many standing orders for procurement of documents and the same are excluded from the study.

Document Selection Procedure

New documents of potential interest of ISAC Library users are normally identified from the following sources: (i) Announcements and catalogues from publishers and suppliers of documents, (ii) Document reviews and announcements in primary periodicals, (iii) Secondary periodicals including bibliographies and current awareness bulletins, (iv) Book exhibitions and books received on approval basis, and (v) Specific document suggestions/indents from users.

Announcements and catalogues, copies of book reviews and relevant parts of secondary periodicals are regularly collected, screened and routed to concerned specialists in the Library Committee. Apart from displaying all such materials in the Library, they are brought to the notice of concerned users. In addition, members of Library Committee peruse books received on approval basis and displayed in the Library and also those displayed in book exhibition for according approval for purchase. Finally, all the suggestions received from users are also examined by the Library Committee for according approval. Thus, indirectly every document undergoes a test of relevance and potential utility (unfortunately, most of the time based on title or abstract or short review of the documents) in the hands of concerned specialist in the Library Committee. Hence, in a broader sense, as the Library Committee itself is a user representative body, there is a hundred per cent indirect user-participation in collection development.

Frequency Distribution of Document Suggestion Data

Table 6.1 depicts the frequency distribution of suggestions for books, reports and periodicals over users. The data regarding suggestions for books when plotted on graph resulted in a very rough asymptotic curve. Reports and periodicals data are too inadequate to plot a smooth graph. It can be seen from Table 6.1 that, maximum number of suggestions for books is 18 per user whereas it is 14 and 9 for reports and periodicals, respectively. The fact that generally more books are suggested by users than reports and periodicals can be explained with the following reasons: (a) Opportunity to know about new books through book exhibitions, display of books received on approval, catalogues and announcements from publishers and suppliers of books and book reviews appearing in periodicals is comparatively more; (b) Suggestions for periodicals are mostly one time suggestions; (c) Browsing report announcement bulletins such as STAR, GRA&I, BRTT, etc., is generally done by limited number of users; (d) Reports themselves being highly specialised in nature, a typical report is expected to be required by a very small set of users.

TABLE 6.1: Frequency Distribution of Number of Suggestions over Number of Users

No. of Sugges-tions	*Books*		*Reports*		*Periodicals*	
	No. of Users	*Total Suggestions*	*No. of Users*	*Total Suggestions*	*No. of Users*	*Total Suggestions*
1	80 (49%)	80	18 (40%)	18	24 (51%)	24
2	27 (16%)	54	9 (20%)	18	11 (23%)	22
3	16 (10%)	48	5 (11%)	15	5 (11%)	15
4	8	32	1	4	2	8
5	8	40	3	15	2	10
6	5	30	2	12	0	0
7	6	42	3	21	2	14
8	1	8	0	0	0	0
9	2	18	1	9	1	9
10	3	30	2	20	0	0
11	0	0	0	0	0	0
12	2	24	0	0	0	0
13	1	13	0	0	0	0
14	1	14	1	14	0	0
15	1	15	0	0	0	0
16	1	16	0	0	0	0
17	1	17	0	0	0	0
18	1	18	0	0	0	0
Total	164	499	45	146	47	102

Again from Table 6.1 one can see that about 40 to 51 per cent of users suggested only one item per year. Similarly, 16 to 23 per cent suggested two and 10 to 11 per cent suggested three items. Interestingly, about 25 per cent (i.e., 41 users) have suggested 64 per cent (i.e., 317) books, reports and periodicals and only 198 users directly participated in the collection building process. Library had about 800 technical staff of the organisation as registered members and more than 1,200 total users during 1982. Thus, the direct and active participation in collection building was made only by less than 25 per cent of users.

Extent of User-Participation in Collection Development

While the overall user-participation in collection development is less than 25 per cent, the ratio of user suggested items to total items ordered by the library during the year is presented in Table 6.2. As could be seen from the table, on this count also, the user-participation in collection development is quite low. Hardly, 18 to 35 per cent of the items ordered (other than standing orders, abstracting, indexing, free and ephemeral periodicals) by the Library are based on direct suggestions from users. Orders for the rest of the items were as a result of document selection work of library staff and Library Committee.

TABLE 6.2: Comparison of User-Suggestions with Total Items Ordered

Document Type	*Total No. of Items Ordered*	*Items Suggested*		*Duplicates*		*Users Participated*		*Average Sugges-tions/ User*
		No.	*%*	*No.*	*%*	*No.*	*%*	
Books	1,046*	366	34.99	133	36.34	164	20.50	3.04
Reports	513*	145	28.27	1	0.65	45	5.63	3.24
Periodicals	552@	102	18.48	0	0.00	47	5.88	2.17

Key: * Excludes standing orders.
@ Excludes abstracting, indexing, free and ephemeral periodicals.

Though duplicate or repeated suggestions for reports and periodicals are almost nil, the suggestions for books had duplication to the extent of 36 per cent. This is mainly due to display of books received on approval basis and book exhibitions attracting simultaneously more than one user for many books of common interest and for other reasons such as specific nature of reports, etc., explained earlier.

It may also be seen from Table 6.2 that, the percentage of users who participated in collection building is little over 5 for reports and periodicals and 20.5 for books. Lastly, average number of suggestions per user per year is around 2 to 3 and this itself is an indication of low user-participation in collection development.

Reasons for Low Participation of Users

Although probing into reasons for low participation of users in collection development calls for more extensive study, a few possible reasons attributable for low participation from the point of view of the Library, based on informal discussions with users are presented below. Firstly, there appears to be reluctance on the part of some users to suggest new documents of their potential interest. In spite of bringing specific announcements to their notice and requesting them to participate in collection development, many users feel that suggesting/selecting and acquiring new documents to the Library is the responsibility of the Library and the Library Committee. Secondly, there is a need for regular induction of new users to library procedures, especially those who have had no acquaintance with the use of a special library. Thirdly, as mentioned earlier, the opportunity for users to know about new documents published is limited. The dealer library plan which regularly brings new books on approval is limited only to a few books in the general fields, mostly by popular publishers and also to the choice of suppliers. On the other hand, many secondary periodicals and announcement bulletins subscribed by the Library are not extensively used. However, the system of changing the constitution of the Library Committee almost every year or two has helped acquainting and involving more and more users in the document selection process as part of their duty in the Library Committee. Fourthly, the nature of work has some implications on use of library and participation of users in collection building. As most of the scientists and engineers are involved in time bound projects with irregular and occasional lean period it becomes difficult for such users to make regular suggestions. Also, when a user is involved in a tightly scheduled project and the design is frozen, new information which leads to rescheduling or delay in reaching the target is not normally desired. Often delayed information in such situations are kept aside. Predicting the requirements of such users in terms of specific titles is very difficult. Lastly, some users feel that the present system of procurement is quite slow and the same discouraged them to suggest more documents (Acquisition delays as demotivator to user-participation is discussed in Case Study 06). Apart from delays on the part of the Library to process orders, it is observed that hardly 50 per cent of the items ordered are supplied within 4 to 6 months (a sizable part of such items supplied are books received on approval basis) and more than 25 per cent of the items were found pending at the end of a year.

Suggestions for Improving User-Participation in Collection Development

Some suggestions to improve user-participation in collection development are: (i) Intensifying current awareness services and disseminating information about new titles/documents to a large cross-section of users, (ii) Systematising literature searching, reference service and other information functions and services to get regular feedback to acquisition system for procuring useful items, (iii) Speeding up procurement of suggested documents to create a drive of achievement motivation in users, (iv) Involving actively the project teams and the information personnel in identifying precise requirements of information and documentary resources of new and on going projects/programmes.

This case study is further extended in Case Study 06 to enumerate the problems of document procurement delays and how such delays act as demotivator to user-participation in collection development. How much time the library has taken to acquire the items suggested by users is also examined.

CASE STUDY 06

BOOK PROCUREMENT DELAY AS A DEMOTIVATOR TO USER PARTICIPATION

In a case study of user-participation in collection development, it was revealed that 35 per cent of total acquisition of books were against specific suggestions of users and only about 21 per cent of total users have ever suggested books to ISAC Library. It was also observed that one of the reasons for such a low participation of users in collection development is book procurement delays. Quick and timely procurement of suggested/on-demand books act as achievement motivator for further suggestions from users. On the other hand, procurement delays could be dangerous disincentives to the meagre 21 per cent of users participating in collection development activity.

Delays in providing on-demand books to users have two major components. Firstly, order processing, classifying, cataloguing and other processing delays at library, which mainly depend on the work environment of the library including quantum of work, available trained manpower and efficiency of the staff. Yet at this stage, by allowing 'line clear treatment' to such books delays can be minimised. The second type of delays are at the book trade/suppliers end and this delay is substantially beyond the control of a library.

A case study is presented here to show the extent of delays on the part of book suppliers for on-demand books. Incidentally the case study also helps by providing some inputs for future collection development policy of the Library.

Before analysing the data one should take note of the background of the data in terms of procurement policies of the library and limitations of the data. Supply position of books ordered by ISAC Library during 1983 were analysed as of mid-September 1984. Orders for theses and reports, standing orders, orders based on approval books and ready stock announcements were excluded from the study for obvious reasons. Most of the orders were placed on more than a dozen carefully selected, fairly known vendors, both Indian and foreign, including exclusive/specialised dealers and direct suppliers.

Few orders placed on miscellaneous suppliers are clubbed with direct suppliers in the analysis. Most of the orders made directly on publishers required advance payments unlike credit supply terms of other vendors. Further, some of the outstation suppliers within the country supply through VPP or Railway parcel or road parcel involving additional marginal delay. Though originally data was tabulated month-wise it was not found much useful as it was not the purpose to analyse the data for 'how soon' books are supplied. On the other hand, taking for granted that there will be some delay, 'how many' books are supplied within a period of 8 to 20 months is examined in the analysis. Hence data is grouped for four quarters of 1983 in Table 6.3.

In addition, the following limitations of the table may be noted. Firstly, all the books for which there are specialised/exclusive representatives were ordered on such Indian suppliers, i.e., IS1, IS2 and IS3 in Table 6.3. Out of the remaining, books of popular publishers such as Academic, Pergamon and McGraw Hill were ordered in batches almost together on Indian suppliers (i.e., IS4 to IS10) with the hope of getting many such books quickly from ready stock. Thirdly, as far as possible, each Indian supplier was provided with orders representing books of all popular publishers. Yet supply position is not analysed here by publisher of the book. Fourthly, most of the books of professional bodies (so called short discount titles) were directly ordered with publishers including Indian publishers, i.e., IS11 and DS3. Fifthly, rest of the books including books of less known/obscure publishers and books which are not likely to be available in local market were ordered with two foreign suppliers (FS1 and FS2 in the table), one in U.K. and the other in U.S.A., based on the nationality and pricing policy of the publishers. Sixthly, all orders except orders made during first quarter were for recently published books. Substantial number of books ordered

TABLE 6.3: Supply Status of On-Demand Books Ordered during 1983

Month of Order		*Indian Suppliers*															*Foreign Suppliers*					*Grand Total*	
		Exclusive/Specialised					*Retailers*					*Direct & Misc.*					*Retailers*	*Direct & Misc.*					
		IS1	*IS2*	*IS3*	*Sub-Total*		*IS4*	*IS5*	*IS6*	*IS7*	*IS8*	*IS9*	*IS10*	*IS11*	*Sub-Total*		*FS1*	*FS2*	*FS3*	*Sub-Total*			
					No.	%									No.	%				No.	%	No.	%
Jan.-March	O	0	13	0	13		18	0	21	26	22	24	32	6	149		18	0	39	57		219	
	S	0	13	0	13	100	3	0	8	6	6	3	6	3	35	23	15	0	22	37	65	85	39
April-June	O	9	14	1	24		3	7	1	5	3	0	10	15	44		31	21	32	84		152	
	S	9	14	1	24	100	2	1	1	1	3	0	0	4	12	27	26	14	12	52	62	88	58
July-Sep.	O	6	2	0	8		0	0	0	4	0	0	4	30	38		60	27	60	147		193	
	S	5	2	0	7	88	0	0	0	0	0	0	0	15	15	39	45	22	34	10	69	23	64
Oct.-Dec.	O	29	6	8	43		0	0	0	0	0	0	3	2	5		62	51	93	206		254	
	S	21	5	2	28	65	0	0	0	0	0	0	2	1	3	60	40	20	39	99	48	130	51
Total	O	44	35	9	88		21	7	22	35	25	24	49	53	236		171	99	224	494		818	
	S	35	34	3	72	82	5	1	9	7	9	3	8	23	65	28	126	56	107	289	59	426	52
	%	80	97	33	82		24	14	41	20	36	13	16	43	28		74	57	48	59		52	

Key: O = Ordered quantity; S = Supplied Quantity; S. Total = Sub-Total.

during first quarter were published during 1970s. Lastly, data is found slightly inadequate in case of suppliers IS3 and IS5. So is the case with third and fourth quarter orders on Indian retailers.

It may be seen from Table 6.3 that out of 818 on-demand books ordered during 1983, only 426 (i.e., 52%) were supplied by September 1984. This is against the usual tall claim of the industry that any book published anywhere in the world can be supplied in about six months time. In other words, 48 per cent of demands of users are not met even after 8/20 months of placing orders. By and large, exclusive/specialised agents have fared fairly better with an overall 82 per cent efficiency. The performance of foreign vendors with an average of 59 per cent efficiency is much better than 28 per cent efficiency of Indian vendors. It may be noted here that though foreign vendors have unilaterally cancelled some titles after lapse of six months/one year, the same are not excluded from the data. Among Indian vendors, highest percentage (i.e., 42%) of books have been bought by direct orders including orders on miscellaneous suppliers. The next highest performance among Indian vendors are by IS6 (41%) (though data is inadequate to generalise) and IS1 (36%).

Among foreign vendors FS1 has been quite better with 74 per cent efficiency than FS2 which supplied 59 per cent of books. However, direct and miscellaneous suppliers (FS3) could supply only 48 per cent understandably due to infrequent contacts of the library and lengthy advance payment procedure involved. Looking at the table for row totals one can see the supply position of orders made during different quarters of 1983. For convenience Table 6.4 presents, by extracting from Table 6.3, percentages of on-demand books supplied by Indian and foreign suppliers for orders of four quarters of 1983. An interesting observation is that the percentage of books supplied is not at all directly proportional to time as far as Indian retail vendors are concerned. However, supply of exclusive/specialised Indian dealers and foreign suppliers show a trend that more books are supplied against older orders. In fact, a reverse trend of more supplies against recent orders than old orders is seen in case of Indian retail vendors. This goes to confirm the general observation that many Indian book vendors make random supply in an accidental way, depending on match of pending orders with stock based on memory of operating staff. There were instances where books pending for supply for long time came as books on approval either from the same vendor or others in the city. As such old orders may not materialise fully and reach 90 to 95 per cent supply even after 2-3 years. Even the feedback about delay or non-availability or cancellation comes rarely from Indian vendors. Vendors should respond with a meaningful report when they cannot fulfil an order within a reasonable period and notwithstanding and vague replies like 'temporarily out of stock'. With the mushrooming of retail book vendors and certain problems of the trade no sign of improvement in supply position of on-demand books is seen in the near future. They try to concentrate on fairly costly books, standing orders on serials, books of popular publishers and prefer dealer library (approval) plan to promote what is available (or what is left?) in their stock than meeting on-demand requirements of users. Very few of them have systematic methods of informing libraries about status of supply and non-supply to enable libraries to take alternate action. In this respect, foreign vendors are quite prompt. With their computerised system, they inform libraries about status of supply as well as cancellation after lapse of stipulated period. Few years ago, a similar experiment was done by ISAC Library with Indian wholesale dealers and the result was not much different from that of Indian retail vendors. Under the circumstances, special libraries may have to explore newer methods of acquiring on-demand books like obtaining by bulk airfreight and/or selective airmail from foreign vendors once convinced about non-availability in local market.

TABLE 6.4: Summary of Supply Status of On-Demand Books in Percentages (as of September 1984)

Month of Order	*Suppliers*			*Total*
	Indian		*Foreign*	
	Exclusive/ Specialised	*Retailers*		
January -March 1983	100	23	65	39
April-June 1983	100	27	62	58
July-September 1983	88	39	69	64
October-December 1983	65	60	48	51
Total	82	28	59	52

Knowing where a library stands in terms of procurement of on-demand books and using the results to frame future procurement and collection development policies are necessary. Since users are not much concerned with the problems faced by libraries due to delays at book trade/suppliers end, all the delays have to be apparently absorbed as delays at library and the acquisitions librarian has to smilingly say user is always right. The problem of procurement delays persists to a great extent.

7

USE OF LIBRARY COLLECTION

CASE STUDY 07

LENT OUT USE OF LIBRARY COLLECTION

Introduction

With the objective of having potentially most useful stock pattern, a library has to strive hard to know optimum size of its collection. In practice it is very difficult to precisely decide how many documents a library should buy and how long they should be kept on active shelves. Yet carefully designed use studies can give some broad guidelines in striking a balance among costs, benefits and utilities.

Use studies contribute to sound acquisition policies. Collection of a library is largely built on anticipated demand based on paternalistic policies. Quite often, document selection itself is based on limited information available at the time of selection. Hence, what has been acquired may or may not be of high utility. The acid test for such acquisitions is the actual use made of the collection.

Apart from evaluating the collection, use studies help to know how much good a library has done. Usage of documents make a quantitative assessment of a library. Use studies help in identifying the need, if only, for promotion and also designing ways and means of promoting use of library documents.

Though everyone agrees that the so-called obsolete documents should be discarded from or weeded out of active collection of a library, it is quite difficult in practice to decide which are the obsolete items. Hence, a defensive strategy to play safe is normally adopted. However, systematic use study strengthen the hands of library authorities to take bold decisions relating to weeding policies.

Use studies normally "... attempt to determine what is used, how frequently it is used, the time span for which material is useful, the national origins of the materials used, etc." (Shaw, 1971, p. 7).

Further, use studies have been helpful in knowing most frequently used documents, how heavily used documents are used, obsolescence and half life of documents, how many titles can satisfy say 60 per cent of user's needs, which ones to be sent for compact, remote, less expensive storage, who are the intensive users, what should be procured in duplicate, what back volumes of periodicals be bought, right type of binding policies, balanced budget for future acquisition, future use pattern, etc. By and large, "... researchers agree that past use is the best indicator of the future use of material" (Kent *et al.*, 1979, p. 49).

It is very difficult to define use of a library document. Even in economics, the term use is vaguely defined. Use of a document is often defined as a process of extracting content of a message to meet a need. Interestingly, it is possible that a document is used without utilising its content or information and *vice versa* (Martin and Lancaster, 1981, p. 88). Leave alone measuring the benefit derived from use, what could be treated as one use of a document is very vague. A document inadvertently or reluctantly taken out of shelf, a document casually glanced, a document curiously browsed, a document seriously consulted in the library, a document borrowed from the library and sublent, returned without reading, read but not put into application or action, renewed without yet reading, etc. are often equated and considered as one use. Further, the ultimate use of library document is not measurable.

Likewise, a 'document' as unitised by use studies has a very wide variations in volume, size and content.

Use of documents when operationally defined essentially constitutes in-house use, circulation or lentout use, inter-library loan use and use through reprographic service. Thus "... total library use can hardly be expressed in terms of circulations statistics which are, at best, only a rough indication of trends in the use of library [and] ... library use cannot be measured merely in terms of loan figures" (Walford, 1975, p. 285).

Use of a library can be viewed from two principal angles. One is looking at use from the angle of a set of documents of the library with its various characteristics such as subject, age, year of acquisition of document, etc. for a given period by a defined set of users. The other is looking at use of a set of documents of the library from the angle of a defined set of users having various characteristics such as psychological, environmental and demographic characteristics.

Based on the method of data collection, use studies could be either synchronous or diachronous. They are also called cross-sectional and historical studies of use of books. "*Synchronous* studies are made on records of users or references at one point in time and compare the uses against the age distribution of the material used or cited and *Diachronous* studies follow the use of particular items through successive observations at different dates" over a certain life span (Line and Sanderson, 1974, p. 52). In other words, diachronous studies are nothing but longitudinal use studies.

The present study was designed predominantly to know the use of ISAC library documents, particularly books, hardcopy reports, standards and journals by scientists, engineers and other technical staff of the Centre. How users of different characteristics have used documents has been taken up as part of a separate study. This study incidentally making use of the data looks at how various types of documents are used based on synchronous method. Since slightly different data collection method and analysis are adopted use of journals is taken up separately (Case Study 10). Thus this study presents use of ISAC library books, hardcopy reports and standards only at the overall level. Longitudinal use, subject-wise analysis of use, distribution of use over year of publication, year of acquisition, etc. of books and reports are presented as two separate (Case Studies 08 and 09).

Data Collection Method and Sample

Due to obvious reasons the entire collection could not be subjected to use study. A 20 per cent stratified, purposeful sample was made for books. Similarly, a simple systematic 20 per cent random sample was adopted for reports and standards. The actual sample reports and standards are checked against the stratified sample.

For the purpose of stratification, UDC class numbers for books, originating organisations as found in primary report numbers for reports and issuing agencies for standards are adopted as the respective criteria. Based on the classified catalogue, the report number catalogue and the standard number catalogue, approximate number of documents in each stratum is measured. To check on this estimation, linear length of shelves of all the subject groups/strata have been measured at a later date when almost entire stock was brought back to shelves for some other purpose.

Actual collection of data is spread over five months and to minimise biases in sample, while choosing sample documents proportional representation was given to documents on shelves, documents being used in the library, documents on circulation (i.e., those issued out) and reserved documents.

The number of times the sample documents are issued out of the library ever since acquired (Library started from the end of 1972) and details of users who borrowed sample documents during last ten months, were noted down based on information found on the due date slips. Rarely due date slips have been replaced with new slips and to that extent data is error prone. In order to have a counter-check on data so collected by 'collection sample', a 'circulation sample' for about three months have also been subsequently collected and examined.

Limitations of the Study

Use and user studies have many built-in limitations and hence expecting more than what they deserve might misguide the reader. As Shaw puts it "These [use] . . . studies can . . . be considered to give no more than very rough outlines of the nature and scope of the problem of communication through literature" (Shaw, 1971, p. 7).

Utility is very difficult to measure ". . . there are not objective means for measuring benefit from materials use" (Kent *et al.*, 1979, p. 2). Though use is not equivalent to usefulness, they are almost made equivalent in use studies. "Recognizing that it is only one of many factors determining 'value', *frequency of use* was chosen as an index of the 'value' or 'usefulness' of book" (Fussler and Simon, 1969, p. 7). Use studies present a quantitative rather than qualitative assessment.

Though use should include in-house use, interlibrary loan use and use through reprographic service apart from lentout use, this study confines to lentout or circulation use of documents. However, an assessment of other types of use is being done as part of separate studies. "The recorded circulation use of books is a reasonably reliable index of all use, including the unrecorded consultative or browsing use within the library" (Fussler and Simon, 1969, p. 3). ". . . external circulation data can be utilised with a high level of confidence to measure total book use . . ." (Kent *et al.*, 1979, p. 10). For example, one of the earlier surveys showed that "Only 5 per cent of stock receives recorded in-library use but does not issue" (Harris, 1977). Similarly, the Fussler and Simon study concluded that "Books that develop little recorded use develop little browsing, and books that develop much recorded use develop much browsing, except for the highest-use books, for which extrinsic factors distort the picture" (Fussler and Simon, 1969, p. 115).

There are an array of factors which affect the use data. Age dependent factors like growth of literature, book publishing rate over years, book publishing rate in different subject groups, collection changes, changes in user population, absence of volumes for binding, etc. affect use considerably. Quite often larger part of the collection consists of recent publications. It is more so in case of ISAC Library which grew fast since 1978. Further, use studies are subjected to internal biases such as library stock and external biases such as readers' knowledge of that stock (Line and Sanderson, 1974, pp. 53-54).

As the collection increases, there is a tendency of decreased marginal utility. In other words as the ratio of collection to user increases, the use per document decreases.

The library system is dynamic. Apart from growth in user and collection components, the objectives, scope and interest of the parent organisation and hence the subject areas of interest of library do not remain constant.

Some of the factors which inflate use data are repeated use by the same user, cursory glance by user, overdue charge system, limited period of issue (lending period), duplicate copies, renewal system, etc. Similarly, the factors deflating use data are lack of physical comforts and congestion in the library (much affects in-house use), limitations of borrowing facility, library timings, nature of work of users, collection to user ratio, extent of reprographic service, etc. In other words "use studies are affected by changes in library policy, issue regulations, accessibility, etc. . ." (Line and Sanderson, 1974, p. 70).

The total number of borrower tickets in use in ISAC Library over years is shown in Table 7.1. Two major limitations on the number of borrower tickets in use are: till 1978 many issuing transactions were also done on registers and though borrower tickets are non-transferable, occasionally users were allowed to borrow on other's tickets.

The data based on 'circulation sample' was collected after one year of 'collection sample' data and by that time there was not only marginal increase in size of collection and users but also a considerable change in the environment. Firstly, the Centre has been shifted to fairly spacious own building in the city. Library was closed for 31 days for the purpose of shifting just prior to collecting 'circulation sample' data. During that time few sections of the centre were not completely shifted to new campus. Lastly, library has been housed in a more spacious centrally located place in the new campus, though the building is unsuitable for library.

TABLE 7.1: Number of Borrower Tickets in Use

Year	*No. of Tickets in Use*	*% Increase Over Previous Year*
1973	520	—
1974	786	51.2
1975	884	12.5
1976	987	11.7
1977	1,451	47.0
1978	1,854	27.8
1979	2,510	35.4
1980	3,191	27.1
1981	3,498	9.6
1982	4,127	18.0
1983	4,889	18.5

Finally, due to limitations of manual lending system, a systematic diasynchronous or longitudinal approach could not be adopted for the present study.

Overall Usage of ISAC Library based on 'Collection Sample'

Two thousand and ninet-one sample books have been issued out 14,674 times so far and of which 3,158 times during last 10 months to 708 library users. Similarly 617 sample reports have been issued 416 times so far and 137 times during last 10 months to 72 users. Use data at this broad level is tabulated in Table 7.2.

TABLE 7.2: Total Use of Sample Books and Reports

Type of Document	*Collection*	*Sample*		*Use During Last 10 Months*		*Cumulative Use so far*		*No. of Users Used*	*Average Use per User*
		No.	*%*	*No.*	*Av.*	*No.*	*Av.*		
Books	10,089	2,091	20.7	3,158	1.51	14,674	7.02	708	22.3
Reports	3,232	617	19.1	137	0.22	416	0.67	72	9.5

As could be seen from Table 7.2, books have been quite heavily used. However, reports have been used much less than books and the number of users using reports are very much less than those using books. It is generally believed that the technical reports are the lifeblood for research workers in the areas of space science, satellite technology, aeronautics, energy, environment, etc. Yet, as revealed in the table, technical reports are almost scarcely used by a limited number of space technologists. The possible reasons for such a low use of reports, as found from informal discussions with users, are as follows. Firstly, the library started building its reports collection from 1978 onwards. Secondly, reports being semiformal publications are available as gratis to many users. Thirdly, many internal and Indian reports received free by library are otherwise accessible to users. Fourthly, fairly adequate and free reprographic service has enabled many users to possess their own copies of reports. Fifthly, since reports deal with specific area of a subject very few defined set of users would be interested in a report. Further, out of about 1,100 members, about 800 members are technical staff and out of these technical staff many have broad specialisation such as mechanical engineering, electronics and computer science. But there are few reports in these broad disciplines in the library. Further, a citation study of papers published on '*Journal of Spacecraft Technology*' (an in-house technical journal of the centre) revealed that the same Space Technologists cited books, reports and journals to the extent of 33 per cent, 26 per cent and 35 per cent respectively in their papers. This very much confirms the criticality of need for technical reports for a limited number of engineers working in the forefront and any reliance on quantitative borrowings of reports from library could be misleading.

It may be seen from the table that books have an average use of 1.51 during last 10 months and an average of 7.02 uses so far.[1]

Average number of uses per user during last 10 months is 22.3 in case of books and 9.5 in case of reports. About 708 users have borrowed books at least once in a 10-month period. In case of reports only 72 have borrowed at least once in 10-months period.

Standards are much less borrowed than even reports. Like reports, standards collection was also started from 1978 and standards other than ISI were acquired much recently. As such, except ISI no other sample standards were borrowed. Secondly, many standards such as MIL, JSS are decentralised and concerned groups have much stronger collection than library. In fact part of library's standards collection was earlier received on transfer from the collection of different groups and few have been given as gratis by individuals. Thirdly, since standards are issued for 3 days without renewing facility, unlike books and reports which are issued for 21 days with renewing facility, users probably would prefer to consult standards within the library.

Overall Use based on 'Circulation Sample'

Before making further observations on use patterns of library documents, the overall picture of use based on three months 'circulation sample' subsequently collected may be examined. As shown in Table 7.3, there were 6,054 lentout uses in all during three months. As could be seen from the table, books constituted 80 per cent of daily issues, followed by journals with 14.8 per cent. The reports have a meagre 5 per cent and standards a negligible 0.2 per cent. In other words, ISAC Library has recorded over 24,000 lentout uses during the year. The data remarkably confirms the upward trend in use, and the lentout use data projected in Table 7.2 based on 'Collection sample' especially the average use per document and average use per user. Table 7.3 also reveals that books, journals and reports, respectively, forming 42 per cent, 30 per cent and 16 per cent of collection account for 80 per cent, 15 per cent and 5 per cent of circulation use.[2]

Trend of Daily Issues

Daily issue statistics for the same period, revealed that average issues per day was 84 (books—69, Reports—3.6, Standards—0.2, and Journals—11.6). Frequently tables made for daily issue statistics have further revealed that number of books issued per day varied from 34 to 112; issue of reports issued varied from 0 to 8 and journals varied from 1 to 25 per day. However, the total issue itself varied from 46 to 125.

TABLE 7.3: Lentout Use as per 'Circulation Sample'

Type of Document	*Circulation Use in 3 months*		*Users (N = 1100)*		*Collection*		*Avg. Use per User per Year*	*Avg. Use per Document per Year*
	No.	*%*	*No.*	*%*	*No.*	*%*		
Books	4,846	80.0	698	63.5	10,500	42.3	27.8	1.8
Reports	302	5.9	123	11.2	4,000	16.1	9.8	0.3
Standards	11	0.2	5	0.5	2,800	11.3	8.8	0.0
Journals	895	14.8	228	20.7	7,500*	30.2	15.7	0.5
Total	6,054	100.0	759	69.0	24,800	99.0	31.9	1.0

Key: *—Includes 4,000 bound Journals and approximately 3,500 loose issues.

Note: A citation study of in-house technical journal revealed that books, reports and journals are cited to the extent of 33 per cent, 26 per cent and 35 per cent respectively.

In another tabulation the average daily issue per day was found to be a maximum of 96 for September 1984 understandably [as explained in Case Study 01 (Sridhar, 1982, p. 153) of library visit and in-house use] due to general season of reviews for departmental promotions.

Table 7.4 presents average number of documents issued per day over a typical week. It is interesting to note that issues are maximum on Saturdays and the daily issues over typical week depicts exactly the reverse pattern of in-house use (Sridhar 1982, p. 182), i.e., minimum in the mid of the week and maximum in the beginning and end of the week. Fig. 7.1 incorporating the results of earlier in-house use study, shows how lentout use over a typical week is in the reverse pattern of in-house use.

TABLE 7.4: Average Daily Issues

Day	*Books*	*Reports*	*Journals*	*Total*
Monday	68	4.3	12.4	85
Tuesday	70	3.5	10.8	84
Wednesday	63	2.7	10.0	76
Thursday	70	3.2	11.4	85
Friday	71	4.1	11.3	86
Saturday	72	4.1	14.4	91
Total	69	3.6	11.5	84

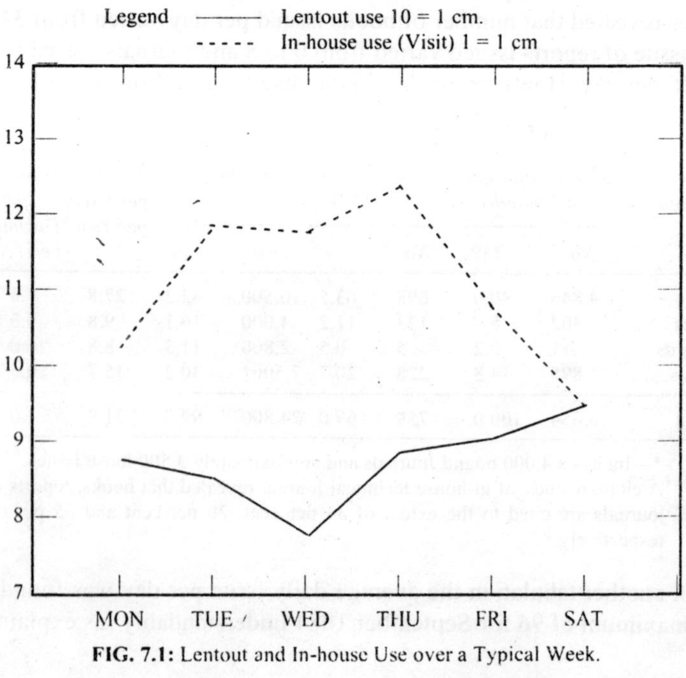

FIG. 7.1: Lentout and In-house Use over a Typical Week.

Frequency Distribution of Use over User based on 'Collection Sample'

Lastly, the use data relating to latest ten months has been tabulated in the form of a frequency distribution over number of users. As noted earlier, 708 users have, in an average, borrowed 22.3 books in a ten months period. Similarly, 72 users have borrowed, on an average, 9.5 reports per user during last 10 months. Use of books per user is quite high. One user has borrowed little more than one book per week and another seven have borrowed almost one book per fortnight. In case of reports, highest borrowing of eight times is done by two users during last ten months.

It may also be seen from Fig. 7.2 which plots cumulative percentage of use over cumulative percentage of users that 20 per cent of users have made 52 per cent and 48 per cent of total use of books and reports respectively. The distribution is very close to a parabolic or asymptotic or Zipfian type distribution.

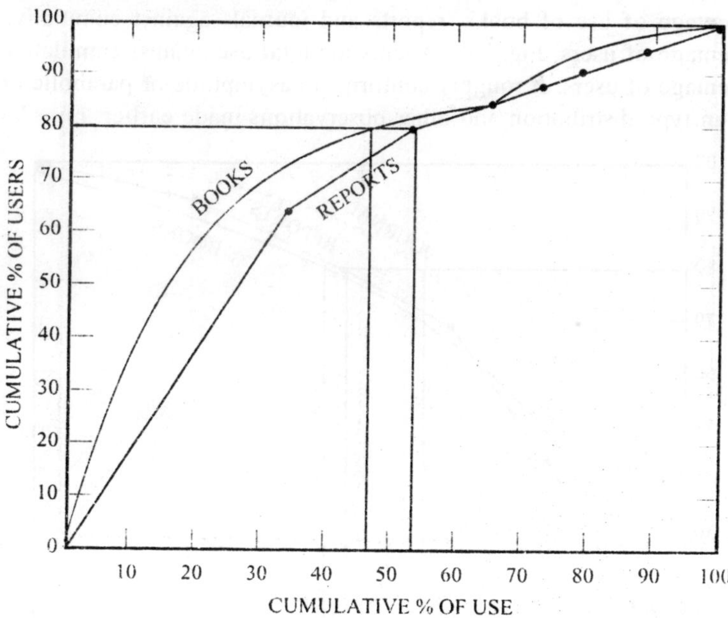

FIG. 7.2: Cumulative Use *Vs.* Cumulative Users (Collection Sample).

By going through the list of 25 intensive users of books and eight intensive users of reports, it is noticed that many intensive borrowers were also intensive in-house users (Case Study 01) and those made relatively more suggestions (Case Study 05) for documents (Sridhar, 1983, p. 171). However a clear picture of cross correlation of borrowed use, in-house use, suggestions, reservations, etc. will be known after completion of a separate study being done. Nine of these intensive users have borrowed books in as many as 7 to 12 different subject groups during last 10 months. This shows the multidisciplinary and heterogeneous nature of the field and varied interest of users.

Frequency Distribution of Use over User based on 'Circulation Sample'

The frequency tables based on 'circulation sample' for books and reports being identical with that of 'collection sample' confirmed the trend seen earlier, though the range slightly differed due to difference in sample sizes.

These two frequency tables together with the frequency table for use of journals has been plotted in Fig. 7.3 in terms of cumulative percentage of use of books, reports and journals against cumulative percentage of users. Fig. 7.4 presents the total use against cumulative percentage of users. It roughly conforms to asymptotic or parabolic or zipfian type distribution and other observations made earlier. Fig. 7.3

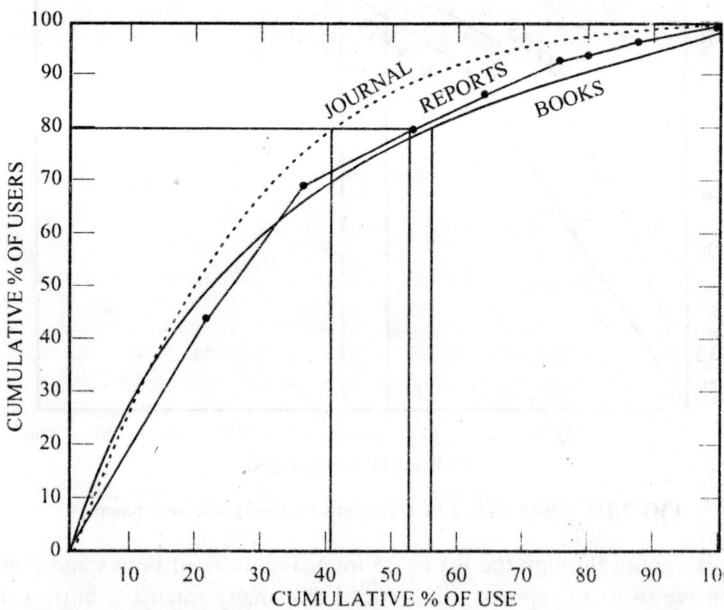

FIG. 7.3: Cumulative User *Vs.* Cumulative Users (Circulation Sample)

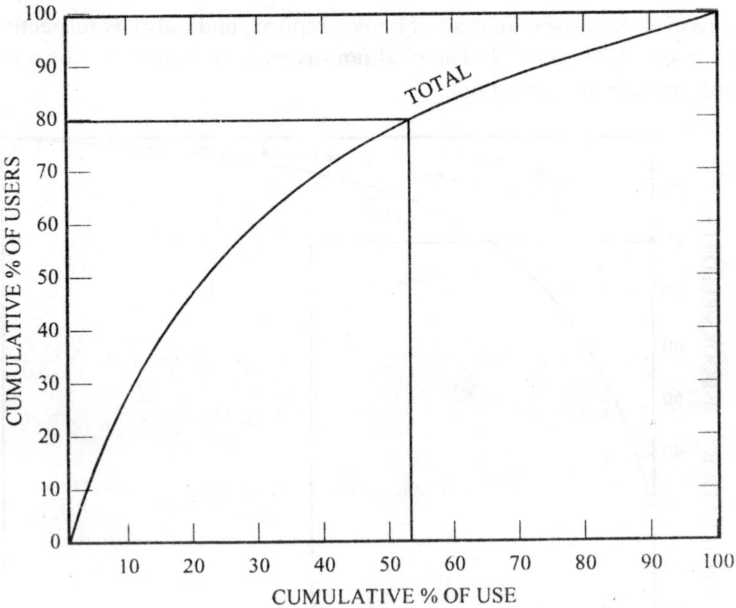

FIG. 7.4: Cumulative Use *Vs.* Cumulative Users (Circulation Sample).

further shows the difference in trend among books, reports and journals. Journals depicted a much sharper curve than the other two, thereby indicating that smaller number of users (say 20%) have made much more use of journals than books and reports. One general observation made from Figs. 7.2, 7.3 and 7.4 is that approximately half of the use is made by 20 per cent intensive users and the remaining half of the use is made by balance 80 per cent of users irrespective of type of document.[3] (Note that non-users are not represented on these diagrams).

Non-users

With approximately 1,000 members at the time of first survey based on 'collection sample', about 292 were non-user members as far as lentout use of books are concerned. Similarly there were 92 non-users of reports.

In case of subsequent survey based on 'circulation sample', 341 registered members out of 1,100 have not borrowed any document during the quarter. These users were holding 890 borrower tickets (excluding 30 division tickets) out of 5,000 tickets. In other words, 39 per cent of members have idled 18 per cent of total borrower tickets during the quarter without borrowing any document from the library.

However, non-users in case of books, reports, and journals respectively were 401, 977 and 872. The total non-users (non-borrowers) of reports and journals are quite high.

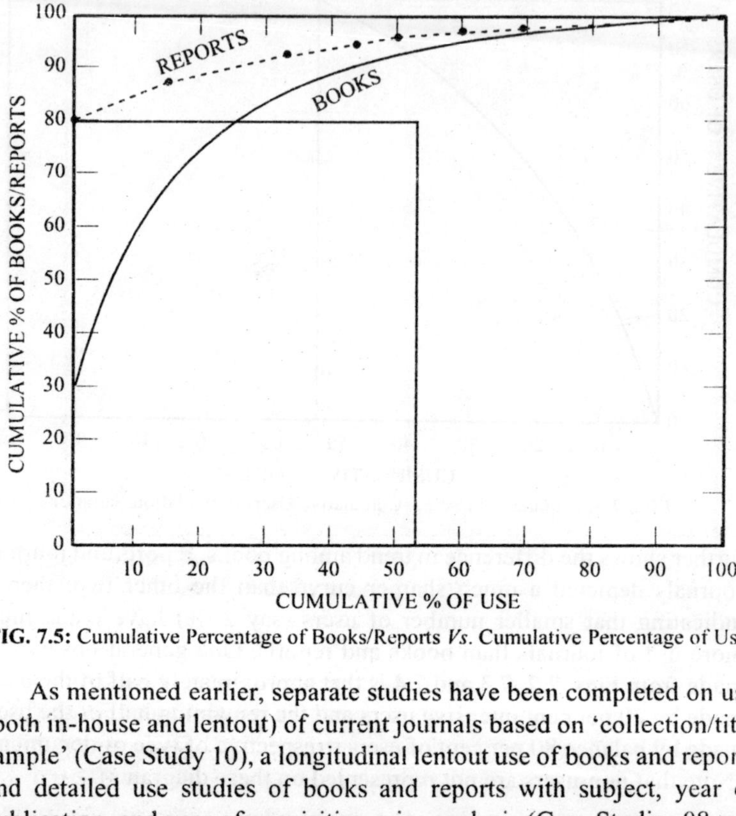

FIG. 7.5: Cumulative Percentage of Books/Reports *Vs.* Cumulative Percentage of Use.

As mentioned earlier, separate studies have been completed on use (both in-house and lentout) of current journals based on 'collection/title sample' (Case Study 10), a longitudinal lentout use of books and reports and detailed use studies of books and reports with subject, year of publication, and year of acquisition-wise analysis (Case Studies 08 and 09). A further study of correlating use with various user characteristics is being done separately (Case Study 20).

Conclusion

To recall certain salient results and observations, books are issued out on an average 1.51 times and reports 0.22 times in a ten months period. However, the same average for lentout use so far, since the establishment of the library in 1972, are 7.02 and 0.67, respectively for books and reports. Average use per user during ten months is 22.3 in case of books and 9.5 in case of reports.

Reports are, by and large, used much less than books and standards much less than reports.

Based on a three months 'circulation sample' it is observed that books constitute 80 per cent of daily issues followed by journals with 14.8 per cent. The reports have a meagre 5 per cent and the standards negligible 0.2 per cent. The circulation sample' data remarkably confirmed the results of 'collection sample' data.

The data further confirmed an earlier observation that the use of library during reviews for departmental promotion reaches maximum. An interesting observation is that lentout use over a typical week is in the reverse pattern of in-house use. This study enabled library to know the overall lentout use of library collection. Use of specific type of documents is dealt in subsequent cast studies.

The frequency distribution of cumulative use over cumulative number of users depicted an asymptotic or parabolic or zipfian type distribution. About 20 per cent users were responsible for nearly 52 per cent of total use. Nearly 39 per cent of members have idled 13 per cent of total borrower tickets during the quarter without borrowing any document from the Library. Non-borrowers of journals, reports and standards are very high.

It was not the intention of this study to examine studies of use of library collections by scientists, engineers and technicians from the angle of: (i) collection development and evaluation with the purposes of identifying highly used to add additional copies, less used to relegate to remote/compact storage and unused for discarding, (ii) promoting better usage of less used and unused, (iii) examining the broad generalisations such as (a) books which are unused during an initial period are more likely to remain in use and those heavily used continue to be used later, (b) use data of a library collection follows reverse J shaped curve or 80/20 rule, (iv) determining life time and obsolescence rate of library materials, relative use in different subjects, etc. The purpose here is to look at the use-studies from the angle of information-use pattern of scientists, engineers and technicians. As such many studies like that of University of Pittsburgh (Kent *et al.*, 1979) are not cited in this case study for comparison.

Like bibliometric and citation studies, use studies also have some limitations. If a use study is not properly designed with adequate reliability and validity, results can cause serious distortions and lead to disastrous decisions.

CASE STUDY 08

USE OF TECHNICAL REPORTS AND STANDARDS

Introduction

A lentout use study of technical reports and standards of ISAC Library based on a simple systematic 20 per cent random collection sample has been carried out during second-half of 1983. An earlier Case Study (07) on lentout use of books, reports, journals and standards has presented results and observations at broad level in addition to highlighting the background, data collection methods and limitations. Six hundred and seventeen sample reports issued out 416 times so far (i.e., since 1978) and 137 times during ten months just prior to survey (to 72 users) are analysed in this study by number of times issued, by issuing agency (organisation) of report, by year of publication and year of acquisition in addition to a longitudinal analysis to see how they are borrowed during latest ten months compared to cumulative use so far.

Frequency Distribution of Use over Number of Reports

Table 7.5 presents the frequency distribution of use over number of reports. As could be seen from the table, 78 per cent of reports have not yet been issued out even once. The balance 22 per cent only belong to the core collection. It is clear that little less than 8 per cent of reports met nearly 67 per cent of total lentout use and 12 per cent were responsible for 85 per cent of use. Plotting cumulative percentage of reports against cumulative percentage of use, an expected parabolic type distribution can be seen.

TABLE 7.5: Frequency Distribution of Use over Number of Reports

No. of Times Issued	*Reports*			*Total 'Lent-out Use' of Reports*		
	No.	*%*	*Cumulative %*	*No.*	*%*	*Cumulative %*
1	2	3	4	5	6	7
0	480	77.8	77.8	0	0.0	0.0
1	63	10.2	88.0	63	15.1	15.1
2	26	4.2	92.2	52	12.5	27.6
3	8	1.3	93.5	24	5.8	33.4

(Contd.)

TABLE 7.5 *(Contd.)*

1	2	3	4	5	6	7
4	10	1.6	95.1	40	9.6	43.0
5	6	1.0	96.1	30	7.2	50.2
6	6	1.0	97.1	36	8.7	58.9
7	6	1.0	98.1	42	10.1	69.0
8	4	0.6	98.7	32	7.7	76.7
9	3	0.5	99.2	27	6.5	83.2
10	0	0.0	99.2	0	0.0	83.2
11—15	3	0.5	99.7	37	8.9	92.1
16—20	1	0.2	99.9	16	3.8	95.9
21—25	1	0.2	101.1	22	5.3	101.2
Error	0	0.0	101.1	–5	-1.2	100.0
Total	617	100.1	101.1	416	100.0	100.0

It is surprising that the reports have been, by and large, scarcely used, though they are believed to be one of the important sources of information in space science and satellite technology areas. It may also be noted that by very nature reports cannot be expected to be used as intensively as books and journals are used. Some of the reasons for low usage of report, as mentioned earlier, are as follows. The development of a centralised reports collection at ISAC Library was started in 1978 though library existed since end of 1972. Secondly, reports being semiformal publications are available as gratis to many users. Thirdly, many internal and Indian reports in the collection are otherwise accessible to most of the users. Fourthly, free reprographic service has enabled many users to possess their own copies of reports. Fifthly, since reports deal with specific topics/problems very few users are interested in a given report. Further, out of about 1,100 members, only 800 were technical staff and of which nearly 400 were lower level operational staff. A majority of 400 higher level technical staff have broad specialisation such as mechanical engineering, electronics, computer science and physics. All these areas have been better covered by books and journals, and there are very few reports in the broad disciplines. On the other hand, the high rate of mishits or non-cost-effective acquisition of reports is attributable to the fact that most of the reports are either acquired on standing order basis or by selections based on titles. There is absolutely no scope for examination of reports before selection (like approval books). Nor critical reviews of reports are available. At the most, stale report announcement bulletins can be consulted which in no way help to screen out any report.

Standards are much less borrowed than even reports. Like reports, standards collection was also started from 1978 and standards other than ISI were acquired much recently. As such except ISI no other sample standards are ever borrowed. Out of 630 sample standards ISI standards have been issued 15 times. Secondly, many standards such as MIL and JSS are decentralised and concerned groups have much stronger collection than library. In fact, Library's standards collection was recently enriched by partially transferring the collections of different groups and by receiving as gratis from individuals. Thirdly, since standards are issued for 3 days without renewing facility (unlike books and reports which are issued for 21 days with renewing facility) probably users would prefer to consult standards within the library.

Relative Use of Technical Reports of Different Issuing Agencies

Table 7.6 presents organisation (or originating agency)-wise use of technical reports and standards. The table also shows a comparison of estimated percentage of stock with percentage of sample in each of the group based on simple systematic random sample. The highest variation is found in NASA reports (+22.3%). Next comes others category reports (–12.1%), internal reports, i.e., ISRO/DOS/PRL reports (+3.8%), GFW (–3.2%) and RAE (–2.7%). The variations in estimation in other groups are very less. In case of standards, BSI has +4.1 per cent and ISI –2.7 per cent variation of estimated stock from stock based on sample. The difference in percentage of estimated stock and sampled stock in case of foreign and Indian reports is 2.5.

It is not surprising that NASA reports forming 27.2 per cent of sample accounted for 55.3 per cent of total use. Next highest usage of 15.1 per cent of total use is made of ESA/ESRO reports which form 9.2 per cent of sample. The percentage of use of all other reports is less than the corresponding percentage of sample. None of the sample reports is issued out at least once in case of AMCP, BARC, COSPAR, GSFC, NAL, NOAA, NRC, TAC and TIFR. This once again suggests that lot of standing order supplies and gratis reports are adding dead-weight to reports collection. Further, foreign reports forming about 85 per cent of sample resulted in 92 per cent of total use as against 15 per cent of Indian reports resulted in 8 per cent of total use.

One important observation regarding reports and to some extent standards is that library should re-examine its policy of accepting reports on gratis, exchange and standing order bases.

TABLE 7.6: Organisation-wise Use of Reports and Standards

Orgn. Code	*Acronym of Originating Agency/Orgn.*	*% of Stock*	*% of Sample*	*Use of Sample Reports/Standards No*	*%*	*% of Stock –% of Sample*	*% of Use - % of Sample*
Reports							
A	AMCP	0.8	0.3	0	0.0	+0.5	–0.3
B	BARC	0.5	0.6	0	0.0	–0.1	–0.6
C	COSPAR	4.6	4.2	0	0.0	+0.2	–4.2
D	ESA/ESRO	8.5	9.2	63	15.1	–0.7	+5.9
E	GEC	0.8	0.6	1	0.2	+0.2	–0.4
F	GFW	1.8	6.0	2	0.5	–3.2	–5.5
G	GSFC	0.9	2.4	0	0.0	–1.5	–2.4
H	ISRO/DOS/ PRL	15.5	11.7	32	7.7	+3.8	–4.0
I	JPL	1.1	0.6	1	0.2	+0.5	–0.4
J	KGD	0.9	1.3	3	0.7	–0.4	–0.6
K	MSFC	1.2	0.2	1	0.2	+1.0	0.0
L	NAL	0.9	1.0	0	0.0	–0.1	–1.0
M	NASA	49.5	27.2	230	55.3	+22.3	+28.1
N	NOAA	0.5	5.7	0	0.0	–0.2	–5.7
O	NRC	0.6	0.8	0	0.0	–0.2	–0.8
P	NTIS/JPRS/PB	2.2	2.8	6	1.4	–0.6	–1.4
Q	RAC	0.6	1.3	4	1.0	–0.7	–0.2
R	RADC	1.7	2.4	6	1.4	–0.7	–1.0
S	RAE	1.7	4.4	15	3.6	–2.7	–0.8
T	TAC	0.6	0.3	0	0.0	+0.3	–0.3
U	TIFR	0.3	0.2	0	0.0	0.1	–0.2
V	OTHERS*	4.6	16.7	52	12.5	–12.1	–4.2
Total		99.8	99.9	416	99.8	—	—
	Foreign	82.4	84.9	382	91.8	–2.5	+6.9
	Indian	17.6	15.1	34	8.2	+2.5	–6.9
	Total	100.0	100.0	416	100.0	—	—
Standards							
W	ANSI	1.3	1.3	0	0.0	0.0	–1.3
X	BSI	5.4	1.3	0	0.0	+4.1	–1.3
Y	IEEE	1.3	2.1	0	0.0	–0.8	–2.1
Z	ISI	89.6	92.3	15	100.0	–2.7	+7.7
S	JSS	0.6	2.0	0	0.0	–1.4	–2.0
H	MIL	1.8	1.0	0	0.0	+0.8	–1.0
	Total	100.0	100.0	15	100.0	—	—

Note: * Others include about 56 organisations. Some of them are NSSDC/NDC, IISc, ONERA, UTIAS, CRC, AD, etc.

It is not economical to accept a gratis report and spend considerable processing and maintenance cost on it when the same is not even issued out once. All those reports or series of such reports which are never used may be considered for weeding out of library including transferring to concerned sections of the centre. Internal reports even though less used for obvious reasons may have to be maintained in the library to meet the archival function for internally generated information.

The frequency scores are also tabulated individually for reports of each issuing agency. It is noticed in the frequency table that in case of NASA reports, 4 had 11 or more uses and 29 never used out of 167 sample reports. In case of ESA/ESRO reports 37 out of 57 were never used. Other reports were scarcely used and hence found not worth probing further.

Longitudinal Use of Reports

Use of reports during last 10 months is compared with the cumulative use so far in this section. Table 7.7 presents a picture of longitudinal use of reports of different agencies. Foreign reports have recorded an increase in use by 6 per cent during last 10 months whereas Indian reports have faced 6 per cent decline in use. Ignoring the non-used categories of reports, ESA/ESRO reports have found 4.6 per cent increased use during last 10 months followed by RAE (+2.3%), RAC (+1.9%), NASA (+0.9%) and NTIS/JPRS/PB (+0.1%). Highest decline in use (–5.5%) is faced by internal reports, i.e., DOS/ISRO/PRL reports. Other reports which showed marginal decrease in use are RADC (–1.4%), reports in 'others' category (–0.8%), KGI (0.7%), GFW (–0.5%) and GEC, JPL and MSFC (each –0.2%).

Frequency Distribution of Use over Age (Year of Publication) of Report

There is a general belief that use of document declines with age in a negative exponential pattern. This section deals with use against age and the next deals with use against year of acquisition of reports. The data of year of publication of reports *versus* use is presented in Table 7.8. Since the survey started in 1983 itself, the data about 1983 and to some extent 1982 reports are quite inadequate. It can be seen from the table that maximum number of reports in the collection (14.1%) are published in 1979 which is followed by 1978 (13.1). Nearly 96.8 per cent of reports

TABLE 7.7: Longitudinal Use of Reports

Origination Agency/ Orgn. Code	*% of Sample*	*Use of Sample Reports*				*% of Use During Last 10 Months – % of Cumulative Use, i.e., (4) – (6)*
		During Last 10 Months		*Cumulative Use so far*		
		No.	*%*	*No.*	*%*	
(1)	(2)	(3)	(4)	(5)	(6)	(7)
A	0.3	0	0.0	0	0.0	0.0
B	0.6	0	0.0	0	0.0	0.0
C	4.2	0	0.0	0	0.0	0.0
D	9.2	27	19.7	63	15.1	+4.6
E	0.6	0	0.0	1	0.2	–0.2
F	6.0	0	0.0	2	0.5	–0.5
G	2.4	0	0.0	0	0.0	0.0
H	11.7	3	2.2	32	7.7	–5.5
I	0.6	0	0.0	1	0.2	–0.2
J	1.3	0	0.0	3	0.7	–0.7
K	0.2	0	0.0	1	0.2	–0.2
L	1.0	0	0.0	0	0.0	0.0
M	27.2	77	56.2	230	55.3	+0.9
N	5.7	0	0.0	0	0.0	0.0
O	0.8	0	0.0	0	0.0	0.0
P	2.8	2	1.5	6	1.4	+0.1
Q	1.3	4	2.9	4	1.0	+1.9
R	2.4	0	0.0	6	1.4	–1.4
S	4.4	8	5.9	15	3.6	+2.3
T	0.3	0	0.0	0	0.0	0.0
U	0.2	0	0.0	0	0.0	0.0
V	16.7	16	11.7	52	12.5	–0.8
Total	99.9	137	99.9	416	99.8	—
Foreign	84.9	134	97.8	382	91.8	+6.0
Indian	15.1	3	2.2	34	8.2	–6.0

in the library are published within last 12 years and 70.7 per cent of reports are published since 1975 (It may be noted here that library was started from end of 1972). It is also revealed by the table that there is no clear correlation of use with age of reports. The average use per report increases steadily as we go backwards (except 1982 and 1983) understandably due to the fact that reports of earlier years might have been acquired early by the library and hence circulated more number of times. Almost all reports published earlier to 1961 are not used at all.

TABLE 7.8: Year of Publication of Reports *Vs.* Use

Year of Pub.	*Sample Reports Covered*		*Lent Out 'Use'*		*Average 'Use' per Report*
	No.	*%*	*No.*	*%*	
83	1	0.2	5	1.2	5.00
82	9	1.5	12	2.9	1.33
81	12	1.9	0	0.0	0.00
80	63	10.2	23	5.5	0.37
79	87	14.1	32	7.7	0.37
78	81	13.1	53	12.7	0.65
77	60	9.7	36	8.7	0.60
76	75	12.2	24	5.8	0.32
75	56	7.8	33	7.9	0.59
74	35	5.7	25	6.0	0.71
73	30	4.9	33	7.9	1.10
72	20	3.2	36	8.7	1.80
71	23	3.7	26	6.3	1.13
66—70	44	7.1	52	12.5	1.18
61—65	14	2.3	27	6.5	1.93
56—60	2	0.3	0	0.0	0.00
51—55	0	0.0	0	0.0	0.00
Upto 50	2	0.3	0	0.0	0.00
n.d.	2	0.3	0	0.0	0.00
Error	+1	+0.2	–1	0.2	—
Total	617	98.7	416	100.1	0.67

An analysis of mode year of publication of the sample reports based on issuing agency did not reveal any clear trend as most of the reports are acquired in last 4-5 years. However, it may be noted that ESA/ESRO reports showed four mode years of publications, viz., 1973, 1977, 1979 and 1980 and NASA reports have 1976 as mode year of publication as against the mode year 1979 for reports as a whole.

Frequency Distribution of Use over Year of Acquisition of Report

In the above analysis of age of reports, the year of acquisition of reports would have a much stronger effect on total use than mode year of publication of report. Table 7.9 presents data about distribution of use over year of acquisition of reports. Also presented in the table is the total number of reports acquired in the year by the library for comparison purpose. No clear trend in the average use per report can be seen in this table. Number of reports acquired in each year differs considerably and maximum were acquired in 1983 (1085) which is followed by 1980 and 1979.

TABLE 7.9: Year of Acquisition of Reports *Vs.* Use

Year of Acq.	*Total Acquired*		*Sample Reports Covered*		*Lentout 'Use'*		*Average 'Use' per Report*
	No.	*%*	*No.*	*%*	*No.*	*%*	
83	1,085	21.6	14	2.3	28	6.7	2.00
82	919	18.3	91	14.7	54	13.0	0.59
81	515	10.3	62	10.0	13	3.1	0.21
80	1,064	21.2	196	31.8	98	23.6	0.50
79	1,037	20.7	182	29.5	176	42.3	0.97
78	400	8.0	72	11.7	42	10.1	0.58
Error	0	0.0	0	0.0	+5	+1.2	—
Total	5,020	100.1	617	100.0	416	100.0	0.67

Results and Observations

To recall some of the observations, NASA and ESA reports have been relatively more used, library has to re-examine its present policy of accepting gratis, exchange and standing order supplies of reports and standards and weed out appropriate categories and series of unused reports. Foreign reports have recorded an increase in percentage of use in recent months. About 78 per cent of reports are not issued out even once and nearly 9 per cent of reports accounted for about 74 per cent of total use. About 97 per cent of reports in the library are published within last 12 years and 71 per cent of them are published since 1975. A further study of correlating use of reports with various user characteristics is also being done separately (Case Study 20 and Sridhar, 1995).

It may be concluded that, by and large, reports are scarcely used and use of standards is negligible. This survey has enabled the library to identify majority of unused and least used reports and also to know how use is distributed among different issuing agencies and other criteria of report. This served as a useful feedback for future collection development policies. But unfortunately, one important question remains unanswered. That is, the use study has indicated the unused categories for weeding out and also to properly control free reports and standing order supplies in future. Due to certain inherent problems in selection and procurement of technical reports can anything substantially be done to make reports acquisition a better cost-effective?

CASE STUDY 09

SUBJECT AND LONGITUDINAL USE OF BOOKS

Introduction

A study of lentout use of books of the ISAC library based on a 20 per cent stratified collection sample was made in 1983 (Sridhar, 1985) and the same presented as case study 07. In addition to results and observations at the broad level, the background of the study, data collection method and limitations are already enumerated. Two thousand and ninety-one sample books accounting for 14,674 loans since end of 1972 when the ISAC library began and 3,158 loans to 708 borrowers during the last ten months (January/March to October/December 1983) are analysed in this study by the number of times loaned, by subject, by year of publication and by year of acquisition. In addition, a longitudinal study is made of how books were borrowed during the ten months prior to the survey is being carried out as compared with the cumulative use from end 1972 to date.

Table 7.10 presents a frequency distribution of use over number of books. Nearly 27 per cent of the books in the sample were not loaned even once.[4] The balance, 73 per cent of all books in the collection, could be deemed to belong to the "core collection".[5] The Kent study suggests that "if a minimum of two uses were arbitrarily established expost-facto as a criterion for a cost-effective acquisition programme, 54.2 per cent of titles purchased in 1969 would not have been ordered; if three uses, then 62.5 per cent would not have been ordered" (Kent *et al.*, 1979, p. 10). As against this, 40.8 per cent and 49.9 per cent of books in the ISAC library can be thought of as non-cost-effective acquisitions with two uses and three uses as threshold criteria respectively.

It may be seen from Table 7.10 that 4.5 per cent of the books account for 25.2 per cent of borrowings (in the Kent's study by contrast 4.06% of items accounted for 20% of transactions); 9.9 per cent of the books contributed 44.9 per cent of total use (as against 11.59% of items meeting 40% of use in the Kent study) and 20.6 per cent of the books account for 82.7 per cent of use (as against 42.41% of items producing 80% of transactions in the Kent study, Kent *et al.*, 1979, p. 38).[6] Thus a smaller part of the collection has accounted for a much larger part of use in ISAC library. Table 7.10, when plotted as a graph in which the cumulative percentage of books is shown against the cumulative percentage of use, produces a parabolic or asymptotic or zipfian type distribution of values.

TABLE 7.10: Frequency Distribution of Use over Number of Books

No. of Times Issued	*Books*			*Total Lentout 'Use' of Books*		
	No.	*%*	*Cumulative %*	*No.*	*%*	*Cumulative %*
0	556	26.6	26.6	0	0.0	0.0
1	296	14.2	40.8	296	2.0	2.0
2	190	9.1	49.9	380	2.6	4.6
3	131	6.3	56.2	393	2.7	7.3
4	118	5.6	61.8	472	3.2	10.5
5	89	4.3	66.1	445	3.0	13.5
6	75	3.6	69.7	450	3.1	16.6
7	82	3.9	73.6	574	3.9	20.5
8	68	3.3	77.0	544	3.7	24.2
9	52	2.5	79.5	468	3.2	27.4
10	44	2.1	81.6	440	3.0	30.4
11—15	166	7.9	89.5	2,280	15.4	45.8
16—20	101	4.8	94.3	1,841	12.5	58.3
21—25	63	3.0	97.3	1,410	9.6	67.9
26—30	51	2.4	99.7	1,476	10.1	78.0
31—40	59	2.8	102.5	1,987	13.5	91.5
> 40	36	1.7	104.2	1,717	11.7	103.2
Error	–86	–4.1	100.1	–499	3.4	99.8
Total	2,091	100.1		14,674	99.8	—

Relative Use of Books in Different Subject Groups

Space science and satellite technology are heterogeneous, multi-disciplinary subjects. As such, knowing the composition of different subjects in a collection and their respective use is of value, as Martyn and Lancaster suggest (Martyn and Lancaster, 1981, p. 78). Table 7.11 shows the subject use of books. Also presented in the table, for comparative purposes, are the approximate percentage of the total number of users specialising in the subject under review, the length of shelf space in feet that the subject occupies, the approximate percentage of total book stock and the percentage of sample in each subject. A word of caution about the specialisation of users. The figures given are only approximate. They are based on what appears in the users' educational qualifications and not on their present area of work. While working out this percentage, 681 technical staff as of January 1982 were considered; non-technical staff members were not included in the calculation. Hence, subject groups such as the social sciences, the natural sciences in general, arts, literature, etc., have been marked NA (not applicable). Subject groups such as astronomy and astrophysics form part of physics; telecommunication is a specialisation of many in the electronics groups. Thus, specialisation data should not be regarded as strictly accurate data but only indicative.

The percentage of use is substantially greater than the percentage of the sample which is more or less the same as the percentage of total stock in the case of D (mathematics), N (energy), O (electronics), P (telecommunication), Q (mechanical engineering) and W (manufactures). Of these D, N, O, P and Q are given substantial specialist usage. As expected, more books are borrowed in the field of specialisation of users than in other fields. The only exception to this apart from generalities (A) occurs in physics (E and F), and this might be explained by the fact that physics is fundamentally a pure science and that very few scientists and engineers in the Centre other than small groups of physicists themselves are engaged in research in this field, although 8.8 per cent of technical staff members have physics as their academic specialisation. Further, the percentage of stock in physics is more than double the percentage of users.

The last column of Table 7.11 shows use per linear foot of shelf. To arrive at this the actual use is multiplied by five, the sample factor, and divided by the linear shelf length in feet. While the average use per linear foot of shelf is 69.2, usage varies from 22 to 128.3. Subject groups B (social sciences, etc.), D (Mathematics), K (engineering and technology in general), O (electronics), Q (mechanical engineering), U (management) and X (arts, etc.) undergo a greater than average use per linear foot of shelf.

It may be noted here that the number of books per linear foot in the case of social sciences (B), management (U) and arts (X) is naturally greater than that in the case of the science and engineering fields. Thus, the usage per linear foot of shelf space confirms, more or less, the relatively greater use made of some subjects than of others. Least use per linear foot of self occurs in subject groups A (generalities), H (geology, etc.), M (energy) and T (agriculture, etc.) One reason for low use of books in group A is laid to the fact that bibliographies and library science books are kept separately in broken sequence from others in A, and some of them are subjected to restricted access.

Frequency scores have been tabulated individually for each subject group. Considering books loaned 31 or more times as "highly used", and those for which no loan record is available as "never used",

TABLE 7.11: Subject Use of Books

Subject Code	UDC Class Number	Subject	% of User Speciali-sation	Linear measurement in Feet of Shelf Space occupied	% of Stock	% of Sample	Use of Sample Books No.	Use of Sample Books %	% Use – % of Sample	Use per Linear foot of Shelf
(1)	(2)	(3)	(4)	(5)	(6)	(7)	(8)	(9)	(10)	(11)
A	0	Generalities	3.2	24	4.1	3.9	104	0.7	–3.4	21.7
B	1, 2, 3 & 4	Philosophy, Religion, Theology, Social Sciences, Phylology, Linguistics & Languages	NA	21	3.8	3.7	490	3.3	–0.5	116.7
C	5	Natural Sciences (General)	NA	9	0.8	0.9	146	1.0	+0.2	34.8
D	51	Mathematics	5.3	75	8.9	8.6	1,575	10.7	+1.8	105.0
E	52	Astronomy, Astro-physics, etc.	Included in F	78	6.2	6.3	840	5.7	–0.5	53.9
F	53	Physics	8.8	147	12.8	12.6	1,472	10.0	–2.8	50.1
G	54, 56, 57, 58 & 59	Chemistry, Paleontology, Fossils, Anthropological & Biological Sciences	0.6	9	1.5	1.4	90	0.6	–0.9	50.0
H	55	Geology, Meteorology, etc.	NA	24	2.1	2.2	113	0.8	–1.3	23.5
I	6	Applied Science, Technology etc. (General)	NA	2	0.3	0.3	31	0.2	–0.1	77.5
J	61	Medical Sciences, Health & Safety	NA	15	1.2	1.2	68	0.5	–0.7	22.7
K	62	Engineering & Technology (General)	NA	5	0.9	1.0	121	0.8	–0.1	121.0

(Contd.)

TABLE 7.11 (*Contd.*)

(1)	(2)	(3)	(4)	(5)	(6)	(7)	(8)	(9)	(10)	(11)
L	620.1	Material Science	NA	30	2.5	2.5	181	1.2	–0.7	30.2
M	620.8/9	Energy	NA	15	1.2	1.1	66	0.4	–0.8	22.0
N	621.3	Electrical Engineering	2.4	90	7.5	7.6	1,315	9.0	+1.5	73.1
O	621.38	Electronics	46.1	81	8.6	9.0	2,078	14.1	+5.5	128.3
P	621.39	Telecommunication	Covered in O	54	4.5	4.5	823	5.6	+1.1	76.2
Q	621.4/9	Mechanical Engineering	33.2	35	4.1	4.0	852	5.8	+1.7	121.7
R	624	Civil & Structural Engineering	0.4	27	2.4	2.3	206	1.4	–1.0	38.2
S	629.7	Aeronautics, Space Vehicles, etc.	Covered in R	114	6.2	6.4	821	5.6	–0.6	36.2
T	63, 64 & 69	Agriculture, Domestic Science, Building Industry, etc.	NA	11	0.9	0.9	59	0.4	–0.5	26.8
U	65	Management	Covered in A	33	3.8	3.7	678	4.6	+0.8	102.7
V	66	Chemical Technology	Covered in G	21	1.7	1.7	198	1.3	–0.4	47.1
W	67/68	Manufactures	NA	129	12.4	12.1	2,088	14.2	+1.8	80.9
X	7, 8 & 9	Arts, Recreation, Literature, Geography, Biography, etc.	NA	12	1.7	1.8	259	1.8	0.0	107.9
	Total		100.0	1,061	101.1	99.7	14,674	99.7		69.2

Table 7.12 indicates the number of such highly used and never used books in different subject groups. The samples in subject groups D, E, F, N, Q, P, S, V, W and X contain at least one highly used book. Of these groups D, N, O, P, Q, S and W contain greater than average number of highly used books (i.e., 4.5). On the other hand, subject groups A, F, H, I, J, K, L, M, S, T and W have more than average number (i.e., 2.6) of never used books. While the percentage of non-hits (i.e., never used books) is quite high in A, J, K, M and T, while have no highly used books, groups F, S and W have both never used and highly used books.

TABLE 7.12: Least and Highest Used Books by Subject

Subject Code	*Sample Size*	*Books with Zero Use*		*Books with 31 or More Use*	
		No	*%*	*No*	*%*
A	82	56	68.3	0	0.0
B	78	1	1.3	0	0.0
C	19	0	0.0	0	0.0
D	180	28	15.6	13	7.2
E	132	34	25.8	4	3.0
F	264	83	31.4	8	3.0
G	30	7	23.3	0	0.0
H	46	16	34.8	0	0.0
I	7	2	28.6	0	0.0
J	25	10	40.0	0	0.0
K	21	9	42.9	0	0.0
L	52	14	26.9	0	0.0
M	24	8	33.3	0	0.0
N	158	36	22.8	8	5.1
O	189	37	19.6	18	9.5
P	95	25	26.3	11	11.6
Q	84	9	10.7	5	6.0
R	48	10	20.8	0	0.0
S	134	40	29.9	7	5.2
T	19	7	36.8	0	0.0
U	78	10	12.8	0	0.0
V	36	8	22.2	1	2.8
W	252	89	35.3	19	7.5
X	38	7	18.4	1	2.6
Total	2,091	556	26.6	95	4.5

Longitudinal Use of Books

How books are used during the latest ten months as compared to their cumulative use is discussed in this section. Table 7.13 presents a picture of the longitudinal use of books of different subject groups. As can be seen from the table, a positive increase in use of books occurred in the case of medical sciences (J), engineering and technology in general (K), material science (L), electronics (O), aeronautics and space vehicles (S), and manufactures (W). The intensity of increase is high in W (+7.6%), marginal in O (+2.0%) and negligible in case of J (+0.1%), K (+0.3%) and L (+0.1%). In all the remaining subject groups there is a decline in use. In most cases, however, this decline is marginal or negligible.

TABLE 7.13: Longitudinal Use of Books

Subject Code	*% of Sample*	*Use of Sample Books*				*% of Use during Last 10 Months – % of Cumulative Use i.e., (4) – (6)*
		During Last 10 Months		*Cumulative Use so far*		
		No.	*%*	*No.*	*%*	
(1)	(2)	(3)	(4)	(5)	(6)	(7)
A	3.9	15	0.5	104	0.7	–0.2
B	3.7	96	3.0	490	3.3	–0.3
C	0.9	20	0.6	146	1.0	–0.4
D	8.6	286	9.1	1,575	10.7	–1.6
E	6.3	100	3.2	840	5.7	–2.5
F	12.6	278	8.8	1,472	10.0	–1.2
G	1.4	15	0.5	90	0.6	–0.1
H	2.2	11	0.3	113	0.8	–0.5
I	0.3	3	0.1	31	0.2	–0.1
J	1.2	19	0.6	68	0.5	+0.1
K	1.0	36	1.1	121	0.8	+0.3
L	2.5	40	1.3	181	1.2	+0.1
M	1.1	7	0.2	66	0.4	–0.2
N	7.6	269	8.5	1,315	9.0	–0.5
O	9.0	507	16.1	2,078	14.1	+2.0
P	4.5	167	5.3	823	5.6	–0.3
Q	4.0	170	5.4	852	5.8	–0.4
R	2.3	33	0.9	206	1.4	–0.5
S	6.4	207	6.6	821	5.6	+1.0
T	0.9	11	0.3	59	0.4	–0.1
U	3.7	104	3.3	678	4.6	–1.3
V	1.7	39	1.2	198	1.3	–0.1
W	12.1	687	21.8	2,088	14.2	+7.6
X	1.8	38	1.2	259	1.8	–0.6
Total	99.7	3,158	99.9	14,674	99.7	—

Frequency Distribution of Use over Age (Year of Publication) of Book

It is generally believed that use of library documents declines with age in a negative exponential pattern. In other words, frequency of use is a function of the age of the document. Here the actual date (or year) of acquisition of the document plays a significant role, and this matter is treated in the next section. Knowledge of the composition of library stock by age (year of publication) as well as by year of acquisition along with some indication of relative use is important in planning for future library acquisitions.

Table 7.14 illustrates the use recorded books by year of publication. Since the time survey was begun in 1983, many 1982 and 1983 publications were yet to be acquired, processed and released for use, the use of such books is naturally under-represented.

TABLE 7.14: Year of Publication of Books *Vs.* Use

Year of Publication	*Sample Books Covered*		*Loans*		*Average Use/Book*
	No	*%*	*No*	*%*	
83	1	0.0	0	0.0	0.00
82	29	1.4	102	0.7	3.52
81	76	3.6	268	1.8	3.53
80	148	7.1	475	3.2	3.21
79	232	11.1	1,435	10.1	6.19
78	248	11.9	1,621	11.0	6.54
77	232	11.1	1,392	9.2	6.00
76	176	8.4	1,011	6.9	5.74
75	116	5.5	921	6.3	7.94
74	117	5.6	737	5.0	6.30
73	95	4.5	673	4.6	7.00
72	108	5.2	894	6.1	8.28
71	96	4.6	759	5.2	7.91
66—70	258	12.3	1,905	13.0	7.38
61—65	148	7.1	969	6.6	6.55
56—60	67	3.2	502	3.4	7.50
51—55	13	0.6	182	1.2	14.00
Upto 50	22	1.1	68	0.5	3.00
Error	–91	–4.4	+760	+5.2	—
Total	2,091	99.9	14,674	100.3	7.01

The distribution of sample documents over year of publication gives some idea about currency of the collection. It is apparent that books published in 1978 are most heavily represented in the collection (11.9%). Twelve per cent of books in the library were published earlier than 1971. In other words, 88 per cent of the books in the library are published within the last 12 years and 60.1 per cent published since 1975.

On examination of the use of books of different ages indicates that the percentage of total use for each year is more or less the same as the percentage of the sample. The average use per book increases steadily as the years recede. It must be borne in mind of course that books published in earlier years have had the chance to circulate more number of times if acquired immediately after publication and considerable increase in number of users (and hence number of borrower tickets,) There is no clear evidence that use correlates with the age of the books.[7]

Adding another dimension, i.e., the subject of the document, to the use data of books, the frequency distribution of use over age of books in different subject groups was examined. It was observed that the mode year of publication of books changes from one subject to other. Table 7.15 presents the mode year of publication of books in different subject groups. For example the mode year of publication of items in applied science and technology, electronics, mechanical engineering, aeronautics and space vehicles is ahead of the mode year of publication of the entire

TABLE 7.15: Mode Year of Publication of Books in Different Subject Groups

Mode Year of Publication	*Subject Codes*	*Subjects*
72	D	Mathematics
74	H	Geology, Meteorology, etc.
75	R*	Civil and Structural Engineering
76	J, P	Medical Sciences, Health and Safety; Telecommunication
77	A, B*, C, K,	Generalities; Philosophy, Religion, etc.
	L, M, U	Natural sciences; Engineering and Technology; Material Science; Energy; Management
78	E, F, G*, N,	Astronomy, Astrophysics, etc.; Physics;
	T, V, W, X	Chemistry; Paleontology, etc.; Electrical Engineering; Agriculture; Domestic Science, etc., Chemical Technology; Manufactures; Arts, Recreation, etc.
79	B*, I, O, Q, S	Philosophy, Religion, etc.; Applied Science and Technology; Electronics, Mechanical Engineering, Aeronautics, Space vehicles etc.
80	G*, R*	Chemistry, Paleontology, etc.; Civil and Structural Engineering

* Bimodal distributions.

sample (1978). On the other hand, the mode year of publication of books in mathematics, geology, medical science, generalities, social sciences, energy, etc., is behind the mode year of publication of the entire sample. Subjects with bimodal distributions in Table 7.15 are not too reliable as the absolute size of samples in these groups is quite small. Though no decisive inference can be drawn from this it may be noted that in certain disciplines such as electronics only the latest books are sought by users.

Since the library has existed for only about 10 years and no weeding has yet been done, every subject has the same chance of having 1978 as the mode year of publication. It was found, for example, that 37 books out of 252 sample books in manufactures (W) were published in 1978. And that in the case of physics (F), books published during the 1950s, 1960s, 1970s are recorded relatively more use than similar books in other groups and even the latest books in physics itself. Finally, none of the sample books in applied science and technology in general (I) was published before 1975.

Frequency Distribution of Use over Year of Acquisition of Book

It appears that how soon after publication a document is acquired has a stronger effect on total use of the document than does the year of publication of the document. As Line and Sanderson indicate, "the pattern of usage over time appears quite different if the standing point is taken as the publication date or three or four years after" (Line and Sanderson, 1974, p. 51).

Table 7.16 presents data concerning distribution of use over year of acquisition of books. Also presented for comparative purposes is the total number of items acquired during the year. As in the previous section, data about documents acquired during 1982 and 1983 should be viewed with caution.

The percentage of sample items and the percentage of items acquired in a particular year are more or less the same. The representativeness of the sample is thus confirmed. Moreover, the average use per book increases more uniformly, steadily and steeply in the case of use over year of acquisition than in the case of use over age (of Table 7.14). Except for 1974 and 1978 in which a marginal fall in average use per book takes place, all other years have a uniformly increasing average use per book.

The number of books acquired per year is not uniform, although the number acquired during 1978 and later (except for 1981) is more or less constant. The largest number of books was acquired in 1978, and the second largest in 1979.

TABLE 7.16: Year of Acquisition of Books *Vs.* Use

Year of Acquisition	*Total Acquired*		*Sample Books*		*Lent-out Use*		*Average Use Per Book*
	No	*%*	*No*	*%*	*No*	*%*	
83	1,286	10.1	26	1.2	57	0.4	2.19
82	1,477	11.6	231	11.0	900	6.1	3.90
81	944	7.4	188	9.0	892	6.1	4.96
80	1,401	11.0	290	13.9	1,762	12.0	6.26
79	1,898	14.9	378	18.1	2,718	18.5	7.61
78	1,980	15.5	397	19.0	2,210	15.1	6.38
77	1,032	8.1	180	8.6	1,509	10.3	8.54
76	509	4.0	68	3.3	685	4.7	11.96
75	413	3.2	82	3.9	737	5.0	10.18
74	578	4.5	90	4.3	889	6.1	9.93
73	1,230	9.6	267	12.8	2,879	19.6	10.75
Error	0	0.0	–106	–5.1	–564	–3.8	—
Total	12,748	99.9	2,091	100.0	14,674	100.1	7.01

Frequency distributions of use over year of acquisition of book in different subject groups are also tabulated and examined. Some observations on these distributions follow. The mode year of acquisition of all the subject groups except social sciences (1982), natural sciences in general (1980), mathematics (1973), astronomy and astrophysics (1980), electrical engineering (1973), chemical technology (1980) and manufactures (1982) is close to 1978. In mathematics and electrical engineering the largest number of books was acquired during 1973. This might explain why the mode year of publication in mathematics appears in Table 7.15 as 1972. In the other subject groups mentioned above the mode year of acquisition is 1980 or later, and hence naturally their mode year of publication is 1977 or later (see Table 7.15).

Although the sample books have been found to be representative, relatively more use (or more accurately average use per year) is made of books procured during 1978-1980. One of the obvious reasons for this as mentioned earlier, is an increase in user strength and a general predilection for novelty of stock.[8]

Results and Observations

To recapitulate, books in the subjects of specialisation are given relatively greater use than others. The average use per linear foot of shelf space is 69.2, and this varied from 22 to 128.3, depending upon subject. In an analysis of data on longitudinal use, it is found that books in certain subject such as electronics and manufactures have shown an increase in percentage of use in recent months.

Nearly 27 per cent of books are never borrowed and about 21 per cent account for 83 per cent of total use. In some subjects like generalities, geology, and medical sciences, the percentage of never used books is higher than the overall percentage of such books in the sample. Subjects such as physics, aeronautics, space vehicles and manufactures have both never used and highly used books.

Nearly 88 per cent of books in the library were published in the last 12 years, and 60 per cent were published since 1975. Use did not clearly correlate with age of books. The mode year of publication of books in subject groups such as electronics, mechanical engineering, aeronautics and space vehicles is later than the mode year of publication of the entire collection. Books published between 1950 and 1970 are recorded relatively more use in case of physics than in other groups.

The average use per book increases more uniformly, steadily and steeply in the case of use over year of acquisition than it does in the case of use distribution over age of book. The sample has been found to be adequate in terms of year of acquisition. The mode year of acquisition of all subjects except mathematics and electrical engineering coincides more or less with the mode year of acquisition of the entire sample.

A further study of correlating use of books with various user characteristics and a rigorous statistical test of the data are being done separately. By and large, books have been fairly well used in the ISAC library. The study assisted the library in determining how use of books is distributed among different subject groups and in pinpointing which books in the collection are highly used and which receive little or no use. It is expected that this information will prove useful in future collection development activities.

CASE STUDY 10

USE AND COST BENEFIT ANALYSIS OF CURRENT JOURNALS

Introduction

More bibliometric, cost-benefit, cost-effectiveness, citation, use, and other studies have been done on journals than on other types of documents in libraries. It is frequently heard that journal librarians faced severe stresses from many directions. The soaring cost of journals, the need to subscribe to important core journals by airmail (or speed mail), the increasing importance of interdisciplinary studies and rapid growth in number of journals in some fields are some of the factors that have prompted librarians to seek more funds and foreign exchange. On the other hand, the librarians feathers are clipped by inelastic buying power or even reduction in buying power as a result of inadequate budgets and inflation. This has led journal librarians to scrutinise existing subscriptions to find out whether any unused or little used titles are being subscribed to. Methods of ranking journals by decreasing order of utility (or, more accurately, use) are devised to eliminate lesser used titles whenever a reduction in buying power occurs, as it is deemed preferable to borrow such journals from other libraries or procure reprints or copies of selected articles than to subscribe. Though most of the methods have their own limitations, use study is generally simple and straight forward.

Actual usage, of course, describes the present demand pattern. Further, usage patterns help in determining optimum binding arrangements, subscription priorities and the finding of substitutes when a journal is cancelled. A simple limited synchronous use study of current journals of the ISAC library is described, and the results presented in this chapter.

Methodology, Sample and Limitations

The two latest issues of almost all current journals subscribed to by the library were selected as samples as and when received during September 1983 and December 1983. Pre-planned data noting sheets were stuck to them to monitor and record in-house use and circulation/lent-out use of three months from the data of first display in the library (latest issues are not allowed to circulate outside in the first week). Journals are loaned for three days with no renewal privileges. Secondary journals, loose leaf journals and some journals are not allowed to leave the library. While recording lent-out use, information about users is noted for comparison of use of the journals against user characteristics. A journal issue left on a reading table is treated as one in-house use in this study. In-house use of journals is recorded while replacing them on the shelves. As many as four uses a day have been recorded for a single issue of a journal. Kent's definition of use as physical selection and the act of leafing through pages is adhered to (Kent, 1979, p. 61). Thus, if a journal was picked up, a use is recorded. The present study, then, is biased in favour of less than actual usage as far as in-house activity is concerned, since practical considerations stood in the way of recording every usage.

Out of 630 current journals in the library, data for 485 titles were collected by the end March of 1984. The remaining journals were made up largely of gratis newsletters, popular and semi-popular journals, news journals, loose leaf journals, and items that had just been cancelled or were newly subscribed to. A few were secondary journals, journals from the areas of medicine and library science, those kept in closed access and titles for which no issues were received during the survey period. All of these have been deleted from consideration. Some titles with partial data were also excluded. However, some important titles in the above categories for which either in-house use or lent-out use alone was known were included with an appropriate note.

The present study of journals suffers from all the limitations of any typical use study. Since only two issues of a title are selected as a sample, use of the titles in general and in-house use in particular is under-represented. However, the data of lent-out use is reasonably accurate and unambiguous. It should be added that in-house use is very much affected by inadequate display space and congestion in the library. More than one title was held in a single compartment because of shortage of display space. Further, in-house use and lent-out use are very much interdependent as only two issues of a title were monitored for three months in this study. For example, an issue of a journal which is in continuous circulation necessarily suffers decreased in-house use, and *vice versa*.

For clarity's sake, it may be noted here that back volumes of journals were not included in the study. Hence, analysis by age is omitted.

The study also faces other limitations. These have to do with: difficulties in measuring use, equating use with usefulness and excluding the use of journals obtained/sent through inter-library loan; the availability of current awareness and reprographic services; age dependent factors; internal biases such as size of actual stock and external biases such as users knowledge of the stock; ratio of collection to users; changes in user population structure, the scope of journals and areas of interest of users, and lending regulations. During survey library had about 1,100 members and about 4,800 borrower tickets were in vogue and all lent-out use of journals is accounted by these tickets. (The same tickets were also meant for borrowing other types of documents.)

Lastly, some of the limitations of use studies pointed out by the University of Pittsburgh's Senate Library Committee in its criticism of Kent's study are worth noting. The Committee quotes a physics faculty member about fluctuation in use as "... when writing a research proposal or paper the use of journals may be extraordinarily heavy for a few days. Thus, it would not surprise me to find that 90 per cent of an individual's annual journal use occurs during a ten-day period, with only 10 per cent occurring during the remaining 350 days" (University of Pittsburgh, 1979, p. 30).

Further, the Committee emphasises that biases are inherent in the use of bound journals during a library's peak attendance hours. The Committee says "... some types of journal users will shun the hours of heavier attendance and come to the library when it is poorly attended so that they can spread out the bound journals with which they are working" (*ibid.*, p. 30). The Committee makes clear also that methods of assessing cost and benefits differ according to type of material. It indicates that support cannot be given to the claim that "... the relatively infrequent use of journals such as Nuclear Physics makes it less beneficial to the user community than very frequently used journals such as Nature and Science ... it is not a fact that all journal uses are commensurable. There are many significantly different types of journal uses and each type should have been investigated by appropriate, possibly separate methods, and counted separately" (*ibid.*, p. 38).

Use of Journals

At the broad level, the use of current journals at ISAC library is found to be moderate. Nine hundred and fifty issues (i.e., two issues each of 475 journals) were used 4,475 times within the library during the quarter immediately after their arrival. Similarly, 918 issues (i.e., two issues each of 459 journals) were borrowed 1,120 times by 351 users in the first quarter. The average in-house use per issue per quarter is 4.71, and the average lentout use per issue per quarter is 1.22. This amounts to a total average use of 5.93 per issue per quarter. Lentout use per person per quarter per single issue of all journals studied is 1.6.[9]

Frequency Distribution of Total Use over Number of Journals

It is stated in Kent's study that "... in order to make use of a cut-off threshold, we must be able to identify which journals fall above that point, and which fall below. This requires knowing the number of times a title was consulted, not just whether or not a particular title was or was not consulted at least once. In view of this, it would seem that a more labour-intensive, but also more fruitful method of tracking usage must be found" (*ibid.*, p. 74).

Table 7.17 presents a frequency distribution of use over number of journals and a ranking of all journals based on use. This table helps identifying unused, least used and most used journals. It may be seen from the table that less than 10 per cent of journals were made use of and that these account for nearly 30 per cent of total use. It is seen also that little more than 20 per cent of journals contributed nearly 52 per cent of total use.

TABLE 7.17: Frequency Distribution of Use over Number of Journals

No. of Times Used	*No. of Jls*	*% of Jls*	*Cumulative % of Jls*	*Total Use*	*% of Use*	*Cumulative % of Use*
(1)	(2)	(3)	(4)	(5)	(6)	(7)
00	60	12.4	12.4	00	0.0	0.0
01	15	3.1	15.5	15	0.3	0.3
02	19	3.9	19.4	38	0.7	1.0
03	23	4.7	24.1	69	1.2	2.2
04	21	4.3	28.4	84	1.5	3.7
05	25	5.1	33.5	125	2.3	6.0
06	25	5.1	38.6	150	2.7	8.7
07	23	4.7	43.3	161	2.9	11.6
08	26	5.4	48.7	208	3.7	15.3
09	21	4.3	53.0	189	3.4	18.7
10	19	3.9	56.9	190	3.4	22.1
11	19	3.9	60.8	209	3.7	25.8
12	24	4.9	65.7	288	5.1	30.9
13	21	4.3	70.0	273	4.9	35.8
14	20	4.1	74.1	280	5.0	40.8
15	10	2.1	76.2	150	2.7	43.5
16	5	1.0	77.2	80	1.4	44.9
17	10	2.1	79.3	170	3.0	47.9
18	7	1.4	80.7	126	2.3	50.2
19	11	2.3	83.0	209	3.7	53.9
20	4	0.8	83.8	80	1.4	55.3
21	6	1.2	85.0	126	2.3	57.6
22	4	0.8	85.8	88	1.6	59.2
25	1	0.2	89.7	25	0.4	67.1
26	5	1.0	90.7	150	2.7	69.8
27	5	1.0	91.7	135	2.4	72.2
28	6	1.2	92.9	168	3.0	75.2
29	9	1.9	94.8	261	4.7	79.9
30	5	1.0	95.8	150	2.7	82.6

(Contd.)

TABLE 7.17 (*Contd.*)

(1)	(2)	(3)	(4)	(5)	(6)	(7)
31	2	0.4	96.2	62	1.1	83.7
32	1	0.2	96.4	32	0.6	84.3
33	4	0.8	97.2	132	2.4	86.7
34	5	1.0	98.2	170	3.0	89.7
35	0	0.0	98.2	0	0.0	89.7
36	2	0.4	98.6	72	1.3	91.0
37	4	0.8	99.4	148	2.6	93.6
38	1	0.2	99.6	38	0.7	94.3
39	0	0.0	99.6	0	0.0	94.3
40	2	0.4	100.0	80	1.4	95.7
41	0	0.0	100.0	0	0.0	95.7
42	1	0.2	100.2	42	0.8	96.5
43	1	0.2	100.4	43	0.8	97.3
44	1	0.2	100.6	44	0.8	98.1
46	1	0.2	100.8	46	0.8	98.8
52	1	0.2	101.0	52	1.0	100.8
58	1	0.2	101.2	58	1.0	100.8
63	1	0.2	101.4	63	1.1	101.9
Error	—	—	—	–104	–1.9	100.0
Total	485	101.4	101.4	5,595	100.0	100.0

Sixty journals or 12.4 per cent of journals at ISAC library are neither consulted within the library nor borrowed from the library in the first quarter. Naturally, the chance that these journals will be used later is very bleak. All these titles including marginally used journals (i.e., those used once or twice) whether subscribed to or obtained free of charge are strongly recommended for cancellation. However, for obvious reasons, news magazines, highly specialised journals with limited specialist users and a few secondary journals may have to be exempted from such action.

Nearly 28 journals were used more than 30 times in a three-month period. In these cases it may be worthwhile subscribing by airmail, subscribing to second copies and using strong bindings to withstand the wear and tear of constant use.

In-house Use

In-house use and lentout use of ISAC library journals are considered separately in this section and the next. A frequency table of in-house use is presented in Table 7.18. It is seen from this table that 20 per cent of journals accounted for more than 47 per cent of total use and less than

48 per cent of journals contributed to more than 82 per cent of use. Eighty-three journals or slightly more than 17 per cent were not used at all. By including journals used once or twice during the sampling period, 106 journals or nearly 22 per cent of journals can be considered least used journals. Fourteen journals were used more than 30 times within the library in the period studied.

TABLE 7.18: Frequency Distribution of In-house Use over Number of Journals

No. of In-house Uses	*No. of Jls*	*% of Jls*	*Cumulative % of Jls*	*Total In-house Use*	*% of In-house Use*	*Cumulative % of In-house Use*
(1)	(2)	(3)	(4)	(5)	(6)	(7)
00	83	17.1	17.1	00	0.0	0.0
01	6	1.2	18.3	6	0.1	0.1
02	17	3.5	21.8	34	0.8	0.9
03	27	5.6	27.4	81	1.8	2.7
04	28	5.8	33.2	112	2.5	5.2
05	27	5.6	38.8	135	3.0	8.2
06	21	4.3	43.1	126	2.8	11.0
07	21	4.3	47.4	147	3.3	14.3
08	25	5.2	52.6	200	4.5	18.8
09	21	4.3	56.9	189	4.2	23.0
10	23	4.7	61.6	230	5.1	28.1
11	20	4.1	65.7	220	4.9	33.0
12	15	3.1	68.8	180	4.0	37.0
13	16	3.3	72.1	208	4.6	41.6
14	18	3.7	75.8	252	5.6	47.2
15	11	2.3	78.1	165	3.7	50.9
16	9	1.9	80.0	144	3.2	54.1
17	8	1.6	81.6	136	3.0	57.1
18	10	2.1	83.7	180	4.0	61.1
19	6	1.2	84.9	114	2.5	63.6
20	4	0.8	85.7	80	1.8	65.4
21	6	1.2	86.9	126	2.8	68.2
22	7	1.4	88.3	154	3.4	71.6
23	11	2.3	90.6	253	5.7	77.3
24	4	0.8	91.4	96	2.1	79.4
25	5	1.0	92.4	125	2.8	82.2
26	5	1.0	93.4	130	2.9	85.1
27	5	1.0	94.4	135	3.0	88.1
28	2	0.4	94.8	56	1.3	89.4
29	1	0.2	95.0	29	0.6	90.0
30	1	0.2	95.2	30	0.7	90.7
31	3	0.6	95.8	93	2.1	92.8
32	4	0.8	96.6	128	2.9	95.7
33	1	0.2	96.8	33	0.7	96.4

(Contd.)

TABLE 7.18 *(Contd.)*

(1)	(2)	(3)	(4)	(5)	(6)	(7)
34	2	0.4	97.2	68	1.5	97.9
39	2	0.4	97.6	78	1.7	99.6
40	1	0.2	97.8	40	0.9	100.5
44	1	0.2	98.0	44	1.0	101.5
NA	10	2.1	100.1	—	—	—
Error	—	—	—	-82	-1.8	99.7
Total	485	100.1	100.1	4,475	99.7	99.7

Lentout Use

Table 7.19 illustrates lentout use. Two hundred and eleven journals or 43.5 per cent of journals were never borrowed in their first three months. It is not possible to use the number of lentout use alone as a criterion for subscription or cancellation of journals since many journals are used for current awareness purposes within the library and quite a few journals carrying current news and brief communications may not be worth taking out of the library. Further, borrowing of journals is very much affected by free and adequate reprographic services in the library. Interestingly, out of these 211 journals, about 128 journals are used within the library and not literally borrowed at all (compare Tables 7.18 and 7.19). Table 7.19 reveals that 10 per cent of journals represent 20 per cent of total borrowings and 19.5 per cent of journals account for nearly 60 per cent of lentout use.

TABLE 7.19: Frequency Distribution of Lentout Use over Number of Journals

No. of Lentout Uses	*No. of Jls*	*% of Jls*	*Cumulative % of Jls*	*Total Lentout Use*	*% of Lentout Use*	*Cumulative % of Lent-out Use*
(1)	(2)	(3)	(4)	(5)	(6)	(7)
00	211	43.5	43.5	0	0.0	0.0
01	48	10.0	53.5	48	4.3	4.3
02	51	10.5	64.0	102	9.1	13.4
03	38	7.8	71.8	114	10.2	23.6
04	28	5.8	77.6	112	10.2	33.6
05	14	2.9	80.5	70	6.3	39.9
06	11	2.3	82.8	66	5.9	45.8
07	9	1.9	84.7	63	5.6	51.4
08	12	2.5	87.2	96	8.6	60.0
09	8	1.6	88.8	72	6.4	66.4
10	6	1.2	90.0	60	5.4	71.8
11	6	1.2	91.2	60	5.4	77.2

(Contd.)

TABLE 7.19 (*Contd.*)

(1)	(2)	(3)	(4)	(5)	(6)	(7)
12	6	1.2	92.4	72	6.4	83.6
13	3	0.6	93.0	39	3.5	87.1
14	2	0.4	93.4	28	2.5	89.6
15	3	0.6	94.0	45	4.0	93.6
21	1	0.2	94.2	21	1.9	95.5
22	1	0.2	94.4	22	2.0	97.5
24	1	0.2	94.6	24	2.1	99.6
NA	26	5.4	100.0	00	0.0	99.6
Error	—	—	—	+06	+0.5	100.1
Total	485	100.0	100.0	1,120	100.1	100.1

Fig. 7.6 shows the curves of in-house use, lentout use and total use compared with the number of journals. Here the cumulative percentage of journals is plotted against the cumulative percentage of use. As the lentout use curve is much flatter than the other two it is clear that a much smaller percentage of journals are borrowed than the percentage consulted within the library. In other words, in-house use of current journals is much higher than lentout use.

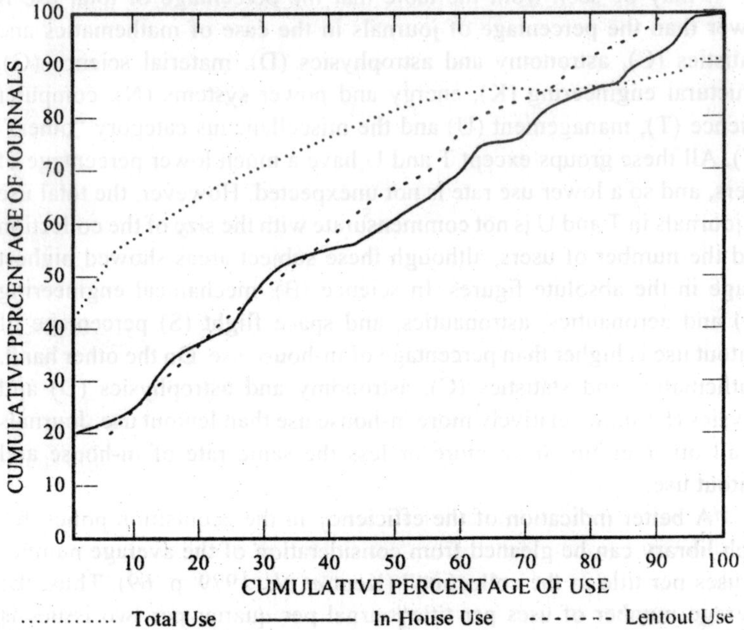

FIG. 7.6: Cumulative Percentage of Journals *Vs.* Cumulative Percentage of Use.

Use of Journals in Different Subject Groups

The subject use of journals is depicted in Table 7.20. In this table, percentage of use is presented against percentages of journals and users. Abstracting and indexing journals are not normally allowed out of the library. Total use and average use per title in this group should be viewed with this limitation in mind. Even so, it is apparent that abstracting and indexing journals are less used than might have been expected.

Areas such as computer science (Q), electronics (T) and aeronautics, astronautics and space flight (S) are better represented in the collection than are other subjects. It is in these subject groups that use is at its maximum point.

Other factors aside, usage depends on size of the collection and number of users interested in a particular subject. It may be noted in this connection that a high majority of users have physics (9%) or electronics (46%) or mechanical engineering (33%) as their broad specialisation. The number of users of each subject groups of journals shown in the table is based on actual usage and roughly indicates the area of interest/ work of these users and not the specialisation.

It may be seen from the table that the percentage of total use is lower than the percentage of journals in the case of mathematics and statistics (C), astronomy and astrophysics (D), material science (G), structural engineering (K), energy and power systems (N), computer science (T), management (U) and the miscellaneous category "others" (V). All these groups except T and U have a much lower percentage of users, and so a lower use rate is not unexpected. However, the total use of journals in T and U is not commensurate with the size of the collection and the number of users, although these subject areas showed highest usage in the absolute figures. In science (B), mechanical engineering (O) and aeronautics, astronautics, and space flight (S) percentage of lentout use is higher than percentage of in-house use. On the other hand, mathematics and statistics (C), astronomy and astrophysics (D) and Physics (E) show relatively more in-house use than lentout use. Journals in all other groups have more or less the same rate of in-house and lentout use.

"A better indication of the efficiency in the acquisition policy for each library can be gleaned from consideration of the average number of uses per title in the collection" (Kent *et al.*, 1979, p. 69). Thus, the average number of uses per title/journal per quarter per two issues is also shown in Table 7.20.[10] The average number of uses per journal is

TABLE 7.20: Subject Use of Journals

Subject Code	*Subject*	*No. of Journals*	*% of Journals*	*No. of Users*	*% of Users*	*No. of In-house Uses*	*% of In-house Uses*	*No. of Lentout Uses*	*% of Lentout Uses*	*Total No. of Uses*	*% of Total Uses*	*Av. Quarterly Use for Two Issues*
(1)	(2)	(3)	(4)	(5)	(6)	(7)	(8)	(9)	(10)	(11)	(12)	(13)
A	Abstract and index journals	26	5.4	*	*	142	3.2	1	0.1	143	2.6	5.5
B	Science (includes biological sciences, chemistry, etc.)	36	7.4	98	27.9	131@	8.3	138	12.3	509	9.1	14.1
C	Mathematics and statistics	18	3.7	7	2.0	126	2.8	8	0.7	134	2.4	7.4
D	Astronomy and astrophysics	20	4.1	12	3.4	184	4.1	33	2.9	217	3.9	10.9
E	Physics (includes acoustics, optics, cryogenics, vacuum science and nuclear science)	21	4.3	13	3.7	267	6.0	23	2.1	290	5.2	13.8
F	Environment, earth science and remote sensing	28	5.8	25	7.1	276@	6.2	39	3.5	315	5.6	11.3
G	Material science	11	2.3	6	1.7	85	1.9	10	0.9	95	1.7	8.6
H	Engineering and technology	18	3.7	34	9.7	143	3.2	41	3.7	184	3.3	10.2
I	Instrumentation	6	1.2	7	2.0	57	1.3	10	0.9	67	1.2	11.2
J	Control engineering	9	1.9	5	1.4	80	1.8	10	0.9	90	1.6	10.0
K	Structural engineering	12	2.5	5	1.4	83	1.9	5	0.4	88	1.6	7.3
L	Thermal engineering	9	1.9	3	0.9	72	1.6	4	0.4	76	1.4	8.4
M	Quality and reliability engineering	5	1.0	3	0.9	27	0.6	10	0.9	37	0.7	7.4
N	Energy and power systems	17	3.5	9	2.6	95	2.1	25	2.2	120	2.1	7.1
O	Mechanical engineering	19	3.9	37	10.5	133	3.0	51	4.6	184	3.3	9.7
P	Electrical engineering and electromagnetism	7	1.4	4	1.1	73@	1.6	9	0.8	82	1.5	11.7

(Contd.)

TABLE 7.20 (*Contd.*)

(1)	(2)	(3)	(4)	(5)	(6)	(7)	(8)	(9)	(10)	(11)	(12)	(13)
Q	Electronics	51	10.5	111	31.6	681	15.2	177	15.8	858	15.3	16.8
R	Communication engineering	26	5.4	34	9.7	228	5.1	54	4.8	282	5.0	10.8
S	Aeronautics, astronautics and spaceflight	43	8.9	69	19.7	482	10.8	171	16.3	653	11.7	15.2
T	Computer science and information theory	65	13.4	76	21.7	504	11.3	173	16.4	677	12.1	10.4
U	Management, behavioural science, industry and economics	22	4.5	35	10.0	154@	3.4	52	4.6	206	3.7	9.4
V	Others (includes photography standardisation, safety engineering etc.)	16	3.3	11	3.1	126	2.8	13	1.2	139	2.5	8.7
	Error	0	0.0	0	0.0	+86	+1.9	+63	+5.6	+149	+2.7	—
	Total	485	100.0	(351)#	—	4,475	100.1	1,120	100.0	5,595	100.2	12.0

Notes: * Normally not allowed for borrowing.

@ In-house use of 4 titles in B, 1 in F, 2 in Q and 3 in U are not available.

\# As a single user can use journals in more than one group, the total does not tally.

very high in the case of science (B), physics (E), electronics (Q) and aeronautics, astronautics and space flight (S). As mentioned earlier, the lowest average use is recorded by abstract and index journals (5.5), followed by energy and power systems (7.1), mathematics and statistics (7.4) and quality and reliability engineering (7.4). All other groups have moderate and high average use per title.

Frequency Distribution of Lentout Use over Number of Users

Lentout use alone is analysed in this section with respect to users. The ISAC library was serving about 1,100 members at the time of conducting the use study. Of these about 800 were technical staff of the centre, including scientists and engineers. As mentioned earlier, only 351 users borrowed journals during the same study period. In other words, more than half of ISAC library members did not borrow sample journals during the quarter.[11] Table 7.21 presents a frequency distribution of lentout use over number of users. Nearly 44 per cent of these users

TABLE 7.21: Frequency Distribution of Lentout Use over Number of Users

No. of Lentout Uses	*No. of Users*	*% of Users*	*Cumulative % of Users*	*Total Use*	*% of Use*	*Cumulative % of Use*
01	155	43.9	43.9	155	13.8	13.8
02	67	19.1	63.0	134	12.0	25.8
03	48	13.7	76.7	144	12.9	38.7
04	15	4.3	81.0	60	5.4	44.1
05	17	4.8	85.8	85	7.6	51.7
06	7	2.0	87.8	42	3.8	55.5
07	10	2.8	90.6	70	6.3	61.8
08	10	2.8	93.4	80	7.1	68.9
09	2	0.6	94.0	18	1.6	70.5
10	7	2.0	96.0	70	6.3	76.8
11	6	1.7	97.7	66	5.9	82.7
12	1	0.3	98.0	12	1.1	83.8
13	2	0.6	98.6	26	2.3	86.1
14	0	0.0	98.6	0	0.0	86.1
15	2	0.6	99.2	30	2.7	88.8
16	0	0.0	99.2	0	0.0	88.8
17	1	0.3	99.5	17	1.5	90.3
25	1	0.3	99.8	25	2.2	92.5
86	1*	0.3	100.1	86	7.7	100.2
Total	351	100.1	100.1	1,120	100.2	100.2

Note: * A high level executive to whom 43 journals are regularly issued on standing instructions.

borrowed only once. About 10 per cent were responsible for 38 per cent of total lentout use, and 38 per cent have made 74 per cent of total borrowings of journals. The frequency distribution data in Table 7.21 together with frequency distribution of lentout use of all issues and volumes of journals during a quarter are plotted against number of users in Fig. 7.7. The lentout use of sample issues. By and large, the distribution appears to be parabolic or asymptotic or Zipfian type.

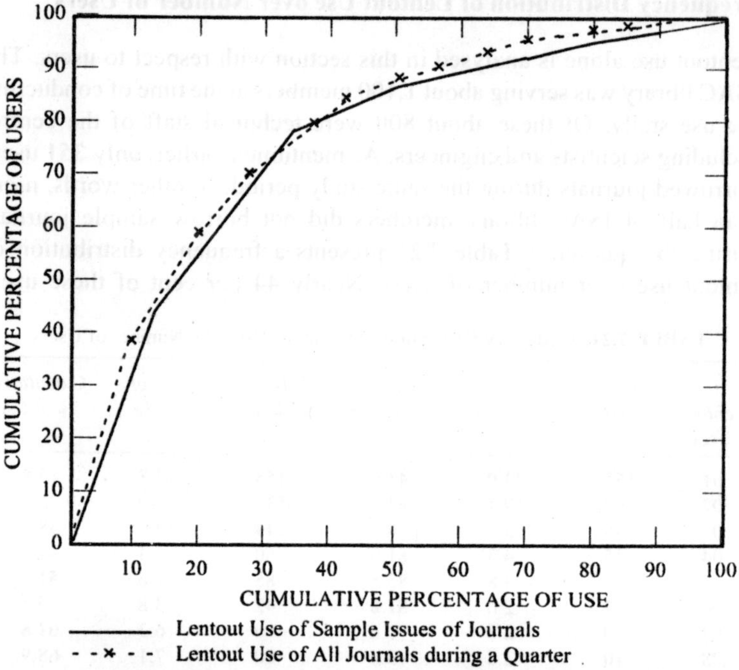

FIG. 7.7: Cumulative Percentage of Lentout Use *Vs.* Cumulative Percentage of Users of Current Journals.

Table 7.22 shows how many different journals/titles are regularly borrowed (i.e., used) by ISAC library users. This frequency distribution indicates the range of titles on which users depend. It is obvious from the table that more than half of the users borrow issues of a single journal/title in the area of their interest. Nearly 22 per cent of users borrow issues of two journals/titles, and 10 per cent borrow issues of three journals/titles. Quite a few users (i.e., 15.5%) borrow issues of 4 to 10 journals/titles regularly. Issues of 11 or more journals/titles are borrowed by 6 users.

TABLE 7.22: Frequency Distribution of Number of Journals over Number of Users

No. of Journals Used	*No. of Users*	*% of Users*	*Cumulative % of Users*
01	178	50.7	50.7
02	77	21.9	72.6
03	35	10.0	82.6
04	21	6.0	88.6
05	9	2.6	91.2
06	6	1.7	92.9
07	7	2.0	94.9
08	4	1.1	96.0
09	4	1.1	97.1
10	4	1.1	98.2
11	1	0.3	98.5
12	0	0.0	98.5
13	2	0.6	99.1
14	1	0.3	99.4
21	1	0.3	99.7
43	1*	0.3	100.0
Total	351	100.0	100.0

Note: * A high level executive to whom 43 journals are regularly issued on standing instructions.

Considering the use of current journals from the angle of users, one might be curious to know the number of different subject groups in which users borrow journals. It may be noted here that space science and satellite technology are heterogeneous, multidisciplinary areas. The frequency Table 7.23 gives the number of subject groups in which ISAC library users are interested. More than 60 per cent of users use journals from a single subject group. Nearly 24 per cent use journals from two subject groups. Seven and 6 per cent of users respectively depend on journals from 3 and 4 subject groups. The remaining 12 (3%) users depend on 4 to 10 different subject groups, as shown in Table 7.23 for their journal literature.

Three other informal observations may be made. By and large, journals of a highly theoretical nature and those in highly specialised subjects are less used. Among journals of the same subject group, American journals are more used than journals from Great Britain and other countries. Thirdly, users who make more intensive/frequent use of journals by and large make use of more journals from more subject groups than other users.

TABLE 7.23: Frequency Distribution of Number of Subject Groups in which Journals are Used over Number of Users

No. of Subject Groups in which Journals are Used	*No. of Users*	*% of Users*	*Cumulative % of Users*
01	211	60.1	60.1
02	84	23.9	84.0
03	24	6.8	90.8
04	20	5.7	96.5
05	7	2.0	98.5
06	2	0.6	99.1
07	1	0.3	99.4
08	1	0.3	99.7
09	0	0.0	99.7
10	1*	0.3	100.0
Total	351	100.0	100.0

Note: * A high level executive to whom 43 journals are regularly issued on standing instructions.

Cost Benefit Analysis of Journals

The McGraw Hill encyclopaedia of professional management defines cost-benefit analysis (CBA) as determining "... the ratio of the benefits of a given project to its cost, taking into account the benefits and costs that cannot be directly measured in dollars" (Bittel ed., 1978, p. 242). A closely related concept of Cost-Effectiveness Analysis (CEA) "... is defined as a way of finding the least expensive means of reaching an objective or a way of obtaining the greatest possible value from a given expenditure" (Bittel ed., 1978, p. 242). Either to arrive at a benefit to cost ratio of a single project or to assess relatively the effectiveness of different projects, the identification and pertinent measure of all the costs and benefits of projects on identical scale of measure (e.g., dollars or Rupees) is necessary. While CBA seeks to develop standards and criteria for determining how well the existing services of a library meet the requirements of its users, CEA aims at discovering new, improved procedures and devices for providing better services to the users (Leimicuhler, 1978). CBA has been considered as a valuable tool for increasing people's awareness of the costs and benefits of information and documentation as a production factor and to provide better basis for budgeting and strategic planning (Lungberg *et al.*, 1976).

Libraries are largely service-oriented paternalistic systems and are not susceptible to precise quantitative assessment. The cost of establishing and running a library can be estimated, but how does one measure its intangible benefits? In the past, mixed reactions have greeted the use of CBA in Librarianship in general and in dealing with journals in particular. Yet, the need for CBA in libraries has been stressed by many (White, 1979; Leimicuhler, 1978). Though a substantial amount of literature has been brought out on CBA, very little has been done to demonstrate the use of CBA in libraries.[12]

Wills and Oldman (1977) reviewing some cost-benefit studies of libraries, question the assumption that "use" equals "value", and criticise the use of CBA for two reasons: (1) economic analysis is inappropriate where decisions have to be based on political factors, (2) it is essential to explore how information supplied by libraries is used. Jenson (1978) also concludes that the CBA is not applicable in assessing library service. The upper hand of non-economic considerations (Sridhar, 1985) in decision-making in libraries has been stressed by Rafeel (1974), who says that the more critical the decision, the less useful a CBA to library decision-makers.

The numerous use studies of libraries have never attempted to measure "utility" or "value" (it is almost impossible to measure precisely the utility of a document or a library) but have made certain assumptions about the operational definition of "use" of a document. Francis (1976), for example, finds an absence of costing standards and suggests that many problems exist in translating the statistics of book circulation into equivalent social benefits.

Apart from exploring the difficulties of applying CBA to journals, it is attempted here to relate the subscription cost of a journal issue to its "use" during the first-three months after its arrival. Kent's definition of "use" as physical selection and the act of leafing through pages of journal was adopted for the purpose (Kent *et al.*, 1979, p. 61). Incidentally, the "cost per use" of a journal appears to be a useful figure both in ratio analysis (Sridhar, 1986) in libraries and in ranking journals in decreasing order of cost per use.

Given a fixed budget, a library has to allocate its funds judiciously to various activities and services, while at the same time ensuring that it maximises benefit to cost ratio. In other words, libraries do carry out benefit-maximising and cost-minimising programmes. For example, if the cost of maintaining an old bound journal is much higher than borrowing it from other libraries, the library may opt to weed it out. Similarly, if in-house reprographic or micrographic work is costlier than having this work done outside, the library may decide to go outside for it. These are traditional make or buy decisions, and they are often, influenced by non-economic considerations.

Much has been written about cost minimising efforts in dealing with journals. Use studies, bibliometric studies, cost-benefit studies, cost-effectiveness studies, citation studies, etc., are common. All such studies have directly or indirectly attempted to rank journals subscribed to by a library (or published in a particular field) in decreasing order of productivity, "utility" or "use". In the process, assumptions are sometimes made with little attempt to isolate factors/variables that affect both the cost of the journals and the benefit they provide. A sort of straight relation between cost and benefit may be brought forth on the assumption that other factors remain constant. Such a ranked list of journals is supposed to be used, depending upon availability of funds, in making borrow or buy decisions.

Robertson and Hansman (1979) felt that the traditional Bradford approach to bibliographic scatter involving ranking of journals according to productivity must be modified in order to answer more directly questions concerning the cost-effectiveness or cost-benefit of journal acquisition. The results obtained in using the Bradford analysis alone appeared to them to depend upon the particular journals that contribute to a field.

As far as cost-benefit analysis of journals is considered, Byrd and Koenig (1978) have pleaded for an objective cost-benefit ratio for each serial title. They point to an unfortunate situation in which selection is often based on user opinion. In addition to subscription cost, they considered many other factors in assessing values. These included coverage, impact factor, use, location, inter-library loan requests, etc. Similarly, a model for selection of journals' titles based on cost-benefit ratios was developed by Kraft and Polacsek (1978), who analysed factors such as usage, relevance and availability of a title elsewhere.

Kent's study at the University of Pittsburgh was another major study in which use of books and journals was related to cost of their acquisition and maintenance (Kent *et al.*, 1979). But controversy arose concerning implementation of the findings of this report (University of Pittsburgh, 1979).

In late 1983 a use study of current journals by Indian space technologists was carried out (Sridhar, 1986). As part of the study in-house use as well as lentout use of two latest issues of 485 current journals subscribed to by the Indian Space Research Organisation (ISRO), Satellite Centre (ISAC) Library were monitored and recorded over three months from the date of their arrival and display in the library. For the purpose of applying CBA to journals, the use data of this study has been extracted in the case of about 6 per cent of the titles. The actual sample was picked by selecting every 15th title from the list of current journals arranged alphabetically by title. Thus, this study is restricted to a sample of 33 titles. The purpose of the study was to see how effective the CBA of journals is in a special library, to determine how the findings of CBA of journals differ from those of a simple use study and to assess how far other factors influence the decision to retain an item or not, based on its CBA. The subscription cost of the sample journals in Rupees for the year 1983 as well as their periodicity have been noted to determine cost per issue. The sample journals are analysed and compared for their cost per use.

Table 7.24 provides the data on 33 sample journals subscribed to by ISAC library in terms of title, periodicity, subscription cost, use and cost per use. As already mentioned, the use data in the table is extracted from an earlier use study of current journals (Sridhar, 1986). The intention here is to extend the analysis done in the use study by incorporating the cost component and assessing to what extent the findings and recommendations of the use study hold good in the CBA. It is intended also to see whether or not further clues are provided by CBA in assessing the relative worth of a journal for a given library.

TABLE 7.24: Cost Per Use of Selected Journals Subscribed to by ISAC Library

Sl. No.	*Title*	*Periodicity*	*Subscription Cost in Rs. per Year*	*Use of Two Issues in First 3 Months*	*Cost per Use per Issue for First 3 Months*
(1)	(2)	(3)	(4)	(5)	(6)
1.	Acta Astronautica	M	4,545	29	26.12
2.	Applied Mechanics Reviews	M	3,636	11	55.09
3.	Astronomy and Astrophysics	F	7,948	11	55.58
4.	Aviation Week and Space Technology	W	667	43	00.60
5.	Celestial Mechanics	8/yr	750	17	11.03
6.	Control Engineering	M	707	29	4.06
7.	Defence Electronics	M	364	22	2.76
8.	Electrical Communication	M	82	12	1.14
9.	Electronics and Communications in Japan	M	4,245	10	70.75
10.	Energy	BM	2,828	0	NA

(Contd.)

TABLE 7.24 (*Contd.*)

(1)	(2)	(3)	(4)	(5)	(6)
11.	Hydraulics and Pneumatics	M	505	5	16.83
12.	IEE Proceedings. B: Electrical Power Applications	BM	5,298	6	294.33
13.	IEEE Trans. on Biomedical Engineering	M	1,197	8	24.94
14.	IEEE Trans. on Engineering Management	Q	364	10	18.20
15.	IEEE Trans. on Plasma Science	Q	545	7	32.43
16.	International Journal of Control	M	3,227	8	67.23
17.	Journal of Applied Photographic Engineering	Q	808	2	202.00
18.	Journal of Engineering Physics	M	5,383	2	448.58
19.	Journal of Photographic Science	BM	587	0	NA
20.	Journal of the Acoustic Society of America	M	1,869	3	103.83
21.	Journal of the Optical Society of America	M	1,818	7	43.29
22.	Machine Design	F	505	24	1.62
23.	Microelectronics and Reliability	BM	2,172	34	21.29
24.	Nature	W	2,820	38	2.85
25.	Optics Communication	M	3,648	13	46.77
26.	Plating and Surface Finishing	M	404	6	11.22
27.	Radio and Electronic Engineer	M	885	10	14.75
28.	Satellite Communication	M	151	52	0.48
29.	SIAM Journal on Control and Optimisation	BM	889	7	42.33
30.	Solar Physics	8/yr	6,779	15	112.98
31.	Space World	10/yr	167	21	1.15
32.	Telecommunication Journal of Australia	3/yr	198	1	132.00
33.	Wireless World	M	277	29	1.59

Key: NA—Not Applicable; M—Monthly; F—Fortnightly; W—Weekly; Yr—Year; BM—Bimonthly; Q—Quarterly.

Note: 1. Average use per journal issue for first quarter is $\left(\frac{492}{66}\right) = 7.5.$

2. Average cost of an issue of journal is Rs. $\left(\frac{66,268}{431}\right) = 153.75.$

3. The average cost per use of single issue in first quarter is Rs. $\left(\frac{2 \times 33}{492} \times 153.75\right) = 20.63.$

It may be noted from Table 7.24 that the average use per issue of a journal (in the sample) during the first-three months of its arrival and display in the ISAC Library is 7.5. The average subscription cost of an issue of a journal in the sample is Rs. 153.75 and the average cost per use of a single issue over the three months is Rs. 20.63.

As the journals *Energy* and the *Journal of Photographic Science* were not used during the sample use study, their cost per use is not worked out in Table 7.24, and hence they are excluded from the CBA. Incidentally, these are 2 of the 60 unused journals at ISAC library recommended for cancellation in the use study. In addition, there were another 34 marginally used titles (used once or twice during the first-three months of their arrival) suggested for cancellation. The sample list of journals in Table 7.25 contains three such marginally used titles: the *Journal of Applied Photographic Engineering, the Journal of Engineering Physics* and *the Telecommunication Journal of Australia.*

On the other hand, it was recommended that 28 heavily used journals (used more than 30 times during the course of the use study) be obtained by airmail subscription and/or additional copy(ies) be subscribed to. Four of them, namely, *Aviation Week and Space Technology, Microelectronics and Reliability, Nature* and *Satellite Communication* occur in Table 7.24.

Table 7.25 presents the sample journals (31 titles, ignoring 2 that were unused) in increasing order of their cost per use. In addition, their respective ranks as per decreasing order of use and increasing order of cost are also indicated in the table. It is interesting to note that the rank order of these journals by cost per use correlates fairly high with the rank order by use per issue as well as rank order by cost per issue. The respective values of the Spearman Rank order correlation coefficient are 0.70 and 0.85 at 0.005 significance level which indicate that as much as 70 per cent of the result of CBA is affected by the use data (i.e., benefits) and 85 per cent of the result by cost data.

An examination of Table 7.25 reveals that the news oriented popular journals score low in cost per use. For example, *Satellite Communication* received the lowest cost per use of Re. 0.48. This is followed by *Aviation Week and Space Technology* (Re. 0.60), *Electrical Communication* (Rs. 1.14), *Space World* (Rs. 1.15), *Wireless World* (Rs. 1.59), *Machine Design* (Rs. 1.62), *Defense Electronics* (Rs. 2.76), *Nature* (Rs. 2.85) and *Control Engineering* (Rs. 4.06). Of four heavily used journals (used more than 30 times), three have the lowest scores in cost per use. The journal *Microelectronics and Reliability*, though used heavily, scores a moderate Rs. 21.29 per use because of its relatively high subscription cost. Hence, it would not be proper to recommend airmail subscription and/or subscribing to an additional copy in its case. The journal *Electrical Communication*, which had a quite low use score (12), is at the top of the list as a result of its low cost. In other words, it has a low cost/low use profile.

TABLE 7.25: Ranked List of Journals by Cost Per Use

Rank in Increasing Order of Cost Per Use		*Title*	*Rank in Decreasing Order of Use*	
1	(0.48)	Satellite Communication	1	(52)
2	(0.60)	Aviation Week and Space Technology	2	(43)
3	(0.14)	Electrical Communication	14	(12)
4	(1.15)	Space World	10	(21)
5	(1.59)	Wireless World	6	(29)
6	(1.62)	Machine Design	8	(24)
7	(2.76)	Defense Electronics	9	(22)
8	(2.85)	Nature	3	(38)
9	(4.06)	Control Engineering	6	(29)
10	(11.03)	Celestial Mechanics	11	(17)
11	(11.22)	Plating and Surface Finishing	25.5	(6)
12	(14.75)	Radio and Electronic Engineer	18	(10)
13	(16.83)	Hydraulics and Pneumatics	27	(5)
14	(18.20)	IEEE Trans. on Engineering Management	18	(10)
15	(21.29)	Microelectronics and Reliability	4	(34)
16	(24.94)	IEEE Trans. on Biomedical Engineering	20.5	(8)
17	(26.12)	Acta Astronautica	6	(29)
18	(32.43)	IEEE Trans. on Plasma Science	23	(7)
19	(42.33)	SIAM Journal of Control and Optimisation	23	(7)
20	(42.29)	Journal of the Optical Society of America	23	(7)
21	(46.77)	Optics Communication	13	(13)
22	(55.09)	Applied Mechanics Review	15.5	(11)
23	(55.58)	Astronomy and Astrophysics	15.5	(11)
24	(67.23)	International Journal of Control	20.5	(8)
25	(70.75)	Electronics and Communication in Japan	18	(10)
26	(103.83)	Journal of the Acoustic Society of America	28	(3)
27	(112.98)	Solar Physics	12	(15)
28	(132.00)	Telecommunication Journal of Australia	31	(1)
29	(202.00)	Journal of Applied Photographic Engineering	29.5	(2)
30	(294.33)	IEE Proceedings B: Electrical Power Applications	25.5	(6)
31	(448.58)	Journal of Engineering Physics	29.5	(2)

Note: The Spearman Rank Order Correlation between two rankings is $r_s = 1 - \frac{6 \times DI^2}{n\left(n^2 - 1\right)} = 0.7068$. The t-test value based on $t = r_s \sqrt{\frac{n-2}{1-r_s^2}}$ is 5.3805. By looking at the tabulated value of *t*, it is found that correlation is statistically significant at 0.005.

On the other hand, the highest cost per use of Rs. 448.58 is scored by the *Journal of Engineering Physics*. Next in line are: the *IEEE Proceedings B: Electrical Power Applications* (Rs. 294.33), the *Journal of Applied Photographic Engineering* (Rs. 202.00), the *Telecommunication Journal of Australia* (Rs. 132.00), *Solar Physics* (Rs. 112.98) and the *Journal of the Acoustic Society of America* (Rs. 112.98). Interestingly, all three of the marginally used (used once or twice during the sample use study) titles mentioned earlier are included in the high cost per use group. In addition, another 3 journals, namely the *IEEE Proceedings B: Electrical Power Applications, Solar Physics* and the *Journal of the Acoustic Society of America*, have also become cost ineffective because of their exorbitant subscription cost. It is these high cost per use journals that should be considered for cancellation and alternative arrangements, such as the buying of xerox copies of relevant articles, made. All six of the high cost per use (> Rs. 100.00) journals are specialised journals dealing with a specific aspect of a subject and are relatively high-priced.

The findings of the journal use study were put before a representative user body for a final decision on cancellation of unused and least used journals and for a decision regarding additional copies and/or airmail subscription in the case of heavily used journals. Not all of the journals recommended for cancellation were actually cancelled. Nearly half were retained on the plea of subject specialists. In very few cases was the airmail/second copy arrangement approved. The cost dimension added to the use study has nevertheless substantially influenced the decision-makers in cutting down the number of highly priced subscriptions. An exception occurs only in the case of a few specialised journals.

Another factor considered was the nature of journals. For example, most of the local (Indian) journals were not only cheaper but also were demanded as a means of supporting the indigenous publishing efforts.

Two further considerations were taken into account. One had to do with whether a journal is published by a professional body or by a commercial publisher. Normally journals published by professional bodies are lower in subscription cost than are those published by commercial publishers. The second consideration dealt with whether a journal is a news/current-awareness journal meant for generalists or one that deals with a subject of interest primarily to specialists.

CBA is helpful in furthering the findings of the use study by grouping the journals of a library into four profiles, as depicted in Fig. 7.8.

		COST	
		LOW	HIGH
USE	LOW	1	4
	HIGH	2	3

FIG. 7.8: Four Profiles of Journals.

Cell 1: Low cost and low use journals. A library does not mind having such journals as long as they are not creating an abnormal maintenance cost. Alternatively, as long as they are not to be kept in the library for a long time, they are desirable.

Cell 2: Low cost and high use journals. These are the ideal journals from a CBA angle for any library.

Cell 3: High cost and high use journals. These need a separate ranking to see whether or not some with a very high cost per use can be cancelled and xerox copies of needed articles acquired and whether or not the journal can be shared with local cooperating libraries.

Cell 4: High cost and low use journals. These need to be carefully considered for cancellation. Strong user opinion and non-economic considerations need to be given attention.

Conclusion

This use study has enabled the library to take note of unused, least used and most used journals. The overall use of ISAC library is found to be moderate, with 5.93 average uses per issue for the first quarter. The lentout use per person per quarter per one issue of all journals covered is 1.6. Nearly 20 per cent of journals met 52 per cent of total use and 10 per cent met 30 per cent of total use. Sixty (12.4%) journals were never used during the first quarter following their arrival and hence are recommended for cancellation. One hundred and twenty eight journals were used once or more within the library during the sample study, but never borrowed formally in that three months period. In other words, lentout use is catered to by a much smaller part of journal collection than the part used within the library, and in-house use of current journals is much higher than lentout use.

It was found out that abstracting and indexing journals were little used. Journals in the areas of computer science and management are relatively little used when compared with percentage of collection and percentage of users. Journals in the areas of mathematics and statistics, astronomy and astrophysics and physics are given more use within the library than journals of other subjects. On the other hand, journals in the areas of science, mechanical engineering and aeronautics, astronautics and space flight were borrowed more frequently than journals of other subject groups. The average number of uses per journal is very high in the physics, electronics, science, aeronautics, astronautics and space flight groups.

Out of 351 users who borrowed journals during the survey, just 10 per cent were responsible for 38 per cent of total borrowings, and 38 per cent of users made 74 per cent of total borrowings. Nearly 44 per cent of users borrowed sample journals only once during the three months period. More than half of the users borrowed issues of a single journal/ title. Nearly 16 per cent of users borrowed issues of 4 to 10 journals/ titles. Six users borrowed issues of 11 or more journals/titles. More than 60 per cent of users borrowed journals of a single subject group. Three per cent of users depended on journals from 4 to 10 different subject groups.

It was concluded that CBA may not provide a completely satisfactory solution to problems of journal retention or cancellation. It does, however, provide some clues as to how to proceed over and above those provided by a simple use study. CBA increases the awareness of librarians, administrators and users concerning collection prerogatives, but must be used in conjunction with intuitive judgment. Above all, non-economic considerations and user opinion dominate the decision-making in journal subscription.

Correlating journal use with various characteristics/parameters of journals such as country of origin, mode of supply, year from which subscribed by ISAC library, periodicity, language paid or free journal, etc., was also planned and will be carried out at a future date. Correlation of use of journals with various user characteristics including user preference in publishing articles and citing articles and use of journals through reprographic service is likewise being taken up as part of a separate study.

CASE STUDY 11

NON-USE AND NON-USERS OF LIBRARIES

Introduction

Business enterprises with the objective of maximising their profits strive hard to increase their sales which in turn require them to enlarge their market share. Market share is a concept meaningful in the context of total population/market and in relation to one's competitors. Market share is enlarged either by increasing the number of customers or increasing the quantity of consumption of the product by existing customers or both. It is essentially the market penetration by which a business enterprise enrolls more customers to its products. In other words, not only it tries to satisfy and sustain existing customers but also tries to attract non-users of their products. It is a game of survival and growth in business.

Libraries are yet to play marketing games in the strict sense. The least is to worry about non-users. The so called user-research has totally ignored the study of non-users leading to unbalanced ratio of user to non-user research due to extremely difficult nature of non-user studies (Slater, 1984, p. 1). One of the salient points noted by Line (1974, p. 53) while summing up the 47th Aslib Annual Conference deliberations is that the need for "Exploration of the Unserved and Underserved: Who They Are, What They Need, How to Reach Them, and Who is to Reach Them". In the same conference Grose (1974) highlighted the deprived users and their information malnutrition especially among practitioners like doctors, dentists, solicitors, teachers, social workers, etc., and the negligence of library systems. Even after 15 years of such deliberations not much attempts have been made to look into the non-users, underprivileged, unserved, underserved and deprived users and their problems of information malnutrition.

Use of a library is believed to be a minority event, i.e., a small segment of rightful users of a library really use their library. The number of users who have need for information far exceed those who actually use information (Atherton, 1977, p. 7). Even among users, the use of a library typically follows Matthew effect,[13] 80/20 role, inverse law and success-breeds-success phenomenon resulting into the fact that a very small cross-section of users account for a large chunk of the use and the rest of large number of users account for a small part of the use.

The ratio of actual users to potential users of a library serves as a rough measure of the impact of the library and its market penetration capability. At the same time one should be aware of limitations of use studies, including spill over effect of use (Wilson, 1977, p. 83), indirect use of a library and various interactions of users with a library. Use of a library by its users and its utility to its users are often quite different. "An information-system may be used, then, but not be useful; it may also be useful, but not used. It may even be neither useful nor used. It is ideal if it is both used and useful" (Kochen, 1976, p. 150).

The purpose here is to examine the non-use and non-users of libraries, possible reasons for non-use and how to overcome this problem together with the nature, characteristics and quantum of non-use and non-users of ISRO Satellite Centre (ISAC) library as a case study in the light of a series of user and use studies completed by the author.

Definition and Types of Non-users

The terms 'non-use' and 'non-user' are difficult to define without answering the questions such as 'non-use of what?' and 'how much use or how frequently using can be termed as non-use?' A non-user of a library is one who has a right to use the library but he does not do so over a specific period and/or for a specific sample of collection or transactions. Here we are not concerned with involuntary non-users who unfortunately do not have a library to use, but interested in voluntary or wilful non-users (Slater, 1984, p. 2) of a given library. For Grose (1974, p. 9) non-users are the "... groups of people in an affluent society who are never given the means to satisfy their needs, or are geographically cut off from centres of provision which are theoretically open to them or are so occupied that even while surrounded by all they need never stop to enjoy it and suffer a form of (information) malnutrition ...". These non-users live in an information-rich society and yet voluntarily suffer from information malnutrition. Deprived users are usually considered to belong to the first group (i.e., involuntary non-users).

A library can have some non-users who do not use library or its collection or services at all and such non-users are absolute non-users. However, a substantial number of users who make marginal use of a library can be called marginal users. The result of some absolute non-users and many marginal users makes a library under-used. In other words, a library may be under-used due to absolute non-users and marginal users but absolute non-use of a library is quite hypothetical.

Under-usage of a library is equally important in the study of non-use and non-users of libraries because from the angle of the library there is no measure or standard to say how much use can be called fair usage.

Conceptual Framework for Use and Non-use of Information

It may not be out of context, while studying the problem of non-use, underuse and non-users of libraries, to briefly look at the process of seeking and collecting information by users. These aspects are already discussed in Chapter 2. The process of a user coming in contact with a source of information (including a library) depends on many factors which can be grouped under the following three categories: (i) the need, (ii) the user, (iii) the source (or library). The process of matching a (specific subject) requirement or need for information with a source of information or library is subjected mainly to cost-efficiency of the process, errors in matching, ignorances of user about the source and the degree of interpretedness of the source. The process is also dependent on the alternatives available, the degree to which the source adopts to the needs of the user and relative cost of generating new knowledge rather than expensive and possible fruitless search. The alternatives include relying on memory (reserve), skirting around the issue, accepting incomplete, vague or relatively unsatisfactory information, abandoning the requirement and not pursuing to continue the search, etc.

The Need

The need is roughly identified as wanting to know or an awareness or recognition of not knowing or existence of an uncertainty. The strength, urgency, clarity and certainty of a need substantially contribute towards use or non-use of a source of information. The strength of a need in conjunction with the perception of possible efforts required to satisfy the need determines whether or not a user pursues his or her search and if pursued how far he pursues it. The urgency of a need or requirement will determine when a search is pursued and how it varies over a period of time. The more clear and unambiguous the need, more likely that it will be perceived as strong need by user. Lastly, the more certain the need the better the perception of opportunity to do something to satisfy the need.

The User

The user includes the non-user, marginal user and sometimes the delegated user and delegatee user. The initiative, drive, self-motivation, objectivity, habits, styles, idiosyncrasies, past experience, cultural and social settings and expertise in searching for information matter very much in moving user towards a source of information. The expertise in searching includes personal knowledge as well as cognitive skills.

The Source

The source of information could be a document or a group of documents, a system like library, an individual or a group of individuals like institutions. The existence or availability, knowledge about existence, physical proximity, accessibility, ease of use and perceived utility of a source determine whether or not a source of information will be approached and used by a user. Ignorance about existence of a source of information has often caused the non-use of a source. Though technologies like telecommunication, on-line systems and mass storage media can overcome the geographical barrier, use of a library as well as quantity or intensity of interpersonal communication are found to be inversely proportional to the square of the distance between the user and the source (Frohman, 1969). Sometimes the source or the information system itself is so complex and it requires assistance to explore.

Accessibility

Accessibility means bringing together physically or technologically the source and the user so as to enable user to become informed or learn from a source and accede to the evidence that the source will yield the information required. Access to a source can be better understood by looking at the possible barriers to access. Barriers are of two kinds. Firstly, *non-intellectual barriers* are those which are not directly concerned with communication or transfer of information from the source to the user but concerned with bringing physically the source and the user together. Following are some important non-intellectual barriers. (i) *Lack of indicative or bibliographic access:* The indicative or bibliographic access is concerned with the way of ascertaining existence of a source and having knowledge about existence of a source. Or identification of a source. (ii) *The Physical barrier:* The physical access or the document delivery which is a logical extension of bibliographic access, depends on available logistics and technology. Classified nature of a source, policy of the information system and other logistics play their own roles in creating physical barriers between user and the source. (iii) *Cost barrier:* 'Cost of access' is the cost in terms of money, time, efforts and discomfort or inconvenience to be incurred by the user. (iv) *Barrier of system cost:* Cost to the system or the source or provider of information in terms of money, time, efforts and discomfort or inconvenience. Non-monetary values like social, cultural and political values including the reasons of national security, private or corporate vested interest and indecent or irreligious materials can also contribute to the cost of the system.

The second kind of barriers are *intellectual barriers* directly concerned with communication or transfer of information from the source to the users. These barriers are more or less created by or concerned with the user and his limitations. There are two groups of intellectual barriers. (i) *Lack of expertise:* Inability to have cognitive and conceptual access (or subject and knowledge access) due to insufficient expertise of user to understand a source. In other words, the user need better understanding of basic concepts of the subject before he uses a source of information which could be intensely theoretical and goes over head. There are two ways to overcome this barrier of cognitive and conceptual access to a source of information. Firstly, more explanation can be provided to the source of information in terms of providing a translation (if the failure is due to linguistic access) or easily understandable summary or informal explanation or interpretation to the source. In other words the source is augmented with explanation to ease the cognitive and conceptual access. Second approach (which is quite traditional to libraries) is concerned with helping and providing education to the user including consultation of dictionaries, encyclopedias, experts, etc. (ii) *Unacceptability of the source:* Choice of a source is a matter of judgment depending on purpose. Information found in a source could be 'soft' and the user might be seeking 'hard' information. Unacceptability of the source may be due to individual's attitude as well as misperception of the source and/or the need. The user could be reluctant to accept the source of information as credible source or find it not having adequate 'cognitive authority'. It could also be due to 'cognitive dissonance', i.e., users unwillingness to accept the evidence of the source as it conflicts with his other beliefs.

Further, three very interesting aspects of access to the source of information need mention here. Firstly, the access itself could become a barrier to use of a source of information when it becomes excess. This problem of 'information explosion', 'information indiscipline', 'information overload' or 'access to excess' is the result of ill effects of luxuries of 'information revolution' and quite opposite to information malnutrition. In addition, inevitable duplication, deliberate redundancies and representations of information in different sources or within the same source further add up to the pollution. For example, the observations like "90 per cent of all scientific papers are unread by anyone but their authors" (Longuet-Higgins, 1970) and "it is cheaper to conduct an experiment to find something out rather than to attempt to discover whether the experiment has previously been performed" (Kemp, 1976, p. 131) speak of the intensity of problem of 'access to excess' and are much against the principle of 'reinventing the wheel'.

Secondly the technological affluence has also caused some barriers. With easy and cheap way of reproduction of reading materials and abundant xerox machines, the document delivery and physical access to information sources have so much improved that the users have started 'accumulating' xerox copies rather than attempting to 'assimilate' all that is copied and possessed. Possession of large amount of xerox copies of would-be-reading materials itself has become barrier to access, retrieve and use information. Otherwise, 'access to excess' is a problem could also exist in the minds of the users and cause stress and frequently increased errors. Some of the possible solutions for this problem are increased specialisation of users, frequent delegated approach to search and collection of information, more efficient ways of processing information including information analysis and consolidation services with greater selectivity, evaluation, review and synthesis.

The third unusual barrier in accessing the source of information is none other than the organiser or the intermediary (i.e., librarian) himself. One may wonder how the organiser of information sources could become a barrier. In the normal process of organising a library and its collection and establishing a system lot of rules and procedures are instituted restricting access to the source of information with punitive measures for those who violate the rules. Traditionally, libraries have many restrictive practices like closed access, chained books, restricted membership, restricted borrowing facilities for a limited time, restricted hours of opening, punitive fines for late returning etc. Further, the means and techniques like classification schemes, storing mechanisms, etc., and tools like catalogues, bibliographies, etc. created in the process could also be hurdles between the user and the source if these tools and techniques are badly developed or excessively deployed. The very effort of librarians to linearly store multidimensional information embodiments rather than having a 'hyperstack' is a classic example of access limitations to users. Knowingly or unknowingly, intentionally or unintentionally many such barriers have been evolved or created by librarians.

Ease of Use

Ease of use is another important condition for an user to use a source of information. This condition has far reaching and very large implications on the physical and other organisation of the sources of information. Physical storing and arrangement, classification, indexing and cataloguing of documents at the system level and the physical medium, organisation and presentation of contents at document level might cause barrier to use of sources of information. The popular Mooer's law (1960, p. 204) states that "an information retrieval system will tend not to be used whenever it is more painful and problemsome for a customer to have information than for him not to have it".

The role played by the building, layout, interior decoration, furniture, lighting, fixtures, colour, etc., which create 'conducive environment' in a library, on ease of use cannot be undermined. A thorough understanding of 'zones in personal distances' and 'types of human territories' within library environment are necessary. The design influences of libraries on user-behaviour are not yet known fully (Shlechter, 1979).

Perceived Utility

Perceived utility of the source also matters very much for a user to select the source. How the user perceives the source about its usefulness to him is very important irrespective of the intrinsic worth of the source. This is basically a user related factor and depends on the quality and quantity of information expected from the source by the user. Perception involves detection, selection, organisation and interpretation of sensory stimuli/information. Perception can be seen as an active and constructive process affected by internal factors like interests, needs expectation, emotion and motivation as well as external factors (physical characteristics) like intensity, size and contrast. Above all perception is also selective. Perception is the sensation reinforced by memories, images, etc., derived from past experience and called up by association. Both the processes of falling back on past experience and calling up by association while perceiving a source can cause havocs. For example, if a user is already exposed to an inefficient, irrelevant and difficult-to-use type of source, his perception of the utility of that or other similar sources is obviously be very low. Similarly, if an user has an 'ill' feeling about or an 'unpleasant' experience with an institution, it is likely that by association, he perceives very low utility of library of that institution.

Subjectivity in perception of utility of a source could be caused by 'perceptual constancy' as well as misperception. The error due to 'perceptual constancy' occurs when a user attributes qualities to an object in perception which are not merely additional to but incompatible with the qualities that are actually sensed. In case of misperception, the perception is greatly influenced by the preliminary direction of user's attention, by expectation, or by desire. In other words, familiarity, expectation or interest or wishful thinking of user may lead to sub-excitement of brain pattern before the actual perception occurs. The subjectivity in perception of utility of a source is not necessarily be adverse or negative. For example, bewilderness of a user at large collection or huge library building could lead him to perceive it as highly useful collection or source of information.

Perceived utility of the source talks of the 'psychological distance' between the user and the source. And often, the 'psychological distance' may be more serious barrier than physical distance (Line, 1974, p. 48).

Reasons for Non-use of Library Collections

Another interesting question is what are the reasons for non-use of a library by its rightful users. All the factors discussed so far, have their own contributions in the success or failure relating to use of a source of information by a user to satisfy a need for information. These factors and their several interplay need to be understood to know why library collections are under used or not used. Analysis of these factors tell us the reasons for underuse and non-use of a source of information and what can be done about the non-use and non-users.

As discussed under the conceptual framework, non-use of a library may be due to lack of strong need or lack of awareness of need on the part of non-users. It could also be due to lack of initiative on the part of non-users. Another possibility is that non-users may wrongly perceive the usefulness of a library. Lastly, it is quite possible that the difficulties in accessing and using a library may also act as barriers and do not encourage a less motivated non-user. They may not perceive that the benefits of use of a library commensurate with the efforts they need to put forth in order to access and use a library (Mooer's law and law of least efforts). Grose (1974) analyses his survey results to show how practitioners like doctors, dentists, solicitors, teachers, social workers are partly or totally neglected by library systems because of geographical distance, lack of time and inclination on the part of practitioners, the very special nature of their need, limitations of available type and form of information and many other inhibiting factors. In other words, he points out how practitioners and field workers are doing without proper and adequate information.

'Belling the Cat'

At this stage one might ask a question that what are we going to do with a study of non-use and non-users of a library and even express a pessimistic view about converting non-users into active users of a library which is not only costly (Luckham, 1971) but difficult. It is also believed that any promotion of services in terms of attracting the non-user is ineffective and such actions may increase the level of usage among existing users than attracting non-users (D'Elia, 1980). It is further argued that it is better to increase the quality and quantity of service to existing users than trying to take non-users into fold. On the contrary, the paternalistic and missionary view could be that the less fortunate non-users be made as users of library (Vermaelen, 1981). Irrespective of encouraging users or non-users by a library, the 'rich become richer' phenomenon (Matthew effect) holds good about users. In other words, it is quite evidently established that those who use one type of document/ service have a better chance to use other type of documents/services and those who use library documents tend to interact more with library and *vice versa* (Sridhar, 1987, 1988).

The problem of non-use or non-users of a library is akin to the problem of not exercising franchise in a democracy. Though such persons (non-users) can put forth logical arguments about not using a library or not exercising franchise in the election, it cannot always be considered as a rational action or attitude. Library professionals are divided on the issue of tackling this problem. While one group feels that libraries should forget hard core (absolute) non-users and should not spend time, money and efforts to change such non-users who are unlikely to change, the other group feels that the non-users need the library most and all stimulating, persuading and marketing efforts of libraries should be concentrated on absolute non-users. A via media of trying to see whether the characteristics of these hard core (absolute) non-users vary and if so can they be divided into two or more subgroups so that identify among those who could be changed into users by stimulating and persuading them as well as modifying the provision of library services to suit their requirements. In other words, if anything can be done about the problem of non-use we must not only analyse the non-use and non-users to see for any pattern among themselves, but also see whether the problem is in the factors relating to the need for information or the user himself or the source of information (i.e., library) or any combination of these factors.

Case Study of Non-use and Non-users of ISAC Library

Let us now look into the non-use of documents and services of ISAC library and the characteristics of non-users of ISAC library. Table 7.26 provides a summary of non-use and non-users of ISAC library with

TABLE 7.26: Non-Users of ISAC Library (N = 807)

Sl. No.	*Type of Use/ Interaction*	*Sample Size*	*Not Used*		*NA*	*Error*
			No.	*%*		
1.	Borrowed use	3 months 'circulation sample'	248	31.6*	22	0
2.	Borrowed use	5% random 'collection sample'	98	14.0	106	0
3.	Library visits (in-house use)	3 months sample	369	47.7	33	1
4.	Reprographic service	One year sample	449	69.1	157	0
5.	Inter-library loan service	One year sample	699	95.2	72	1
6.	Library-use Index	(Based on 1 to 5 above)	75	11.9	179	0
7.	Procurement services	One year sample	462	73.6	177	2
8.	Suggestions for new documents	One year sample	463	73.5	176	1
9.	Document reservations	One year sample	336	50.8	146	0
10.	Literature search service	One year sample	726	98.9	75	–2
11.	Reference service	One year sample	606	82.2	73	–3
12.	Library-Interaction Index	(Based on 7 to 11 above)	253	40.2	178	0

Key: *—the percentage of users who did not borrow any book, journal, report and standard over a quarter respectively are 36.5, 79.3, 88.8 and 99.5. NA—Since data are collected over a period of two years, cases partially represented due to resignation and long absence are excluded.

Note: Percentages are worked out ignoring not applicable cases and error from total defined population of 807.

number and percentage of non-users of library documents and services together with the extent of non-usage in terms of 'library-use index' and 'library-interaction index'.[14] While nearly 12 per cent of the population are absolute non-users of documents as revealed by library-use index, as many as 40 per cent are non-users of various library services and had no interactions with library. Yet the absolute non-users can make 'delegated' or 'spill over' use of library documents (Wilson, 1977, p. 83) through other users. It may also be noted that it is not necessary that user should make use of every type of document or every type of service of a library.

It is interesting to note from Table 7.26, that if 31.6 per cent of users have not made borrowed use of documents as per three-months 'circulation sample', only 14 per cent were found to have not made borrowed use of documents as per 5 per cent systematic random 'collection sample'. This indicates that 5 per cent collection sample is a better sample than 3 months circulation sample to define non-use and non-user. This is exactly the difficulty of definitions of non-use and non-user discussed earlier.

From Table 7.26, it is obvious that among the components of library-use index (i.e., Sl. Nos. 1 to 5) the inter-library loan use is made by least number of users followed by use of library documents through reprographic service and in-house use of library documents. It is also not proper to expect a user to make inter-library loan, reprographic or in-house use without making borrowed use of library documents. Secondly, it is the borrowed use which is primary, traditional and more popular service and a way of using documents than others. Lastly, any library is hardly equipped to serve effectively if every user makes frequent demand on inter-library loan, reprographic and in-house use of documents. In other words, there is an unwritten understanding that the later services or facilities are provided to a limited extent to supplement the borrowed use of documents.

As far as library interaction index is concerned the least interaction is made regarding literature search service followed by reference service, document reservation facilities and finally interactions and suggestions for procurement services (Sl. Nos. 7 to 11 in Table 7.26). Document reservation service is a complementary activity to lending service of the library and naturally had interaction from maximum number of users. Surprisingly, low participation of users in collection development (procurement services and suggestions for new documents) has been discussed (Case Study 05) in detail (Sridhar, 1983). The long range reference service and literature search service are meant to be used by a handful of users. These services require adequate professional manpowers if more users avail them and normally users who do not make use of other fundamental services like lending service of library may not expect and seek these services.

Having seen how the use of library documents and interactions with library varied over different types of facilities and services, let us try to look at the non-usage of library documents and services in relation to the background of non-users. More particularly, seeking how the (lent-out) non-use of books, reports and journals, absence of in-house use, and not availing reservation and procurement (participation in collection development) services varied with status, academic qualifications, nature of work, specialisation, length of experience and professional activities and achievements of these hard-core non-users.

Table 7.27 presents how the percentage of non-users varied with their status in the organisation. From Table 7.27, it is amply clear that proportion of non-users regards borrowed use of library books and journals has linearly decreased as their status increased (except for those in status E). The same is true about borrowed use of reports but linearity at higher echelon is not that clear. The activity of document reservation which is closely related to borrowed use of documents has identical result of decrease in non-users as status increases but the highest status (i.e., A to E) claim exception. There is slightly higher proportion of non-users in these grades regarding reservation of books and reports. This could indicate a slightly relaxed attitude of these highly placed persons in not pursuing specific title search through reservation or more easily

TABLE 7.27: Status-wise Distribution of Non-Users (in %)

Status	*Books (N = 800)*	*Reports (N = 803)*	*Journals (N = 801)*	*In-house Use (N = 772)*	*Document Suggestion (N = 630)*	*Document Reservation (N = 650)*
A, B, C & D	11.5	88.5	57.7	25.9	50.0	40.7
E	33.3	80.6	58.3	27.1	64.3	41.4
F	18.6	78.8	54.1	32.3	62.5	37.8
G	19.0	88.1	54.2	28.7	62.7	38.3
H	19.5	94.8	62.3	39.4	66.7	42.0
I	21.3	96.3	68.5	48.1	75.3	42.9
J	21.6	98.0	73.5	67.1	90.6	61.8
K	51.4	97.3	91.9	83.8	97.3	89.2
L	66.1	00.0	91.3	85.5	96.8	88.7
M & N	66.7	98.1	92.2	91.3	100.0	96.3
Total	28.9	91.3	66.9	47.8	73.5	51.7

Note: Status A to N are in the descending order of hierarchy.

finding a substitute document when something is issued out than persons at lower grades. Again in-house use of documents and participation in collection development (through document suggestion) are positively and linearly related to status of users (except those with status F and E respectively). In other words, the proportion of non-users has decreased with increase in status for in-house use and procurement service. It can also be noted from the table that the percentage of non-users at the lowest bracket of the organisation is as many as six times that of highest bracket in case of use of books, more than three and a half times in case of in-house use of library and more than two and a half times in case of document reservations.

Table 7.28 presents the percentage of absolute non-users of books, reports, journals, in-house mode of use, reservation service and document suggestion interactions against their academic qualifications. As could be seen from the table the number of non-users regarding borrowed use of reports, reservation service and document suggestion interactions with library has linearly decreased as the qualifications increased. The same is true about borrowed use of books and journals as well as in-house use of library but for postgraduates having much smaller proportion of non-users than doctorates. Interestingly, the percentage of non-users of books among undergraduates is more than three times that of postgraduates. Similarly those who does not make in-house use of library among undergraduates are four times that of postgraduates.

TABLE 7.28: Qualifications-wise Distribution of Non-users (in %)

Qualifications	*Books (N = 691)*	*Reports (N = 693)*	*Journals (N = 692)*	*In-house Use (N = 674)*	*Document Suggestion (N = 587)*	*Document Reservation (N = 605)*
Under-graduates	56.3	97.2	90.1	83.7	97.0	86.8
Diploma Holders	28.2	98.6	75.3	60.8	81.2	58.0
Graduates	20.7	89.9	55.3	35.9	62.6	38.8
Post-graduates	17.5	84.7	52.6	22.8	60.4	32.9
Doctorates	20.0	67.7	56.7	26.7	44.4	27.6
Total	28.7	90.8	65.9	46.6	72.7	51.2

How non-users are distributed against nature of their work is presented in Table 7.29. It is obvious from the table that those involved in planning and system analysis work have least (proportion of) non-users followed by those involved in design, development, management and supervision. Maximum (proportion of) non-users are found in those involved in fabrication, testing and operational activity. (The only exception appears to be that of those involved in management and supervision activities who have least proportion of non-users of journals and document suggestion interactions.) If we compare the proportion of non-users among those involved in management and supervision work with those involved in design and development, we find substantial higher proportion of non-users among managers and supervisors as far as use of technical reports, in-house use of library and document reservation services are concerned. However, ratio of non-users among those involved in fabrication and testing is almost same as that of those involved in operational activity.

TABLE 7.29: Nature of Work-wise Distribution of Non-users (in %)

Nature of Work	*Books (N = 458)*	*Reports (N = 458)*	*Journals (N = 458)*	*In-house Use (N = 439)*	*Document Sugges-tion (N = 362)*	*Document Reserva-tion (N = 371)*
Management/ Supervision	21.4	90.5	52.4	48.8	55.3	53.8
Planning/Systems Analysis	15.1	81.1	56.6	28.8	64.1	27.5
Design & Development	20.5	86.5	55.8	24.3	56.8	39.0
Design, Development, Fabrication and Testing	22.2	92.6	63.0	40.7	75.0	54.2
Fabrication & Testing	32.8	93.8	77.3	65.8	83.7	60.6
Operational Activity	38.2	97.1	73.5	63.6	88.0	59.3
Others	44.4	100.0	55.6	58.8	92.9	71.4
Total	25.8	90.0	63.3	43.5	69.9	49.1

How do these non-users of ISAC library stand against their subject of specialisation (in the highest academic qualification) is presented in Table 7.30. Mathematicians have least proportion of non-users in respect of borrowed use of books (5%), in-house use of library (10%) and document reservation service (11.8%). They have second lowest proportion of non-users in use of journals. However, mathematicians have highest (95%) proportion of non-users of technical reports. This may be an indication of forms of literature required by mathematicians.

Physicist have the least proportion of non-users of journals and relatively low percentage of non-users of books, reports and even other services. In other words, physicists have relatively low non-users in almost all aspects of use of library and user-interactions with library. It is quite interesting that aeronautical and structural engineers have least (proportions of) non-users of technical reports. They also have relatively less non-users of books and reservation services. However, they have highest proportion of non-users (75%) of journals (like that of mechanical engineers). It is mechanical and electrical engineers who have very high proportion of non-users of library documents and services. The situation of electronics engineers is equally bad and even worse in some cases (for example use of books and reports) but they have very low proportion of non-users regarding in-house use of library. To put it in nutshell, scientists (i.e., physicists and mathematicians) have less non-users than aeronautical and structural engineers and aeronautical and structural engineers than other engineers.

TABLE 7.30: Specialisation-wise Distribution of Non-users (in %)

Speciali-sation	*Books (N = 431)*	*Reports (N = 431)*	*Journals (N = 431)*	*In-house Use (N = 415)*	*Document Sugges-tion (N = 355)*	*Document Reserva-tion (N = 361)*
Physics	19.5	87.8	53.7	24.4	54.8	43.8
Mathematics	5.0	95.0	55.0	10.0	75.0	11.8
Mechanical Engineering	38.5	92.6	75.4	68.1	80.0	67.9
Aeronautical & Structural Engineering	12.5	56.2	75.0	37.5	66.7	30.8
Electrical Engineering	47.1	82.4	58.8	58.8	81.2	50.0
Electronics	80.3	94.9	62.8	37.6	66.9	44.1
Total	26.7	91.6	65.4	44.3	70.7	49.3

Table 7.31 presents the distribution of non-users of library documents and services against their length of experience. Though there is no clear and strong pattern emerging from the table one or two weak indications are worth noting. New-comers with least experience have least non-users of books, journals and in-house use followed by those with more than eight years of experience. However less experienced have maximum non-users of technical reports.

TABLE 7.31: Experience-wise Distribution of Non-users (in %)

Experience (in years)	*Books (N = 379)*	*Reports (N = 398)*	*Journals (N = 394)*	*In-house Use (N = 397)*	*Document Suggestion (N = 398)*	*Document Reservation (N = 398)*
< 2	20.0	97.4	61.5	41.0	76.9	53.8
2—3	37.5	90.5	61.0	42.9	73.8	50.0
4—5	35.6	97.9	72.9	62.5	83.3	52.1
6—8	39.7	92.6	78.2	60.0	78.8	58.8
9—11	31.6	82.7	66.7	41.2	58.0	42.0
12—14	28.6	88.1	62.7	40.7	71.2	50.8
> 14	34.7	91.8	77.1	63.3	83.7	65.3
Total	33.2	91.0	69.3	50.4	73.9	52.8

Lastly, Table 7.32 presents the distribution of non-users against professional activities and achievements index[15] specifically developed for a study of information behaviour of space technologists (Sridhar, 1987). The main study has already indicated a positive and strong relation between professional activities and achievements index and use of library documents and services. It is very interesting that all the non-users of reports and all the non-users who did not suggest documents to library have zero score on professional activities and achievements index, thereby indicating that any effort to increase the professional and academic activities of non-users of library could help and might lead to better use of library.

TABLE 7.32: Professional Activities and Achievements-wise Distribution of Non-users (in %)

Professional Activities and Achievement Index	*Books (N = 171)*	*Reports (N = 181)*	*Journals (N = 179)*	*In-house Use (N = 181)*	*Document Suggestion (N = 180)*	*Document Reservation (N = 181)*
0	50.0	100.0	80.8	80.8	100.0	84.6
1—3	34.4	93.9	72.7	48.5	69.7	54.5
> 3	18.6	86.1	55.8	26.2	51.2	27.9
Total	26.3	89.5	62.6	38.1	61.7	50.8

Conclusion

Information malnutrition, under usage and non-usage are common features in libraries. Yet systematic efforts have not gone into understanding the non-users, underprivileged, unserved, underserved and deprived users. Only a minority of rightful users account for a large majority of usage of libraries. The profession is even divided about the concern for non-users. The problem is more serious in case of voluntary or wilful non-users than involuntary non-users or underprivileged, unserved, underserved and deprived users.

Several factors relating to the need for information, the user and the source and their interplay cause underusage and non-usage of information and libraries. Delineating and identifying these factors affecting non-usage can help libraries to tackle the problem. Identifying the characteristics of these non-users and their specific needs and characteristics of such libraries go long way to increase market penetration of libraries.

A case study of hard core or absolute non-users of ISAC library has revealed several patterns of the non-users. Various services of the library forms a hierarchy and users do not reach advanced information services without going through rudimentary services like lending service and in-house use. The omnibus library facilities and services to some extent fail to meet requirements of diverse set of users having different status and other characteristics. It was revealed in the survey that increased status in the organisation lead non-users to become users of the library. Further, as academic qualifications and the status in the organisation are highly correlated, the non-users are more among less qualified persons. Those who are involved in planning, system analysis, design, development and management have better chances of becoming users of the existing pattern of library system than those having fabrication, testing and operational activity as nature of work. Interestingly physicists and mathematicians (i.e., scientists) are less likely to be non-users than aeronautical and structural engineers and aeronautical and structural engineers than other engineers. It appears that too little (less than 2 years) and too much (may be about 8 years or more) experience is related to increased use of libraries and decreased the proportion of non-users. Promotion of professional and academic activities of non-users and thereby professional achievements is likely to make many non-users of library to use library.

Lastly, designers of library systems should not be carried away by the present users of library but look into some of the basic factors which prevented some rightful users from using the library.

NOTES AND REFERENCES

1. "For all items circulating externally during the period 1969-1975, the average was 5.024 transaction per item" (Allen Kent *et al.*, 1979, p. 29). Though the magnitude, methodology and environmental parameters differ and Kent's study is very much disputed as "remarkably superficial and unidimensional", "simultaneously aggressive and evasive", "highly subjective and political" and "question the validity of the hypothesis, research methods, conclusions and recommendations" *vide* the Senate Library Committee, University of Pittsburgh, "The Study of Library Use of Pitt" by Professor Allen Kent *et al.*, *A Pittsburgh Reply*, Pittsburgh: University of Pittsburgh, July 1979, the same has been cited in this study for comparison purpose.
2. This confirms the low usage of serials reported in Kent's study vide Allen Kent *et al.*, *Idem*, p. 65 and p. 67 and the LC Study's result that serials forming 39.8 per cent of the collection accounted for 24 per cent of use vide Metz, 1979, p. 430.
3. A detailed account of this inverse relation called 80/20 rule, i.e., "approximately 80 per cent of the circulations are accounted for by about 20 per cent of the holdings" may be seen vide Question L. Burrell "The 80/20 rule: library loan or statistical law?", *Journal of Documentation*, 41(1), March 1985, p. 24-39. In this respect, by including the unused (zero used) documents approximately 80 per cent of circulation use accounted for by about 26 per cent in case of books, 22 per cent in case of journals and 10 per cent in case of reports.
4. During seven years and two months period at Pittsburgh University Library 48.37 per cent of the collection did not circulate at all (Kent *et al.*, 1979, pp. 12-13). Under 55 per cent of books had no recorded use during a nineteen-month period at Newcastle Upon Tyne Polytechnic Library (Harris, 1977, p. 119).
5. Kent defines an item as being in the core collection if it circulates externally one or more times (Kent *et al.*, 1979, p. 49).
6. In the case of Harris study loans account for just over 45 per cent of stock (Harris, 1977, pp. 119-20).
7. A previous study on the effect of age upon book use revealed a similar result (Sridhar, 1983, pp. 39-48).
8. Harris study showed that ". . . a greater proportion of material acquired in 1972 was used than of that acquired prior to 1972 (and) . . . material acquired after 1972 is more heavily used than that material acquired during 1972, reflecting a general presence for novelty of stock" (Harris, 1977, p. 121).
9. Though the present study is not on comparable grounds with Kent's study, similar data from Kent's study are provided at appropriate places. The use (both in-house and lentout) per person per trimester is 16.6 for physics, 0.67 for engineering, 2.5 for computer science and 1.7 for mathematics. Hence, Kent concluded that the usage of journals was generally very low (Kent *et al.*, Idem, pp. 65 and 67).
10. It may be compared with the average number of uses per year (includes all issues and bound journals unlike the present study) of 33.2 in physics, 9.3 in computer science, 7.2 in mathematics and 4.0 in engineering of Kent's study (*Ibid.*, p. 69).
11. Daily issues data for three months subsequently collected revealed that on an average books constituted 80 per cent of daily issues followed by journals with 14.8 per cent. There were 895 issue transactions for journals in the quarter

which amounted to an average of 3.7 uses per user. During the period 228 users (or 21% of registered members) borrowed journals at least once.

12. Some attempts to apply CBA to certain areas of library works like library unionisation and networking, union catalogue, electronic security system, catalogue automation, library automation network, catalogue system, library delivery systems, manpower planning, etc., have already been made.
13. Merton (1968) first proposed "Matthew effect" which was based on Matthew's Gospel 'For unto everyone that hath shall be given, he shall have abundance; but from him that hath not shall be taken away even that which he hath'.
14. In order to simplify the analysis of various modes of use of library documents and user-interactions with library, these two indexes were developed in the original study based on individual frequencies of component data. Library use index has as its components xerox copies of reading materials taken, inter-library loan, in-house and borrowed use of library documents. Library interaction index consisted of documents suggested to and procured by library, reservations made for library documents, literature search and reference services availed (Sridhar, 1987, 1995).
15. The index consisted of lectures delivered, seminars, symposia and conferences attended, internal documents/reports prepared, papers published, patents obtained, awards and citations received, memberships of professional associations, societies, board of studies, editorial committees, internal committees as well as official tours, in-service trainings and part time studies undertaken.

8

USER INTERACTIONS WITH LIBRARY

CASE STUDY 12

DOCUMENT RESERVATION PATTERN

Introduction

Collection and membership of ISRO Satellite Centre Library have almost doubled in the last four years resulting in manifold increase in lending activity and use of documents. With the objective of maximising the use of documents among those who are in need, provisions for reservation of documents and levying overdue charges for late returning of documents were introduced during 1979. The factors which have direct bearing on reservation activity are size and homogeneity of users as well as collection, simultaneous demand for documents by more than one user, duration of issue of documents, fine system, user attitude and perseverance in borrowing a document, etc.

Objectives and Scope

In order to know the trend in reservation and also to have feedback for better lending system and collection development policy all reservations for books and paper copy reports received at charging desk of the Library during 1982 were collection and analysed for this study. These documents are normally issued for 21 days with a provision to levy overdue charge of 10 Paise per day Per document till three months from the date of issue and recover the 'replacement cost' of the document together with overdue charges thereafter. If a particular document has more than three reservations at a time the issue period is often reduced to 7 or 14 days in order to make it available to all those in the reservation list within a reasonable period. About 1,500 reference and restricted documents which are not issued for 21 days and hence not covered under reservation provision are excluded from the study.

Due to limitation of manually operated lending system including lack of complete details of documents as well as users for every reservation transaction, a detailed analysis for a larger data could not be undertaken. Incorporating the total number of books published in the subjectwise analysis and comparison of results with statistics of similar special libraries are much desired. However, a detailed analysis of reservations against different user characteristics is being done as part of a separate study (Sridhar, 1995).

Frequency Distribution of the Data

The frequency distribution of number of documents against number of reservations is depicted in Table 8.1. When this data is plotted on a graph, a fairly smooth wide angled 'L' shaped curve with long tail along number of reservations can be seen.

TABLE 8.1: Frequency Distribution of Documents against Reservations

No. of Reserva-tions	*Books*		*Reports*		*Total*	
	No. of Books	*Total Reserva-tions*	*No. of Reports*	*Total Reserva-tions*	*No. of Docu-ments*	*Total Reserva-tions*
1	260	260	47	47	307	307
2	102	204	7	14	109	218
3	52	156	3	9	55	165
4	28	112	2	8	30	120
5	23	115	2	10	25	125
6	31	186	0	0	31	186
7	12	84	0	0	12	84
8—10	22	192	0	0	22	192
11—13	14	166	0	0	14	166
14 & above	4	68	0	0	4	68
Total	548	1,543	61	88	609	1,631

As expected almost one-half of reserved documents had only one reservation during the year. Many of these are as a result of initial curiosity about a new book on display. A little less than one-fifth of reserved books had two reservations. As number of reservations increase the number of titles fall sharply. No report had more than five reservations during the year whereas some books had as many as 14 to 20 reservations.

This can be explained by the facts that (i) many reports are otherwise accessible to users as gift from authors or from organisations of issue (ii) reports normally deal with highly specialised area which is in the forefront of R&D and attract a definite small set of users and (iii) finally, books are more popular than reports for meeting 'continuing education' requirement of large number of users.

Library has about 1,000 registered members and from Table 8.2 it is clear that little over one-third of these members have availed reservation facility during 1982. Among those availed little less than one-third have reserved only one book. The number of members decreases sharply as number of reservations increase. This frequency distribution of users against reservations when plotted on graph results in a typical simple asymptote curve. It is very interesting to note that one member has made 54 reservations in the year amounting to an average of one per week. Also there are four members each with 23, 24, 27 and 29 reservations. There are 45 members (or 12% of the members) who availed reservation facility each with more than 8 reservations represented 684 reservations or 42 per cent of total reservations during the year.

TABLE 8.2: Frequency Distribution of Users against Reservations

No. of Reservations	*No. of Users*	*Total Reservations*
1	118	118
2	81	162
3	48	144
4	22	88
5	22	110
6	19	114
7	15	105
8	12	96
9	8	72
10	8	80
11	5	55
12	3	36
13	3	39
14	1	14
15—20	11	184
21—54	6	204
Total	382	1,631

Comparison of Reservation Statistics with Collection and Membership

Table 8.3 summarises reservation, collection and membership statistics of the Library for comparison. About 5.5 per cent of total books and 1.7

per cent of total reports are reserved during the year. Average reservation per document is 2.8 for book and 1.4 for reports. Average reservation per member is little over four.

TABLE 8.3: Reservation, Collection and Membership Statistics

Sl.No.	*Description*	*Books*	*Reports*	*Total*
1.	Total reservations	1,543	88	1,631
2.	Collection	10,000	3,500	13,500
3.	No. of documents reserved	548	61	609
4.	Percentage of collection reserved (3/2 × 100)	5.48	1.74	4.51
5.	Average reservation per document (1/3)	2.78	1.44	2.68
6.	No. of members who availed reservation facility			382
7.	Average reservation per member (1/6)			4.25
8.	Total members			1,000

Further analysis of reservations against year of acquisition, year of publication (age) and subject of the document is made only for 40 books having more than 7 reservations and 7 reports having more than 2 reservations. As could be seen from Table 8.1 these 47 documents constituting 7.72 per cent of reserved documents account for 453 reservations or 27.77 per cent of total reservations.

Reservation *Vs.* Year of Acquisition of Document

It is clear from Table 8.4 that except few fundamental classic books in the field acquired during initial years (i.e., 1973, 1974 and 1977) all other highly reserved documents were acquired during last four years. Again as expected maximum reservations are made for books acquired during 1982 and the number of reservations steadily decreases as we go backwards. The data indicates that except classic books which are needed repeatedly by many new as well as old members, other books are less likely to have reservations after 3-4 years. However in case of reports, all highly reserved reports were acquired during 1982. Thus the data establish that recency/currency of the acquired document has a direct bearing on reservation.

Reservation *Vs.* Age of Document

The same data presented against year of publication of the document reveal that reservations are concentrated among documents published during latest four years. However, it is obvious from Table 8.5 that books published as early as 1966 and 1967 are also in great demand. Thus reservations are spread over almost last 15 years of the publications. To some extent, this may be an indication of the technological gap. The data appears to be inadequate for above generalisation as far as reports are concerned.

TABLE 8.4: Reservation *Vs.* Year of Acquisition of Document

Year of Acquisition	*Books*		*Reports*	
	No. with more than 7 Reservations	*Total No. of Reservations*	*No. with more than 2 Reservations*	*Total No. of Reservations*
1982	18	186	7	27
1981	4	57	0	0
1980	6	62	0	0
1978	0	0	0	0
1977	1	9	0	0
1976	0	0	0	0
1975	0	0	0	0
1974	1	13	0	0
1973	4	36	0	0
Total	40	426	7	27

TABLE 8.5: Reservation *Vs.* Year of Publication (Age) of Document

Year of Publication	*Books*		*Reports*	
	No. with more than 7 Reservations	*Total No. of Reservations*	*No. with more than 2 Reservations*	*Total No. of Reservations*
1982	1	8	1	3
1981	9	98	0	0
1980	9	95	2	9
1979	6	70	0	0
1978	4	49	0	0
1977	1	9	0	0
1976	1	11	0	0
1975	1	13	0	0
1974	0	0	3	10
1973	1	8	0	0
1971	2	21	0	0
1967	2	18	0	0
1966	0	0	1	5
Total	40	426	7	27

Reservation *Vs.* Subject of Document

A subject-wise distribution of reservations for books, library members and the total book stock based on UDC divisions are presented in Tables 8.6(a) and 8.6(b). It is not a surprise that out of 7 highly reserved reports, 6 are NASA reports and one is Aerospace Corporation report as NASA reports from over 50 per cent of the present hardcopy collection.

TABLE 8.6(a): Reservation *Vs.* Subject (Based on main divisions of UDC)

Main Divisions of UDC	*Approx. % of Members*	*Approx. % of Stock*	*Reservations for Books*		
			No. with more than 7 Reservations	*Total No. of Reservations*	*% of Reservations*
0	—	4	0	0	0
1, 2, 3 & 4	—	4	1	8	1.8
5	12	32	5	46	10.7
6	85	58	34	372	87.4
7, 8 & 9	—	2	0	0	0
Total	97	100	40	426	100.0

TABLE 8.6(b): Reservation *Vs.* Subject of Documents (for classes in main division 6 of UDC)

Class No. of UDC	*Approx. % of Stock*	*Reservations for Books*		
		No. with more than 7 Reservations	*Total No. of Reservations*	*% of Reservations*
6 (General)	0.3	0	0	0
61	1.1	0	0	0
62	38.5	20	204	47.9
64, 64 & 60	0.8	0	0	0
65	3.7	0	0	0
66	1.6	0	0	0
67/68	12.0	14	168	39.5
Total	58.0	34	372	87.4

It is obvious from Table 8.6(a) that almost all users and 90 per cent of books collection fall under main divisions 5 (Mathematics and Natural Sciences) and 6 (Applied Sciences and Technology). Both put together account for 98 per cent of reservations. A comparison between main divisions 5 and 6 shows that books in 6 are in much more demand than those in 5. Books under main division 5 constituting 32 per cent of collection represent only about 11 per cent of reservations whereas books under main division 6 constituting 58 per cent of collection represent 87 per cent of reservations . The subject-wise analysis shows that the percentage of reservations in a subject correlates better with percentage of members than percentage of stock.

A further analysis of reservations for books in main division 6 presented in Table 8.6(b) reveals that all reservations fall under class number 62 (Engineering and Technology) and 67/68 (Manufactures). A great majority of members have specialisation as in class number 62 and the only other class which has very meagre representation of members is 67/68. Thus we can safely conclude that high demand for books naturally comes only in the areas of specialisation of users. It may be interesting to note that except one title all other titles in class number 62 were on Electronics and Electrical Engineering (621.3) and all the titles in class number 67/68 were on Data Processing, Computer Science, etc. (681.3). Incidentally these two are high technology, fast growing and all pervasive areas, specialised by more than 50 per cent of users.

Results and Observations

It is assumed in the study that, by and large, document reservation activity in the library reflect awareness and perseverance of users, overall demand for and use of library documents.

To summarise the results, while frequency distribution of documents against reservations gave a fairly smooth wide angled 'L' shaped curve with long tail, frequency distribution of users against reservations resulted in a typical asymptotic curve. Only about one-third of existing members used reservation facility. One-half of reserved documents had only one reservation during the year. Maximum reservations for books and reports were twenty and five respectively.

About 12 per cent of members contributed to 42 per cent of reservation transactions. One member has reserved almost one book per week and four others have reserved one book per fortnight. Average reservation per member is 4.25 and average reservation per document is 2.68. The percentage of collection subjected to reservation during the year was 5.48 in case of books and 1.74 in case of reports.

Maximum reservations were made for books acquired during the current year and most of the reservations were for books acquired during last 3-4 years with the exception of few fundamental classic books in the field. Though slight concentration of reservations on documents published during last 4-5 years is seen, age of document does not clearly correlate with reservation pattern. Reservation is spread over books published during last 15 years.

Most of the reserved reports are NASA reports which form more than 50 per cent of the present collection. While pure science books representing 32 per cent of collection cover only 11 per cent of reservations, Applied Science and Technology books representing 58 per cent of the collection cover 87 per cent of reservations. Reservations for books falling under other main divisions of UDC are almost negligible. Percentage of reservations in a subject correlates better with percentage of members in that subject than with percentage of stock.

All reservations for books under Applied Science and Technology are for books in the areas of Electronics, Electrical Engineering, Data Processing and Computer Science. In other words, most of the reservations were made in high technology and fast growing areas which represent major part of the existing collection and also the specialisation of majority of users.

As a feedback to lending system, it is obvious that more details, especially call number of document and staff number of user, of each and every reservation should be made available preferably as part of automated lending system. The study clearly points that latest documents in UDC class No. 6 need to be acquired quickly and in multiple copies. Lastly, in order to explore the possibility of adding additional copies of high demand books, a comprehensive list of 55 books with 10 or more reservations was made after scanning reservations made during 1980 and 1981. This list included most of the 40 high demand books analysed in this study. A qualitative scrutiny of the list by concerned specialists resulted in recommendation for additional copies of many of these books barring few text-books identified as having temporary demand.

It is quite natural to speculate that the attitude of the users about a book and their reservation behaviour are influenced by the background of those who suggested/indented the book to the library and by those (in the organisation) interested in it. A controlled experiment was carried out during October 1985 to see how far the decision of a user to reserve and use a book is influenced by the interest of other colleagues in it. A carefully selected 30 new books were added to the new arrivals display of the library as usual but with a tag on 16 of them with the names (and their sections/divisions/projects) of the persons who originally indented/suggested them. The same information about indentors of these books was also provided in the weekly list of additions, copies of which were distributed to all sections, divisions and projects just before the display started. The remaining 14 books fairly matching in subject and nature with the 16 books in the experimental group did not carry any such information about indentors either in the weekly list or on the display. After a week's display, there were 25 reservations for 16 books in the experimental group and 14 reservations for 14 books in control group. The average number of reservations per book during the week for books in the experimental group (where interest of other users/colleagues are publicised) was 1.56 as against 1.00 for books in the controlled group. Thus a 56 per cent extra reservations are attracted by making users aware of the fact that other users/colleagues are interested in them. However, there is not much difference in the attitude of the users about books suggested/indented by communication stars, supervisors and section/division heads compared to books suggested/indented by others.

CASE STUDY 13

CARD CATALOGUE CONSULTATION BEHAVIOUR

Introduction

Library catalogues are largely based on a series of assumptions, which are not normally questioned from the point of view of needs of users. The number of studies on use of catalogues reported in the profession has been considerably less compared to large number of document use studies. In a recent study (Drone, J.M., 1984, p. 253), it is estimated that more than fifty major catalogue use studies have been done since 1930. From India, not even few such studies are reported.

In the present day popular card catalogue system, the standard types of catalogues are assumed to be necessary based on traditional so called 'standard approaches' of users. A catalogue code is often meticulously followed for the choice of heading and description of the entry irrespective of type of library and nature of users. Descriptions such as place of publication and collation and entries such as added entry for editor of series are almost unnecessary. As such library catalogues have been silent victims of both over-enthusiastic and disbeliever of catalogue codes. In this connection "Cavan McCarthy (1975) has amusingly described the sanctification of cataloguing in some developing countries as a kind of handicraft art for art sake". In a recent study about the description of catalogue entry by different systems Gorman and Hotsinpiller came to "... the conclusion that, in many library environments, the conventional catalogue entry description is largely useless" (Gorman and Hotsinpiller, 1979, p. 521) and they advised the critics of conventional cataloguing to concentrate on real problems such as silly subject headings, unsought author headings and lack of reader orientation.

Library catalogue is only one of the many means by which users discover bibliographic references of their potential interest. So says Wilson "The catalogue of a particular library is just one more piece of bibliography among thousands of others" (Wilson 1983, p. 6). Analysing in a very unusual yet pragmatic way the objectives and functions of traditional catalogue, keeping in view the requirements of users and the implications on online catalogue, he traces the limitations of card catalogue from its basic stated objectives. He further says ". . . the unique contribution of the catalogue is after all . . . to help locate copies of books and texts that may have been learned about elsewhere" (Wilson 1983, p. 16).

The objective of the present study is to examine the habits and attitudes of users towards the card catalogue of the library by analysing how far the card catalogues of ISAC Library are used by scientists, engineers and other technical staff, which type of catalogue is consulted more frequently (and obviously which is less consulted) and to examine closely the purposes for which the card catalogues are used.

Card Catalogue of the Library

ISAC Library has a classified catalogue for books (about 14,000 in number) based on UDC and a report number catalogue for technical reports (about 6,000 in number) based on alphanumeric report numbers. A subject catalogue based on standard descriptors of NASA thesaurus, an author catalogue and a title catalogue are also maintained for the same books and reports in a combined way with colour codes to distinguish reports from books. A unit card method and AACR-1 for choice of heading and description are roughly followed with provision for analytical entries in selected cases.

Method

Observation and recording of user interactions with catalogues at central catalogue area of the library for about 24 hours randomly spread over a month during January 1985 has been done. Equal representation has been given for all timings of a working day (by dividing working day into eight hourly blocks) and to different days of the week. Thus a sample recording of card catalogue consultation during three working days (at 8 hours a working day) has been done. Each of the users who consulted the card catalogue during the sample period has been questioned immediately after his search by adopting 'critical incidence technique' to ascertain the purpose for which catalogue was consulted. During the period of the investigation, the library had about 1,150 members. The majority of the collection of the library is oriented towards little over 800 core technical staff members of the parent organisation.

Limitations

For clarity's sake we may note here that catalogues of standards and bound (back) volumes of journals kept separately are not covered in the study. Secondly, title catalogue has been developed recently, i.e., since last 3-4 years and hence it covers only about half of the books and reports available in the library. Searching strategies of users, difficulties faced, multifaced search, repeated search, consulting library staff, abandoning a search and results of search such as success/failure rate in retrieving a desired reference, description of the catalogue entry, the length of time spent at catalogue etc. are not examined in this study. Relating use of catalogue to user characteristics is not done. As such, to that extent this should not be thought of as a comprehensive catalogue use study. The study also excluded the use of card catalogue by library staff. Thus it is a simple exploratory catalogue use survey based on observation and interview methods to find out habits and attitudes of users about the library card catalogue. However, the total number of failures of catalogue search and retrieval of desired reference/document are found to be very few due to extensive personal reader assistance rendered by professional staff and the regular corrections carried out in catalogues as and when errors are detected. The two type of failures left out of the study are searches of users with incorrect and/or incomplete details of a document and searches for documents not available in the library. A large majority of former failures have led users to a second trial with either slightly modified author, title or subject heading with the same catalogue or another type of catalogue. As many as 35 users in the survey have attempted, as first trial to consult the author catalogue with incomplete and/or incorrect name of the author and later switched over to subject catalogue. Such unsuccessful first consultations on the author catalogue have been excluded from the data. In other words, data about one consultation of each user is recorded in this study. The data slightly underrepresent the use of catalogue due to obvious difficulties in recording the data.

Data

Table 8.7 gives a picture of consultation pattern of different types of catalogues during the survey period. Thirty two persons have consulted the card catalogue of the library on a working day. Out of total 96 consultations maximum of 52 searches or 54.29 per cent of total searches have been made on subject catalogue followed by 34 searches on author, 8 on title and 2 on report number catalogues.[1] No user has searched the classified catalogue.

TABLE 8.7: Number of Consultations of Catalogue during 24 Hours Sample Period

Catalogue Type	*Consultations*	
	No	*%*
Subject	52	54.2
Author	34	35.4
Title	8	8.3
Report Number	2	2.1
Classified	0	0.0
Total	96	100.0

The same data of card catalogue consultation is presented in Table 8.8 against eight hourly blocks of a working day.

TABLE 8.8: Catalogue Consultation at Different Hours of a Working Day

Hours	*Consultations in a 3-Hour Sample (for each hourly block)*	
	No	*%*
9—10	7	7.3
10—11	11	11.5
11—12	6	6.3
12—13	8	8.3
13—14	17	17.7
14—15	13	13.5
15—16	19	19.8
16—17	15	15.6
Total	96	100.0

By questioning users, different purposes of consulting card catalogue have been elicited. The purposes have been broadly divided into six groups and the same data is presented in Table 8.9.

TABLE 8.9: Purposes of Card Catalogue Consultation

Sl. No.	*Purpose of Consultation (Information Sought)*	*Consultations No*	*%*
1.	Call number to locate document	54	56.3
2.	Accession number to check its issue status in circulation system	24	25.0
3.	References on a topic/subject	9	9.4
4.	Report number to locate document	5	5.2
5.	References of an author	2	2.1
6.	More details of a document	2	2.1
	Total	96	100.1

The natural question which arises out of the inquiring into purposes of searching in card catalogue is that how these purposes are related to different types of catalogues consulted. So the data has been reformatted and presented in Table 8.10 to facilitate how purpose of catalogue consultation is distributed among different types of catalogues.

TABLE 8.10: Purposes of Card Catalogue Consultation *Versus* Type of Catalogue

Type of Catalogue	*Codes for Purposes of Consultation**						*Total*
	1	*2*	*3*	*4*	*5*	*6*	
Subject	30	9	9	3	0	1	52
Author	17	14	0	0	2	1	34
Title	7	1	0	0	0	0	8
Report Number	0	0	0	2	0	0	2
Classified	0	0	0	0	0	0	0
Total	54	24	9	5	2	2	96

Key: * For codes see Sl. No. in Table 8.9.

Discussion

A defined set of about 800 technical staff members of ISAC was earlier asked through a questionnaire (as part of a larger survey) about how they get relevant references of their requirements. Out of 535 responded, 367 (69%) have expressed that library catalogue is one of the sources for getting references, (two have not answered and three have become invalid responses) and the rest of 163 (31%) opined that they do not consider library catalogue as a source for references. As mentioned earlier, library catalogue supplements other sources or means to which users have access. "Based on a review of the literature Meyer summarised, most people avoid the catalogue when they can. Many particularly in public libraries, never use it at all" (Meyer, 1977, p. 69). It was also acknowledged by others that the non-use of card catalogues may not be limited to a particular type of library and it may be a universal phenomenon. Further some users find books by browsing the shelf and consulting the colleagues and library staff. As stated earlier, learning about references may be elsewhere than from catalogue alone. The relative importance of other sources for getting references/documents according to above questionnaire survey in terms of percentage of users depending as against not depending are: Consulting colleagues and fellow professionals (68%), Searching in library shelves (61%), Consulting experts in the field (51%), Citations in current reading materials (48%), Abstracting and indexing periodicals/journals (47%), References from bibliographies and review literature (45%), Consulting library staff (40%), and Current awareness bulletins of library (39%).

Looking at the data presented in the previous section, it is very difficult to say whether 32 consultations of card catalogue by users in a day is adequate or not. But the relative use of different types of catalogues has some lessons for the library. It is evident from Table 8.7 that none of the sample searches are made on classified catalogue. If so, one would wonder at the utility of the classified catalogue. Is it, just to satisfy the theory of cataloguing or cataloguer's or librarian's ego? Keeping in view the fact that the cost, time, and efforts needed to create and maintain classified catalogue are same as that of an author or a title catalogue, it is certain that its non-use does not justify its presence in a special library. In a slightly different context an experimental study showed that ". . . the card catalogue does not have a significant influence on circulation . . ." in a public library and hence the author concluded that "Serious consideration should be given to the amount of time and money expended on cataloguing and classification. Perhaps the less expensive bookstore model, where card catalogues are not available and where users locate materials in a browsing, is worthy of further study and exploration" (Meyer, 1977, p. 183).

The meagre use of the report number catalogue (vide Table 8.7) is partly due to the fact that reports themselves are very much less used than books (Sridhar, 1984). It is widely accepted that technical reports are more frequently known by their report numbers and as such reports are arranged alpha numerically by report number and the report number catalogue is the 'classified catalogue' for reports.

There is a heavy use of subject catalogue suggesting that users depend more on subject approach through natural language than other attributes. This implies that it is worth putting more efforts in subject indexing by the Library.

Table 8.8 has shown how on a typical day the library card catalogues are used. While first half of the day (first 4 hours till lunch) has resulted in one-third of the total use with maximum of 11 searches around morning tea break, in the second half of the day the rest of two-third of consultations are made with maximum of 19 searches around afternoon tea break. This typically matches with visit of users and in-house use pattern of the Library reported earlier (Sridhar, 1982) in Case Study 01.

The data on purposes for which users have consulted card catalogue has shown that a majority (54 out of 96) wanted to know the call numbers of books and another five wanted to know report numbers of reports in order to locate them on shelves. Twenty four of the 96 consultations are made to know the accession numbers of books and reports which is a prerequisite of the circulation system to know checked out status and to reserve a document checked out to other users or sent for binding. Nine searches were made to retrieve references on a particular topic or subject. These are quite comprehensive searches for retrieving multiple references. Lastly, two consultations each were made on catalogues to know documents of specific authors and to know more details of vaguely known documents. In other words, more than half of the use of card catalogue is to locate specific documents, another one-fourth of the use is towards aiding circulation system to find out the checked out status of documents and possibly to reserve if checked out, one-tenth of the use is for comprehensive subject search and the rest for miscellaneous purposes.

Some interesting observations can be made on the data at Table 8.10 wherein the purposes of consulting different types of catalogues have been presented. Nine comprehensive searches for retrieving references of a particular topic are naturally made on subject catalogue. Though classified catalogue could also be of some help for the purpose due to reasons mentioned earlier and also due to two stage search (involving an additional step of finding out class number) no user has consulted classified catalogue. Further two consultations of card catalogue to know documents of specific authors have also been naturally made on author catalogue. In two cases where more details of vaguely known documents are needed subject and author catalogues were consulted once each.

Out of five persons who consulted card catalogue to know report numbers of vaguely known reports three have searched in subject catalogue and two in report number catalogue. Surprisingly, users are not searching for reports in either author or title catalogue questioning thereby the need for author and title catalogues for reports. Of the 24 persons who sought acccssion number of documents, a majority (i.e., fourteen) of them knew names of authors. They are expected to be either repeated users of the documents or those who had correct references through other sources or both. Out of the rest of ten persons seeking accession number, nine searched in subject catalogue and one in title catalogue.

It is quite interesting to note that thirty out of 54 users who wanted to know location or call number of documents have searched in subject catalogue. Out of the rest, 17 used author catalogue and 7 used title catalogue to locate a document. In this process, the flexibility of the subject catalogue has helped majority to concretise vague assertions about documents. Though, no conclusion can be drawn about use of title catalogue (since it is incomplete) it is obvious from the limited data that title catalogue is more used than classified catalogue. On the other hand, author catalogue is approached more when the name of the author is fairly known.

Conclusion

This study clearly establishes the non-use of the classified catalogue of ISAC Library. Under the given circumstances, it may not be necessary for library to keep classified catalogue as well as shelf list. Before a final decision about classified catalogue is taken, it may be worth building, on experimental basis, an alphabetical part of the classified catalogue with class index entries to ascertain that classified catalogue is not needed at all. In case it is established, it may be worth dispensing with classified catalogue and any query to classified catalogue can be tackled with the help of subject catalogue and shelf list. The only difficulty would be in resj ect of compilation of quick and short reading lists based on classified catalogue.

On the other hand, subject catalogue is found to be heavily used and hence more attention and care in subject indexing is worth.

The present practice of providing access by first two authors in case of author catalogue and extent of utility of title catalogue may have to be examined further separately.

The card catalogue consultation at ISAC Library on a typical day follows a bimodal roughly symmetric distribution like user visit to library and in-house use of library documents reported earlier (Case Study 01).

One important result of the present study is that there is a need to change the arrangement of the charged tray (of circulation system) from accession number of the document to call number/report number. The purposes of card catalogue consultation revealed that one-fourth of the total consultations on catalogues are to know accession numbers of the books or reports. Further user is very much burdened by demanding him to know/use both call number/report number to locate a document and accession number to interact with circulation system.

By and large, subject, author and title catalogue were more used than report number and classified catalogues. Subject catalogue with its flexibility of multiple keywords and dictionary arrangement of natural language words has attracted more users seeking books and reports on a particular topic, those searching for call number or accession number of a known document and those seeking more details of vaguely known documents. The author and title catalogues are found unpopular (or unused) as far as technical reports are concerned and the practice of indexing reports by author and title may also be discontinued.

As pointed out earlier, further studies about various other assumptions of the card catalogues from the point of view of needs and approaches of users is necessary. Finally, many other interpretations and inferences of the above data are possible. As an example, one can see the obvious implications of this study on automating the catalogues of the library.

CASE STUDY 14

LIBRARY-USE INDEX AND LIBRARY-INTERACTION INDEX

Introduction

There have been many user and use studies of libraries but only a few have interpreted use data to infer information-behaviour of users and effectiveness of a library. Majority of use-studies have analysed what is used, frequency of use, lifetime and obsolescence rate of material used etc., with varied objectives. At the most, they were thought of as demand-studies. User-interactions with libraries did not receive enough attention in user-research. The critical incident data of specific demands made on typical libraries should reveal behavioural trends, and indicate their underlying motivation better than a theoretical and qualitative investigation (Slater and Fisher, 1969, p. 1). Lack of suitable and adequate standards make it all the more difficult to assess a library based on use statistics.

Theoretical background about use studies and results of some past use studies are presented in greater details in Chapter 2. This case study while consolidating the data from all studies of ISAC library use and user interactions (of the Indian space technologists) (some of which are already presented in detail in earlier case studies), analyses the data at broad level, builds two indexes (namely, library use index and library interaction index) from the data and finally correlated these index values with characteristics of the Indian space technologists.

Background of the Data

As part of a comprehensive information-behaviour study (Sridhar, 1987, 1995), the use of and user-interactions with the 'primary library' by the IST was carried out. Here, then, are presented the extracted quantitative data, at the broad level, about various interactions of the IST with ISAC Library and use of library documents in Table 8.11. The data, as explained below, are gathered partly based on observations for a sample period/ sample collection in a pre-planned way and partly extracted from the records available in the library:[2] (i) Procurement service availed by the IST, i.e., number of books and reports procured against request for the IST during 1982, (ii) The number of new books, reports and journals suggested by the IST during 1982 representing the current demand for new documents and as a measure of user participation in collection development (Case Study 05), (iii) The number of reservations made for books and reports at the circulation counter of the library by the IST during 1982 (Case Study 12), (iv) The number of delegated literature searches made by the library against request for the IST (July 1982-June 1983), (v) The number of short range reference queries answered and the number of times reader assistance was provided for difficult-to-locate type of documents to the IST during July 1982 and June 1983, (vi) The number of documents borrowed by the IST through inter-library loan service from other libraries during July 1982 and June 1983

TABLE 8.11: Frequency Distribution of Use of Library Documents and User-Interactions with the Library

Frequency	*Procurement Services*	*Suggestions for New Documents*	*Document Reservations*	*Literature Search Service*	*Reference Service*	*Inter-Library Loan Service*	*Reprographic Service (in 00's)*	*In-house Use/Library Visits*	*Borrowed Use as per 'Circulation Sample'*	*Borrowed Use as per 'Collection Sample'*
(1)	(2)	(3)	(4)	(5)	(6)	(7)	(8)	(9)	(10)	(11)
00	462	463	336	726	606	699	449*	369	248	98
01	52	74	86	4	80	22	93	124	54	82
02	37	26	72	3	29	8	35	67	48	86
03	11	17	34	1	9	3	20	50	64	72
04	12	14	20	0	4	0	12	28	39	51
05	7	4	21	0	1	1	8	23	33	49
06	11	3	15	0	0	0	1	29	35	55
07	7	3	14	0	1	0	3	24	23	25
08	3	2	13	0	0	1	3	10	24	34
09	2	3	5	0	0	0	4	13	22	21
10	2	3	7	0	1	0	3	7	31	17
11	1	4	4	0	0	0	3	8	18	20
12	4	4	4	0	0	0	1	10	24	12
13	2	2	3	0	0	0	0	3	14	18
14	1	1	1	0	0	0	0	0	22	10
15	3	4	1	0	0	0	3	1	11	6
16—20	2	3	9	0	0	0	4	4	45	24
21—25	2	0	2	0	0	0	2	1	19	11
26—30	2	0	2	0	0	0	2	0	7	4
31—35	1	0	0	0	0	0	2	1	2	2

(Contd.)

TABLE 8.11 (*Contd.*)

(1)	(2)	(3)	(4)	(5)	(6)	(7)	(8)	(9)	(10)	(11)
36—40	1	0	1	0	0	0	0	0	0	3
41—50	2	0	1	0	0	0	1	0	1	0
51—75	1	0	0	0	0	0	1	1	0	1
76—100	0	0	0	0	0	0	0	0	0	0
> 100	0	0	0	0	0	0	0	0	1	1
Not Applicable	177	176	146	75	73	72	157	33	22	106
Error	+2	+1	0	–2	–3	+1	0	+1	0	—
Total	807	807	807	807	807	807	807	807	807	807

Key: * One hundred and eleven users who consumed reprographic service upto 49 pages are treated as zero.

excluding the direct borrowing facility availed with the two major libraries in the city (i.e., IISc and NAL libraries), (vii) The reprographic service of the library availed by the IST in terms of number of pages of xerox copies of library-reading materials provided during 1982, (viii) The number of visits by the IST to the library reading hall and the seat occupancy over three months (16 March 1983-17 May 1983), recorded randomly at every two hours by giving due representation to different timings of a day and different days of a week as an indirect measure of in-house use of library documents (Case Study 01), (ix) Borrowed/ Circulation use of books, reports and journals by the IST based on three-month (July-September 1984) 'circulation sample' (Case Study 07), (x) Borrowed/circulation use of books and reports over ten months (January/March-October/December 1983, based on a 20 per cent 'collection sample' (Case Study 07) and borrowed as well as in-house use of two latest issues of each journal over three months (September 1983/December 1983-January/March 1984) (Case Study 10).

Certain limitations and background of the data in Table 8.11 need to be noted. The library has provided literature search and reprographic services to a limited number of users based on approval of authorised persons of the group. Though more of higher-status persons have availed of these services, everyone has access to such services with the approval of concerned. The procurement service and suggestions for new documents are two stages of the same interaction.[3] The only difference being that the procurement service emphasises the successful meeting of demands of the users and the suggestions for new documents do not speak of whether or not of such suggestions/requirements have been fulfilled. The frequency distribution of borrowed use of library documents as per 'circulation sample' and 'collection sample' are also close to each other which confirms the representativeness and the adequacy of the sample.

Analysis of the Data

It is clear from Table 8.11 that the number of space technologists who did not use/interact with library at all (i.e., zero scored persons) have ranged from 98 to 726 depending on the type of use and user-interaction. While the borrowed use of documents is not made by about 30 per cent of the space technologists, document reservation was not done by 50.8 per cent, and 47.7 per cent have not figured in the in-house use and seat occupancy data. Naturally, as many as 95.1 per cent have not used inter-library loan service, about 82 per cent have not availed of the reference service and 73 per cent have not suggested any documents and hence not directly availed of any procurement service. Further, except one or two, none of the users has availed of reference service and inter-library-library loan service more than five times. In case of borrowed use, in-house use, reprographic service, suggestions and procurement services intensive interactions up to 50 times by few users are observed.

Keeping in view the general drawback of user-studies that they ignore non-users, views of the non-users are elicited through questionnaire, interview and discussions. The major reasons, for not using library are: (i) Lack of time due to the time-bound nature of projects, (ii) The work does not demand a use of literature/documentary information on a regular basis, i.e., they rush to library either when they have to prepare reports or papers or prepare for departmental review for promotion or if they are undergoing part-time studies, (iii) The culture in general and the organisation culture in particular are not in favour of use of formal documentary information and therefore of the library, (iv) The attitude of an individual. For instance, one senior engineer frankly admits that he did not use libraries even for his postgraduate level studies.

Library-Use Index and Library-Interaction Index

In order to simplify the analysis of various types of use of library documents and various user-interactions with the library, two indexes have been developed based on individual frequencies[4] depicted in Table 8.11. The first index called the 'Library-use Index' is defined as the sum of (i) one-hundredth of total number of pages of xerox copies of library reading materials taken during a year, (ii) two times the number of documents borrowed through inter-library loan during a year, (iii) five times the number of visits paid to the library and reading seat occupied during the three months sample survey, and (iv) the mean borrowed/circulation use of books, reports and journals of the circulation and the collection samples. The second index called 'Library-Interaction Index' is defined as the sum of (i) the number of books and reports procured for a user, (ii) the number of new books, reports and journals suggested by a user, (iii) the number of reservations made for books and reports by a user, (iv) two times the number of literature searches provided to a user, and (v) the number of short range reference queries answered and reader assistance service availed by a user during one year duration.

Table 8.12 depicts the frequency distribution of 'library-use index' and 'library-interaction index' values for the population. It is clear from the table that as many as about 40 per cent of the population have no 'interactions' with the library and hence scored zero under 'library-interaction index'. However, the number of users who scored zero under 'library-use index', (i.e., the non-users of library documents) are just about 12 per cent. Further, nearly 28 per cent of the users have scored more than the mean value of 'library-use index' (19) as well as 'library-interaction index' (6). Both the distributions are quite skewed.

TABLE 8.12: Frequency Distribution of Library-Use Index and Library-Interaction Index

Frequency	*Library-Use Index*			*Library-Interaction Index*		
	No. of Users	*% of Users*	*Cumulative % of Users*	*No. of Users*	*% of Users*	*Cumulative % of Users*
00	75	11.9	11.9	253	40.2	40.2
01	51	8.1	20.1	64	10.2	50.4
02	38	6.1	26.1	70	11.1	61.5
03	25	4.0	30.1	46	7.3	68.8
04	27	4.3	34.4	30	4.8	73.6
05	25	4.0	38.4	18	2.9	76.5
06	24	3.8	42.2	13	2.1	78.6
07	21	3.3	45.5	13	2.1	80.7
08	20	3.2	48.7	15	2.4	83.1
09	21	3.3	52.0	11	1.7	84.8
10	13	2.1	54.1	13	2.1	86.9
11—15	58	9.2	63.3	24	3.8	90.7
16—20	60	9.6	72.9	23	3.7	94.4
21—25	35	5.6	78.5	8	1.3	95.7
26—30	24	3.8	82.3	6	1.0	96.7
31—40	43	6.8	89.1	9	1.4	98.1
41—50	22	3.5	92.6	7	1.1	99.2
51—75	37	5.9	98.5	5	0.8	100.0
76—100	7	1.1	99.6	1	0.2	100.2
101—150	2	0.3	99.9	0	0.0	100.2
Total	628	99.9	99.9	629	100.2	100.2

Note: 1. Some components of the indexes were not available/applicable in case of 179 and 178 cases respectively for library-use index and library-interaction index and hence all those cases have been excluded from the Table.

2. The mean values of library-use index and library-interaction index for population as a whole are respectively 19 and 6.

Correlation of Library-Use Index and Library-Interaction Index with Characteristics of the Indian Space Technologists

The results of statistical association/correlation tests of the six characteristics of the IST, namely, status, qualifications, nature of work, specialisation, experience and professional activities and achievements with 'library-use index' values and 'library-interaction index' values are shown in Table 8.13. One can see an almost perfect positive rank order correlation (r_s = 0.99) of status of the users (which supports the findings of Shaw, 1971, pp. 17, 20, 48-49) and a moderate positive correlation (r = 0.4) of professional activities and achievements with both the indexes (which supports the findings of Lufkin and Miller, 1966, p. 180 and Case Institute of Technology, 1960, p. 21). The qualifications, nature of work and specialisation of the users also exhibited statistically significant relation with both the indexes. However, experience has shown a slight negative correlation (r = –0.12) with library-use index supporting the findings of the Bath University Library (1971), Barkey (1966) and Ford (1977, p. 93) and contrary to that found by Scott (1960, p. 29), Lipetz (1970), Fearn and Melton (1969). There is no significant correlation of experience with library-interaction index.[5]

TABLE 8.13: Results of Association/Correlation Tests of Library-Use Index and Library-Interaction Index with User-Characteristics

User-Characteristics	*Library-Use Index*			*Library-Interaction Index*		
	$r_s/x^2/r$	*df*	*Tabulated Value of* x^2 *at* $p = 0.05$	$r_s/x^2/r$	*df*	*Tabulated Value of* x^2 *at* $p = 0.05$
Status (r_s)	0.99*	8	—	0.99*	8	—
Qualifications (x^2)	225.27*	16	26.296	146.86*	8	15.507
Nature of work (x^2)	84.67*	24	36.42	39.50*	12	21.026
Specialisation (x^2)	75.92*	20	31.41	30.53*	10	18.31
Experience (r)	–0.12*	290	—	–0.004	292	—
Professional Activities and Achievements Index (r)	0.38*	174	—	0.39*	178	—

Key: * The association/correlation is statistically significant at 0.05 significance level.

The mean score of 'library-use index' and 'library-interaction index' against status, qualifications, nature of work and specialisation of the users are shown, respectively, in Tables 8.14, 8.15, 8.16 and 8.17. As is evident from Table 8.14, persons in the top ranked status made 27 times more use of library documents and 132 times more interactions with the library than lowest status persons, confirming thereby the under-privileged nature of lower status technicians (Slater and Fisher, 1969, pp. 17-18 and 50). Table 8.15 reveals that the qualification of the user is linearly and positively related to 'library-use index' and 'library-interaction index'. Doctorates being intensive users of the library, used the library nearly seven times that of an average undergraduate, three and a half times that of an average diploma holder, one and a half times that of an average graduate and 1.14 times that of an average postgraduate in the population. As far as the number of interactions with the library are concerned, an average doctorate interacted more than 23 times that of an average undergraduate, nine times that of an average diploma holder, two and a half times that of an average graduate and 2.7 times that of an average postgraduate. This very much supports the findings of Scott (1960, p. 16), Lipetz (1970), Fearn and Melton (1969) and

TABLE 8.14: Status *Vs.* Library-Use Index and Library-Interaction Index

Status	*Library-Use Index (Mean)*	*Library-Interaction Index (Mean)*
A, B, C & D	26.12	15.85
E	22.22	8.63
F	22.84	7.38
G	21.09	5.95
H	17.16	3.96
I	14.92	3.93
J	9.60	1.21
K	3.86	0.27
L	2.80	0.68
M & N	0.96	0.12
Total	18.80	5.90

($r_s = 0.9879, fd = 8, p < 0.001$) ($r_s = 0.9879, df = 8, p < 0.001$)

Note: Status A to N are in the descending order of hierarchical rank.

TABLE 8.15: Qualifications *Vs.* Library-Use Index and Library-Interaction Index

	Qualifications	*Library-Use Index (Mean)*	*Library-Interaction Index (Mean)*
U	Undergraduate	4.9	0.9
D	Diploma Holder	9.7	2.3
B	Graduate	22.9	8.4
M	Postgraduate	29.5	7.8
P	Doctorate	33.5	21.0
	Total	19.0	6.1

($x^2 = 225.27, df = 16, p < 0.05$) ($x^2 = 146.86, df = 8, p < 0.05$)

Note: The actual contingency tables on which chi-square test is made are not shown. The ranges used in the contingency table for library-use index are 0—2, 3—10, 11—20, 21—30 and more than 30. In case of library-interaction index the ranges are 0—2, 3—10 and more than 10.

Shuchman (1981, p. 35). As it could be seen from Table 8.16 those who did planning and system analysis work have made maximum use of the library and interacted to the maximum with the library, followed by design and development personnel and managers and supervisors than others (who have made less than average use of and interactions with the Library). This contradicts the finding that managers and supervisors

TABLE 8.16: Nature of Work *Vs.* Library-Use Index and Library-Interaction Index

	Nature of Work	*Library-Use Index (Mean)*	*Library-Interaction Index (Mean)*
A	Management/Supervision	21.5	8.6
B	Planning/System analysis	30.8	9.0
C	Design & Development	24.6	8.4
P	Design, Development, Fabrication & Testing (C & D)	14.9	4.1
D	Fabrication & Testing	11.0	3.0
E	Operational activity	12.5	2.1
F	Others	9.6	4.3
	Total	18.9	5.9

($x^2 = 84.67, df = 24, p < 0.05$) ($x^2 = 39.50, df = 12, p < 0.05$)

Note: The contingency tables on which chi-square test is made are not shown. The ranges used in the contingency table for library-use index are 0—2, 3—10, 11—20, 21—30 and more than 30. In case of library-interaction index the ranges are 0—2, 3—10 and more than 10.

TABLE 8.17: Specialisation *Vs.* Library-Use Index and Library-Interaction Index

	Specialisation	*Library-Use Index (Mean)*	*Library-Interaction Index (Mean)*
A	Physics	34.5	12.7
C	Mathematics	31.8	8.4
E	Mechanical Engineering	10.7	2.8
F	Aeronautical & Structural Engineering	29.0	10.0
H	Electrical Engineering	15.1	3.8
I	Electronics	17.8	6.0
	Total	18.0	5.8

($x^2 = 75.92, df = 20, p < 0.05$) ($X^2 = 30.53, df = 10, p < 0.05$)

Note: The contingency tables on which chi-square test is made are not shown. The ranges used in contingency table for library-use index are 0—2, 3—10, 11—20, 21—30 and more than 30. In case of library-interaction index the ranges are 0—2, 3—10 and more than 10.

make maximum use of library (Scott, 1960, p. 28; Shuchman, 1981, p. 36; and Raitt, 1984, p. 278). Finally, from Table 8.17 one can see that physicists, mathematicians and aeronautical and structural engineers have made more use of and interaction with the library than all others (who have made less than average use of and interactions with the library). Though this supports the general finding of the earlier studies that scientists make more use of library than engineers, the aeronautical and structural engineers in the present study are exceptions.

Conclusion

Though there are bits and pieces of use studies of various types of libraries, comprehensive use study of a library is quite rare. Interpretation of results of use studies becomes very difficult due to lack of suitable norms and standards. Use of a library and user-interactions with the library can be measured in many ways. As a matter of fact use of library itself involves many components and user-interactions are innumerable resulting in voluminous literature on use studies. Hence developing suitable indexes of use of library and user-interactions with library becomes necessary to comprehend the data. Such indexes developed for each user in the population being served by the ISRO Satellite Centre Library has not only served as a neat and rational summarising devices in understanding information-behaviour of the Indian Space Technologists but also to assess and express the effectiveness of the Library.

NOTES AND REFERENCES

1. "Sidney Jackson in *Catalog Use Study* found that in one study of 7,000 large university users, about 52 per cent of users made subject searches and about 48 per cent made known-item searches", see *Quantitative Methods in Librarianship: Standards, Research, Management.* Proceedings and papers of a Institute held at the Ohio State University, 3-16 August 1969, ed. by Irene Braden and Alice S. Clark. Connecticut: Greenwood Press, 1972 (Contribution in Librarianship and Information Science, No. 4), Pt. 1 Group Discussion, pp. 24-25. Almost same percentage of searches made on subject catalogue is found in the present study.
2. Since data are collected in a series over a period of almost two years, care has been taken to exclude partially represented cases including those who resigned during the survey and those absenting for a long time either on leave or on tour. The data do not represent the complete use or interactions of all the users of the ISAC library as data pertaining to the users not covered in the defined population of the study are excluded.

3. The frequency distribution-pattern of procurement service and suggestions for new documents are almost identical.
4. The multiplying factors or weightages are arrived at based on the relative behaviour of frequency distribution shown in Table 8.11 and the observations such as average number of documents a user has consulted in the library per visit. For example, the frequency distribution of number of pages of xerox copies of reading materials taken is close to that of other types of use of library documents when reduced by a factor of 100 times. Borrowing a document through inter-library loan not only involved extra efforts on the part of the user, but also expected the user to wait for sometime, and the user made a fairly thorough use of such documents compared to documents of the primary library. Users are found to consult on an average 5 documents per visit/reading seat occupied in the survey. The interactions for literature search are more prolonged as compared to other interactions.
5. Women space technologists do not differ from men in making borrowed use of library documents but differed significantly in in-house use and interactions with the library as presented in Case Study 18 (Sridhar, 1987).

9

INFORMATION AND COMMUNICATION BEHAVIOUR

CASE STUDY 15

CO-AUTHORSHIP AND COLLABORATIVE RESEARCH

Introduction

The extent of multiple authorship or co-authorship in published papers depends on many factors such as nature of research, nature of financial support, interdisciplinary and heterogeneous nature of the subject, need for team work, informal networks among research workers and so on. It is often presumed that multiple authorship in a paper is a direct consequence of collaborative research of the authors in a group or team. Similarly, the productivity of research workers, especially those in the areas of social, behavioural and pure sciences, is assessed by the number of papers published in reputed journals. An attempt is made here to study the 'collaboration' in publishing and hence in research and the productivity (in terms of number of papers published) of scientists and engineers of ISRO Satellite Centre (ISAC), Bangalore. It is well known that space research is basically problem and mission-oriented research essentially depending on team work. Further, the space sciences in general and satellite technology in particular are highly interdisciplinary and heterogeneous subjects. Incidentally it may be noted that space research itself is much more than R&D, and unlike other R&Ds it does not end up with just publications or patents.

Methodology, Sample and Limitations

Simple statistical presentation and analysis of productivity and collaboration based on full as well as fractional authorship credits and identification of equivalence classes or non-intersecting clusters of collaborators are made for 224 papers of ISAC scientists and engineers. At least one of the authors in all these papers is from ISAC. For the purpose of this study 'co-authorship' and 'collaboration' are used almost interchangeably and a communication star' is one who co-authors or collaborates with more independent authors and author groups. Fractional authorship credit is based on the following method. Taking a multiple authorship paper as unity, credit to an individual co-author is given on *pro rata* basis depending on total number of authors. Thus if a paper is published by four authors each one is credited with 1/4 or 0.25 authorship and a summation of such credits is carried out for all papers in which he is a co-author.

The sample references of papers (i.e., 224) available for study is estimated to represent about 25 per cent of total papers published by ISAC scientists and engineers. Most of these papers are reprints of articles published in journals and conference proceedings. Very few of them are brief communications to journals, special lectures, radio talks and preprints. Technical reports are excluded from the study (About 200 to 400 internal technical reports are broughtout every year)..

The concept of 'productivity' is not only debatable but also of less relevance as far as space research is concerned. The sample papers under study are not systematically drawn but consist of whatever papers and references were made available by authors against request.

In this connection initially about 800 technical staff (other than medical, transport and library staff and helpers) of ISAC were contacted to know the number of papers published by them. The frequency distribution of 707 papers published by 489 persons who responded is shown in Table 9.1. Out of the 800 persons contacted nearly 400 were scientists and engineers and the rest lower level technical staff.

TABLE 9.1: Frequency Distribution of Number of Papers Published by ISAC Technical Personnel*

No. of Papers	*No. of Persons*	*% of Persons*	*Cumulative % of Persons*	*Total Papers*		
				No.	*%*	*Cumulative %*
(1)	(2)	(3)	(4)	(5)	(6)	(7)
0	382 @	78.12	78.12	00	0.00	0.00
1	35	7.16	85.28	35	4.95	4.95
2	14	2.86	88.14	28	3.96	8.91
3	9	1.84	89.98	27	3.82	12.73
4	9	1.84	91.82	36	5.09	17.82
5	4	0.82	92.64	20	2.83	20.65

(*Contd.*)

TABLE 9.1 (*Contd.*)

(1)	(2)	(3)	(4)	(5)	(6)	(7)
6	6	1.23	93.87	36	5.09	25.74
7	3	0.61	94.48	21	2.97	28.71
8	4	0.82	95.30	32	4.53	33.24
9	0	0.00	95.30	00	0.00	33.24
10	3	0.61	95.91	30	4.24	37.48
11	1	0.20	96.11	11	1.56	39.04
12	2	0.41	96.52	24	3.39	42.43
13	1	0.20	96.72	13	1.84	44.27
14	1	0.20	96.92	14	1.98	46.25
15	6	1.23	98.15	90	12.73	58.98
16	1	0.20	98.35	16	2.26	61.24
18	1	0.20	98.55	18	2.55	63.79
20	1	0.20	98.75	20	2.83	66.62
26	1	0.20	98.95	26	3.68	70.30
30	1	0.20	99.15	30	4.24	74.54
40	2	0.41	99.15	80	11.32	85.86
50	2	0.41	99.97	100	14.14	100.00
Total	489	99.97	99.97	707	100.00	100.00

Note: * This table is based on claims of the authors whereas subsequent tables are based on actual references and papers available in the library.

@ Almost all these persons are other than scientists and engineers (i.e., technical staff at lower levels).

Productivity

A chronological breakdown of papers published by Indian space technologists is depicted in Table 9.2. The productivity is more or less

TABLE 9.2: Productivity of Papers

Year	*No. of Papers*	*Percentage*	*Cumulative Percentage*
Up to 1971	71	31.7	31.7
1972	8	3.6	35.3
1973	11	4.9	40.2
1974	9	4.0	44.2
1975	16	7.1	51.3
1976	16	7.1	58.4
1977	7	3.1	61.5
1978	33	14.7	76.2
1979	10	4.5	80.7
1980	12	5.4	86.1
1981	13	5.8	91.9
1982	13	5.8	97.7
No date	5	2.2	99.9
Total	224	99.9	99.9

uniform except for the year 1978 and to some extent for 1975 and 1976. These were years which followed the completion of major projects and there is a weak indication that slightly more papers are published in such years.

Tables 9.3 and 9.4 present frequency distribution of productivity of ISAC authors with full credit and co-authors with fractional credit respectively. It may be noted here that 224 papers are authored by 170 different persons, of which 107 are from ISAC. Hence overall average number of papers per author is 1.3. Since there are about 400 scientists and engineers at ISAC, only about one-fourth of them have ever published papers. The average number of authors per paper (or 'multiplicity index') is 3.17 and the inverse of which (i.e., 'productivity ratio') is 0.32. This trend and co-authorship measures remained same in the papers published in in-house technical journal, *Journal of Spacecraft Technology*, published since 1991.

TABLE 9.3: Frequency Distribution of Productivity (for ISAC authors only)*

No. of Papers (i.e., Productivity)	*No. of Authors*	*% of Authors*	*Cumulative % of Authors*	*Total Papers at Credit (or Authorship)*	*% of Papers at Credit*	*Cumulative % of Papers at Credit*
1	73	68.2	68.2	73	14.3	14.3
2	10	9.3	77.5	20	3.9	18.2
3	5	4.7	82.2	15	2.9	21.1
4	2	1.9	84.1	8	1.6	22.7
5	1	0.9	85.0	5	1.0	23.7
6	1	0.9	85.9	6	1.2	24.9
7	1	0.9	86.8	7	1.4	26.3
8	1	0.9	87.7	8	1.6	27.9
9	1	0.9	88.6	9	1.8	29.7
10	1	0.9	89.5	10	2.0	31.7
11	1	0.9	90.4	11	2.2	33.9
12	0	0.0	90.4	0	0.0	33.9
13	3	2.8	93.2	39	7.6	41.5
14	2	1.9	95.1	28	5.5	47.0
15	2	1.9	97.0	30	5.9	52.9
29	1	0.9	97.9	29	5.7	58.6
64	1	0.9	98.8	64	12.6	71.2
146	1	0.9	99.7	146	28.6	99.8
Total	107	99.7	99.7	510	99.8	99.8

Note: * All ISAC authors are given full credit in this table even if the paper was co-authored. See Table 9.4 for corresponding table in which fractional credits based on number of co-authors are recorded.

Table 9.3 clearly indicates an inverse relationship between productivity and number of authors. For example, 9.3 per cent of highly productive authors have published 68.0 per cent of total papers. Similarly, 82.2 per cent of least productive authors have contributed only 21 per cent of total papers. Also we may note that the maximum productivity of 146 papers or 28.6 per cent of total papers is from one author and the second and third highest, respectively, have 64 and 29 papers to their credit. Further, the majority of authors (i.e., 68.2%) have only one paper to their credit.

It is amply clear from Table 9.4 that due to high collaboration in publications, the total authorship of 510 in Table 9.2 comes down to 213 in Table 9.4 when fractional authorship credit is assigned to co-authors. The productivity of individual authors in this table ranges from 0.1 to 60. Interestingly, 5 highly productive authors have contributed 50 per cent of total papers and 85 least productive authors have contributed 31.5 per cent of total papers. This once again reemphasises the inverse relationship.

TABLE 9.4: Frequency Distribution of Productivity with Fractional Authorship Credit (for ISAC authors only)

No. of Papers (i.e., Productivity Range)	*No. of Authors*	*% of Authors*	*Cumulative % of Authors*	*Total Papers at Credit/ Authorship based on Mean*	*% of Papers at Credit*	*Cumulative % of Papers at Credit*
0.00—0.25	62	57.9	57.9	10.85	5.1	5.1
0.25—0.50	13	12.2	70.1	48.75	22.9	28.0
0.50—1.00	10	9.4	79.5	7.50	3.5	31.5
1—2	9	8.4	87.9	13.50	6.3	37.8
2—3	4	3.7	91.6	10.00	4.7	42.5
3—4	2	1.7	93.3	7.00	3.3	45.8
4—5	2	1.7	95.0	9.00	4.2	50.0
5—6	0	0.0	95.0	0.00	0.0	50.0
6—7	1	0.9	95.9	6.50	3.1	53.1
7—8	1	0.9	96.8	7.50	3.5	56.6
8—9	1	0.9	97.7	8.50	4.0	60.6
24—25	1	0.9	98.6	24.50	11.5	72.1
59—60	1	0.9	99.5	59.50	27.9	100.0
Total	107	99.5	99.5	213.10	100.0	100.0

Collaboration

Table 9.5 depicts the extent of collaboration of ISAC authors with others. About 37 per cent of co-authors of these 224 papers are outsiders. Collaboration with scientists and engineers of other centres and projects of the parent organisation (i.e., ISRO—Indian Space Research Organisation) is only 6 per cent whereas the collaboration with authors from outside ISRO is about 31 per cent and it is certainly quite considerable from the angle of study of informal communication networks. However, by deleting 71 papers published previously to the establishment of ISAC (i.e., up to 1971) the number of outside collaborators comes down to 27 (i.e., 19.4%). Similarly, the number of co-authors from other centres and projects of ISRO comes down to 7 and total ISAC authors themselves become 105. A cursory look at the outside collaborators reveals that a good majority of them are counterparts in other organisations, one-time colleagues and research guides of ISAC authors. It is not surprising that an almost negligible proportion of the outside collaborators are foreign nationals.

TABLE 9.5: Extent of Collaboration with Outsiders

Author Affiliation	*No.*	*%*
ISAC	107	63
Other Centres and Projects of ISRO	10	6
Outside ISRO	53	31
Total	170	100

Table 9.6 presents frequency distribution of collaboration or multiple authorship. Assuming that collaboration in publishing is a result of collaborative research, the data in Table 9.6 indicate the small size of research teams. The following observations can be made on the data. Only about 19 per cent of the papers are single authored. This comes down considerably if we exclude brief communications, special lectures, radio talks and the like which are mostly single authored papers. Thus more than 80 per cent of papers have two or more authors. The maximum number of authors per paper is ten. Three-authored papers are the most frequent (i.e., 53). About 46.5 per cent of papers are either two or three authored papers. The number of papers steadily decreases as number of authors per paper increases. By and large, the data indicate high collaboration in space research confirming the fact that team work in time-bound projects is one of the important features of space research.

Lastly, when the broad specialisation or subject backgrounds of co-authors of the individual papers are examined, it is noticed that most of the specialised papers have been authored by persons with the same specialisation and hence a sort of division of work took place among specialists. On the other hand, system level papers are authored by persons with different subject backgrounds.

TABLE 9.6: Frequency Distribution of Collaboration

No. of Authors per Paper	*No. of Papers*	*% of Total Papers*	*Cumulative % of Total Papers*	*Total Author-ships*	*% of Author-ships*	*Cumulative % of Authorships*
1	43	19.2	19.2	43	6.0	6.0
2	51	22.8	42.0	102	14.3	20.3
3	53	23.7	65.7	159	22.4	42.7
4	30	13.4	79.1	120	16.9	59.6
5	19	8.5	87.6	95	13.4	73.0
6	15	6.7	94.3	90	12.7	85.7
7	6	2.7	97.0	42	5.9	91.6
8	4	1.8	98.8	32	4.5	96.1
9	2	0.9	99.7	18	2.5	98.6
10	1	0.4	100.1	10	1.4	100.0
Total	224	100.1	100.1	711	100.0	100.0

Informal Communication Networks

One of the important objectives of a study of collaborative research is identification of informal communication networks, communication stars among research workers and size, nature and structure of informal groups. In order to determine the non-intersecting clusters or equivalence classes of collaborators the relationship 'collaborator' or 'co-author' is taken as an equivalence relationship. If A and B are co-authors in at least one of the papers under study the relation 'A co-authored or collaborated with B' holds good.[1] By applying the 'co-author' relationship successively for 107 ISAC authors twelve mutually exclusive groups of authors have been identified. The sizes of these groups with their group productivities are presented in Table 9.7.

The first group consists of persons with the broad subject background of physics including astrophysics, electronics, communication engineering, computer science, etc. The second group also consists of persons with almost similar specialisations except astronomy and astrophysics. However, this group has specialists from mechanical engineering, electrical engineering and control engineering also. Most of the other groups have specialists from one or two areas.

TABLE 9.7: Equivalence Classes or Non-intersecting Clusters of Collaborators (for ISAC authors only)

Group No.	*Total Authors*		*Productivity with Full Authorship*			*Productivity with Fractional Authorship*		
	No.	*%*	*No.*	*%*	*Cumulative %*	*No.*	*%*	*Cumulative %*
1	41	38.3	352	69.0	69.0	118.13	67.8	67.8
2	29	27.1	119	23.3	92.3	45.97	26.5	94.3
3	9	8.4	9	1.8	94.1	1.00	00.6	94.9
4	8	7.5	8	1.6	95.7	1.00	00.5	95.4
5	6	5.6	6	1.2	96.9	1.00	00.6	96.0
6	5	4.7	6	1.2	98.1	2.00	01.2	91.2
7	2	1.9	2	0.4	98.5	1.00	00.6	97.8
8	2	1.9	3	0.6	99.1	1.50	00.9	98.7
9	2	1.9	2	0.4	99.5	0.22	00.1	98.8
10	1	0.9	1	0.2	99.7	1.00	00.6	99.4
11	1	0.9	1	0.2	99.9	1.00	00.6	100.0
12	1	0.9	1	0.2	100.1	1.00	00.6	100.6
Total	107	100.0	510	100.1	100.1	174.32	100.6	100.6

It is clear from the table that there are two large groups and all the remaining groups are smaller ones with number of members ranging from 1 to 9. However, the total group productivity (based on fractional authorship credit) of any small group does not exceed one paper (except group No. 6 which has a productivity of two papers). In other words, almost all highly productive authors are embraced in two large groups. Hence from the point of view of informal communication these two groups deserve more attention than others. It is expected that the members of these groups have access to a wider variety of information through informal networks than others. A further observation of these groups has indicated the following. Highly productive authors have acted as interlinking nodal points in the large groups. Hence most of highly productive authors in these two large groups could be considered as communication stars. There appears to be considerable horizontal or interdivision/interproject collaboration in research and publications. In other words, the members of these groups cut across the formal organisation barriers such as division, section and project.

Lastly, the presentation in Table 9.8 tries to probe, from different angles, the collaboration of ten highly productive authors. As could be seen from the table only four of them have written papers without collaborators (see Column 4). Average productivities of the first two

TABLE 9.8: Collaboration of Highly Productive Authors

Sl. No.	Productivity (Authorship)					Gross No. of Collaborators*	Net No. of Collaborators**	Average Productivity of Authors in the Group		Av. No. of Authors per Paper col (7)/ col (6)	Average Collaboratorship per Collaborator col (7)/ col (8)
	With fractional Credit	With Full Credit	Single Authored Papers	Fractional Credit	Papers with 2 or more Authors			Fractional Credit col (5)/ col (8)	Full Credit col (6)/ col (8)		
(1)	(2)	(3)	(4)	(5)	(6)	(7)	(8)	(9)	(10)	(11)	(12)
1	59.71	146	20	39.71	126	343	41	0.95	3.00	2.72	8.37
2	24.58	64	8	16.50	56	168	30	0.53	1.81	3.00	5.60
3	6.14	29	0	6.14	29	171	25	0.24	1.12	5.90	6.84
4	3.29	15	0	3.29	15	56	8	0.37	1.67	3.73	7.00
5	4.98	15	0	4.98	15	43	11	0.42	1.25	2.87	3.91
6	2.07	14	0	2.07	14	57	16	0.16	0.82	4.07	3.56
7	4.03	14	0	4.03	14	40	12	0.29	1.08	2.86	3.33
8	7.05	13	4	3.05	9	16	11	0.29	0.75	1.78	1.45
9	2.95	13	0	2.95	13	49	11	0.25	1.08	3.77	4.45
10	8.83	13	6	2.83	7	12	7	0.35	0.88	1.71	1.71
Mean											
Total	124.98	336	38	86.98	298	955	172	0.51	1.73	3.20	5.55

Note: * Total number of co-authors in all the papers in which the given person is also an author. This includes repetitive co-authorship.

** This ignores repetitive co-authorship and presents number of individuals co-authored with the given person.

authors (see Columns 9 and 10) are more than the mean productivity. On the other hand the average number of authors per paper (Column 11) is more than mean in case of 3rd, 4th, 6th, and 9th authors. Also the average collaboratorship per collaborator (i.e., Column 12) is very high in case of first-four authors indicating thereby more intensive informal exchange of information by these authors with other authors. It is the highly productive authors who are also communication stars playing a key role. The average productivity per author in the group, average number of authors per group and finally average collaboratorship per collaborator heavily depended on the contribution of these highly productive communication stars. Thus any information input to the groups/networks at these nodal points (i.e., communication stars) is expected to flow faster and disseminate more widely depending on the above indexes than other points in the communication networks.

Conclusion

In summary, we may note that slightly more papers are published in the year following the completion of major projects, only about one-fourth of scientists and engineers at ISAC have the habit of writing and publishing papers, there appears to be an inverse relationship between productivity and the number of authors per paper as less than 10 per cent of authors have published almost 60 per cent of papers and 82 per cent of authors have contributed only 21 per cent of total papers, majority of authors (i.e., 68%) have only one paper to their credit, one author published 146 papers or 28.6 per cent of total papers and five highly productive authors have contributed more than 50 per cent of total papers.

Further, more than 80 per cent of papers have two or more authors (Degree of collaboration is 0.81). There appears to be high collaboration in publishing papers implying high collaboration in space research. Collaboration with authors from outside ISRO is also considerable (i.e., 31%).

By and large, the study has indicated a low productivity and high collaboration and co-authorship pattern among space technologists. It is also observed that the productivity of papers by scientists is much more than that of engineers. Some of the possible reasons for low productivity are as follows. As mentioned earlier the nature of the organisation is more than just R&D and the emphasis in the objective is to produce workable satellites in the given time rather than working papers or establishing patents. Among the authors analysed, a good majority of highly productive authors are scientists. Though the centre has more engineers than scientists the number of papers published by scientists is greater than those published by engineers. It is commonly accepted that scientists are more attuned to publishing papers than engineers and the data support this common belief. Further, a considerable number of scientists and engineers in the centre are young and less experienced. They may need a few years of fruitful experience after settling on the job before starting to write papers. On the other hand, high collaboration in publishing papers is clearly the result of the mission-oriented nature of the organisation necessitating high collaboration in work.

The study has identified two large non-intersecting informal communication groups with 65 per cent of authors contributing 94 per cent of papers. Many highly productive authors have been identified as communication stars. Lastly, there appears to be considerable horizontal collaboration in publishing papers.

A further detailed study of these and other informal communication groups and channels with a larger data base and also by other methods is presented in Case Study 19.

CASE STUDY 16

CITING PATTERNS

Introduction

The principle of "publish or perish" is, perhaps, more applicable to academics and scientists, particularly pure scientists and social scientists, than to engineers and technologists. The practice of assessing the productivity and performance of applied scientists, engineers and technologists based on the number of papers published in reputed journals could be disastrous, although the same practice is extensively followed in the pure science and social science areas. However, engineers and technologists do interact with formal communication channels by publishing papers in journals and presenting papers in conferences apart from using many types of formal documents. This is a cyclical process of production, transference and consumption of information but there is a degree of difference among these activities. One of the methods of knowing what information a research worker uses seriously is to study citation in his articles or papers. This study tries to probe the publishing and citing features or patterns of scientists and engineers of ISRO Satellite Centre (ISAC), Bangalore.

Methodology, Sample and Limitations

A statistical presentation and analysis of "productivity" in terms of the number of papers published by scientists and engineers; sources where published and sources from which cited including the ratio of foreign and Indian sources; frequency distribution of publishing in and citing from journals and conference proceedings; frequency distribution of the number of references cited and number of self-citations; comparison of citing and publishing in different journals and also with use in the case of most frequently published as well as cited journals, are made. Out of 224 total available references (in which at least one of the authors is from ISAC), 148 papers have been published between 1972 and 1982 and the same years are covered in this study. This sample is estimated to represent more than 25 per cent of the total papers published during the period covered. As will be shown in one of the tables later, most of these papers are journal articles and conference papers. Very few of them are preprints, lecture notes and brief communications to journals. Thus the word "publishing" in this study includes presenting a paper in conference, preprints and lecture notes. Thus, technical reports, books, monographs, theses or dissertations and private communications are excluded from the study. However, while analysing citations all such forms are considered. As mentioned earlier the concept of productivity based on the number of papers published is not only debatable but also of less relevance in space research. Further, the sample references or papers under study are not systematically drawn but consist of all those references and papers made available by authors at request.

Lastly, although citation analysis has been extensively used as "an adjunct of the peer review process" in assessing the scientific productivity, and many other related purposes, there is a considerable amount of for and against arguments about the validity of this tool.[2]

Productivity

A chronological breakup of the number of papers published between 1972 and 1982 is presented in Table 9.9. The productivity is more or less uniform except for the year 1978 and to some extent 1975 and 1976. There is a weak indication that slightly more number of papers are published in the year following the year of completion of major projects of the organisation.

Sources in which Published and from where Cited

Table 9.10 depicts various sources in which 148 papers are published and sources from which 713 citations are made by space technologists. The majority of papers (i.e., 57%) are published in 31 journals. Conference papers and journal articles put together constitute more than 90 per cent of sample papers. Even the majority of citations (i.e., 60%) are from 90 journals. The next highest citations are from books and monographs (14%), reports (10%) and conference papers (9%). These sources put together constitute nearly 95 per cent of citations.[3]

TABLE 9.9: Productivity of Papers

Year	*No. of Papers*	*Percentage*	*Cumulative Percentage*
1972	8	5.4	5.4
1973	11	7.4	12.8
1974	9	6.1	18.9
1975	16	10.8	29.7
1976	16	10.8	40.5
1977	7	4.7	45.2
1978	33	22.3	67.5
1979	10	6.8	74.3
1980	12	8.1	82.4
1981	13	8.8	91.2
1982	13	8.8	100.0
Total	148	100.0	100.0

TABLE 9.10: Sources in which Published and from where Cited (No. of journals in brackets)

Sources	*Published*		*Cited*	
	No.	*%*	*No.*	*%*
Journal articles	85 (31)	57.4	432 (90)	60.6
Books and monographs	NA	NA	103	14.4
Reports*	NA	NA	72	10.1
Conference papers	49	33.1	69	9.7
Theses and dissertations	NA	NA	16	2.2
Preprints	5	3.4	14	2.0
Lecture notes	9	6.1	2	0.3
Standards	NA	NA	1	0.1
Product catalogues	NA	NA	1	0.1
Private communication	NA	NA	3	0.4
Total	148	100.0	713	99.9

Key: NA—Not available; *—About 200 to 400 internal reports are broughtout every year.

By comparing the publishing and citing sources in the table we can see that the percentage of conference papers brought out is more than that cited, and the percentage of journal articles published and cited are almost the same. Thus, it may be concluded that space technologists have a flair for oral conference presentation rather than archival publication such as a journal article (assuming that all other factors remain the same). Though the exact data about the publication of books and reports is not presented, it is observed that the percentage of reports brought out is more than that cited and the percentage of books cited is much more than the percentage of books published. A further detailed analysis of publishing in and citing from journals is presented in a later section.

Table 9.11 presents a clear and glaring difference between Indian and foreign sources. If 46 per cent of papers are published in Indian journals only 3 per cent of journal articles cited are of Indian origin. Compared to journal articles, a greater number (67%) of conference papers are presented at foreign and international conferences. By and large both published and cited sources are slanted towards foreign sources, a trend that is more significant in the citations to reports and journal articles. Hence it can be safely said that, as one might expect, Indian journals serve more as publishing outlets to space technologists than sources for citing. In other words, as a corollary we can say that journals which are used for publishing are less cited (excepting self-cited journal articles).

TABLE 9.11: Indian Sources *Vs.* Foreign Sources (No. of journals in brackets)

Sources	*Published*				*Cited*			
	Indian		*Foreign*		*Indian*		*Foreign*	
	No.	*%*	*No.*	*%*	*No.*	*%*	*No.*	*%*
Journal articles	39 (10)	45.9*	46 (21)	54.1*	14 (7)	3.2	418 (83)	96.8
Conference papers	16	32.7	33	67.3	NA†		NA†	
Reports	NA‡		NA‡		15	20.8	57	79.2

Note: * Another recent survey revealed that academics and scientists in India publish, respectively, 57.7 per cent and 41.1 per cent of their articles in Indian journals. See V. Bhavani (1982). "Publication Activities of Indian Scientists a Survey", *Library Science Slan. Doc.* 19(1), 54-68.

† The majority of the conference papers are presented either in foreign conferences or in international conferences.

‡ Obviously all the reports published are Indian.

Publishing and Citing Patterns

To get an overall picture of publishing pattern, as mentioned in previous case study, all the 800 technical staff (other than medical, transport and library staff and helpers) were requested to provide the number of papers published by them. The frequency distribution of 707 papers published by the 489 persons who responded is once again presented in Table 9.12. Out of the 800 persons contacted about 400 were scientists and engineers and the remaining were lower level technical staff.

TABLE 9.12: Frequency Distribution of the Number of Papers Published by ISAC Technical Personnel*

No. of Papers	*No. of Persons*	*Percentage of Persons*	*Cumulative % of Persons*	*Total Papers*		
				No.	*%*	*Cumulative %*
0	382†	78.12	78.12	0	0.00	0.00
1	35	7.16	85.28	35	4.95	4.95
2	14	2.86	88.14	28	3.96	8.91
3	9	1.84	89.98	27	3.82	12.73
4	9	1.84	91.82	36	5.09	17.82
5	4	0.82	92.64	20	2.83	20.65
6	6	1.23	93.87	36	5.09	25.74
7	3	0.61	94.48	21	2.97	28.71
8	4	0.82	95.30	32	4.53	33.24
9	0	0.00	95.30	0	0.00	33.24
10	3	0.61	95.91	30	4.24	37.48
11	1	0.20	96.11	11	1.56	39.04
12	2	0.41	96.52	24	3.39	42.43
13	1	0.20	96.72	13	1.84	44.27
14	1	0.20	96.92	14	1.98	46.25
15	6	1.23	98.15	90	12.73	58.98
16	1	0.20	98.35	16	2.26	61.24
18	1	0.20	98.55	18	2.55	63.79
20	1	0.20	98.75	20	2.83	66.62
26	1	0.20	98.95	26	3.68	70.30
30	1	0.20	99.15	30	4.24	74.54
40	2	0.41	99.15	80	11.32	85.86
50	2	0.41	99.97	100	14.14	,100.00
Total	489	99.97	99.97	707	100.00	100.00

Note: * This table is based on claims of the authors whereas subsequent tables are based on actual references and papers available in the library.

† Almost all of these persons are other than scientists and engineers (i.e., technical staff at lower levels).

At the macro level, out of about 400 scientists and engineers in the centre only 107 (i.e., a little over 25%) have ever published a paper. This percentage may marginally increase when the entire population of papers is studied. As mentioned earlier, 224 references to papers of 107 ISAC authors were initially available for this study. This amounts to an average of 2.09 papers per author. As far as a citing pattern is concerned, the average number of citations per paper is 7.35 (i.e., 713 ÷ 97) and the percentage of self-citation is 16.4 (i.e., {117 ÷ 713} × 100).

Table 9.13 presents frequency distribution of number of references cited. Nearly 25 per cent of the papers studied have no references cited.[4] It is seen from the table that journal articles carry more references (with a maximum of 51 and an average of 8.9 references per paper)[5] than conference papers which mostly (except three papers) have less than five references with an average of 4.2 references per paper. In the frequency distribution one can see that 24 journal articles (i.e., one-third of total journal articles) with 10 or more references cite approximately 484 references (i.e., three-quarters of total references). Similarly, one-fifth of the conference papers cite almost three-quarters of total references.

It may be noted here that most of the conference papers and proceedings cited are from AIAA, IEEE, COSPAR and other foreign and international seminars on space technology. More than 90 per cent of the foreign reports cited are either NASA or ESA reports. Preprints are cited by authors of astronomy and astrophysics articles only. This confirms the view that preprints distribution activity is very high in astronomy and astrophysics area.

The extent of self-citation by space technologists is presented in the frequency distribution Table 9.14. It may be noticed that as many as 35 per cent of papers have one or more self-citations. The average self-citation among these papers is 3.44. However, about 15 per cent of total papers (or 44% of papers having self-citations) have only one self-citation.

Although detailed analysis is not carried out, the following personal informal observations are interesting. Firstly, all the 15 Indian reports cited (out of total 72 citations of reports) are internal reports and most of them are self-citations. Secondly, most of the theses cited are self-citations. Lastly, apart from self-citations, there are a considerable number of citations of papers by other ISAC authors.

Publishing in and Citing from Journals

A comparison of the frequency distribution of the number of papers published in journals with the number of papers cited from journals is

TABLE 9.13: Frequency Distribution of Number of References Cited

No. of References Cited	*No. of Journal Articles*	*Total References Cited*	*No. of Conference Papers*	*Total References Cited*	*Other Documents*	*Total References Cited*	*Total No. of Documents*	*Total References Cited from all Types of Documents*
0	11	0	6	0	7	0	24	0
1	7	7	1	1	0	0	8	8
2	5	10	0	0	0	0	5	10
3	4	12	3	9	0	0	7	21
4	6	24	2	8	0	0	8	32
5	2	10	0	0	0	0	2	10
6	3	18	0	0	1	6	4	24
7	6	42	0	0	0	0	6	42
8	2	16	0	0	0	0	2	16
9	2	18	1	9	0	0	3	27
10	3	20	0	0	0	0	3	30
11—15	11	143*	1	13	1	13	13	169
16—20	3	54*	0	0	0	0	3	54
21—25	1	23*	1	23	0	0	2	46
26 and above	6	234*	0	0	1	39	7	273
Total	72	641	15	63	10	58	97	762

Note: * Worked out based on mean of the range.

TABLE 9.14: Frequency Distribution of Self-citation

No. of Self-citations	Journal Articles		Conference Papers		Others		Total	
	No. of Articles	Total Self-Citations	No. of Papers	Total Self-Citations	No. of Documents	Total Self-Citations	No. of Papers or Documents	Total Self-Citations
0	42	0	12	0	9	0	63	0
1	12	12	3	3	0	0	15	15
2	7	14	0	0	0	0	7	14
3	6	18	0	0	0	0	6	18
4	0	0	0	0	0	0	0	0
5	2	10	0	0	0	0	2	10
6	0	0	0	0	0	0	0	0
7	2	14	0	0	0	0	2	14
8	0	0	0	0	0	0	0	0
9	1	9	0	0	0	0	1	9
37	0	0	0	0	1	37	1	37
Total	72	77	15	3	10	37	97	117

shown in Table 9.15. Out of 31 journals used for publishing articles and 90 journals from which citations are made 23 are common. In other words, nearly 75 per cent of journals used for publishing papers were also used for citing references. As can be seen from the table the number of papers published in journals varies from one to seven. However, there is one exceptional journal which has accommodated 16 articles or papers of Indian space technologists. On the other hand, the number of papers cited from a journal ranges from one to 59. Eight journals (or a little over 25 per cent of the journals) published 53 papers (or more than 62% of the papers) of Indian space technologists. Similarly 10 journals (accounting for a little over 21% of journals) were in all cited 259 times (or nearly 60% of references are from these 10 journals). These most frequently used journals for publishing as well as citing are analysed further in the next section.

The pattern of local and foreign journals used for publishing and citing is depicted in Table 9.16. Out of 98 journals used by space technologists for publishing and for citing, 11 are of Indian origin. As revealed earlier, the contrasting picture of "high publishing and low citing" profile in Indian journals is clear from the fact that while nearly 46 per cent of papers are published in Indian journals, hardly 4 per cent of the references cited are from Indian journals. Only one Indian journal is cited where no paper from an Indian space technologist is published.

TABLE 9.15: Frequency Distribution of Number of Papers Published in and Cited from Journals

No. of Papers	*Published*				*Cited*			
	Journals		*Total Papers*		*Journals*		*Total Papers*	
	No.	*%*	*No.*	*%*	*No.*	*%*	*No.*	*%*
1	14	45.2	14	16.5	35	38.9	35	8.1
2	9	29.0	18	20.2	22	24.4	44	10.2
3	2	6.5	6	7.1	7	7.8	21	4.9
4	0	0.0	0	0.0	10	11.1	40	9.3
5	1	3.2	5	5.9	3	3.3	15	3.5
6	2	6.5	12	14.1	3	3.1	18	4.2
7	2	6.5	14	16.5	1	1.1	7	1.6
8	0	0.0	0	0.0	1	1.1	8	1.9
11	0	0.0	0	0.0	1	1.1	11	2.5
14	0	0.0	0	0.0	1	1.1	14	3.2
16	1	3.2	16	18.8	1	1.1	16	3.7
25	0	0.0	0	0.0	2	2.2	50	11.6
44	0	0.0	0	0.0	1	1.1	44	10.2
50	0	0.0	0	0.0	1	1.1	50	11.6
59	0	0.0	0	0.0	1	1.1	59	13.7
Total	31	100.1	85	101.1	90	99.6	432	100.2

TABLE 9.16: Share of Local and Foreign Journals in Publishing and Citing (Percentages in brackets)

Local or Foreign	*Published*		*Cited*		*Total No. of Journals*
	No. of Journals	*No. of Articles*	*No. of Journals*	*No. of Articles*	
Indian	10 (32.3)	39 (45.9)	7 (7.8)	14 (3.2)	11 (11.2)
Foreign	21 (67.7)	46 (54.1)	83 (92.2)	418 (96.8)	87 (88.8)
Total	31	85	90	432	98*

Note: * Twenty-three journals are common to publishing and citing.

Table 9.17 shows the availability of those journals used for publishing and citing papers at the ISAC library. It may be noted incidentally, that collection of library was not developed systematically till 1978 as it was supposed to serve a small group of workers in the project. It was only after converting the project into a full-fledged centre, the library started growing. As a result many of the journals used for publishing and/or citing earlier to 1978 are not available in the library. It may be seen that about 78 per cent of journals used for publishing and citing are available in the library. In terms of number of papers, nearly 97 per cent of papers published and 91 per cent of papers cited are available in the library. The intention in this study is not to judge the relevance and adequacy of the library collection but to drive home the point that most of the times the authors under study preferred to publish in a journal available in their library and also cite from those available to the library.

TABLE 9.17: Availability of Published and Cited Journals in the Library (Percentages in brackets)

Availability	*Published*		*Cited*		*Total No. of Journals*
	No. of Journals	*No. of Articles*	*No. of Journals*	*No. of Articles*	
Available	28 (90.3)	82 (96.5)	69 (76.7)	390 (90.3)	76 (77.6)
Not available	3	3	21	42	22
Total	31	85	90	432	98

Publishing and Citing *Vs.* Use of Journals

The most popular journals for publishing and citing are presented in Tables 9.18 and 9.19 respectively with publishing, citing and use data. Use of a journal in these tables is sub-divided into the number of pages of xerox copies taken from the journal during 1982; the number of times two issues of the journal are issued out and the number of times the journal is consulted over the three months immediately after receipt in the ISAC library (Case Study 10). The number of pages of xerox copies taken from about 650 journals in the library for one year is about 7,600. Out of the 98 journals covered in this study (of which 87 are available in the library) 40 journals were used for taking 3,215 pages of xerox copies and use data is collected for 56 titles (i.e., 112 issues of 56 journals were monitored over three months to record 921 uses). In other words, a little over 13 per cent of the journals (used for publishing and citing) have been used for taking nearly 42 per cent of total xerox copies.

Thus at this level, there is a correlation between publishing and citing with the use of journals. It may be noted that the number of journals which are common to publishing and citing and those used for taking xerox copies in the study is only 15.

TABLE 9.18: Most Popular Journals for Publishing with Scores of Citation and Use

Title	*Published*		*Cited*		*Use*			
	No.	*%* (*N = 85*)	*No.*	*%* (*N = 432*)	*No. of Xerox Copies Taken*		*In-house and Circulation*	
					No.	*%* (*N = 3215*)	*No.*	*%* (*N = 921*)
Proceedings of the Indian Academy of Sciences (I/AV)	16	18.82	2	0.46	20	0.62	†	†
Astrophysics and Space Science (F/AV)	7	8.24	25*	5.79	253	7.87	8	0.87
Indian Journal of Radio and Space Physics (I/AV)	7	8.24	1	0.23	0	0.00	†	†
Journal of AEU (F/AV)	6	7.06	1	0.23	0	0.00	29	3.15
Journal of the Institute of Electronics and Telecommunication Engineers (I/AV)	6	7.06	4	0.93	111	3.45	28	3.04
Nature (F/AV)	5	5.88	59*	13.66	26	0.81	38	4.13
IEEE Transactions on Industrial Electronics and Control Instrumentation (F/AV)	3	3.53	4	0.93	124	3.86	†	†
JBIS (F/AV)	3	3.53	5	1.16	109	3.39	†	†
Total	53	62.36	101	23.39	643	20.00	103	11.19

Note: * Titles score as highly cited, in Table 9.19.
† Titles for which use data is not available.
Key: I—Indian; F—Foreign; AV—available, NA—Not available.

A close examination of Tables 9.18 and 9.19 reveals that no clear correlation can be found of journals frequently used for publishing and citing with that of the use of these journals. Thus, title by title correlation fails, though at a broad level journals used for publishing and citing have registered considerably more use. The possible reason for non-correlation in this limited data of "use" is that xerox copies of a journal article are taken for many purposes, and writing a paper, citing an article xeroxed and publishing the paper in the same journal are only a few of those purposes. As it is set out in a separate use study, the quantitative use is influenced by many factors like the number of journals in a field, the number of users in a field, journal circulation policy, etc. (Case Study 10, Chapter 7).

TABLE 9.19: Most Often Cited Journals with Scores of Publishing and Use

Title	Cited		Published		Use			
					No. of Xerox Copies Taken		In-house and Circulation	
	No.	% (N = 432)	No.	% (N = 85)	No.	% (N = 3215)	No.	% (N = 921)
Nature (F/AV)	59	13.66	5*	5.88	26	0.81	38	4.13
Astrophysical Journal Letters (F/AV)	50	1.57	0	0.00	0	0.00	8	0.87
Astrophysical Journal (F/AV)	44	10.19	1	1.18	226	7.03	16	1.74
Astrophysics and Space Science (F/AV)	25	5.79	7*	8.24	253	7.87	8	0.87
Journal of Geophysical Research (F/AV)	25	5.79	1	1.18	3	0.09	3	0.33
Journal of Spacecrafts and Rockets (F/AV)	16	3.70	1	1.18	59	1.84	32	3.47
Planetary and Space Science (F/AV)	14	3.24	2	2.35	0	0.00	13	1.41
Space Science Reviews (F/AV)	11	2.55	2	2.35	206	6.41	2	0.22
Solar Physics (F/AV)	8	1.85	1	1.18	0	0.00	2	0.22
Journal of Atmospheric and Terrestrial Physics (F/AV)	7	1.62	0	0.00	0	0.00	†	†
Total	259	59.96	20	23.54	773	24.05	122	13.26

Note: * Titles score as highly published in Table 9.18.
† Titles for which use data is not available.

Key: I—Indian, F—Foreign, AV—Available, NA—Not available.

Again by looking at publishing and citing data in these two tables, we see that not all the journals frequently used for publishing are highly cited and *vice versa* (with the exception of two titles in each table). However, all highly used journals for publishing have one or more citations. Self-citations have played a great role in this direction. It is the self-citations which boosted the score of Indian journals in these tables. On the other hand all but two journals highly cited have been used for publishing one or more papers.

An interesting observation is that all the 18 journals which are highly cited and used for publishing papers are available at ISAC library. Additionally, almost all highly cited journals are foreign journals. But three of the eight journals popular for publishing papers are Indian.

Other observations made, though not statistically proved, in this study are as follows. The majority of the papers are written by scientists (i.e., those possessing science degrees). A considerable number of papers are in the astronomy and astrophysics areas and hence, obviously, journals in these areas have received more citation scores.

Although not relevant in this study, one might be curious to know how others cite Indian space technologists. For this analysis, probably the only tool available is the science citation index (SCI). A search through the 1982 annual indexes of the SCI for source papers as well as citations to 10 highly productive ISAC authors is tabulated in Table 9.20. All the citations except one citation for author at serial number one are made by foreign authors or authors abroad.

TABLE 9.20: Source Papers and Citations to Papers of Ten Highly Productive ISAC Authors by Others (based on 1982 SCI)

Sl. *No.*	*No. of Source Papers*	*No. of Times Cited*
1.	2	5
2.	0	2
3.	0	1
4.	0	1
5.	0	0
6.	0	1
7.	0	0
8.	0	0
9.	0	0
10.	0	1
Total	2	11

As the SCI covers a limited number of Indian journals and there is considerable self-citation among Indian space technologists, the result in Table 9.20 is quite obvious. A small difficulty is also encountered in the collection of the data especially consulting the citation index and segregating the citations of four authors having names identical with other Indian scientists and engineers in other fields. As an illustration one can see as many as 139 source articles listed under A.K. Jain and these articles are cited by 203 papers in various fields like communication, demography, nuclear physics, geology, electronics, astrophysics, medicine, chemistry, etc. It would be of great use if the SCI provides author affiliation of cited papers in the citation index also.

Results and Observations

Subject to the limitations noted earlier, the following results and observations can be made based on the analysis made so far.

Conference papers and journal articles constitute more than 90 per cent of what Indian space technologists write and publish. However, the order of sources used for citation differs and, in order of decreasing use for citation, they are journals, books, technical reports and conference papers. The percentage of journal articles cited and published are almost the same. But the percentage of conference papers cited (in spite of the fact that the majority of conference papers are presented in foreign and international conferences rather than Indian conferences, unlike journal articles) is much less than those brought out. Hence, there is an inclination for oral conference presentation (and possibly semi-formal publications such as technical reports) than archival publication on the part of Indian space technologists. Journal articles cited (3%) from Indian journals is much less than that published (46%). In other words, Indian journals and foreign and international conferences serve more as publishing outlets to space technologists than sources for citing.

Only a little over 25 per cent of scientists and engineers in the Centre have ever published any paper with an average of 2.09 papers per author, an average citation of 7.35 references per paper (The same is of in case of papers published in *The In-house Technical Journal* published since 1991) and 16.4 per cent self-citations. Nearly 25 per cent of papers do not have any citations. By and large, journal articles carry a larger number of references and are cited more frequently than conference papers. One-third of total journal articles covered in this study having 10 or more references, contributed approximately to three-quarters of total references cited.

Self-citation among Indian space technologists is quite high (i.e., 35% of papers have one or more self-citations). The average number of self-citations per paper is 3.44. Obviously, most of the Indian reports cited are self-citations or citations of the colleagues in the same organisation. More than 90 per cent of foreign reports cited are either NASA or ESA reports. Preprint citations appear only in the astronomy and astrophysics areas.

Nearly 75 per cent of journals used for publishing papers were also used for citing references (including self-citations). A little over 25 per cent of the journals published more than 62 per cent of papers, and a little over 21 per cent of them had 60 per cent of the total citations. As stated earlier, Indian journals claim a profile of "high publishing and low citing" as far as space technologists are concerned.

Nearly 97 per cent of journal articles published and 91 per cent journal articles cited are from journals available in the library, which indicates that the library is aware of the needs of the users and that the Indian space technologists mostly publish and cite from journals available at the library.

A little over 13 per cent of journals used for publishing and citing papers have been used by Indian space technologists for nearly 42 per cent of total xerox copies taken in one year. This indicates a slight positive correlation of publishing and citing with use of journals. However, a clear title by title correlation of publishing and citing with use of journals does not exist.

Not all the journals highly used for publishing papers are highly cited and *vice versa*. However, all highly used journals for publishing papers are cited at least once. Self-citations have played a great role in this direction. All but two highly cited journals have been used for publishing at least one paper.

All highly used journals for publishing papers and highly cited journals are available in the library and all highly cited journals are of foreign origin. But three out of eight highly used journals for publishing papers are of Indian origin.

Conclusion

Although the "user" is regarded as the king of any information system, the most neglected aspect of research in Indian librarianship is user studies in its real sense. Looking at users in different contexts and groups, at different angles, using different methods, it is necessary to probe this important, yet scarcely known, component of the information system before making any such system potentially relevant and useful. A study of publishing and citing patterns of users helps as one way of knowing the users and their role and participation in overall (scientific and technical) information transfer cycle. In addition, such a study is useful in collection development and evaluation.

As a feedback of this study, all those journals which are used by space technologists to publish and cite articles but are not available in the library have been presented before a panel of experts for consideration to be included in the library's subscription list.

CASE STUDY 17

CORRELATION OF USE, CITATION AND PUBLISHING IN JOURNALS

Introduction

Journals are the formal primary medium of communication for researchers. The cycle of information consumption, transmission and production is complex. Journals alone cannot represent all phases of the cycle. Nevertheless, the role of journals in information gathering, use and transmission by researchers cannot be over estimated. The interactions of Indian space technologists with journals in terms of usage, citation and publishing papers are examined in this case study to explore possible correlations among these factors. The null hypothesis could be stated as that there is no correlation among these variables other than those attributable to chance.

Background of the Study

As part of a comprehensive user study (Sridhar, 1987, 1995), about 800 defined sets of users of the Indian Space Research Organisation Satellite Centre (ISAC) Library were asked for the number of papers they have published. Out of 489 respondents, only 93 persons (mostly scientists and engineers at fairly higher and middle levels have one or more papers to their credit. When followed up, 224 actual references were made available. However, it was possible to obtain copies of 148 papers published over the last decade. Ignoring conference papers and a few unspecified papers, 85 journal articles were selected for this study.

These 85 sample papers (Sridhar, 1985), in which at least one of the authors is from ISAC, were published in 31 journals, and they in turn cited 432 articles from 90 journals, apart from books, reports and conference papers. Twenty -our journals were common to both publishing and citing activities. In other words, there were 97 distinct journals that covered all of the source articles and cited articles. It may be noted here that 28 of the 31 journals in which Indian space technologists published papers and 69 of the 90 journals from which citations were made by them are subscribed to by ISAC library (Case Study 16).

Subsequently a use study (Sridhar, 1986) of 485 current journals subscribed to by the library was carried out and use data available to the extent of 68 of the above referred 97 journals extracted. In the use study, two latest issues of current journals were monitored for about three months from the date of their first display in the library to record the number of in-house uses as well as lent-out uses. In the case of in-house use, a maximum of four in-house uses a day was recorded for a single issue of a journal (Case Study 10).

The data collected on these three variables of journals (namely, publishing, citing and use) were tabulated to calculate the Pearson correlation coefficient and to test the significance of the coefficient through the t-test.

Limitations of the Study

This study has some limitations. Firstly, the sample journal articles of Indian space technologists were not systematically drawn. All reprints made available by the authors were considered. Secondly, quite a few co-authors of these papers are from outside ISAC. Thirdly, it is not certain that all these papers are the results of work done by researchers at their present place of work, i.e., ISAC. Fourthly, journal use data is not restricted only to authors of sample papers, but it also present consolidated use of journals by all the users of ISAC Library. Owing to certain practical difficulties segregation of journal use data of ISAC authors could not be done. Fifthly, the variables of use, citation and publishing of papers in journals could not be well controlled. For example, ISAC authors could use journals other than those subscribed to by ISAC library by ordering preprints, reprints, visiting other libraries, etc., and hence cite these in their papers. Further, the use study was carried out during September 1983 and March 1984, whereas the sample papers were published during the decade prior to the use study. Above all, use studies and citation studies are themselves imbued with certain drawbacks and presumptions. Lastly the Pearson correlation coefficient was chosen for this study on the assumption that variables are distributed normally.

Calculation of Correlation Coefficient

The following formulae are used for calculating the Pearson correlation coefficient and t-test value:

$$r_1 = \frac{\sum xy - n_1 \overline{xy}}{\sqrt{\left(\sum x^2 - n_1 \bar{x}^2\right)\left(\sum y^2 - n_1 \bar{y}^2\right)}}$$

$$t_1 = r_1 \sqrt{\frac{n_1 - 2}{1 - r_1^2}}$$

where,

x — Number of times two issues of a journal are used in first three months

y — Number of articles published in a journal

z — Number of articles cited from a journal

r_1 — Pearson correlation coefficient between x and y

r_2 — Pearson correlation coefficient between y and z

r_3 — Pearson correlation coefficient between x and z

$\bar{x}$ — Average number of times two issues of a journal are used in the first three months

$\bar{y}$ — Average number of articles of Indian space technologists published in a journal

$\bar{z}$ — Average number of articles cited by Indian space technologists from a journal

n_1 — Number of journals observed for r_1

n_2 — Number of journals observed for r_2

n_3 — Number of journals observed for r_3

t_1 — t-test value of r_1

t_2 — t-test value of r_2

t_3 — t-test value of r_3

p — Significance level as per t-test

df — Degrees of freedom

The calculated value of r_1 is as follows:

$$r_1 = 0.0144; \quad p > 0.10; \quad df = 66$$

The value of r_1 is negligible. Hence the null hypothesis that there is no correlation between use of journals and choosing journals for publishing papers by Indian space technologists is valid.

Similarly, we find

$$r_2 = 0.1918; \quad p < 0.05; \quad df = 95$$

For a significant correlation to exist between two variables, the value of the Pearson correlation coefficient would normally be 0.4 or more. Thus the r_2 indicates a slight positive correlation between choice of a journal for publishing papers and citing papers. However, the value of t_2 at 95 degrees of freedom in the t-distribution table indicates that the calculated value of r_2 is different from zero at 0.05 significance level. Hence, we may conclude that a slight positive correlation exists between publishing in and citing from journals. The null hypothesis that there is no correlation between citing from journals and publishing in journals by Indian space technologists may not be true, though not significantly disproved.

Thirdly, $r_3 = 0.0055$; $p > 0.10$; $df = 66$

The value of r_3 is close to zero, and hence the variables in use of a journal and choice of the same for citing by Indian space technologists are independent. In other words, the null hypothesis here is found valid.

Discussion

It is but natural that researcher gathers and consumes more information than what he or she transmits, cites, generates and publishes. The variable use of a journal is very much constrained by the 'law of least effort,' and an average researcher would like to use as many potentially useful journals in his or her field as possible. On the other hand, when publication of paper is desired, he or she prefers a journal considered more relevant and reputed than others. While use of a journal is constrained by factors such as availability and access, choosing a journal for publishing is restricted by the capability to meet the expectations of the journal. But it is partly obvious that a researcher chooses a journal when publishing that he or she at least occasionally uses. The converse is not always true. As such, no correlation between use of a journal and choosing the same for publishing is found in this study. This is in conformity with an earlier finding of the American Psychological Association (Meadows, 1974, p. 105).

A slight positive correlation between choice of a journal for publishing papers and citing papers by Indian space technologists is found in spite of the fact that the general rule is to publish more often in local journals and cite more often from foreign journals (Case Study 16). Though citation studies have some limitations, it is believed that an article cited is very much used by the researcher and found relevant to his or her work. This correlation is not totally unexpected as the majority of publishing and citing activities take place within a set of journals in the field.

Lastly, the use of a journal and the chance of its being cited have not demonstrated significant correlation and ". . . it is doubtful if reference to documents by an article match the actual uses made in the course of are long it" (Line and Sanderson, 1974, p. 56).. However, a study by Mendez and Blanco (1979) revealed that the most cited journals by a group of dairy research scientists corresponded well with the most requested journals at their library. As mentioned earlier, citing of a journal almost implies use but not necessarily *vice versa*. In other words, one of the major reasons for lack of correlation in this study is that the number of journal articles that a researcher uses is very much larger than that cited. Thus, by restricting the use study to only journals from which sample papers are cited and to those authors who have cited, a better correlation of these two factors can be expected.

Conclusion

The present study with the limitations inherent in incidental use of data from a larger study has shown a slight positive correlation between publishing in and citing from a journal. A third variable use of journals is found to be independent of publishing and citing. It is greatly desirable to have a more tightly controlled experiment with a larger sample and preferably a homogeneous user group as well as journals in a specific subject area to test the hypothesis. Alternatively, an opinion survey of such a user group about journals in their area might also result in a more accurate picture of what is happening.

CASE STUDY 18

INFORMATION AND COMMUNICATION BEHAVIOUR OF WOMEN USERS

Introduction

Research findings in mass communication suggest that '. . . there are consistent differences between men and women in their information processing habits. Women seem to ingest, store and reproduce information with less distortion than do men' (Bauer, 1973). Taking only information related to science and technology into consideration one may hypothesise that women scientists, engineers and technicians are more information conscious and more active in seeking information than men.

As part of a larger and comprehensive information behaviour study of Indian space technologists (scientists, engineers, managers, technocrats and technicians of ISRO Satellite Centre, Bangalore) the data about gender of respondents were also collected (Sridhar, 1987, 1995). The survey covered a population of about 800 persons through the questionnaire as well as a semi-controlled library use study. The response rate for a questionnaire was 68 per cent. This study reports the statistical analysis and gives an interpretation of selected aspects of information behaviour in relation to the gender of the respondents. To analyse the differences between men and women the non-parametric chi-squared test has been employed on contingency tables. The results of the test are accepted at 95 per cent statistical significance level.

Hypotheses

Both Shuchman (1980, 1981) and Raitt (1984) have referred to engineering in general and aerospace in particular as a man's world. Shuchman has further indicated that women engineers are at a disadvantage in the world of engineering in which information transfer is predominantly informal.

Though the first woman cosmonaut from USSR, Valentina Tereschkova, went into space as early as June 1963, women astronauts from America faced a high discrimination in the late 1950s and 1960s. Sheffield (1984) claimed that 'in addition to a handful of astronauts, women now work at all technical and most managerial levels in aerospace, government, and industry, but space, and particularly the aerospace industry is one of the toughest fields for women to seek success in, probably because of its traditional ties to the strongly male-dominated military programmes.'

Neither Shuchman nor Raitt has compared the proportion of women in aerospace engineering with other R&D employment patterns in their countries. Nor has Shuchman explained how women are at a disadvantage in using informal communication sources. His data did not directly support his conclusion that the largest group potentially affected in using informal information networks is women, because engineering has been a predominantly male profession as women make up only about 3 per cent of the engineering in industry (Shuchman, 1980, 1981). The covert assumption appears to be that women hesitate to communicate with and receive communication from men and hence they form a very minor or insignificantly limited network of informal communication among themselves. This assumption appears to be a potential hypothesis for testing.

Background Data of the Study

Compared to 6 per cent females in the overall employment pattern of R&D institutions in India (India, Department of Science & Technology, 1982), the population of space technologists in this study contained 7.6 per cent females. Hence there was no discrimination in female employment patterns in space technology compared to other R&D employment in the country.

Almost all women in the population of the present study were placed in the middle level of the organisational hierarchy. The response of females to the questionnaire was slightly lower (56.9%) than that of males (68.5%).

Professional Activities and Achievements

The professional activities and achievements index developed for the response population of the study took into account, for each respondent, the number of lectures delivered, number of seminars, symposia and conferences attended and number of internal documents/reports prepared in a year, average number of papers published per year of experience, average number of patents obtained and awards and citations received per year of experience (the latter two with a weighting of 5), the number of professional associations, societies, boards of studies, editorial committees on which they served or were members, the number of professional journals personally subscribed to, the number of tours to other centres of ISRO and organisations in a year, membership of committees, in-service training, and number of part-time studies undertaken in the last two years. The men and women respondents scored average professional activities and achievement index values of 9.20 and 6.22 respectively.

Time Spent in Information Gathering

The survey revealed that women did not differ significantly from men in the amount of time spent on information gathering activities. Men and women respondents respectively spend an average of 9.2 and 9.5 hours per week in information gathering (Table 9.21). Nor were women space technologists significantly different from men in the percentage of time spent on formal and informal sources of information (Table 9.22).

TABLE 9.21: Time Spent on Information Gathering Activities

		Men		*Women*		*Total*
		No.	*%*	*No.*	*%*	
A	More than 20 hours per week	15	3.2	1	3.1	16
B	16 to 20 hours per week	24	5.1	1	3.1	25
C	11 to 15 hours per week	105	22.4	8	25.0	113
D	7 to 10 hours per week	183	39.1	15	46.9	198
E	4 to 6 hours per week	88	18.8	6	18.8	94
F	Less than 4 hours per week	53	11.3	1	3.1	54
	Total	468	99.9	32	100.0	500

($X^2 = 2.65$, $df = 5$, $p > 0.05$).

TABLE 9.22: Relative Time Spent on Formal and Informal Sources of Information

	Men		*Women*		*Total*
	No.	*%*	*No.*	*%*	
More time on formal than informal sources of information	228	85.4	22	95.7	250
More time on informal than formal sources of information	39	14.6	1	4.3	40
Total	267	100.0	23	100.0	290

($X^2 = 1.87$, $df = 1$, $p > 0.05$).

Note: Those who claimed to have spent equal time on formal and informal sources of information are not shown.

Relative Dependence on Formal and Informal Sources of Information

Even in the relative dependence on formal and informal sources of information, women were identical with men respondents (Table 9.23).

TABLE 9.23: Relative Dependence on Formal and Informal Sources of Information

		Men		*Women*		*Total*
		No.	*%*	*No.*	*%*	
A	Almost entirely on informal sources	78	17.8	3	9.7	81
B	More on informal sources than formal sources	43	9.8	1	3.2	44
C	Equally on both informal and formal sources	192	43.7	19	61.3	211
D	More on formal sources than informal sources	105	23.9	8	25.8	113
E	Almost entirely on formal sources	21	4.8	0	0.0	21
	Total	439	100.0	31	100.0	470

($X^2 = 5.95$, $df = 4$, $p > 0.05$).

Informal Communication/Sources of Information

It would be expected from Shuchman's argument that women space technologists would depend less on informal and inter-personal sources of information, would contact fewer persons for information than do men, consult fewer experts in the field, colleagues and fellow professionals and library staff, delegate information-gathering work much less than would men. It was surprising that women did not differ from men in any of these aspects.

As could be seen from Table 9.24 women respondents depended almost to the same extent on informal, intrapersonal and inter-personal sources of information as men. The table presents weighted mean from responses recorded on a five-point scale from 0 to 4 (0—No dependence; 1—Rare dependence; 2—Occasional dependence; 3—Frequent dependence; 4—High dependence).

TABLE 9.24: Dependence on Informal, Intrapersonal and Interpersonal Sources of Information

	Informal, Intrapersonal and Interpersonal Sources of Information	*Weighted Mean on a Five Point Scale*		
		Men	*Women*	*Total*
A	Personal experience	3.06	3.18	3.07
B	Superiors	2.31	2.70	2.34
C	Peers and colleagues (in ISRO)	2.11	2.27	2.12
D	Subordinates and juniors	1.74	1.80	1.74
E	Fellow professionals outside ISRO	1.19	1.26	1.19
F	Results of one's own experiments	2.54	2.74	2.55
G	Professional meetings, seminars, symposia and lectures	1.71	1.58	1.70
H	Educational and training courses	1.68	2.16	1.72

Note: The chi-square non-parametric test was carried out on each of the sources with respect to five points on the scale. The differences between men and women were not significant for any source of information.

The number of persons contacted for information within the organisation as well as outside the organisation (ISRO) did not vary significantly between men and women (Tables 9.25 and 9.26). By decreasing the statistical significance level to 0.10 (from 0.05) one can see that the difference in number of persons contacted outside the organisation varied from men to women. Women tended to have fewer contacts outside the organisation than men, an expected natural result (Table 9.26).

Sources of Bibliographic Information and Degree of Delegation of Information Gathering Work

Consulting experts in the field, colleagues and fellow professionals and library staff for bibliographic references (Tables 9.27, 9.28 and 9.29) did not significantly differ between men and women. However, women seem to consult experts slightly more than men, which is quite opposite to expectations (significance level 0.10).

TABLE 9.25: Number of Interpersonal Contacts within the Organisation

Number of Persons Contacted	*Men*		*Women*		*Total*
	No.	*%*	*No.*	*%*	
None	4	1.1	0	0.0	4
1 to 5	141	37.8	11	37.9	152
6 to 10	120	32.2	11	37.9	131
11 or more	108	29.0	7	24.1	115
Total	373	100.1	29	99.9	402

($X^2 = 0.8$, $df = 3$, $p > 0.05$).

TABLE 9.26: Number of Interpersonal Contacts Outside the Organisation

Number of Persons Contacted	*Men*		*Women*		*Total*
	No.	*%*	*No.*	*%*	
None	83	27.5	5	23.8	88
1 to 5	133	44.0	14	66.7	147
6 or more	86	28.5	2	9.5	88
Total	302	100.0	21	100.0	323

($X^2 = 4.89$, $df = 2$, 0.10, $p > 0.05$).

TABLE 9.27: Consulting Experts in the Field for Bibliographic References

	Men		*Women*		*Total*
	No.	*%*	*No.*	*%*	
Consulted	237	50.6	22	66.7	259
Not consulted	231	49.4	11	33.3	242
Total	468	100.0	33	100.0	501

($X^2 = 2.2$, $df = 1$, $p > 0.05$).

TABLE 9.28: Consulting Colleagues and Fellow Professionals for Bibliographic References

	Men		*Women*		*Total*
	No.	*%*	*No.*	*%*	
Consulted	310	66.2	26	78.8	336
Not consulted	158	33.8	7	21.2	165
Total	468	100.0	33	100.0	501

($X^2 = 2.2$, $df = 1$, $p > 0.05$).

TABLE 9.29: Consulting Library Staff for Bibliographic References

	Men		*Women*		*Total*
	No.	*%*	*No.*	*%*	
Consulted	193	41.2	16	48.5	209
Not consulted	275	58.8	17	51.5	292
Total	468	100.0	33	100.0	501

($X^2 = 0.67$, $df = 1$, $p > 0.05$).

The degree of delegation of information gathering work did not differ significantly between men and women (Table 9.30).

TABLE 9.30: Degree of Delegation of Information Gathering Work

Degree of Delegation		*Men*		*Women*		*Total*
		No.	*%*	*No.*	*%*	
A	No delegation	233	53.4	14	46.7	247
B	Occasional delegation	87	20.0	8	26.7	95
C	Moderate delegation	90	20.6	7	23.3	97
D	Frequent delegation	26	6.0	1	3.3	27
	Total	436	100.0	30	100.0	466

($X^2 = 1.3$, $df = 3$, $p > 0.05$).

Information Value Potential

In the survey respondents had been asked to cite names of five persons most often contacted for information. By sociometric analysis Case Study 19), it was found that 423 (unique) individuals within the population have been mentioned in all 1,263 times by 391 respondents. In other words, on average, a person cited has been a source of information to about 3 respondents.

By assuming that a communication star is one who is contacted as an informal source of information by more than one standard deviation over and above the mean number of contacts by respondents, (i.e., 2.99 + 3.03 = 6.02), 44 communication stars who were frequently contacted by 7 or more respondents were identified. Of these only one female frequently contacted by seven respondents qualified to be a communication star. The rest of the women technologists were not communication stars. In fact, one was contacted by 3 others, another by 2, and 10 others by one each in the response population. The rest of the 48 females in the population scored zero information potential on this ground. In other words, 13 women were mentioned as most frequently contacted persons for information 22 times (average 1.69) but 410 men were mentioned as most frequently contacted persons for information 1,241 times (average 3.03). This is a substantial difference in the information potentiality for interpersonal communication in the given environment between men and women. In addition as many as 48 out of 61 women technologists (i.e., 78.7%) were not considered by any of the 391 respondents to be one of the five persons most frequently contacted for information.

From the above analysis the potential of women space technologists for imparting information in the informal communication structure/network is highly limited. It is also obvious that there is an inhibition on the part of men to contact women colleagues for information, and not necessarily the other way round, even though women in principle have just as much information to impart as men.

Use of Library Documents and User Interactions with the Library

In addition to the questionnaire survey, a semi-controlled usage study was carried out recording the number of library documents borrowed by space technologists. It was based on a 20 per cent systematic random sample of books and reports over 10 months and two latest issues of 487 current journals over three months (Sridhar, 1985, 1986). Similarly their interactions with the library in terms of the number of books and reports reserved in a year and number of times the primary library was visited/reading seats were occupied in a three months period were also collected (Sridhar, 1982, 1983) (Chapters 7 and 8).

TABLE 9.31: Number of Books Borrowed

Number of Books Borrowed	*Men*		*Women*		*Total*
	No.	*%*	*No.*	*%*	
None	220	29.8	12	19.7	232
1—2	184	24.9	18	29.5	202
3—5	166	22.5	12	19.7	178
6—10	115	15.6	11	18.0	126
11 or more	54	7.3	8	13.1	62
Total	739	100.1	61	100.0	800

($X^2 = 5.32$, $df = 4$, $p > 0.05$).

It was found that the gender of respondents had no influence on number of books, reports and journal issues borrowed in the use study (Tables 9.31, 9.32 and 9.33). However, there was a significant difference in number of journal titles used by men and women space technologists (Table 9.34). The average number of journal titles used by men and women, respectively, were 0.87 and 1.13.

TABLE 9.32: Number of Reports Borrowed

Number of Reports	*Men*		*Women*		*Total*
	No.	*%*	*No.*	*%*	
None	675	90.8	58	95.1	733
1 or more	68	9.2	3	4.9	71
Total	743	100.0	61	100.0	804

($X^2 = 1.26$, $df = 1$, $p > 0.05$).

TABLE 9.33: Number of Journal Issues Borrowed

Number of Journal Issues	*Men*		*Women*		*Total*
	No.	*%*	*No.*	*%*	
None	503	68.0	33	54.1	536
1—2	130	17.6	18	29.5	148
3—5	66	8.9	5	8.2	71
6 or more	41	5.5	5	8.2	46
Total	740	100.0	61	100.0	801

($X^2 = 6.7$, $df = 3$, $p > 0.05$).

TABLE 9.34: Number of Journal Titles Used

Number of Journal Titles	*Men*		*Women*		*Total*
	No.	*%*	*No.*	*%*	
None	498	67.8	33	54.1	531
1—2	157	21.4	22	36.1	179
3—5	56	7.6	3	4.9	59
6 or more	23	3.1	3	4.9	26
Total	734	99.9	61	100.0	795

($X^2 = 8.09$, $df = 3$, $p < 0.05$).

In in-house use of the primary library women space technologists have significantly differed from men (Table 9.35). The average number of times women and men space technologists were observed making in-house use of library documents respectively were 3.92 and 2.48. This has disproved earlier informal observation that men make more in-house use than women users (Case Study 01). The same is true as far as the number of documents reserved by women respondents was concerned (Table 9.36). The average number of reservations made by men and women respondents respectively were 2.19 and 2.84.[6]

TABLE 9.35: In-house Use of Library Documents by Seat Occupancy

Frequency of Use/Seat Occupancy in Three Months Sample	*Men*		*Women*		*Total*
	No.	*%*	*No.*	*%*	
Nil	348	48.7	20	35.1	368
1—5	273	38.2	19	33.3	292
6—10	68	9.5	15	26.3	83
11 or more	25	3.5	3	5.3	28
Total	714	99.9	57	100.0	771

($X^2 = 17.03$, $df = 3$, $p < 0.05$).

TABLE 9.36: Number of Reservations Made

Number of Reservations	*Men*		*Women*		*Total*
	No.	*%*	*No.*	*%*	
None	326	53.3	10	27.0	336
1	80	13.1	5	13.5	85
2	63	10.3	9	24.3	72
3—5	67	10.9	8	21.6	75
6—10	50	8.2	4	10.8	54
11 or more	26	4.2	1	2.7	27
Total	612	100.0	37	99.9	649

($X^2 = 14.77$, $df = 5$, $p < 0.05$).

Conclusion

From the analysis of the data so far presented it is clear that women space technologists did not differ significantly from men in (1) amount of time spent in information gathering; (2) relative time spent on formal and informal sources of information; (3) relative dependence on formal and informal sources of information; (4) degree of dependence on various informal and interpersonal sources of information; (5) number of interpersonal contacts within the organisation; (6) number of interpersonal contacts outside the organisation; (7) consulting experts in the field for bibliographic references; (8) consulting colleagues and fellow professionals for bibliographic references; (9) consulting library staff for bibliographic references; (10) degree of delegation of information gathering work; and (11) the number of books, reports and current journal issues borrowed. However, the women tended to have fewer interpersonal contacts outside the organisation than men (significance level 0.10). Surprisingly, they tended to consult experts for bibliographic references more than men (significance level 0.10). Above all, women space technologists have made *significantly* (significance level 0.05) more interactions with the primary library sources than men in terms of in-house use and number of reservations made for books and reports as well as journal titles used.[7]

From the result of this study it is clear that women space technologists were more information-conscious and active than men as far as seeking information from formal sources of information like library documents and contacting interpersonal sources of information within the organisation are concerned. Hence, women are intrinsically more capable of supplying information than men. However, the women have had a natural obstacle in accessing interpersonal sources of information outside their organisation. The disadvantageous position of women, if any, relates to their inability to move out of the organisation in tapping interpersonal sources of information. On the other hand there appeared to be an inhibition on the part of men due to socio-cultural background in contacting women colleagues for information, and not necessarily *vice versa*. As a result the potential of women as information suppliers is not realised. The result is that they never become information stars. There may be other factors like the placement of women at middle level in the organisational hierarchy and qualities and abilities of women space technologists in transmitting information, which are not explored in this study.

CASE STUDY 19

SOCIOMETRIC ANALYSIS OF INFORMAL COMMUNICATION

Introduction

Some of the factors which decide the choice of a source of information by user, apart from task and purpose of seeking information, are physical proximity, accessibility, perceived quality and utility, ease of use and previous experience about the source or acquaintance with the source. It is fairly established that the least effort principle operates in the choice of alternative sources or channels of information by users. This does not mean that many sources of information are non-complementary. Another simple principle on which use or non-use of a source of information is based is Mooers [1960, p. (ii)] law. It states that "an information retrieval system will tend not to be used whenever it is more painful and troublesome for a customer to have information than for him not to have it".

The most popular way of classifying sources of information is formal and informal or non-formal sources. The other overlapping criterion often used are internal and external sources, interpersonal and intrapersonal sources, seeker generated sources and sources external to the seeker, personal and impersonal sources, written or documentary and oral sources, auditory and visual sources, etc. No way of classifying sources of information is fully satisfactory and the groups are neither exhaustive nor mutually exclusive. For example, participation in a conference could be both formal and informal and information obtained in a conference could be written as well as oral. Some have labelled such sources of information as semi-formal sources.

In the arena of information user research, librarians appeared to have concentrated more on formal sources of information and the non-librarians particularly sociologists, psychologists, communication specialists, educationists, managers, have concentrated on informal communication. Hatt (1976, p. 96) says "... Librarians seem to be ignoring the below-ground network of informal incidental communications while the D&U (Dissemination and Utilisation) workers are ignoring the mushrooms of formal communication in organised stores. What is needed, perhaps, is an approach that views the two kinds of growth as one system, rather than two".

Many past studies have confirmed that both formal and informal sources of information are equally important for a user. There appears to be a neat interlinking of formal and informal sources that each stimulates the use of the other in many situations and thus acts as mutually supportive dependent and complementary sources of information. Hence it is more appropriate that librarians know about the informal and interpersonal communication of their clientele in order to suitably supplement it by formal sources of information. In fact the broad purpose of an information system is to establish effective communication between people (Kunz *et al.*, 1977, p. 6). Communication as a complex phenomenon forms an integral part of day to day scientific and technical work. One of the approaches of quantitative analysis in librarianship is to explore or inquire the morphology of information flow or the unknowns in the communication process (Gertrude, 1972, pp. 113-14). "Work in this area is less rigorous than the bibliometric techniques, purely because the survey data is difficult to collect. To study citations is far easier than studying people" (Rowley and Turner, 1978, p. 45).

It is attempted in this chapter to highlight the importance of informal and interpersonal communication, and examine the informal and interpersonal communication network, patterns and behaviour of Indian satellite technologists in the form of a sociometric analysis based on the data collected as part of a larger and comprehensive information behaviour study (Sridhar, 1987, 1995).

Importance of Informal Communication

Communication is considered successful if it brings desired change in the receiver. It is very difficult to say that reading is a superior way of transferring or acquiring information than hearing or other ways of transferring or acquiring information. Many past user studies have confirmed that informal, oral and interpersonal sources within the organisation are very important sources of information for engineers whether they are direct or indirect (two step/multistage flow), vertical or horizontal in the organisation structure and it is estimated that ". . . professional researcher may receive upto 55 per cent of his useful technical information by informal means" (Bodensteiner, 1970).

The relatively greater role played by informal communication for practitioner is emphasised by Brittain (1971, p. 15) especially under the conditions of uncertainty and/or anxiety which make him to seek out others similar to him for comparison (Havelock 1969, pp. 4, 12) and for a tailor-made solution synthesised to support a finding (Ackoff, 1976, p. 148).

Hall (1972, p. 14) in his review of user studies summarises and says, "first, the information which scientists and engineers want is frequently some detail concerning procedures or experiments which is therefore unlikely to be easily found in a written source, and it may be more conveniently obtained by word-of-mouth. Second, professional interaction is an important source of confidence. When a scientist or engineer is uncertain about the reliability of information he needs, he is likely to turn to colleagues for judgment. There are other possible reasons for predominance of oral communication such as reassurance or just wanting to cut the lag in publication time".

It is well known that the word-of-mouth experts play significant role in getting across the message through mass media. Crane (1971, p. 30) has traced the reason why technologists depend more on informal source than scientists to the fact that many technological problems have to utilise knowledge from a very diverse set of research areas and hence expert assistance is needed in locating published material rather than information concerning unpublished material. Crane (1972, p. 117) further observes that "Scientists who have no informal contacts with the large groups of collaborators in their research areas have the greater difficulty in locating information since . . . the latter serve to link the smaller groups and isolates". It is also established that members of invisible college do decide the direction of research in a given area and technological gatekeepers and communication stars exert substantial influence on others when they transmit information.

Wolek (1970) based on the intensive interpersonal communication in mission-oriented research hypothesise that the need for interpersonal communication varies directly with the complexity of messages to be communicated. Kunz and others (1977, p. 9) conceive the same reason in a more general way as "the gap between supply of and demand for information is bridged to a large extent by informal means of communication. . .". Glass and Norwood (1959) reported that casual conversation was the most-mentioned first source of information on items chosen by each scientist-respondent as representing scientific concepts and research of major or crucial significance to the development of his own work. A similar result was found in DOD's Project Hindsight (Sherwin and Inemson, 1966) that in 70 per cent of the cases information and ideas originated (in the development of 20 successful weapons systems) from personal contact. The studies of Rosenbloom and Wolek (1970), also confirmed that verbal sources inside the organisation were the most important sources of information for technologists. Among the verbal sources, Gralewska-Vickery (1976, p. 269) found that the most used verbal sources were colleagues (80%), conferences (58%) and external personal contacts (49%) and the least used were manufacturers (16%) and consultants (17%). Kelly (1986, p. 46) found almost universal praise for casual table-talks following a conference as most important sources of new ideas for scientists. He quoted an award winning biologist that, "I have the impression that a great body of information is getting around by a mechanism that can only be termed gossip".

'Transceiver' Role of Information User

The study of informal communication emphasises the 'transceiver' role of scientists, engineers and technologists. A user of information is often producer and transmitter of information and hence information users are also interpersonal 'sources' of information. While the information seeking behaviour emphasise the 'user' role, the communication behaviour emphasise the role as a 'source' of information. In the informal and interpersonal communication, the flow of information from person to person also highlights the information potential of participants of communication, identification of communication networks, communication stars, technological gatekeepers, isolates and invisible colleges.

The morphology of information flow in the context of an organisation is described in three types, viz., input, throughput and output. The throughput could be horizontal or vertical one and the vertical in turn could be downward or upward and the horizontal could be intragroup or intergroup flow of information (Havelock *et al.*, 1969, pp. 63-65). The informal communication studies are almost similar to that of the multistep flow of communication referred to in mass communication. The important differences being that in science and technology, informal communication is more audience motivated, the links are more cognitive than in mass communication and the massages often precede the appearance in print (Menzel, 1966, p. 1001).

The Measures of Communication Network Analysis

The patterns of communication among members of a group are referred as communication network or sociogram (constructed by sociometric analysis or by snowball technique). There has been a suggestion to classify a subject based on its communication structure than its contents (Pitchard, 1977). Brittain (1971, p. 11) observes that "each area of scholarship and practice may be associated with special communication networks, and fundamentally different information requirement". The network analysis has been applied in many subjects and some of the measures of network analysis borrowed from other subjects are density, connectedness, centrality and cluster (Jones, 1981, p. 63).

The density measures the degree to which members of a network are in touch with one another and is the ratio of the actual number of links to the maximum possible. The connectedness is the average number of relationships that each person has with others in the same network. The centrality of a network location is the ratio of the communication activity at that location to the mean communication activity over all locations in the network. The cluster is a set of persons who have many links with one another, with a density of not less than 80 per cent.

Informal and Interpersonal Communication of the Indian Satellite Technologists

Size of Informal Communication Network

The entire population of little over 800 Indian Satellite technologists of ISRO Satellite Centre (ISAC) were asked though a questionnaire (Sridhar, 1987, 1995) to give approximate number of persons they generally contact regularly for work related information. The respondents were requested to indicate the size of informal communication network in two ways, viz., the number of persons contacted within ISRO and those outside ISRO and the responses are shown in Table 9.37. The frequency distribution shows 10 as the mode number of persons contacted within ISRO and 5 outside ISRO. Naturally, the mode is in the range of 11—15 under the column 'total number of persons contracted' in the Table. It is also clear from the table that contact of upto 5 persons (both within ISRO and outside ISRO) are made by 27 per cent and upto 15 persons by 65 per cent of the Indian satellite technologists. As the cumulative percentages in the table shows contact of more than 25 persons within ISRO and outside ISRO are respectively maintained by about 8 per cent and 4 per cent of the respondents. A considerable number (i.e., 94 or 27.5%) of the respondents do not contact persons from outside ISRO for information (and it corroborates well with the fact that 29.4 per cent of the respondents said that they do not consider fellow professionals outside ISRO as a source of information in the broader study). The average number of contacts per person within ISRO and outside ISRO respectively are 11.8 and 6.6.

TABLE 9.37: Frequency Distribution of Number of Persons Contacted as Informal Sources of Information

No. of Persons Contacted	*Within ISRO*			*Outside ISRO*			*Total*		
	No.	*%*	*Cum. %*	*No.*	*%*	*Cum. %*	*No.*	*%*	*Cum. %*
0	4	1.2	1.2	91	27.5	27.5	NA	—	—
1	2	0.5	1.7	10	2.9	30.4	2	0.5	0.5
2	32	7.5	9.2	59	17.3	47.7	30	6.7	7.2
3	32	7.5	16.7	18	5.3	53.0	26	5.8	13.0
4	29	6.8	23.5	23	6.7	59.7	22	4.9	17.9
5	65	15.3	38.8	44	12.9	72.6	42	9.4	27.3
6	24	5.6	44.4	1	0.2	72.8	22	4.9	32.2
7	12	2.8	47.2	1	0.2	73.0	21	5.0	37.2
8	9	2.1	49.3	3	0.9	73.9	11	2.5	39.7
9	1	0.2	49.5	1	0.2	74.1	12	2.7	42.4
10	92	21.6	71.1	41	12.0	86.1	29	6.5	48.9
11—15	41	9.6	80.7	8	2.3	88.4	73	16.4	65.3
16—20	23	5.4	86.1	16	4.7	93.1	34	7.6	72.9
21—25	24	5.6	91.7	9	2.6	95.7	40	9.0	81.9
26—30	7	1.6	93.3	6	1.8	97.5	17	3.8	85.7
31—35	0	0	93.3	0	0	97.5	14	3.2	88.9
36—40	0	0	93.3	1	0.2	97.7	9	2.0	90.9
41—50	19	4.5	97.8	2	0.5	98.2	12	3.0	93.9
51—60	1	0.2	98.0	1	0.2	98.4	10	2.3	96.2
61—70	0	0	0	0	0	98.4	2	0.5	96.7
71—80	1	0.2	98.2	0	0	98.4	6	1.4	98.1
81—90	0	0	98.2	0	0	98.4	0	0	98.1
> 90	6	1.4	99.6	4	0.3	98.7	11	2.5	100.6
Total	424	99.6	99.6	339	98.7	98.7	445	100.6	100.6

Key: NA—Not applicable.

Note: Not answered, and invalid responses to the extent of 111 (69+42) for 'within ISRO' and 196 (179+17) for 'outside ISRO' are excluded. In the total column the partial responses to either 'within ISRO' or 'outside ISRO' are not excluded. The number of 'not answered' and invalid responses in total column is 202.

Correlation of Number of Regular Informal and Interpersonal Contacts with User Characteristics

Results of association/correlation tests of the number of regular informal, interpersonal and intraorganisational contacts with the user characteristics are shown in Table 9.38 (the individual contingency tables are not shown). As revealed in the Table, there is a linear and positive association of status, qualifications and management/supervision content of job with the number of interpersonal contacts within the organisation. There is also a slight positive correlation ($r = 0.17$) of number of interpersonal contacts within the organisation with the professional activities and achievements[8] of the satellite technologists. Specialisation and experience, on the other hand, have no bearing on the number of interpersonal and intraorganisational contacts.[9]

TABLE 9.38: Results of Association/Correlation Tests of Number of Regular Interpersonal Contacts within ISRO (for Information) with Selected User Characteristics

	Status (X^2)	*Qualifications* (X^2)	*Nature of Work* (X^2)	*Specialisation* (X^2)	*Experience* (*r*)	*Professional Activities & Achievements Index* (*r*)
X^2/r	71.80*	61.27*	28.93*	16.66	0.07	0.17*
Degree of freedom (*df*)	14	8	12	10	308	153
Tabulated value of X^2 at $p = 0.05$	23.69	15.51	21.03	18.31	—	—

Key: * The association/correlation is statistically significant at 0.05 significance level.

Table 9.39 presents the results of association/correlation tests of number of regular informal/interpersonal interorganisational contacts with selected user characteristics. The number of contacts outside the organisation, like the number of contacts within the organisation, also shows positive and linear relationship with status, qualifications and management /supervision content of the job of the users. It also shows a low positive correlation ($r = 0.20$) with professional activities and achievements and a slight positive correlation ($r = 0.14$) with experience of the satellite technologists (the individual contingency tables are not shown). On the other hand, specialisation of the satellite technologists has no bearing on the number of interpersonal contacts outside the organisation.[10]

TABLE 9.39: Results of Association/Correlation Tests of Number of Regular Informal Contacts Outside ISRO (for Information) with Selected User Characteristics

	Status (X^2)	*Qualifications* (X^2)	*Nature of Work* (X^2)	*Specialisation* (X^2)	*Experience* (*r*)	*Professional Activities & Achievements Index* (*r*)
X^2/r	39.41*	42.51*	31.68*	17.93	0.14*	0.20*
Degree of freedom (*df*)	14	8	12	10	261	132
Tabulated value of X^2 at $p = 0.05$	23.69	15.51	21.03	18.31	—	—

Key: * The association/correlation is statistically significant at 0.05 significance level.

Pattern of Informal Communication Network

In the second part of the above discussed question the respondents were requested to name the five most often contacted persons for work related information. Though this part of the questionnaire was rather embarrassing to the respondents, as many as 391 (out of 535) have positively reacted (i.e., excluded are 138 who did not answer, 4 who made invalid answers and two for whom the question was not applicable). However, as a special case 29 generic type responses mentioning 'Division/Section/Project staff' are included in the response group. But generic responses, like library staff, project manager or other designations and names of outside organisations without specific names of individuals are invalidated. Among the not answered, about ten expressed their inability to answer in the following words: 'persons are contacted only occasionally depending upon the problem and situation; 'many', 'not interested to reveal', 'no regular contact for information, but will meet persons regarding work related problems', 'I do not want to mention', 'not interested in giving any names', 'find it difficult to name such person', etc. Further, a very few individuals outside ISAC have figured in more than one respondent's list of names and hence further analysis of all outside ISAC individuals is restricted to the names of the organisations to which they belong (Sridhar, 1987, 1995).

Thus, all the responses having names upto five most often contacted persons (i.e., individuals most frequently chosen as sources of informal information) have been processed to examine the nature of relations that exist between the respondent and the named individuals within ISAC (i.e., within the population under study) or names of other centres, units and projects of ISRO/DOS (Department of Space, Government of India) or organisations outside ISAC. Totally 391 respondents (out of 535) have provided names of 515 individuals/organisations and mentioned them 1,538 times as most frequently chosen informal sources of information. The break-up of the number of individuals and organisations contacted together with number of times cited by the satellite technologists is shown in Table 9.40 and Fig. 9.1. It is clear that 87 per cent of the contacts are within the organisation (i.e., ISRO) and inter-organisational communication is represented by a meagre 13 per cent. Satellite technologists as practitioners have maintained a very high

TABLE 9.40: Pattern of Informal Communication Network

	No.	*No. of Times Cited*	*Percentage of Total Citations*
Individuals within ISAC	423	1,263	82.1
Section/Division/Project staff within ISAC	3*	39	2.5
Other ISRO/DOS Centres/ Units/Projects	9	36	2.3
Other organisations within the country	58	162	10.5
Organisations abroad	22	38	2.5
Total	515	1,538	99.9

Key: * Refers to three types of generic statements. 'Section staff': 'division staff' and 'Project staff'.

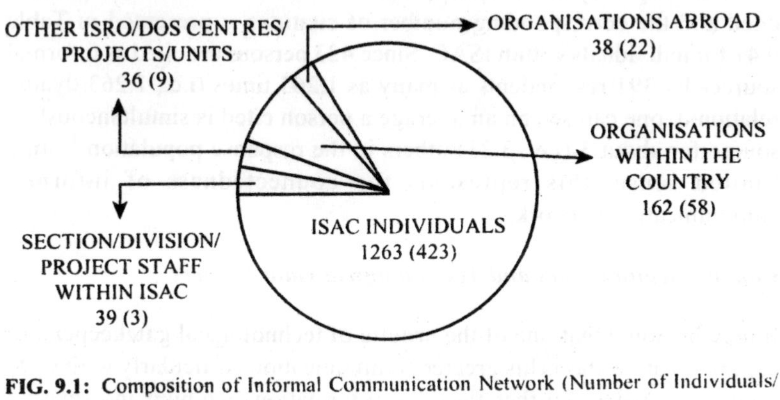

FIG. 9.1: Composition of Informal Communication Network (Number of Individuals/ Organisations within Brackets).

intraorganisational communication. About 19 per cent of the respondents in aerospace establishments communicated with people outside their organisations in Raitt's study (1984, pp. 213-14). A slightly higher percentage of external communication which is noticed in Raitt's study is attributable to the fact that his sample consisted of only higher level scientists and engineers.

Informal and Interpersonal Communication Behaviour and Interpersonal Information—Potential

While the contacts of the satellite technologists with individuals within ISAC are discussed further in this sub-section, the contacts outside ISAC (i.e., 58 Institutional and Individual Sources Outside the Organisation) are discussed in a subsequent sub-section.

Now by looking at the same data from the angle of most often contacted persons within ISAC (i.e., individuals most frequently chosen by the respondents as informal sources of information), we can get a lot of insight into the informal communication network and the informal and interpersonal communication behaviour of the Indian Satellite technologists. Incidentally, as far as interpersonal communication within the population is concerned, seeking as well as communicating information are complementary to one another. Here, a respondent mentioning the name of another respondent or any member of the population is treated as a 'relation' in the informal communication network. However, one limitation of the data at this level of analysis is that the official superior-subordinate relations are not excluded.

The frequency distribution of the five most often contacted persons cited and the corresponding number of citations is presented in Table 9.41 for individuals within ISAC. Since 423 persons are cited as informal sources by 391 respondents as many as 1,263 times (i.e., 1,263 dyadic relations), one can see on an average a person cited is simultaneously a source for about 3 (i.e., 3.23) others in the response population.[11] In a limited sense, this represents the connectedness of informal communication network.

Communication Stars and Technological Gate Keepers

It may be noted that one of the criteria of technological gatekeeper and communication star is his greater communication particularly with wide range of persons. Further they are information rich/high information potential, sociable, most accessible persons holding high status, they

make greater use of literature, they are experienced, professionally active, well educated senior members or first line supervisors.

TABLE 9.41: Frequency Distribution of Most Often Contacted Persons within ISAC as Informal Sources

Frequency Score of Citation	*Persons Cited*			*Citations*		
	No.	*%*	*Cum. %*	*No.*	*%*	*Cum. %*
1	180	42.6	42.6	180	14.3	14.3
2	83	19.6	62.2	166	13.1	27.4
3	48	11.3	73.5	144	11.4	38.8
4	33	7.8	81.3	132	10.5	49.3
5	22	5.2	86.5	100	9.0	58.3
6	13	3.1	89.6	78	6.2	64.5
7	5	1.2	90.8	35	3.0	67.5
8	13	3.1	93.9	104	8.2	75.7
9	6	1.4	95.3	54	4.3	80.0
10	4	0.9	96.2	40	3.2	83.2
11	6	1.4	97.6	66	5.2	88.4
12	2	0.5	98.1	24	2.0	90.4
13	1	0.2	98.3	13	1.0	91.4
14	2	0.5	98.8	28	2.2	93.6
15	1	0.2	99.0	15	1.2	94.8
16	1	0.2	99.2	16	1.3	96.1
17	1	0.2	99.4	17	1.3	97.4
18	1	0.2	99.6	18	1.4	98.8
23	1	0.2	99.8	23	1.8	100.6
Total	423	99.8	99.8	1,263	100.6	100.6

Note: 1. Persons from outside ISAC are tabulated in the name of their respective organisations in the previous Table.
2. One hundred and thirty-eight not answered, 2 not applicable and 4 invalid responses are excluded.
3. The mean and standard deviation of number of times a satellite technologist is cited are respectively 2.99 and 3.03.

Assuming that communication star is one who is contacted as an informal source of information by more than one standard deviation over and above mean number of contacts by respondents (i.e., 2.99 + 3.03 = 6.02 in Table 9.41), there are 44 such communication stars or High Information Potentials (HIPs) in the population. These 44 stars forming just 10.2 per cent of the total persons cited, account of 36 per cent of total citations as most often contacted persons for information. Compared with general formula that the population of size '*n*', approximately contains $\sqrt{n}$ elites, the star-elites or HIPs identified is

much more than square root of the population (i.e., $\sqrt{807} = 28.4$). Further, excluding 423 who have been cited by one or more of others in Table 9.41, the remaining 384 persons in the population could be considered 'isolates' or Low Information Potentials (LIPs).

Such of the stars who link the organisation to external environment can be called technological gatekeepers. Out of 44 stars spotted in this method, 29 are found to have responded to the questionnaire. But only 19 of them provided upto five names of most often contacted persons for information. Out of a total of 88 such citations made by these 19 stars, 41 (46.6%) to other stars, 28 (31.8%) to non-stars within the population and the rest of 19 (21.6%) to persons outside the organisation. As against a 13 per cent outside contacts by the response population as a whole, the communication stars have 21.6 per cent outside contacts. The 'discussion stars' in Hall's study (1972, p. 121) have maintained much lower (15%) outside contacts. It is interesting that communication stars have maintained almost half of their contacts among themselves. However, outside the organisation contacts of communication stars are marginally more than others. Though all the 19 respondent communication stars do not appear to be technological gatekeepers, six of them who have higher than average external contacts for information could be considered as technological gatekeepers.[12]

The characteristics of forty-four communication stars as compared to characteristics of the population/response population as a whole have differed significantly in some respects (Table 9.42). Firstly, the communication stars are predominantly males (with the sole exception of one). Secondly, they are more aged (average age of communication star is 36 years against the average age of 31 years in the population) and they are more experienced (the average total experience of star is 11.8 years as against the average total experience of 7.4 years in the population).[13]

Surprisingly there is no difference between communication stars and others in their job satisfaction. However, the communication stars have tended to acquire more promotion than others (75.7 per cent have secured two or more promotions as against 35.5 per cent in the population). In fact all the communication stars (i.e., 16 for whom normalised data was available) were considered high performers based on frequency of promotion. They also scored a very high professional activities and achievements index values.[14] This is in conformity with findings of earlier research that performance and communication are highly correlated. For example, Bethell (1972, p. 72) found that stardom in the oral communication network has a strong tendency to depend on the number of laboratory reports written and on the amount of attention that is paid to them. He also found that a high performance informal communication is a significant characteristic of a communication star in the informal network.

TABLE 9.42: Characteristics of Communication Stars

Sl. No.	*Characteristics*	*Population*	*Communication Stars*
1.	Average Age (in years)	31	36
2.	Males (in %)	92.4	97.7
3.	Average Experience (in years)	7.4	11.8
4.	Secured 2 or more Promotions (in %)	35.5	75.7
5.	Professional Activities and Achievements (Index)	7.6*	23.8
6.	Status H and above (i.e., Gazetted Officers in %)	45.4	95.5
7.	Technocrats (in %)	13.3	100.0
8.	Managers, Supervisors, Planners and System Analysis (in %)	20.5	56.0
9.	Change in Nature of Work (in % having changes)	28.9	55.2
10.	Postgraduates and Doctorates (in %)	31.8	66.6
11.	Library Use (index)	15.4*	21.4
12.	Library Interactions (index)	5.1*	13.7

Key: * The score is based on indexes developed and for an average non-star and not for a typical satellite technologist in the population.

Note: Communication stars do not differ from others in their job satisfaction.

Communication stars tend to be higher status persons (95.5% of communication stars are in gazetted rank as against 45.4% in the population). They tend to have jobs with more of management/ supervision contents than operational activities (while 56% of stars have management/supervision and planning/system analysis jobs, only 20.5 per cent have these jobs in the population). Further, all the communication stars (i.e., 23 for whom data is known) are found to be technocrats and 55.2 per cent of the communication stars have some change in their nature of work in recent years as against 28.9 per cent for the response population as a whole.

Communication stars are also found to be better qualified than others (while 31.8% are post graduates and doctorates in the population, the same is 66.6% among communication stars). There are disproportionately more communication stars among physicists and electronics engineers and disproportionately less stars among mechanical engineers.

Lastly, though the library membership status remained same among communication stars and others, the former are found to be heavy users of library (average library use index[15] value of a star and non-star, respectively, are 21.4 and 15.4) and they interact more frequently with their primary library (the average value of library interaction index of a star is 13.7 and the same for a non-star is 5.1). Interestingly, there is no non-user (zero score in library use index) of library among the communication stars.

Discussion with selected communication stars and technological gatekeepers revealed that it is part of their duty to collect information from others particularly outsiders and pass on the same to appropriate persons working with them. They also felt that their contacts with information potential persons (especially those from outside the organisation) are their assets. They appear to read widely on general interest from library books and reports. They had a feeling of self-sufficiency as far as work related information is concerned.

Dyadic or Mutual or Reflexive Communication in the Network

Another interesting observation of the most-often-contacted persons cited by 391 respondents (as far as 423 ISAC individuals within population are concerned) is that 72 cited persons (i.e., 36 dyadics or pairs) have mutually cited each other as one of the most-often contacted persons. However, there are only 56 unique persons in 36 pairs or relations.[16] Further, out of 36 pairs of such reflexive relations, 34 pairs are between persons from the same divisions and of which 32 pairs are between persons from the same sections.[17]

Interestingly, ten pairs of persons are of exactly equal status in terms of their designations and of which eight pairs are in the same sections. Out of the remaining 26 pairs of reflexively related persons, the status differences between the persons are, 3 levels in 2 pairs, 2 levels in 11 pairs and just 1 level (or grade) in the rest of 13 pairs.

By assuming that the above 'reflexive relations' satisfy the other conditions of 'equivalence relation', one can decompose the above set of 56 unique respondents into mutually exclusive groups of persons called 'equivalence classes'. Such an analysis has resulted in identifying one class of 9 persons, another class of four persons and other five classes of three persons each. The rest of them form independent small classes of two each. This has also given an indication that respondents with codes C0068, C0095, C0110, C0136, C0209, C0255, C0344, C0482, C0565, C0587, C0719, C0768 and C0774 act as linking pins[18] in the first seven classes and the nine respondents of the largest class form a cluster of the network in a limited sense.

Similarities and Dissimilarities of Participants in Informal Communication

The communication behaviour and the information potential of the Indian satellite technologists are further examined in this sub-section to find out whether some of the characteristics such as technocrat nature, experience, status, specialisation, field of activity, division and section affiliation have any relation for a satellite technologist in seeking another satellite technologist as interpersonal source of information. It has been noted that the average number of times a person (in ISAC) is cited by the respondents is about 3. In other words, an average satellite technologist is a regular informal source of information for three others. However, when we segregate all persons with functional designation (representing technocrat, i.e., managerial and supervisory nature in addition to technical nature) from the rest, the data of Table 9.41 could be grouped as shown in Table 9.43.

TABLE 9.43: Information Potential of Technocrats as Informal Source

	No.	*No. of Times Cited*	*Mean Citation*
Technocrats	45	279	6.2
Others	378	984	2.6
Total	423	1,263	3.0

Technocrats

From the data in Table 9.43, one can see that an average technocrat communicates frequently and informally within the population with more than double the number of persons an average non-technocrat communicates. At the same time, the technocrats in general having sought by more than six others (i.e., over and above one SD on mean contacts), satisfy one of the criteria of technological gatekeepers and communication stars.

Experience

Two hundred and sixty-eight out of 423 most often contacted persons (whose length of experience is known) are further examined and the Table 9.44 presents their experience against the number of persons contacting them for information. As contacts by more than 6 persons (i.e., meant one SD) is the basic criterion for one to be a technological gatekeeper or communication star, we find 29 persons in the Table with 7 or more contacts. Further, except one person with 18 years of experience all these communication stars have an experience from 5 to 13 years. In other words, both highly experienced as well as less experienced are not communication stars. Looking at the overall data in the Table, it appears that more experienced persons are slightly more information potential than less experienced. In fact, the Pearson Product Movement Correlation (*r*) between the experience and number of informal contacts is +0.27 which indicates a slight positive correlation between the two variables. In other words, the null hypothesis that there is no correlation between the number of years of experience of the satellite technologist and the number of other satellite technologists considering him as an informal source for work-related information cannot be completely rejected. The *t*-test has indicated that the correlation value is significant much beyond 95 per cent significant level. Thus, some minimum experience appears to be a prerequisite for a 'technological gatekeeper' or 'communication star' but too much of experience appears to be working in the opposite direction. The finding that new recruits do not communicate to many is in agreement with what Gerstberger (1971) has reported, but the highly experienced do not communicate to many colleagues, is a totally new and unexpected result.

Table 9.44 also reveals to a limited extent that the number of satellite technologists to whom another satellite technologist communicates is curvilinearly related to the experience of the person communicating. In the initial years it appears that he communicates with less number of persons and as the experience exceeds the initial period of say 5 years, he communicates to more colleagues and again declines after about 12 years. In other words, both less experienced and highly experienced technologists communicated to relatively less number of colleagues and those with 6-12 years of experience communicated to the maximum.

Status

As noted in the previous section, 391 space technologists (as respondents

TABLE 9.44: Experience in ISRO *Vs.* Frequency Score of Most Often Contacted Persons within ISAC

Freq. Score	*Experience in Years*																*Total*
	1	*2*	*3*	*4*	*5*	*6*	*7*	*8*	*9*	*10*	*11*	*12*	*14*	*16*	*17*	*23*	
00	04	01															05
01	17	04		03	02												26
02	06	03	02	01	01												09
03	04	03			02												09
04	09	02			01	01		01									14
05	24	06	07	01	02	01	01										42
06	10	06	04	01	01	01	01	01	01								27
07	10	05	02														17
08	02	02		01	01				01								07
09	02	01	04	01		01		02									11
10	20	08	02	03		03	01	02		01	01	01					42
11	04	06		04	01	02		02		01	01				01	01	23
12	01	02	01		02					01		01	01	01			10
13	02		02	02	02		02			01							11
14			01			01											02
15			03	01		01											05
16					01												01
17	01																01
18											01						01
22	01																01
Total	117	49	28	18	16	11	03	10	02	04	04	02	01	01	01	01	268

to the questionnaire) have cited 423 names from the same population as their most often contacted persons for information and the number of times cited is 1,263. By considering the organisational status (or grade) of both citing as well as cited persons (upto five in each case) one can examine the nature of seeking as well as communicating information informally and inter-personally. By eliminating such of the cases where the designation of citing person or cited person or both persons are not known, 330 respondents whose designations are known and the designation of at least one of the persons cited by them is known, have been listed. The total citations of persons are reduced to 1223 from 1263. The results are tabulated in Table 9.45.

TABLE 9.45: Relative Status of Most Often Contacted (Information Potential) Persons

Status	*Information Sought ONLY from*		*Information NOT Sought from any*		*Most Often Contacted (citing) Relations*	
	No.	*%*	*No.*	*%*	*No.*	*%*
Lower	9	2.7	244	73.9	146	11.9
Equal	2	0.6	209	63.3	186	15.2
Higher	163	49.4	18	5.5	891	72.9
Total	174†	52.7†	471*	142.7*	1,223	100.0

Key: * The categories are not mutually exclusive.
† Mixed types are not shown and hence total do not tally to 330. However, percentages worked out are based on 330.

It is obvious from the table that almost half of the respondents have informal and interpersonal linkage for information with persons of higher status only. A negligible 2.7 per cent and 0.6 per cent have such contacts with lower status and equal status persons respectively. On the other hand, nearly three-fourth of the respondents have not sought informal and interpersonal contacts with collegues of lower status. About 63 per cent have not considered equal status colleagues as informal sources of information. However, a marginal 5.5 per cent have not cited any person of higher status. This indirectly supports two of the earlier findings. Firstly, the technological gatekeepers tend to be of higher status or senior persons. Secondly, seeking of information from the informal and interpersonal source of information, is largely confined to higher status persons. Further, even when number of citing relations or dyadics (i.e., 1,223) are examined it is seen from the table that nearly three-fourth (72.9%) of such relations are with higher status persons. The equal status and lower status relations are 15.2 per cent and 11.9 per cent respectively.

Though not totally surprising, by and large, the results indicate that the Indian satellite technologists are status conscious in seeking informal and interpersonal communication. It may be noted that, this does not naturally apply for communicating to others. Hence, it can be concluded that the satellite technologists seem to have considered status as a self-created artificial barrier for free interpersonal communication with colleagues.

This finding partly confirms the findings of Allen and Cohen (1970, p. 16), i.e., there is a greater volume of communication from a higher status person to lower status person but not as much as that takes place between equistatus persons. But it very well supports the findings of another Indian study (Pruthi and Nagpaul, 1978, p. 55) where more communication flourished among persons of different status than equistatus. However, Raitt (1986, p. 254) found more lateral communication among peers than others.

It is also found in the larger survey that the Indian satellite technologists believed that peers and colleagues share information more freely compared to the superiors and subordinates. Thus, in spite of the fact that superiors and subordinates feel less free in sharing information, the amount of communication among persons of different status (not necessarily superiors and subordinates) is more than among persons of same status.

Specialisation and Field of Activity[19]

The broad specialisation and field of activity of persons citing as well as cited are compared and the results are presented in Table 9.46. All such relations where specialisation and field of activity of either citing or cited persons is not known are excluded. The result appears to be inconclusive as far as relation of field of activity to information seeking though interpersonal communication is concerned, as slightly more persons of different fields of activity have been contacted than persons of the same field of activity. As regards specialisation, slightly more interpersonal contacts are found among persons of similar specialisations than different specialisation. One can safely conclude that the Indian satellite technologists not only have regular contact for information with colleagues of the same specialisation and field of activity, but also with persons of different specialisations and fields of activity. This probably, is a reflection of system engineering and multidisciplinary nature of work and a way of cross fertilisation of ideas.

TABLE 9.46: Specialisation and Field of Activity of Most Often Contacted Persons

	Specialisation		*Field of Activity*	
	No.	*%*	*No.*	*%*
Same	325	57	223	45
Different	245	43	272	55
Total	570	100	495	100

Division and Section Affiliation

The divisions and sections to which the persons contacting as well as contacted for informal communication belong are examined and the results are presented in Table 9.47. The data in the Table indicates that while little less than half of the informal and interpersonal communications cut-across the official section-barrier, only one-fourth of such communication relations are beyond division barrier. The following inferences can be drawn from the table: (i) Intra-division contacts (74.3%) are almost three times the inter-division contacts (25.7%); (ii) Intra-section contacts (53.6%) are slightly higher than inter-section contacts (46.4%); (iii) Intra-division contacts (74.3%) are considerably higher than the intra-section contacts (53.6%); (iv) Inter-section contacts (46.4%) are nearly double the inter-division contacts (25.7%). Raitt's (1984, pp. 163-64) finding that 53 per cent of contacts were within the division or project is comparable with 53.6 per cent of contacts found within the same section or project in the present study.

TABLE 9.47: Division and Section Affiliations of Most Often Contacted Persons

	Division of Contacting and Contacted Persons		*Section of Contacting and Contacted Persons*	
	No.	*%*	*No.*	*%*
Same	913	74.3	653	53.6
Different	316	25.7	566	46.4
Total	1,229	100.0	1,219	100.0

In Bethell's study (1972, p. 47) of communications in an international research laboratory, the intersection choices for discussion were 51 out of 183 (28%) which is quite comparable with interdivision contacts (25.7%) in the present study. Shuchman (1981, pp. 40-41) also reported that "for many engineers, contact with colleagues takes place exclusively in their own work group" and the contacts within work group were rated useful by about 90 per cent of respondents whereas contacts outside the work group were rated useful by 40 per cent in case of within the firms and 47 per cent in case of outside the firms.

Qualifications

Since doctorates represented a much smaller fraction (4.5%) of the total population in the present study, the earlier findings of Allen and Cohen, Bethell and many others that 'doctorates choose other doctorates for discussion and non-doctorates tend to contact doctorates', could not be clearly validated.

Thirteen doctorates have cited 56 names as most often contacted persons for information. Only one-fourth of such contacts of doctorates are with other doctorates and they have a slightly higher rate of contacts outside the organisation than others (30.4% as against 13% by response population as a whole and 21.6% by communication stars). The doctorate communication stars tend to be the technological gatekeepers.

Out of 32 doctorates, 'communication stars' and 'isolates' are eight each. Twenty-four doctorates are cited totally 132 times by 391 respondents. In other words, an average doctorate is a frequent informal source of information to 5.5 persons in the response population (this is against the average citation score of 2.99 for population as a whole in the questionnaire among the persons cited as sources of information).

Institutional and Individual Sources of Information Outside the Organisation

Lastly, any user of information has to depend on information outside one's own organisation. The present sub-section examines the interactions of the satellite technologists with the institutions and individuals outside ISAC who act as informal sources. The number of outside ISRO contacts (i.e., roughly same as number of persons) has already been discussed and it is found that on an average a respondent expressed that he has regular contact with 6.6 persons outside ISRO and it is almost half of the average number of persons with whom regular contacts are maintained within ISRO (i.e., 11.8). One observation at this juncture is that the average number of persons contacted within ISAC does not differ much from that within ISRO. It is also, noted that the outside ISAC contacts of the Indian satellite technologists amount to about 18 per cent (13%

outside ISRO) of the total contacts. The further break-down with frequencies of these contacts are presented in Table 9.48. As noted earlier, though the respondents have cited names of individuals, the analysis is restricted to names of institutions as very few individuals of other organisations have scored more than one in the frequency list. The contacts of the respondents, though limited within other centres, units and projects of ISRO and moderate with organisations abroad, are widespread over 58 different institutions within the country. A very large number of contacts are made with organisations or their wings, which are situated within the Bangalore City. Secondly, the number of contacts with 15 academic institutions within the country are alone almost equal to the number of contacts made with remaining 43 organisations (i.e., research organisations, industries, business firms, and other organisations) within the country. However it is noticed that contacts are more with research organisations than industries and with industries than business firms. Thirdly, almost all the business firms contacted are computer or electronics related firms for the purposes of product information. Fourthly, the educational institutions contacted are mainly the almamaters of the satellite technologists. Lastly, the large majority of the rest of the organisations within the country, have projects

TABLE 9.48: Frequency Distribution of Most Often Contacted Organisations* Outside ISAC as Informal Sources

Frequency Score of Citations	*Other Centres, Units Projects of ISRO/ DOS*	*Organisations within the Country*	*Organisations Outside the Country*
01	2	38	14
02	0	9	4
03	3	3	3
04	1	0	0
05	0	1	0
06	0	3	0
07	3	0	0
08	0	1	1
09	0	1	0
10	0	1	0
47	0	1	0
Total	9	58	22

Key: * Respondents were asked to name individuals with their organisations. Since very few individuals from outside ISAC have been cited by more than one respondent, all such responses have been coded by the name of the organisation of the person cited.

sponsored by ISRO or joint projects with ISRO or got ISRO as their customer or are themselves user agencies/customers of ISRO. Among the organisations contacted abroad, NASA and ESA (with their subsidiaries) are significant.

Conclusion

In conclusion, we may recapitulate that an engineer seeks informal communication to circumvent the uncertainties and/or anxieties of his work, to get a tailor made solution to a problem, for details concerning procedures or experiments, to build the confidence in the unique work he does, for quick professional judgments on issues, to gain reassurance on the work he does, in order to cut time lag in publications, for expert assistance in locating published material in diverse subjects, to overcome the problem of formally communicating the complex messages and to fill the gap between supply of and demand for information. It is very clear that even-though some of the above needs are met by informal communication system, libraries do have a role to play, both directly and indirectly to fulfil these needs. To highlight one or two, however unique the work of an engineer he claims it to be, the ongoing research and bibliographic databases could yield references close to one's work. The grey literature like technical reports do provide details about procedures or experiments. Other semiformal publications like preprints do help cutting time lag in publications. A different type of tailor made library services are needed by engineers. The expert assistance an engineer seeks in locating published documents in diverse subjects is a challenge to the organised information system.

The linear and positive relation of number of persons contacted for information with status, qualifications, professional activities, experience and management/supervision content of the job indicates that more provision for formal services is needed to those who have been denied access to intensive informal communication networks.

In a highly intra-organisation oriented communication like the one discussed so far, there is a need for cutting recirculation of ideas or information among members of tight and closed loop informal network of 'old boys'.

The marginal inter-organisation communication due to communication stars and technological gatekeepers and tours and visits abroad (mostly of higher status persons) may have to be increased by encouraging more contacts outside the organisation especially at middle and lower levels. As communication stars have maintained almost half of their communication with other stars, a more liberal organisation structure which places communication stars accessible to more number of colleagues and make many of them as 'linking pins' in the organisation structure might optimise use of such high information potentials. In addition increasing the ratio of technocrats to non-technocrats, periodic reassignment of jobs, more encouragement of inter-section, inter-division and inter-project communication bringing 'isolates' to the communication network is needed. In addition high information potentials, communication stars, technological gatekeepers and linking pins should be provided with extra formal information services so that they act as disseminating agents for formal informal system.

The 'psychological cost' or 'status inhibition' exhibited in seeking information has to be overcome by process of confidence building among lower level workers and colleagues.

Apart from accelerating informal communication among respondents and between respondents and sources outside the organisations, a systematic effort to blend the formal and informal services of information should take place. Development of 'components databank', 'components coordination group', 'panel of experts' from different specialisations, in-house technical seminars, colloquia, in-house technical journal,[20] information bank of internally generated information, journal clubs, etc. may go long way in this direction.

These are only a few implications of the sociometric analysis of informal communication of Indian satellite technologists. Many more can be deduced from the detailed interpretation of communication structure presented above and results are useful to both management and the formal information system.

NOTES AND REFERENCES

1. For background details about equivalence relation and equivalence classes any fundamental book on set theory or the first part of the following paper of the author may be seen: 'A Mathematical Approach to Relations in Thesauri', *Journal of Library and Information Science*, 5(1) June 1980, 77-79.
2. N. Wade (1975), "Citation Analysis: A New Tool for Science Administrations", *Science*, 188, 429-32.
3. A general average is that 80 per cent of references cited in papers are to serial publications. In the case of Indian space technologists 60.6 per cent of references are made to journal articles. See D.J. de Solla Price (1965), "Networks of Scientific Papers", *Science*, 149, 56-64.

4. In case of journal articles 11 out of 72 or 15.3 per cent have no references. This is against a general average of "10 per cent of the papers contain no references at all". See D.J. de Solla Price, *op. cit.*, pp. 56 and 58.
5. "On the average there are 15 references per paper", vide *ibid.*
6. Women space technologists have scored much higher than men in both 'library use index' and 'library interaction index' developed in the study. The average use index value of men and women space technologists, respectively were 15.51 and 20.96. The average interaction index values of men and women were 5.09 and 5.41 respectively (Case Study 19).
7. It is quite interesting to note that similar observations were made in a twin survey on attitudes of students to the Southampton University library in May 1965. It was concluded that one of the two special features of the survey was '. . . the greater use made of libraries by women. They used the University library far more for recreational reading, and borrowed more from it for vacations; they used the catalogue more and were more satisfied with the catalogue entries; they had more confidence in the library staff, but were more reluctant to ask them queries and were more 'intimidated' by the library on first arrival;. . . . These differences exist within each faculty, and are all statistically significant (most of them highly significant). The explanation must surely lie in personality factors; presumably women are on the whole more amenable and perhaps more conscientious than men, more ready to admit they need help and less ready to criticise' (Line and Tidmarsh, 1966).
8. An Index of professional activities and achievements of the respondents is developed based on activities like papers published, patents held, conferences attended, tours, lectures delivered, etc. (Sridhar, 1987, 1995).
9. Contrary to expectation women and men respondents did not differ significantly in number of persons contacted regularly for information within the organisation (Sridhar, 1987, p. 303) (Case Study 19).
10. Again as found in intra-organisational contacts, women and men respondents did not differ in number of interpersonal contacts outside the organisation (Sridhar, 1987, p. 303) (Case Study 19).
11. It is interesting to note that 13 women space technologists were mentioned as most frequently contacted persons for information 22 times (average 1.69) and 410 men space technologists are mentioned as most frequently contacted persons for information 1241 times (average 3.03). Further as many as 48 out of 61 women space technologists in the population (i.e., 78.7%) are not considered as one of the five most frequently contacted persons for information by any of the 391 respondents. This shows a substantial difference in the information potentiality for interpersonal communication between men and women in the given environment. In other words, the information potential of women space technologists in the informal communication structure/network is limited. There appears to be an inhibition on the part of men to contact women colleagues for information even though women are intrinsically information potential as they have all other information related activities almost on par with men. Women space technologists apparently appear low information potentials in the sociometric analysis possibly due to socio-cultural background (Sridhar, 1987) (Case Study 19).
12. The stars or gatekeepers could not be clearly identified by both Shuchman and Raitt in their studies.
13. Bethell (1972, p. 63) found that age is not a significant point of difference but the length of service of a communication star is.

14. The average professional activities and achievements index values of communication stars and non-stars respectively are 23.8 and 7.6.
15. The library use index and library interaction index are also developed in the study for each user (Case Study 14).
16. A relation between elements '*a*' and '*b*' is reflexive if '*b*' chooses '*a*' whenever '*a*' chooses '*b*'. For background details of concepts of relations, any fundamental book on set theory or the first part of following paper may be seen. M.S. Sridhar, "A Mathematical Approach to Relations in Thesauri", *Journal of Library and Information Science*, 5, No. 1 (June 1980), 77-79.
17. Section is a narrower concept than division in the organisation structure, i.e., a division has one or more sections within it.
18. 'Linking Pin' concept is originally propounded by Rensis Lickert (1959, p. 194).
19. Specialisation refers to Specialisation in highest degree (e.g., physics, electronics, etc.) whereas field of activity is more related to work and much narrower and/or interdisciplinary in nature.
20. It is heartening to note that not only in-house seminars with many invited outside speakers have become common but also a technical in-house formal entitled '*Journal of Spacecraft Technology*' is regularly published by the centre since 1991.

10

INFORMATION SEEKING AND GATHERING BEHAVIOUR

CASE STUDY 20

SUMMARY OF A CLUSTER OF STUDIES ON INFORMATION SEEKING AND GATHERING BEHAVIOUR

Introduction

Information Behaviour in General and Information Seeking Behaviour (ISB) in particular of Indian Space Technologists (IST) comprising of scientists, engineers, managers, technocrats and technicians of ISRO Satellite Centre (ISAC), Bangalore are investigated. The study is timely as there is a greater need for continuous, focused, localised and organisation oriented user-research for design and operation of better information systems in the country.

Objectives and Hypothesis

The main objectives of this study are to probe information transfer process and to determine ISB of IST, various characteristics of IST as variables of their information behaviour and relate selected characteristics with their information behaviour. The positive hypothesis of the study is that ISB of space technologists has a definite relation to their characteristics like status, qualifications, nature of work, specialisation, experience and professional activities and achievements based 'performance'.

Scope and Limitations

The study confined to the current work-related scientific and technical information in all its manifestations. While the term 'information behaviour' includes information seeking, gathering, receiving and communicating, the ISB is defined to include aspects like motives and purposes of seeking information, the nature and types of information sought, the ways and means of accessing, searching, identifying and acquiring information, the communication behaviour and use of and interactions with the 'primary library'.

The study is primarily an 'applied' user-research and not 'basic' user-research, i.e., why a user behaves as he does is outside the scope of the study.

Some of the related aspects which are not covered under ISB are how information is applied to work, the satisfaction or dissatisfaction of users about information system, frequency and urgency with which information is needed, nature of demand for information, information search strategies adopted, the success/failure rates, stimulus value of information, user assimilation capacity, problems of information overload and redundancy in information system.

Not all characteristics of IST are covered in the study. For example, psychological factors/variables, personality traits, social roles, semiofficial roles, etc., are kept outside the scope and only six characteristics as mentioned under objectives and hypothesis are tested for their relation with ISB of the space technologists without implying any cause and effect relationship. The study has not attempted for exploring inter-correlation of various aspects of ISB as well as user characteristics, multiple and partial correlation, factor analysis of ISB with two or more characteristics of the space technologists.

This is not a participative user-research and hence respondents are naturally conditioned by what is known to them and available to them presently. Lastly, the study has not attempted for generalising the findings.

Research Design and Methods

An exploratory survey approach and a cross-sectional research design with emphasis on norms of critical incident technique and occasionally on longitudinal approach and activity sampling technique are followed in the study. Multiple investigation methods and data collection tools and techniques are employed in the study.

Different methods are applied in a helpful sequence such that each tries to gain from and supplements the preceding method/s. At the same time all methods are directed towards the core problem so as to depict different perspectives like users' opinions, researcher's observations, results of discussions, self-reported activities of users, historical records, etc.

About 180 men-weeks of summary of information related activities to a maximum of six consecutive weeks per respondent (with a 20% response from 20% systematic random sample) is collected. In addition, a near census survey of over 800 space technologists through largely self-administered independently designed and tested questionnaire with 68.5 per cent response yielded rich, adequate and representative data. Thirty space technologists are interviewed for about an hour each with a semi-structured interview schedule designed and tested for the purpose. A semi-controlled/quasi-experimental study of use of library documents and observations of user-interactions with the library and analysis of records of the 'primary library' provided further rich and critical incident data. In addition, certain indirect methods are also employed.

The chi-square non-parametric test, Spearman rank order correlation (r_s), Pearson product moment correlation (r) and t-test are employed in the analysis and interpretation of the data.

Summary of Findings

Realisation of Objective 1: Information-seeking Behaviour of the Indian Space Technologists

Motives and Purposes of Seeking Information

Unlike scientists, the space technologists are not motivated much by recognition, competition, visibility among peers and urge to write and publish (in the decreasing order of priority) while seeking information. On the other hand they are primarily motivated by a need for self-improvement, the desire to be up-to-date in the field of specialisation, maintaining professional competence, self-satisfaction and achieving the desired result in work (in that order).

This is in conformity with Shuchman's (1981, p. 29) observation about American industrial engineers that "most professionals are concerned with appearing technically competent to their colleagues". A typical respondent says "I gather information mainly to improve my knowledge. . . . I want to spend my leisure time for information gathering". The findings are also on line with Menzel's (Columbia University, 1958) observation that achievement, curiosity, self-evaluation and affiliation are the main motives of seeking information. Keeping up-to-date with latest developments in the field of specialisation/activities and relating present work with the current body of knowledge are the main/purposes of seeking information by the space technologists. This again is close to the findings of Menzel (Columbia University, 1958, pp. 67 and 80) and Voigt (1959, pp. 177-79). To quote a respondent "information is gathered to increase the general sense of awareness about the state-of-the-art in the area of work, to see how it can be applied in the work and to identify and pursue desirable degree of professional competence".

The space technologists do not seek information much for the purpose of data treatment and processing, crystallising broad and vague assertions, participating in seminars and conferences, writing papers and delivering talks (in that rank order).

Nature and Type of Information Required

In consistency with the high ranked motives and purposes of seeking information, the requirements of S&T news and basic S&T information have ranked high for the space technologists. In addition, the space technologists seek more of theoretical background, experimental results, methods, processes and procedures, product, material, equipment and apparatus information and physical, technical and design data (in that rank order) than state-of-the-art, review literature, standard and patent specifications (Case Study 03).

The ranking is almost close to that of Shuchman (1981, pp. 32-83; 1982, pp. 106-09) about American industrial engineers, Rawdin (1975, pp. 41-42) about American users of technical libraries, Wood (1967, p. 217) about British mechanical engineers and Slater and Fisher (1969, pp. 32-33, 36, 47 and 49) about users of British technical libraries and roughly close to the findings of Auerbach (1965, pp. 1-19), Cole (1958), Herner and Herner (1959, p. 67) and Raitt (1984, pp. 204-08). Discussions with respondents revealed that general information to keep abreast with current developments and specific work related information to solve practical problems are two main types of information required by the space technologists. Further, Information is sought only when it is utmost needed and there is a strong need for internally generated information and product information. A respondent says "when I want some information on any component or equipment I will go through the text books to build up the theoretical background and then refer to data and product catalogues and application notes. Then I will go through the journals, if necessary".

This shows the intermittent and intermixed use of different types of information by the space technologists depending on the nature of work.

Further, change in the nature of work of the space technologists is found to affect both the intensity of need and the type of information required. The problem of information overload, enlargement of boundaries of interest and intensification of space activities in the country, impact of electronics boom and resultant need for condensed information-services and need for fast serving information intermediaries or agents are felt by the IST.

Sources of Bibliographic Information Used

Library catalogues, colleagues and fellow professionals, direct browsing of library shelves, experts in the field, citations in current reading materials (in that order) are major sources of bibliographic information to the space technologists.

Except higher dependence on library catalogues (which need further probing) the rest of the sources of bibliographic information are almost in the same order as found in many earlier studies (Voigt, 1959; pp. 179-80; Hanson, 1964, p. 71; Raisig, *et al.*, 1966; B.N. Singh, 1981, p. 172). As against 38 per cent of British physicists, 48 per cent American physicists (Gray, 1950, p. 417, Urquhart, 1965), 33.5 per cent American engineers (Davis, 1965, p. 31) and 14.9 per cent British mechanical engineers (Wood, 1967, p. 220), 46.6 per cent of the IST used abstracting and indexing journals.

The space technologists have consulted library catalogues half of the time to locate specific documents, one-fourth of the time to interact with loaning system, one-tenth of the time for literature search. The subject catalogue is consulted most frequently (Sridhar, 1986) (Case Study 13).

A respondent says "searching in library shelves may not be scientific but more practical". The space technologists felt that relevant references are rarely available in a ready to use way, but a lot of browsing, searching and digging is necessary. In the process they have sought free reprints and reports and used indirect methods like cyclic way of generating references. Thus intermittent use of various sources of bibliographic information and interdependence among the sources, indirect cyclic way of generating useful references and more practical way of directly searching the shelves are adopted by the IST for bibliographic references. The following report of a respondent in his weekly summary of information related activities makes it clear:

"I needed more information on Realising switching function. I went to library and scanned through latest books. I wondered that there are so many new techniques. I selected a latest book on digital design which I have not yet read. A colleague suggested another book; when I searched in the library through author and subject indexes, I could not get more details of the book. I found it is better to take some other book available on the shelf with the required information than searching through indexes".

Delegation of Information-gathering Work

Just 6 per cent of the space technologists have frequently, and another 40 per cent moderately or occasionally, delegated information-gathering work to juniors and subordinates, mainly due to lack of time and/or for involving team members.

Though the degree of delegation by the space technologists is close to social scientists (Line, 1971, p. 425), it is slightly lower than that found with atomic scientists (Hogg and Smith, 1959, p. 33) and industrial technologists (Scott, 1960, p. 33).

The reasons for delegation are unique to the IST. The tasks delegated are mainly collection of factual data, documents/literature and latest references on specific topics. The nature of information gathering work delegated conformed to that found by Raitt (1984, p. 304) as well as Line (1971, p. 425) except that IST have delegated more of (even) current search for latest references (48.6%) than retrospective and exhaustive search (26.6%) and analysed and digested literature (34.2%). Those who tend to seek more of physical, technical and design data have delegated more of factual, design and physical data and those who tend to seek more of state-of-the-art and review literature have naturally delegated more of retrospective and exhaustive searches.

Those who do not have assistants and those who believe strongly in serendipity value of information-searching process have naturally tended not to delegate information-gathering work. A respondent says "while searching there are ample chances for me to sight other titles which will be of immense help in my field". Though it is felt possible to communicate to others and train others in one's way of information gathering, it is felt that there are not many people in the organisation with similar background to delegate. Majority of the space technologists do regular unfocused browsing of current literature which lead them, at times, to highly useful accidental or chance acquisition of needed information. This is on line with the observations of earlier studies (Rosenbloom *et al.*, 1965; Columbia University, 1958; Scott, 1959; Bernard *et al.*, 1963/1964; Shuchman, 1981, p. 15). Respondents have narrated specific incident of accidental acquisition of information while skimming through the current journals, unintentionally looking here and there, browsing library shelves and reorganising personal and departmental collections.

Time Spent on Information-gathering Activities

The IST have spent, on an average, 9.2 hours per week or one-fourth of their working time for gathering work-related information which is close to that found by Raitt (1984, pp. 151-54) and higher than 7 hours per week spent by Indian scientists in another study (Garg and Ashok Kumar, 1984, p. 71). Nearly 80 per cent of the space technologists spent 4-15 hours per week on information-related activities and is slightly lower than that found in many earlier studies (Schussel, 1969; Halbert and Ackoff, 1959; Jahoda, 1969; and Gilmore *et al.*, 1967, pp. 41-42).

As many as 86 per cent of the IST have spent more than half of such time in seeking/gathering information from formal and documentary sources of information. This is in conformity with what Raitt (1984, p. 153) has found but differed from that found by Halbert and Ackoff (1959).

The helplessness about lack of time is reflected in the following statements of respondents:

"I could not find enough time for information related activities as I was more involved in routine works such as development and testing"; "It is not possible to have information gathering activity on a regular basis due to pressure of work. Hence, it is done as and when time permits"; "Pressure of routine works has prevented me from collecting information as much as possible as regularly as possible and as much as I would like to do".

The space technologist could not spend as much time as they wished (a reinforcement of a finding of Raitt, 1984, p. 228). By and large, more time is spent in the initial phases of projects for information-gathering (except where the project is a feasibility study or the project itself is defined and assigned from outside the group) than during later stages. The reverse is true with engineers not involved in conception and definition of projects.

Dependence on Sources of Information

The space technologists indicated slightly more dependence on formal and documentary sources of information compared to informal and inter-personal sources.

This does not support the general findings of DOD user study (Auerbach, 1966, pp. 106-07; 1965, pp. 1-12) and that of Raitt (1984, pp. 209, 211 and 214) and Shuchman (1981, pp. 30, 53-55) that users depended heavily on informal sources. A typical statement like the following indicates the primacy of 'ease of use' in accessing a source of information: "My information gathering habits are mostly dependent on things easily come across in everyday life".

Among the formal sources, they depend heavily on journals followed by books, reports, trade literature and internal reports in that rank order. This is in conformity with the findings of Tornudd (1959), Herner and Myatt (1954) and Davis (1965, pp. 30-34). However, in Raitt's study (1984, p. 253) reports occupied more predominant position than books for his respondents. Conference proceedings, reprints and preprints, standard and patent specifications and theses and dissertations have ranked lowest (in that order) for the IST. The degree of dependence on journals showed a low positive correlation with degree of requirement of S&T news ($r = 0.25$).

The IST have qualitatively stressed the importance of trade literature, technical reports, data sheets, conference papers and proceedings, personal and departmental collections and even newspapers. The following statements of respondents make it clear that trade literature is a significant source of information to the IST and they have greater dependence and need for it.

"I depended mainly on the trade catalogues and data sheets available in the section to meet the information needed during the week"; "I always use the readers service cards in the journals to get catalogues and more information from the manufacturers"; "I collect information by scanning journals like 'Machine Design', 'Industrial Product Finder', etc., contacting suppliers, studying product catalogues and visiting other similar installations elsewhere"; "I make regular correspondence with manufacturers and their representatives, visit exhibitions and other centres where information about products are displayed".

Personal and departmental collections of the space technologists consist mainly of internally generated information, free reading materials, preprints, journals, trade catalogues, standard specifications, reprints, reports, diagrams, handbooks, manuals and are not generally well organised.

A typical respondent says "I get most of the information required for my work from the departmental collection and from books in the library".

Among the informal sources, the space technologists have depended heavily on two intra-personal sources, namely, personal experience and results of their own experiments.

This very well goes with the observation of Shuchman (1982, p. 5) about American engineers that "the primary source of engineering information is largely what the engineer keeps in his head". The discussion with respondents revealed that the "personal experience plays a major role and only when there is a vague resemblance one is lead to formal literature". Due to high specialisation and need for practical processes the nucleus of information-gathering activities of the IST is often oneself. The inter-personal contacts are mainly for opinion, suggestions and references.

The high dependence on intra-personal source is followed by inter-personal sources like superiors, peers and colleagues in the organisation. This again is on par with findings of Glass and Norwood (1959), Sherwin and Inemson, (1966), Rosenbloom and Wolek (1970) and Gralewiska-Vickery (1976, p. 269).

The IST have depended least on fellow professionals outside-the-organisation for work-related information.

Some ways of blending formal and informal sources of information are: (1) organisation of internally-generated information, (2) in-house technical journal, (3) databank of expertise, (4) component co-ordination group, (5) in-house seminars, (6) liberal tours, (7) presentations from outside speakers, and (8) journal clubs.[1]

In order to keep up-to-date in the field, over 52 per cent of the respondents depend mainly on journals (similar to that found by Shuchman, 1981, p. 44), another 13 per cent on discussion with colleagues and 9 per cent on trade literature. In addition seminars, newspapers, preprints, lectures and sales representatives are considered quite useful for keeping up-to-date. As found in the past, discussion with similar minds and conscious reading are the two activities which stimulate new ideas to the IST. The tolerable delay in supplying information and documents ranged widely depending on specific instances. Many instances of late detection of information are pointed out by the respondents. Depending on the specific field of work, the technological gap is found to be 5-15 years. The respondents are, by and large, fairly satisfied with the sources of information presently available to them. But they are optimistic on their devoting increasingly more time in future to explore various sources of information.

Inter-personal Information-sharing

There exists greater and more free inter-personal communication among peers and colleagues than among subordinates and superiors. There is a general lack of confidence or trust among the respondents about their superiors freely sharing information even though many depend on superiors for information and even superiors claim that they collect information for the purpose of sharing it with other members in the team.

Information sharing is dependent on content (information), context (time and space) and personality (person with whom information is shared). Some covert inhibitions and conditions that exist for free interpersonal flow of information are professional jealousy, potential threat arising out of competition, lack of motivation, conducive atmosphere, team spirit and group discussions, compartmentalised organisation structure, status consciousness and fear of getting ridiculed about ignorance on the part of seeker of information.

A typical engineer frankly says "I do withhold information on selective basis". Another admits that "a great deal of improvement results if one overcomes the inherent hesitation to admit ignorance". Yet another says "when approached people give information if they can readily and easily do so. But they are not likely to take extra trouble to give information". This is very much close to the findings of Collins (1974) and Wolek (1984, p. 226). The degree of dependence for information by respondents related much better with the degree of information sharing in case of subordinates and peers as interpersonal sources of information than superiors.

Intra- and Inter-organisational Communication

A very high intra-organisational communication exists among the space technologists (similar to practitioners vide Wilkin, 1981, pp. 2-10) as 87 per cent of the five most often-chosen persons for information are from within the organisation and less than one-third of the respondents kept absolutely no inter-personal contacts outside-the-organisation. The most often-contacted persons outside-the-organisation for information are spread over 50 organisations within the country and 22 outside the country. A large majority of communication outside-the-organisation is confined to the persons within the same city and nearly half of such communication is with persons in the academic institutions, where the space technologists have had their education earlier (Case Study 19).

Informal Communication Behaviour

The communication network based on five most frequently-chosen persons for information revealed that on an average a space technologist is chosen by 3.23 respondents (i.e., average inter-personal information-potential is 3.23). An average 'technocrat' communicated (informally) most often with more than double the number of persons an average non-technocrat communicated. Those with 6-12 years of experience have maximum informal communication ($r = 0.27$). The findings that new entrants do not communicate to many is in agreement with findings of Gersberger (1971) but highly experienced also do not communicate to many colleagues is a totally new and unexpected result.

Status or organisational rank is a self-created barrier in inter-personal information-seeking as nearly three-fourth of the contacts are with higher-status persons but status is not a barrier in providing information.

Relatively more lateral communication among peers found by Raitt (1984, p. 254) and more communication among persons of different status found by Pruthi and Nagpaul (1978, p. 55) are in conformity with this result. But the finding of Allen and Cohen (1970, p. 16) that there is a greater volume of communication from a higher status persons to lower status persons but not as much as that takes place between equi-status persons is partly supported.

Similar barriers do exist in the form of official organisation structure especially divisions, as just one-fourth of the contacts are outside-the-divisions.

This is comparable with 28 per cent intersection choices of respondents of Bethell (1972, p. 47). On the other hand Raitt's (1984, pp. 163-64) finding that 53 per cent of contacts are within the division or project is comparable with 53.6 per cent similar contacts found within the same section or project in the present study.

There exists substantial cross fertilisation of ideas among the IST as almost half of the inter-personal communication are among persons of different specialisations and fields of activities. Doctorate space technologists are high (informal) communicators even though equal number of 'stars' as well as 'isolates' exist among them. Doctorates (30.4%) are twice likely to receive communication from outside-the-organisation than others (15.3%) and 50 per cent more than 'communication stars' (21.6%). Information-potential of an average doctorate space technologist (5.5%) is double that of an average person in the population (2.99%). One-fourth of the frequent contacts of doctorates for information is with other doctorates (Case Study 19).

Communication Stars and Technological Gatekeepers

Forty-four 'communication stars' (including six 'technological gatekeepers') in the response population have maintained nearly half (47%) of their informal communication among themselves. They have marginally higher communication (21.6%) outside-the-organisation than an average respondent (15.3%). The 'stars' are characterised by higher age, experience, status, qualifications, professional activities and achievements, use of library and interactions with the library. They are predominately male technocrats with a confidence of self-sufficiency and satisfaction with respect to information-use and transfer and more willing to share information with others. Communication stars do not differ from others in their job satisfaction but they acquired promotion more frequently than others.

This is close to the general finding of the past studies that performance and communication are positively related (Rothwell and Robertson, 1975, p. 393; Bethell, 1972, p. 93; Pelz and Andrews, 1976, p. 47; Hall and Ritchie, 1975, pp. 234-44 and Hagstorm, 1965).

Formal Communication Behaviour

The formal communication through internal reports has been a more popular method than publishing research papers in journals as space technologists of different status, qualifications and nature of work are involved in preparing internal reports.

This goes well with the observation of Shuchman (1982, p. 5) that the most important output of American engineers is in-house technical reports. The percentage (25%) of the IST involved in publishing papers is same as that found by Shuchman (1981) but less than that (35%) found by Tornudd (1959).

The space technologists have shown an inclination for oral conference presentation of papers rather than archival publications in journals. Indian journals have served more as publishing outlets for the space technologists than sources of information and sources for citation.

The ranking of various forms of literature in citations of the IST is journals (61%), books (14%), reports (10%), conference papers (10%), theses (2%), preprints (2%) and lecture notes, standards, product catalogues and private communications (1%).

This is close to that found by Herner *et al.* (1979); and Srinivasan (1970), but differed from that of others. Citations to reports and self-citations (16%) are on a higher side compared to results of other studies

(Burton and Green, 1961, p. 35; B.N. Singh, 1981, p. 179; Srinivasan, 1970; Herner *et al.*, 1979; Meadows and O'Conner, 1969, p. 160). Almost 97 per cent of journal articles and 79 per cent of reports cited by the IST are of foreign origin (Case Study 16).

The IST have a high co-authorship and collaboration in publishing and research as 81 per cent of the sample papers are multi-authored papers with a 'multiplicity index' of 3.17 and 'productivity ratio' of 0.32. There exists sufficient vertical as well as horizontal co-authorship and collaboration as nearly 80 per cent of co-authorship relations are between persons of different status. Further, 42 per cent and 52 per cent of co-authorship relations are respectively between persons of different divisions/sections and different fields of activities (Case Study 15).

Use of the Library and User-interactions with the Library

The 'primary library' is used by a large majority, i.e., 88 per cent used library documents and 60 per cent interacted with library.

As against, 50 per cent of UK electrical engineers (Scott, 1960, p. 3); 26.3 per cent and 22.6 per cent in UK industrial firms and government laboratories (Slater and Fisher, 1969, p. 21) and 37 per cent at MIT (Bush *et al.*, 1956, p. 94) used their respective libraries.

But it is mainly for keeping up-to-date rather than for increasing their work performance. The space technologists are aware of the consequences of using as well as not using formal sources of information like the library. While the theoretical and basic science oriented persons considered 'papers' as their 'backbones', developmental persons felt that the information from written documents are not often directly applied in the work but are used to have an intuitive guess about future work. After a certain basic level of use, the amount of use of the library is not commensurating with the results of work. The innovative ideas cannot always be put into use due to risk, reliability and cost factors.

The frequency-distribution of use of journals is less skewed than that of books, and books than that of reports. In other words, the interest of the IST is more widely spread among different journals than in case of books and more widely among books than in case of reports. Unusually, more use of the library is made during reviews for promotion although the space technologists do not attribute seeking information for getting promotion as a major motive or purpose. The borrowed use of books is quite intensive (80%), journals moderate (14%), reports marginal (5%) and standards negligible (0.2%). The in-house use of journals is much more than borrowed use.

Though the use of journals is much less than that of books, the average time spent by the users in journals section of the library is much longer than that spent in books and reports area. Interestingly, there exists a statistically significant moderate positive rank order correlation ($r_s = 0.55$) between in-house use of library documents and the nearness of the functional division/project of the user to the library. The average in-house use by project personnel is maximum and that of the service sector personnel is minimum.

Interestingly enough, the chances of reserving a document by the IST increases by 56 per cent when the interest of colleagues in the new books is publicised. A user who used library documents has greater chances of interacting with the library for other purposes and *vice versa*. Even a user of a single type of document has a greater chance of using other types of documents and one who interacts with the library for one purpose/service has a greater chance to interact for other purposes/services (Chapters 7 and 8).

Realisation of Objective 2 : Characteristics of the Indian Space Technologists

The Indian space technologists are working in a young organisation and are themselves quite young. The average age of the IST is (31-years) much less than that of respondents of Raitt (1984, p. 191) and DOD user study (Auerbach, 1965, p. B-3). The response population of the study consists of 6.5 per cent females which is slightly more than the overall employment pattern in R&D institutions in the country (India, DST, 1982, p. 5) and much higher (2.8%) than that found by Raitt (1984, p. 121). The average experience of the respondents in ISRO, and before joining ISRO, are respectively, 5.9 years and 2.5 years. The frequency distribution of age of space technologists is close to that of DOD user study (Auerbach, 1965, p. B-6). A large majority of the respondents brought prior experience from industry (41%), R&D organisations (30%) and academic institutions (18%). A reverse trend was found by Raitt (1984, p. 129) in aerospace establishments of U.K.

The space technologist are motivated mainly by 'self-improvement' followed by 'work progress' in seeking information. Of the respondents, nearly three-fourths (73%) are fairly or fully satisfied with their present jobs. They have shown a high job mobility within and outside-the-organisation. The performance rating by peers has mostly coincided with the promotion based performance measure. Based on frequency of promotion, 158 'high performers' are identified. The frequency distribution of performance based on professional activities and achievements shows that about 13 per cent claim zero value, 37 per cent score a low value of 1 to 5, 45 per cent score 6 to 10 and the rest of 5 per cent a high value of 11 or more.

Nearly 55 per cent of the population are scientists and engineers by designation and the rest are non-gazetted technical staff. About 12 per cent of the space technologists are technocrats and a little over 5 per cent are working exclusively in project management offices and core teams. Of the respondents, over two-thirds (68%) are involved in design, development, fabrication and testing activities and about one-fifths (20.5%) in management, planning and system-analysis work (as against 60% in Raitt's study, 1984, p. 123). Large-scale developmental work has necessitated more middle and lower-level and less qualified personnel, particularly in various service sectors. The space technologists show a wide professional diversity in terms of their specialised fields of activities. A majority of the respondents work in the areas of mechanical engineering, communication engineering, computer science, instrumentation and physics which is close to that found in DOD user study (Auerbach, 1965, p. B-8).

The population consists of just 4.5 per cent doctorates, which is lower than that (11%) found elsewhere in the country (India, DST, 1982, p. 5). On the other hand undergraduates and diploma holders who constitute 40 per cent of the population are more than (28%) the country's average (India, DST, 1982, p. 5). By the criterion of subject of specialisation, there are 44 per cent electronics engineers, 27 per cent mechanical engineers, and 8 per cent physicists. Nearly two-third of the respondents are from applied science, engineering and technology, one-eighth from pure science and a meagre 1.3 per cent from management disciplines. The low percentage of doctorates as well as pure science personnel indicate lack of 'pure research' nature in the space technologists.

By and large, the IST is a heterogeneous group in terms of their characteristics. But the response-population is highly representative of the total population of the study by almost all characteristics. Many user-characteristics of the IST are highly related to each other and status, nature of work, qualifications, specialisation and performance (based on professional activities and achievements) fairly represent the characteristics of the IST for a correlational study of ISB (Chapter 3).

Realisation of Objective 3: Correlation of Information-seeking Behaviour of the Indian Space Technologists with their Characteristics

A summary of correlation/association test results of various aspects of ISB with status, qualifications, nature of work, specialisation, experience and professional activities and achievements of the IST revealed that almost all the aspects of ISB are related to one or more characteristics of the IST. Though experience of the IST is related to their ISB, only in 28 of the 108 aspects, other-characteristics relate significantly in 57 to 81 aspects. Thus the null hypothesis that there is no significant relation, other than due to chance, between the ISB and the characteristics of the IST is, by and large, rejected. Hence it can be concluded that the ISB of the IST varies significantly with status, qualifications, nature of work, specialisation and professional activities and achievements.

A majority of the significant relations of the status of the IST with information-seeking activities are positive. However, seeking information for the purpose of equipment setup and use, need for standard and patent specifications, consulting library card catalogues and library staff for bibliographic references, chances of delegating information-gathering work due to unfamiliarity with the sources, dependence on standard and patent specifications, superiors and educational and training courses as sources of information and relative dependence on informal and inter-personal sources compare to formal and documentary sources of information decrease as the status of the IST increases.

Even in case of qualifications of the IST, most of the correlations/associations are positive. However, the motive of gaining promotion while seeking information, consulting library card catalogues and library staff for bibliographic references, delegating information-gathering work due to unfamiliarity with the sources, dependence on superiors as sources of information and relative dependence on informal sources compared to formal sources of information decrease as the level of qualifications of the space technologists increases.

The nature of work of the IST arranged in the ascending order of management/supervision content or descending order of operational activity of the job is highly interrelated to their status structure and level of qualifications. As such, the relation of the nature of work to information-seeking activities runs almost parallel to that found with status and qualifications. However, a strict linear positive relation to the ascending order of management/supervision content of the job is found in the case of seeking information for the purposes of participating in seminars, keeping abreast with developments, crystallising broad and vague assertions and evolving innovative ideas/techniques, seeking state-of-the-art and review literature, degree of delegation of information-gathering work, involving team members as a reason for delegation, dependence on fellow professionals outside-the-organisation and professional meetings and seminars as sources of information, the number of inter-personal contacts both within and outside-the-organisation, communication stardom, inter-personal information-potential and use of reprographic service of the library. Yet, the relative dependence on informal sources compared to formal sources decreases as management/supervision content of the job increases. Interestingly, the amount of time spent on information-gathering activities is independent of the nature of work of the IST.

The IST is a heterogeneous group by considering the subject of specialisation of its members. Some of the information seeking activities of specialists within the IST differed from one another. Physicists, mathematicians, mechanical engineers, aeronautical and structural engineers, electrical engineers, electronics engineers have their own profiles of information-behaviour. Physicists, being scientists, are highly active in seeking information and are oriented to literature and formal information-system. Mathematicians are also active seekers of information but not to the extent of the physicists. Among engineers, aeronautical and structural engineers are most active in seeking information and they are close to scientists in their information-behaviour. Out of the rest, electronics engineers are more active seekers and users of information than mechanical engineers and electrical engineers within the IST. The specialisation of the IST has no bearing on the delegation of information-gathering work. Even the motives of seeking information, use of sources of bibliographic information and communication-behaviour are almost independent of specialisation of the space technologists.

As mentioned earlier, the experience of the IST is found to be correlated with just one-fourth of the information-seeking behaviour items tested for correlation. Interestingly, experience correlated positively with building professional competence as a motive and guiding the team as a purpose of seeking information, need for state-of-the-art and review literature, standard and patent specifications, S&T news, dependence on citations in current reading materials, involving team members as a reason for delegation of information-gathering work, dependence on conference proceedings and papers, journals, standard and patent specifications, reprints and preprints, subordinates, professional seminars as sources of information, inter-personal information sharing by subordinates, number of inter-personal contacts outside-the-organisation and the chances of becoming communication star. The aspects negatively related to the length of experience of the IST are: data treatment and processing as a purpose of seeking information, need for theoretical background, computer programs and model building information, time spent on information-gathering activities, percentage of time spent on informal sources of information, dependence on books, internal reports, superiors, educational and training courses as sources of information and library-use index. Yet experience is not significantly related to majority of the motives and purposes of seeking information, use of bibliographic sources, delegation of information-gathering work, use of library documents and interactions of the IST with the library.

The professional activities and achievements-index developed in the study appears to be a good measure of the intensity of information-seeking activities of the users. A majority of the information-seeking aspects correlated positively with this index. The aspects of ISB which correlate negatively with the professional activities and achievements-index are: getting promotion as a motive of seeking information, equipment set and use as a purpose of seeking information, the need for standard and patent specifications, consulting experts and library staff for bibliographic references, unfamiliarity with the sources as a reason for delegating information-gathering work, dependence on standard and patent specifications, trade literature, superiors as sources of information and relative dependence on informal sources of information compared to formal sources of information. Yet majority of the nature and type of information sought and bibliographic sources used are independent of professional activities and achievements of the IST.

Implications of the Results and Findings

It is not feasible to enumerate all the implications of the results and findings of this study. However, an attempt is made here to highlight selected, significant and direct implications of the findings. The multifaceted approach in seeking and collecting information adopted by the heterogeneous group of the IST makes generalisation too difficult. The IST are specialised in different disciplines, yet have a common mission and thereby exhibit the duality of the discipline and mission orientation (Weinberg, 1967) in their information-behaviour and provision of uniform or common service to all is highly unsuitable.

The formal information system should be clear about its objectives (including derived and assumed objectives, if any). Information-services for increasing productivity and enhancing work performance, self-progress, departmental promotion, continuing education do differ very much from one another. The excessive dependence on library for departmental promotion and for continuing education has to be taken note of. For example, a text book bank facility either in a centralised or semicentralised way would not only meet the bulk of such needs of continuing education of the space technologists, but also substantially relieve the burden on central work-related information facility or the 'primary library' of providing information-services to enhance work performance.

Provision of increased opportunity to browse latest literature in both core as well as related/peripheral areas and carrying current awareness services to the workspots and laboratories of otherwise busy IST is necessary. Yet provision for secondary journals, state-of-the-art and review literature can be reduced at the 'primary library'. On the other hand, the library should house more of primary news magazines, trade journals, reference books, data manuals for providing quick and up-to-date information and factual data. More efforts need to be made to provide extensive subject catalogues in the 'primary library'. The resources needed for maintaining author and title catalogues for reports be reallocated for updating the subject catalogues and providing extensive reference service in selection and location of documents by the users.

There is a necessity to provide information-services of the 'primary library' on a regular basis right at the place where the space technologists work. Further, a provision for trained information specialists in an adequate ratio with user-strength be made so that the space technologists can be persuaded to delegate some information-gathering tasks to them whenever they lack sufficient time to undertake such work or whenever their time can be better utilised more productively elsewhere.

A large part of the work-related information needed by the space technologists can be met from a well-organised, comprehensive and internally-generated information in the form of technical reports (of various kinds), preprints and reprints of journal articles, conference papers, software documents, design drawings, photographs, slides, transparencies, etc. Since all such information cannot be put at the disposal of all the users, surrogates of such documents should be made available with a note about their location and security clearance, if so needed. The 'reinventing of the wheel' within the organisation can be avoided with a well organised system of internally-generated information. Due to security reasons or lack of clear policy on security classification many such internally produced documents are not collected, processed and organised at one place within the organisation.

The product catalogues and trade literature, which are considerably sought after by the space technologists are not systematically collected, indexed, organised, stored and updated at one place. Though trade catalogues are normally available free, they are, at times, arbitrarily priced for those not buying the concerned product, component or equipment. Enormous trade literature is getting 'buried' in the purchase files denying current information to prospective buyers, and servicing and maintenance personnel. Such literature should be taken care of as multiple requests for free copies of manuals and other related trade literature from the same organisation are normally discouraged by the manufacturers and even when they wish to supply either free or on nominal payment, copies may not be available for equipments and components sold earlier. A fairly centralised data bank of trade literature which acquires indexes, organises and systematically weeds obsolete product literature is necessary.

There is a need for intermediary information-specialists who can act as data and information-gathering and analysing agents and support the local information-analysis centre. There intermediaries should work closely with the senior space technologists, projects and the 'primary library'. They should screen and sift the reading material to be browsed by the senior space technologists and provide highly reliable and accurate data/information to those who need it.

A process of generating confidence among subordinates and juniors for seeking information from superiors and seniors is necessary to overcome the 'psychological cost' or 'status inhibition' exhibited in the transfer of information. In a highly intra-organisation-oriented communication of the space technologists, there is a need for cutting re-circulation of ideas or information among members of tight and closed loop informal network of 'old boys'. The marginal inter-organisational communication due to communication stars and technological gatekeepers and tours and visits abroad (of mostly of higher-status persons) may have to be increased by encouraging more contacts outside-the-organisation especially at middle and lower-levels. A more liberal organisation structure which places communication stars accessible to more number of colleagues and makes many of them 'linking pins' in the organisation structure might optimise use of such high-information-potentials. In addition, increasing the ratio of technocrats to non-technocrats, periodic reassignment of jobs, more encouragement of inter-section, inter-division and inter-project communication bringing 'isolates' into the communication network is needed.

Encouraging and giving due credit for publishing activity is more likely to result in an increased use of literature more frequently and systematically and intensify engineers' information-behaviour.[2] The publishing activity also encourages more co-authorship and collaboration and in turn informal communication. Further, a proper security classification scheme could be evolved to give publication status to all unclassified and declassified internal reports of the organisation. This not only aids internal generation of information but also motivates authors to be more literature and documentation oriented in production of internal reports. Moreover, the cost of production and distribution of such reports can be recovered by charging those buying such reports and/or by exchanging such reports with reports of other similar organisations.

For the purpose of blending formal and informal sources of information the following options can be considered: (i) Developing 'components databank' and 'components co-ordination group', (ii) disseminating various technical information and activities through the in-house technical journal, (iii) developing a panel of experts on whom technologists in the organisation can look upon for getting authentic information quickly on a given specific area without much 'psychological cost', (iv) conducting regular in-house technical seminars, and circulation of brief summaries, detailed summaries and the complete documents relating to such seminars, reviews, etc., to appropriate persons, (v) establishing 'journal clubs' and (vi) creating more opportunities for the space technologists to meet fellow professionals outside the organisations by allowing liberal tours and/or by inviting outside professionals for presentation of papers/reports in in-house seminars.

The formal information facility, i.e., the primary library, needs to be strengthened in respect of nature and type of information needed by the IST. The overall organisation planning in general and planning of various projects and activities (including TDPs) in particular, have to make provision for information-support needed. The members of the projects and groups should be made to develop the habit of participating in the collection-development process of their primary library. It is necessary to see that each section, division and project formulates a systematic way of circulating current awareness services and other surrogates, announcements about documents and summaries among members of their sections, divisions and projects.

The primary library, on its part, should evolve a more liberal policy of promoting the use of journals, reports, standards and trade catalogues among the users concerned without expecting the space technologists to visit the library to consult a document or to reserve a document or to borrow a document for a limited period and, at times, pay a heavy fine as penalty for having not returned in time. This may necessitate a need to be more flexible in the application of library rules and regulations excepting a few areas like textbooks and popular books. For example, nearly three-fourths of the sample reports of the primary library which are not borrowed could be sent to the work tables of the potential users concerned (atleast copies of the title pages, abstracts and document control data sheets) for perusal rather than passively storing them on library shelves. Above all, the primary library has to find the ways and means of inducing and inducting the non-users. There is a need to give orientation programmes to the space technologists (especially to new entrants and less frequent users) in the use of the primary library. The experimental services like the 'pathfinder' and 'aid to space science and satellite technology orientation' have been well received and efforts need to be continued on similar lines. The space technologists also need an informal training in organising their personal information system consisting of references, notes, abstracts and documents in various forms like registers, notebooks, files, loose sheets, cards and desk diaries.

It is necessary that the organisation and the primary library take cognizance of various information-behaviour aspects and activities which are shown to be functions of one or more variables and accordingly plan, design and operate the information-system. These relations of the user-characteristics to information-behaviour may be kept in view in providing information-services to various groups within the IST.

The professional activities and achievements index developed in this study has fairly represented the intensity of information-seeking, information-orientedness, the information-potential and the library/literature orientation of the space technologists which could be made use of in repatterning the information-services.

Suggestions for Further Research

The present study is confined to pursuing and achieving the three objectives and testing the hypothesis stated earlier. In this pursuit many related issues/problems are noticed. Though they are delimited as outside the scope of the study, many of them are worth considering as areas for further research. Here, then, are presented such areas as well as areas for further research on ISB of the IST.

User-Research in General

There is a strong need for a meta-analysis[3] (i.e., the analysis of several analyses) of many past user-studies over the last four decades in science and technology areas so that a thorough sifting and stock taking as well as consolidation of the findings of user-research takes place. It is worthwhile to arrive at a generalised user-behaviour research model using the pattern of the present and other past studies as bases so that each one of the major organisations, disciplines and missions within science, engineering and technology in the country could be studied preferably by the information-specialists 'living with the tribe'.[4] Further comparisons and meta-analysis would become meaningful and dependable only if such a research model is adopted for series of studies covering different user populations. Such a model could also be used for periodic information-behaviour studies of the same set of users.

There is also a need for a national level multidisciplinary research organisation in India on par with BASR (ISR), CRUSK, CRUS, etc., of the western countries to take care of continuous research on communication and information-behaviour of the Indian scientists, engineers, technicians and technologists.

The basic aspect of user-research, namely, 'why does the information-seeker behave as he does?', 'Why does ISB vary with user-characteristics?", "Is ISB contingent to the work atmosphere or dependent on attributes of individuals?" are some of the fundamental areas which demand in-depth studies.

More surveys are necessary not only to confirm general patterns of information-behaviour but also to identify departures from the norm (Hanson, 1974). Some of the areas needing urgent attention are assessing the impact of different kinds and levels of presentation of reading materials, ways of measuring accessibility to information and ascertaining the effects of such accessibility, impact of information on its recipient and on the progress and outcome of his work. In addition, extensive local, organisation, discipline and mission oriented user-research within the country is needed.

Other Aspects of Information Behaviour

An intensive multidisciplinary research of motives of seeking information, a study of how unmet needs of users get dissipated, ways of measuring 'information overload' and impact of 'information overload' on use of information are some of the other areas for further research. A thorough review of the need for catalogues and indexes in libraries and their functions in serving engineers and technologists, how they can be made more attractive and useful to users in providing bibliographic information, how the library can aid specialists and experts in providing bibliographic information and how subject specialists be developed as information intermediaries for providing information-services so that scientists, engineers and technologists can confidently delegate their information-gathering work to them are the other wider avenues for further research.

More research is also needed about the information-processing behaviour of scientists, engineers, technicians and technologists, i.e., the way they use documents and information as well as relating use of information to the purposes of seeking information and the requirements of information. How the use of information varied at different stages of a work or project, what sources of information under what setting (bringing text and user together) generates new/novel ideas, increases 'accidental acquisition' of information and reduces chances of 'late find' of information need to be explored.

More research by librarians about informal and inter-personal sources of information as well as informal communication of scientists, engineers, technicians and technologists is needed. In particular, the ways and means of increasing effectiveness and efficiency of informal communication have to be explored. A semi-controlled experiment to test the hypothesis that 'high performance causes high communication and not *vice versa*' would be quite interesting. Similarly, a study to distinguish the effects of formal organisation structure and informal social relationships on communication of scientists, engineers, technicians and technologists is highly desirable. One specific hypothesis could be that "the effect of informal social relationship is much stronger than the formal organisation structure on communication". Another potential hypothesis to be tested could be that "the informal communication among peers and colleagues is much more effective and cordial than between a superior and a subordinate".

Further, can communication stars and technological gatekeepers be formally appointed? and, if so, how do they differ from self-chosen communication stars and technological gatekeepers in their effectiveness? Such issues require systematic studies. To put it in the form of a hypothesis "the communication stardom and technological gatekeepership are intrinsic to individuals and not contingent to a particular organisation.

Another less explored area is that of informal communication among co-authors. There is a need to compare the characteristics of co-authors and also to determine the nature and amount of work shared by co-authors in producing a paper or a document. "Does co-authorship-relations result in lasting and highly effective informal communication among co-authors?" is quite speculative in nature. A qualitative study of citations which could throw light on how use of information is related to its citation is necessary. Why one cites a reference and whether all the references cited have been read and used by the author are to be answered. Further, research regarding various interactions of scientists, engineers, technicians and technologists with formal sources like a library is needed to assess their real time responses for arriving at their information-behaviour as well as their attitude towards information.

Further Research on Information-Behaviour of the Indian Space Technologists

The present study may be extended to cover other scientists, engineers, technicians and technologists, in general, and space technologists working in sister organisations in particular, in India, so that results could be compared. There is a vast scope for further research in terms of different types of users, different aspects of user-behaviour and attitudes and comparison of user-behaviour and attitudes of different types of users. In addition, the basic research aspect of ISB of the space technologists could also be explored. The information requirements of about 100 industries which worked with ISRO and supplied materials, equipment and services and another 25 industries which used ISRO-developed technology for non-space uses as well as the organisations which undertook sponsored projects and contracts of ISRO are worth probing. Many other user-characteristics/attributes including personality traits and psychological dimensions of information-seeking and using need to be identified and their relation with information-behaviour of the IST tested.

Further analysis of the database created in the present study could also be taken up especially by cross tabulating the data. For example, the nature and type of information sought against the sources of information preferred and ranking of various factors within ISB aspects (like motives and purposes of seeking information, nature and type of information required, dependence on sources of information, etc.) can be compared for different user-characteristics. There is ample scope for finding inter-correlation among various factors within each aspect of information-behaviour as well as inter-correlation of various aspects of information-behaviour. Thus, the findings of the present study as well as its database could serve as a starting point for many independent short and long range research projects which may in turn throw better light on the ISB of the IST.

Use of Refined Methodologies and Data-Analysing Techniques

From the point of view of methodology and data-analysing techniques, there is a need for the use of semi-controlled experiments, multiple correlation, partial correlation, factor and cluster analysis, analysis of variance, regression-analysis and other techniques. For example, the quantitative data like age, experience, professional activities and achievements, library-use and library-interactions of the space technologists can be subjected to linear regression-analysis.

NOTES AND REFERENCES

1. Raitt (1984, p. 275) also make similar observations.
2. It is heartening to note that not only in-house seminars with many invited outside speakers have become a regular activity but also a technical journal entitled '*Journal of Spacecraft Technology*' is regularly published by the Centre since 1991.
3. Meta-analysis is a methodology quantitatively cumulating and integrating findings across studies (Gooding and Wagner, 1985, p. 465).
4. This should have been the foremost task of the apex bodies like NISSAT in the country.

BIBLIOGRAPHY

Ackoff, Russell L. *et al.*, *Designing a National Scientific and Technological Communication System* (The SCATT Report), Pennsylvania: University of Pennsylvania Press, 1976.

Aims, A., "Survey of Information Needs of Physicists and Chemists", *Journal of Documentation*, 21(2), June 1965: 83-112.

Aina, S.A., "Stimulating the Non-user", *in* A. Van Derbaan and A.A. Winters, ed., *The Use of Information in a Changing World*, Proceedings of the Forty Second FID Congress held in the Hague, The Netherlands, 24-27 September, 1984, Amsterdam: North-Holland, 1984: 57-63.

Allen, Thomas J., *Utilisation of Information Sources during R&D Proposal Preparation*, MIT-97-64, Cambridge: MIT, Alfred P. Sloan School of Management, 1964.

————, *Managing the Flow of Technology: Technology Transfer and the Dissemination of Technological Information within the R&D Organisation*, Cambridge: MIT Press, 1977.

Allen, Thomas J. and Maurice P. Andmen Jr., *Time Allocation among Three Technical Information Channels by R&D Engineers*, MIT-131-65, Cambridge: MIR, Alfred P. Sloan School of Management, 1965.

Allen, Thomas J. and P.G. Gerstberger, *Criteria for Selection of an Information Source*, MIT-284-67, Cambridge: MIT, Alfred P. Sloan School of Management, 1967.

————, "Criteria Used by Research and Development Engineers in the Selection of an Information Source", *Journal of Applied Psychology*, 52(4), 1968, 272-79.

Allen, Thomas J. and Stephen I. Cohen, "Information Flow in R&D Laboratories", *Administrative Science Quarterly*, 14(1), January-February 1970: 12-19.

Allen, Thomas J. *et al.*, *Time Allocation among Three Technical Information Channels by R&D Engineers*, MIT Working Paper No. 184-66, Cambridge, Massachusetts: MIT, Alfred P. Sloan School of Management, 1966.

Amba, S. and Raghavan, K.S. "Information Science in India: An Analysis", *Library Science with Slant to Documentation*, 22(3), September 1985: 129-40.

Anthony, L.J. *et al.*, "Growth of the Literature of Physics", *Reports of Progress in Physics*, 32, 1969: 709-67.

Atherton, Pauline, "Views of the Communication Network of Scientific and Technical Information", *International Forum on Information and Documentation*, 1(1), 1975: 10-12.

————, "Research in Information Science: An Assessment", *in* A. Debons and W.J. Cameron, eds., *Perspectives in Information Science*, Leyden: Noordhoff, 1975: 665-79.

————, *Handbook for Information Systems and Services*, Paris: Unesco, 1977.

Auerbach Corporation, *DoD User Needs Study*, Phase I. Final Technical Report, 2 Vols., DoD 1151-TR-3: AD 615 501, 2. Philadelphia, Pa.: Auerbach Corporation, 1965 (1969).

————, "What's Wrong with Information Retrieval?", *Machine Design*, 38(16), 7 July 1966: 106-09.

Back, Kurt H., "Behaviour of Scientists: Communication and Creativity", *Sociological Inquiry*, 32(1), Winter 1962: 82-87.

Bailey, Robert L., *Disciplined Creativity for Engineers*, Michigan: Ann Arbor Science, 1978.

Barkey, P., "Patterns of Student Use of College Library", *College and Research Libraries*, 27, 1966: 277-82.

Barber, Bernard, "Resistance by Scientists to Scientific Discovery", *Science*, 134(3479), September 1961: 596-602.

Bath University Library, *Comparison of Results of Science User with INFROSS*, Bath: Bath University Library, 1971.

Bauer, Raymond A., "The Audience", *in* I.S. Pool *et al.*, eds., *The Handbook of Communication*, Rand McNally College Publishing Co., Chicago, 1973, p. 146.

Bernal, J.D., "Preliminary Analysis of Pilot Questionnaire on the Use of Scientific Literature", in *Report of the Royal Society Scientific Information Conference*, 21 June-2 July 1948, London: Royal Society, 1948: 589-637.

Bernard, Jessie *et al.*, *Informal Communication among Bio Scientists*, Washington, D.C.: George Washington University, 1963/1964.

Bethell, John P., *Communications in an International Research Laboratory*, London: The City University, Centre for Information Science, 1972.

Bhavani, V., "Publication Activities of Indian Scientists: A Survey", *Library Science with Slant to Documentation*, 19(1), March 1982: 54-68.

Bittel, Lester Robert, ed., *Encyclopaedia of Professional Management*, New York: McGraw Hill, 1978, p. 242.

Bodensteiner, W.D., *Information Channel Utilization under Varying Research and Development Project Conditions: An Aspect of Interorganisational Communication Channel Usage*, Ph.D. Thesis, Austin: University of Texas, 1970. Quoted from Winford E. Holland, "The Special Communicator and his Behaviour in Research Organisations—A Key to the Management of Informal Technical Information Flow", IEEE Transactions on Professional Communication, PC-17, No. 3/4, Sep.-Dec. 1974, p. 48.

Braden, Irene and Alice S. Clark, "Quantitative Methods in Librarianship: Standards, Research, Management". Proceedings and Papers of a Institute held at Ohio State University, 3-16 August 1969, ed. by Irene Braden and Alice S. Clark, Connecticut: Greenwood Press, 1972 (Contributions in *Librarianship and Information Science*, No. 4), Pt. 1 Group discussion, 1969: 24-25.

Brember, V.L., "Linking a Medical User Survey to Management for Effectiveness: II Checklandsoft Systems Study", *Journal of Documentation*, 4(12), June 1985: 59-74.

Brittain, J. Michael, *Information and its Users: A Review with Special Reference to Social Sciences*, Bath: Bath University Press, 1970.

————, *Information and Its Users—A Review with Special Reference to Social Sciences*, New York: Wiley Interscience, 1971.

————, *User Studies in Education and the Feasibility of an International Survey of Information Needs in Education*, Bath: Bath University, 1971.

————, "Information Needs and Applications of Results of User Studies", *in* Anthony Debons and Williams Cameron, (eds.), *Perspectives in Information Science*, Leyden: Noodhoff, 1975: 425-47.

Buckland, Michael K., *Library Services in Theory and Context*, 2 Edition, New York: Pergamon Press, 1988.

Burton, R.E. and B.A. Green, "Technical Reports in Physics Literature", *Physics Today*, 14 October 1961: 35-37.

Bush, G.C. *et al.*, "Attendance and Use of the Science Library at MIT", *American Documentation*, 7(2), April 1956: 87-109.

Byrd, Gary D. and Michael E.D. Koenig, "Systematic Serials Selection Analysis in a Small Academic Health Sciences Library", *Bulletin of Medical Libraries Association*, 66, No. 4, October 1978: 397-406.

Campbell, David E. and Theodore M. Shlechter, "Library Design Influences on User Behaviour and Satisfaction", *Library Quarterly*, 49(1), January 1979: 26-41.

Canisius, Peter P., "Stimulating the Use of Information", *in* A. Van Derbaan and A.A. Winters, ed., *The Use of Information in a Changing World*, Proceedings of the Forty-second FID Congress held in the Hague, the Netherlands, 24-27 September, 1984, Amsterdam: North-Holland, 1984: 65-68.

Case Institute of Technology, Operations Research Group, "Study of the Dissemination and Use of Recorded Scientific Information", Pt. I—*Journal Reading by Physicists and Chemists*; Pt. II—*Cost of Journal Publication*; Pt. III—*Effect of Condensation on Comprehension of Journal Articles*, Cleveland, Ohio: Case Institute of Technology, 1960.

Chafin, Roy L., "User Characteristics for Information System Design", *in* Alan R. Benenfeld and Edward John Kazlauskas, eds., *Communicating Information—Proceedings of the 43rd ASIS Annual Meeting, 1980*, Anahein, California, 5-10 October 1980, New York: ASIS, 1980, 17: 317-19.

Cole, P.F. "Analysis of Reference Questions Records as a Guide to the Requirements of Scientists", *Journal of Documentation* 14(4), December 1958: 197-207.

Collins, H.M., "TEA Set: Tacit Knowledge and Scientific Networks", *Science Studies* 4(4), 1974: 165-86.

Columbia University, Bureau of Applied Social Research, *Flow of Information among Scientists: Problems, Opportunities and Research Questions* (Study Director: Herbert Menzel), New York: Columbia University, BASR, 1958.

————, Bureau of Applied Social Research, *Review of Studies in the Flow of Information among Scientists* (Study Director: Herbert Menzel), 2 Vols., New York: Columbia University, BASR, 1960.

Cooper, William S., "Why Bother Theory of Information Usage", *Journal of Informatics*, 2(1), April 1978: 2-5.

Cott, Van, "National Information System for Psychologists: A Proposed Solution for a Pressing Problem", *American Psychologist*, 25(5), May 1970: i-xx.

Crane, Diana, "Information Needs and Users", *in* Carlos A. Cuadraed, *Annual Review of Information Science and Technology*, Chicago: Encyclopaedia Britannica Inc. 1971: Vol. 6, 3-39.

————, *Invisible College: Diffusion of Knowledge in Scientific Communities*, Chicago: Chicago University Press, 1972:, p. 117.

Crawford, Susan, "Information Needs and Uses", *in* Martha E. Williams, ed., *Annual Review of Information Science and Technology*, New York: Knowledge Industries Inc. for ASIS, 1978: Vol. 13, 61-81.

Cronin, Blaise, "Assessing User Needs", *Aslib Proceedings*, 33(2), February 1981: 37-47.

————, "Invisible Colleges and Information Transfer: A Review and Commentary with Particular Reference to the Social Sciences", *Journal of Documentation*, 38(3), September 1982: 212-36.

Davis, R.A., "How Engineers Use Literature", *Chemical Engineering Progress*, 61(3), March 1965: 30-34.

D'Elia, George, "The Development and Testing of a Conceptual Model of Public Library User Behaviour", *Library Quarterly*, 50(4), October, 1980: 410-30.

Dervin, Brenda, "Everyday Information Needs of the Average Citizen: A Taxanomy for Analysis", *in* Manfred Kochen and Josephe Donhue, eds., *Information for the Community*, Chicago: ALA, 1976: 19-38.

Dhawan, Sathish, *Space and Industry*, Sriram Memorial Lecture, N.p.n.p., 1983: 4-5.

Drone, Jeanette M., "A Use Study of the Card Catalogs in the University of Illinois Music Library", *Library Resources and Technical Services*, 28(3), July/September 1984, p. 253.

Fearn, Robin A.C. and Jessica S. Melton, "Information Centre User Study", *in* Jeanne B. North, ed., *Proceedings of the 32nd Annual Meeting of ASIS, San Francisco, California, 1-4 October 1969*, Westport, Connecticut: Greenwood Publishers, 1969: 463-70.

Ford, Geoffrey, "Research in User Behaviour in University Libraries", *Journal of Documentation*, 29(1), March 1973: 85-106.

Ford, N., *User Studies: An Introductory Guide and Select Bibliography*, CRUS Occasional Paper 1, Sheffield: University of Sheffield, CRUS, 1977.

————, "Relating Information Needs to Learners Characteristics in Higher Education", *Journal of Documentation*, 36(2), June 1980: 99-114.

Francis, D. Pitt, "Cost-benefit Analysis and Public Library Budgets", *Library Review*, 25, 1976: 189-92.

French, Wendell L., *The Personnel Management Process: Human Resources Administration and Development*, 4 Edition, Boston: Houghton Mifflin Company, 1978.

Frohman, Alan, *Determinants of Library Use in an Industrial Firm*, Term Paper, Cambridge, Massachusetts: MIT, Alfred P. Sloan School of Management, 1969.

Fussler, H.H. and J.L. Simon, *Patterns in the Use of Books in Large Research Libraries*, Chicago: University of Chicago, 1969: p. 3. Quoted from Kent, Allen and others, "Use of Library Materials: The University of Pittsburgh Study", New York, Marcel Dekker Inc. 1979: p. 31.

Garg, Kailash Chandra and Ashok Kumar, "Information Gathering of R&D Scientists: A Survey", *Annals of Library Science and Documentation*, 31(1-2), March-June 1984: 63-73.

Garvey, William D., *Communication: The Essence of Science*, Oxford: Pergamon, 1979.

Garvey, William D. *et al.*, "Scientific Information User", *in* Anthony Debons and William J. Cameron, eds., *Perspectives in Information Science*, Leyden: Noodhoff, 1975.

Gerstberger, Peter G., *The Preservation and Transfer of Technology in Research and Development Organisations*, Thesis, Massachusetts: MIT, Jan. 1971, Alfred P. Sloan School of Management. Quoted from Nan Lin and William D. Garvey, "Information Need and Uses", *in* Carlos A. Cavdra, ed., *Annual Review of Information Science and Technology*, Chicago: Encyclopaedia Britannica Inc., for ASIS, 1972: Vol. 7, 14-15.

Gerstberger, Peter G. and Thomas J. Allen, "Criteria Used by Research and Development Engineers in the Selection of an Information Source", *Journal of Applied Psychology*, 52(4), August 1968: 272-79.

Gertrude, H. Lamb, "The Rediscovery of Librarianship", *in* Irene Branden Hoadley and Alice S. Clark, ed., *Quantitative Methods in Librarianship: Standards, Research, Management*, Proceedings and Papers of an Institute held at the Ohio State University, 3-16 August 1969, Connecticut: Greenwood Press, 1972: 113-14.

Gilmore, John S. *et al.*, *Channels of Technology Acquisition in Commercial Firms and the NASA Dissemination Program*, NASA-CR-790, Washington, D.C.: Denver Research Institute, University of Denver, Colorado for NASA, 1967.

Glass, B. and S.H. Norwood, "How Scientists Actually Learn of Work Important to Them", in *Proceedings of the International Conference of Scientific Information*, Washington, D.C., 16-21 November 1958. (Washington, D.C.: National Academy of Sciences, National Research Council, 1959), Vol. 1, 195-97. Quoted from Edwin B. Parker and William J. Paisley, "Research for Psychologists at the Interface of the Scientists and his Information System", *in* Tefko Saraevic Comp and ed., *Introduction to Information Science*, New York: R.R. Bowker Co., 1970: p. 86.

Goldberg, L.C. *et al.*, "Local-cosmopolitan: Unidimensional or Multidimensional?" *American Journal of Sociology*, 70(6), May, 1965: 704-10.

Gooding, Richard Z. and Wagner III, John A., "A Meta-analysis Review of the Relationship between Size and Performance: The Productivity and Efficiency of Organisations and their Subunits", *Administrative Science Quarterly*, 30(4), December 1985: 462-81.

Gopinath, M.A., "Information Needs of Design Engineers", *Library Science with a Slant to Documentation*, 17(3), September 1980: 58-61.

————, *Current Trends in Information Sources and Communication Media*, The Working Document Prepared for the 15th DRTC Refresher Seminar, 12-14 December 1984, Bangalore: DRTC, 1984.

Gorman, Michael and Jami Hotsinpiller, "ISBD: Aid or Barrier to Understanding?" *College and Research Libraries*, 40(6), November 1979, p. 251.

Gralewska-Vickery, A. "Communication and Information Needs of Earth Science Engineers", *Information Processing and Management*, 12(4), 1976: 251-82.

Gray, Dwight E., "Physics Abstracting", *American Journal of Physics*, 19(7), October 1950: 417-24.

Gray, John and Brian Perry, *Scientific Information*, New York: Oxford University Press, 1975.

Grose, Dophna, "Some Deprived Information Users", *Aslib Proceedings*, 26(1), January 1974: 9-27.

Gupta, B.M., "Information, Communication and Technology Transfer: A Review of Literature", *Annals of Library Science and Documentation*, 28(1-4), January-December 1981: 1-13.

Hagstrom, Warren O., *Scientific Community*, New York: Base Books Inc., 1965.

Halbert, Michael H. and Russel L. Ackoff, "Operations Research Study of the Dissemination of Scientific Information", in *Proceedings of the International Conference on Scientific Information*, Washington, D.C., 16-21 November 1958, Washington, D.C.: National Academy of Sciences, National Research Council, 1959: Vol.1, 97-130 (Preprints p. 87-120).

Hall, Kevin R. and Eric Ritchie, "Study of Communication Behaviour in an R&D Laboratory", *R&D Management*, 5(3), July 1975: 243-45.

Hall, Robert W., *Personal Effectiveness in Industrial Research*, Ph.D. Thesis, Indiana: Indiana University, Graduate School of Business, 1972.

Hanson, C.W., "Research on User's Needs: Where It Is Getting Us?" *Aslib Proceedings*, 16(2), February 1964: 64-78.

————, *Review of Research and Experimentation on Engineering Information particularly in Mechanical Engineering*, OSTI Report No. 5202, 1974.

Harris, Colin, "A Comparison of Issues and in Library Use of Books", *Aslib Proceedings*, 29, 1977: 199-22.

————, "Studying the Non-user", *in* A. Van Derbaan and A.A. Winters, ed., *The Use of Information in a Changing World*, Proceedings of the Forty-second FID Congress held in the Hague, The Netherlands, 24-27 September, 1984, Amsterdam: North-Holland, 1984: 69-75, 121.

————, *User Needs and User Education*, A Paper Presented at Fifth Information Officers Training Course (INFOTRAC), 6-31 May 1985, Manila, Philippines. Organised by TECHNONET ASIA and APCTT National and International Transfer and Development, N.p.n.p., 1985.

Hatt, Frank, *Reading Process: A Framework for Analysis and Description*, London: Clive Bingley, 1976.

Havelock, Ronald G., "Research Utilization of Knowledge", *in* Manfred Kochen and Joseph C. Donohue, eds., *Information for the Community*, Chicago: ALA, 1976, Chapter 13, 200-13.

Havelock, Ronald G. *et al.*, *Planning for Innovation Through Dissemination and Utilization of Knowledge*, Michigan: The University of Michigan, The Institute for Social Research, CRUSK, 1969.

Herner, Saul and Dewitt O. Myatt, "Building a Functional Library", *Chemical and Engineering News*, 32, 1954: 4980.

Herner, Saul and N. Herner, "Determining Requirements for Atomic Energy Information from Reference Questions", in *Proceedings of the International Conference on Scientific Information*, Washington,

D.C., 16-21 November 1958, Washington, D.C.: National Academy of Sciences, 1959, 1: 181-87.

Herner, Saul *et al.*, *Evaluation of the Goddard Space Flight Centre Library*, NASA-CR-159969, Washington, D.C.: Herner & Co., 1979.

Hiscock, Jane E., "Does Library Usage Affect Academic Performance?: A Study of the Relationship between Academic Performance and Usage of Libraries at the Underdale Site of the South Australian College of Advanced Education", *Australian Academic and Research Libraries*, 17(4), December 1986: 207-14.

Hoadley, Irene Braden and Alice S. Clark, eds., "Quantitative Methods in Librarianship: Standards, Research, Management", Proceedings and Papers of an Institute held at the Ohio State University, 3-16 August 1969, *Contributions in Librarianship and Information Science*, No. 4, Connecticut: Greenwood Press, 1972.

Hogg, I.H. and J.R. Smith, "Survey of the Communication of Information in the Research and Development Branch of the United Kingdom Atomic Energy Authority", in *Proceedings of the International Conference on Scientific Information*, Washington, D.C., 16-21 November 1958, Washington, D.C.: National Academy of Sciences, National Research Council, 1959, 1: 131-62 (Preprint 1, 235-52).

India, Department of Science and Technology, Research and Development Statistics 1980-81, New Delhi: India, DST, 1982.

Indian Association of Special Libraries and Information Centres, *Users and Library and Information Services*, IASLIC Special Publication No. 5, Pt. I, Calcutta: IASLIC, 1965.

Jahoda, G., "Information Gathering and Use Habits of Chemists", *Journal of Chemical Documentation*, 9(5), 1969: 153.

Jenson, Neils, "Cost-benefit and the Library Service Just Don't Go Together", *Bibliotek*, 70, No. 12, 1978: 310-11 (In Danish).

Jones, Pat, *Some Social Aspects of Information Transfer*, London: Polytechnic of North London, School of Librarianship, 1981: 63.

Kanaka Rekha, T., *Communication Behaviour Patterns of Scientists in Research Organisation: A Case Study of CFTRI*, M.Lib. Sc. Thesis, Mysore: University of Mysore, 1984.

Kelly, Kevin, "Information as a Communicable Disease: Infected by Ideas", *Computers Today*, 1(11), January 1986: 45-48.

Kemp, D.A., *Nature of Knowledge: An Introduction for Librarians*, London: Clive Bingley, 1976.

Kent, Allen *et al.*, *Use of Library Materials: The University of Pittsburgh Study*, New York: Marcel Dekker, 1979.

————, *Usage of Journals was Generally Very Low*, 1979: 65-74.

Kochen, Manfred, "What Makes a Citizen Information System Used and Useful", *in* Manfred Kochen and Joseph C. Donhue, eds., *Information for the Community*, Chicago: American Library Association, 1976, Chapter 10, 149-70.

Kothari, C.R., *Research Methodology: Methods and Techniques*, 2nd Edition, New Delhi: Vishwaprakashan, 1990.

Kraft, Donald H. and Richard A. Polacsek, "A Journal Worth Measure for a Journal Selection Decision Model", *Collection Management*, 2, No. 2, Summer 1978: 129-39.

Krikelas, James, "Information-seeking Behaviour: Patterns and Concepts", *Drexel Library Quarterly*, 19(2), Spring 1983: 5-20.

Krishan Kumar, "Users Survey Concerning Teachers and Research Scholars in the Department of Chemistry, University of Delhi", *Annals of Library Science and Documentation*, 15(4), December 1968: 175-205.

————, "Users Survey: Identification of Users and their Information Needs in Health Sciences Libraries", *ILA Bulletin*, 18(1-2), April-September 1982: 44-50.

Kumar, P.S.G., "Doctorates and Doctoral Studies in Librarianship in India: A Statistical Study", *Library Herald*, 22 (2&3), July-December 1983: 85-91.

Kunz, Werner *et al.*, *Methods of Analysis and Evaluation of Information Needs: A Critical Review*, Munchen: Verlag Documentation, 1977.

Landau, Robert *et al.* (Working Group V), "User Needs", *in* Anthony Debons and William J. Cameron, eds., *Perspectives in Information Science*, Leyden: Noodhoff, 1975.

Langrish, L. *et al.*, *Wealth from Knowledge*, London: Macmillan, 1972.

Leimicuhler, Ferdinand F., *Evaluation of Costs and Benefits of Libraries*, Arlington, VA: ERIC Document Reproduction Service, 1978. ERIC-Report-ED-163947. (A Paper Presented at the Annual Conference of the Special Libraries Association, Kansas City, Missouri, June 1978).

Lickert, Rensis, "Motivational Approach to Organisations", *in* M. Haire, ed., *Modern Organisational Theory*, New York: Wiley, 1959: 194.

Lin, Nan and William D. Garvey, "Information Needs and Uses", *in* Carlos A. Cuadra, ed., *Annual Review of Information Science and Technology*, Chicago: Encyclopaedia Britannica Inc., 1972: Vol. 7, 5-37.

Line, Maurice B., "Social Scientist and His Information Needs", in *Proceedings of the 16th Annual Conference of the Library Association*, Durham, 1968, London: The Library Association, 1968.

Line, Maurice B., "Information Uses and Needs of Social Scientists: An Overview of INFROSS", *Aslib Proceedings*, 23(8), August 1971: 412-34.

————, "Fortyseventh Aslib Annual Conference Summing Up: The Information Service in Practice", *Aslib Proceedings*, 26(1), January 1974: 47-53.

————, "Draft Definitions: Information and Library Needs, Wants, Demand and Uses", *Aslib Proceedings*, 26(2), February 1974: 87.

————, *Library Surveys: An Introduction to the Use Planning Procedure and Presentation of Surveys*, 2nd Edition, London: Clive Bingley, 1992.

Line, Maurice B. and A. Sanderson, "Obsolescence and Changes in the Use of Literature with Time", *Journal of Documentation*, 30, 1974: 51-70.

Line, Maurice B. and Mavis Tidmarsh, "Student Attitudes to the University Library: A Second Survey at Southumpton University", *J. Doc.*, 22, 1966: 123-35.

Lipetz, Ben-Ami, "Information Needs and Uses", *in* Carlos A. Cuadra, ed., *Annual Review of Information Science and Technology*, Chicago: Encyclopaedia Britannica Inc., 1970: Vol. 5, 3-32.

Longuet-Higgins, H.C., "Language of Science", *Times Literary Supplement*, UK: 558, 7 May 1970: 505-06.

Luckham, B., *The Library in Society: A Study of the Public Library in an Urban Setting*, London: The Library Association, 1971.

Lufkin, J.M. and E.H. Miller, "Reading Habits of Engineers: A Preliminary Survey", *IEEE Transactions on Education*, E-9 (4), December 1966: 179-82.

Lungberg, Sixton *et al.*, "Investigation on the Use of Information in R&D at a Research Intensive Company, Phase II: Possibilities of Economic Evaluation", *Tidsk Dokum*, 32, No. 2, 1976: 17-23.

Maguire, Carmel, "What Qualifies as Research in Librarianship", *in* Allen, G.G. and Exon, F.C.A., ed., *Research and the Practice of Librarianship: an International Symposium*, Perth: The Library, Western Australian Institute of Technology, 1986, 1-10.

Markee, Katherine M., "Where is the Library Researcher", *in* Irene Braden Hoadley and Alice S. Clark, eds., *Quantitative Methods in Librarianship: Standards, Research, Management*—Proceedings and Papers of an Institute held at Ohio State University, 3-16 August 1969, Connecticut: Greenwood Press, 1972: 119-21.

Marquis, Donald G. and Thomas J. Allen, "Communication Patterns in Applied Technology", *American Psychologist*, 21(11), November 1966: 1052-60.

Martin, Miles W., "Use of Random Alarm Devices in Studying Scientist's Reading Behaviour", *IRE Transactions on Engineering Management*, 9(2), June 1962: 66-71.

Martyn, John, *Report of Investigation on Literature Searching by Research Scientists*, London: Aslib, 1964.

————, "Information Needs and Uses", *in* Carlos A. Cuadra, ed., *Annual Review of Information Science and Technology*, Washington, D.C.: ASIS, 1974: Vol. 9, 3-23.

Martyn, John and Wilfred F. Lancaster, *Investigative Methods in Library and Information Science: An Introduction*, 1981, Virginia: Information Resources Press, 88.

McCarthy, Cavan, "Colonial Cataloguing", *New Library World*, 76(897), March 1975: 55-56. Quoted from, Ken Jones, *Conflict and Change in Library Organizations: People, Power and Service*, London: Clive Bingley, 1984: 29.

McGarry, Kevin, *Communication, Knowledge and the Librarian*, London: Clive Bingley, 1975.

Meadows, A.J., *Communication in Science*, London: Butterworths, 1974: 105.

Meadows, A.J. and J.G. O'Connor, *Investigation of Information Sources and Information Retrieval in Astronomy and Space Sciences*, OSTI 5044, Leicester: University of Leicester, Astronomy Department, 1969.

Mendez, A. and Blanco, C., "Differences between Requested and Cited Literature in a Group of Dairy Research Scientists", *Journal of Information Science*, 1, 1979: 113-16.

Menzel, Herbert, "Information Needs and Uses", *in* Carlos A. Cuadra, ed., *Annual Review of Information Science and Technology*, New York: Interscience Publishers for ADI, 1966: Vol. 1, 41-69.

————, "Sociological Perspectives on the Information Gathering Practices of the Scientific Investigator and the Medical Practitioner", *in* D. McCord, ed., *Bibliotheca Medical: Physician for Tomorrow, Dedication of the Countway Library of Medicine*, Boston: Harvard Medical School, 1966.

————, "Scientific Communication: Five Sociological Themes", *American Psychologist*, 21(11), November 1966: 999-1004.

————, "Informal Communication in Science: Its Advantages and Its Formal Analogues", *in* C. Rawski, ed., *Toward a Theory of*

Librarianship—Papers in Honour of Jesse Shera, New York: Syracuse University Press, 1966/1971.

Merton, A., "Report on the Results of Experimental Investigation into the User Needs and Requirements in the Czechoslovak Academy of Science", in *Second Symposium of Information Specialists of the Czechoslovak and Polish Academies of Science*, Smolenice, Czechoslovakia, October 1967, Prague: Library of the Czechoslovakia Academy of Science, 1968.

———, "Matthew Effect in Science", *Science*, 159(3810), 5 January 1968: 56-63.

Merton, Robert K., *Social Theory and Social Structure*, New York: Free Press, 1957.

Metz, Paul, "The Use of the General Collection in the Library of Congress", *Library Quarterly*, 49(4), October 1979: p. 30.

Meyer, Alan, "Some Important Findings in Catalog Use Studies", *in* F.W. Lancaster, ed., *The Measurement and Evaluation of Library Services*, Washington, D.C.: Information Resources Press, 1977: 69. Quoted from William Aguilar, "Influence of the Card Catalog on Circulation in a Small Public Library", *Library Resources and Technical Services*, 28(2), April/June 1984: 175-83.

Mick, Colin K., "Human Factors in Information Work", *in* Alan R. Benenfeld and Edward John Kazlauskas, eds., *Communicating Information: Proceedings of ASIS 1980 Meeting*, Ananheim, California, 5-10 October 1980, New York: ASIS, 1980: 17, 21-23.

Mooers, Calvin N., "Mooer's Law or Why Some Retrieval Systems are Used and Others Are Not", *American Documentation*, 11(3), July 1960: ii.

Moor, William Chattle, "Development and Preliminary Test of Behaviour Related Dimensions of Information Systems", *Journal of the American Society for Information Science*, 23(1), January-February 1972: 50-57.

Morris, Ruth C.T., "Toward a User-Centered Information Service", *Journal of the American Society for Information Science*, 45(1), 1994: 20-30.

Myers, J.M., "Information as a Saleable Commodity", in *Accelerating Innovation*, Papers given at a Symposium held at the University of Notingham, March 1969. Organised by Aslib, U.K. Ministry of Technology and Research Associations, London: Aslib, 1970, 26-29.

Nagarajan, K.S., "Needs of Scientific, Technical and Managerial Information among Technocrats in Indian Industries: A Survey", in

Users of Documentation: Papers presented at the 35th Conference and International Congress of Documentation, Buenos Aires City, 14-24 September 1970, Paris: FID, 1970.

Nagpal, P.S. and Pruthi, S., "Problem-solving and Idea-generation in R&D: The Role of Informal Communication", *R&D Management*, 9(3), July 1979: 147-49.

Oldman, Christine, "Value of Information", *Library Research Occasional Paper No. 1*, Bradford: MCB Publications, 1976.

Orr, Richard H., "Scientist as an Information Processor: A Conceptual Model Illustrated with Data on Variables Related to Library Utilization", *in* C.E. Nelson and D.K. Pollock, eds., *Communication among Scientists and Engineers*, Massachusetts: D.C. Heath Lexington, 1970: 143-90.

Paisley, William J., *Extent of Information Seeking as a Function of Subjective Certainty and the Utility of the Information*, Ph.D. Thesis, Stanford University, California, 1965.

————, "Information Needs and Uses", *in* Carlos A. Cuadra, ed., *Annual Review of Information Science and Technology*, Chicago: Encyclopaedia Britannica Inc., 1968: Vol. 3, 1-30.

Pelz, Donald C. and Frank M. Andrews, *Scientists in Organisations: Productive Climates for Research and Developments*, Michigan: The University of Michigan, Institute for Social Research, 1976.

Pings, Vern M. and Fanny Anderson, *Study of the Use of Wayne State University Medical Library*, Pt. 1, Detroit, Michigan: Wayne State University, School of Medicine Library and Biomedical Information Service Centre, 1965.

Price, Derek J. DeSolla, "Is Technology Historically Independent of Science?: A Study of Statistical Historiography", *Technology and Culture*, 6(4), Fall 1965: 553-68.

————, "Structures of Publications in Science and Technology", in William H. Gruber and Donald G. Marquis, eds., *Factors in Transfer of Technology*, Massachusetts, MIT Press, 1969: 91-104.

Pringgoadisurjo, Lawarsih, "Stimulating the Use of Information in a Developing Community", *in* A. Van Derbaan and A.A. Winters, ed., *The Use of Information in a Changing World: Proceedings of the Forty-second FID Congress held in the Hague*, the Netherlands, 24-27 September, 1984, Amsterdam: North-Holland, 1984: 77-82.

Pitchard, A., *Information Transfer: Some Applications of Graph Theory and the Geography of Transport*, Unpublished report, London: The City of London Polytechnic, 1977. Quoted from Pat Jones, *Some*

Social Aspects of Information Transfer, Research Report No. 4, London: The Polytechnic of North London, School of Library, 1981: 72.

Pruthi, S. and P.S. Nagpaul, "Communication Patterns in Small R&D Projects", *R&D Management*, 8(2), April 1978: 53-58.

Rafeel, Jeffrey A., "From Economic to Political Analysis of Library Decision-making", *College and Research Libraries*, 35, No. 6, November 1974: 412-23.

Raisig, Miles L. *et al.*, "How Biomedical Investigators Use Library Books", *Bulletin of the Medical Libraries Association*, 54, April 1966: 104-07.

Raitt, David Iain, *Communication and Information Seeking and Use Habits of Scientists and Engineers in International Organisations and National Aerospace Research Establishments in Europe*, Ph.D. Thesis, Loughborough: Loughborough University of Technology, 1984.

Rajagopalan, T.S. and Rajan, T.S., "Use of Information in Science and Research with Emphasis on National Development: Some Indian Experiences", *International Forum on Information and Documentation*, 9(3), July 1984: 3-9.

Ranganathan, S.R., "Psychology and the Nature of the Work of Users", *in* International Federation for Documentation, *Users of Documentation: Papers presented at the 35th Conference and International Congress of Documentation*, Benos Aires City, 14-24 September 1970, Paris: FID, 1970: 1-10.

Rao, N.P., *Survey of Scientific Literature and Information Activities in India (R&D) and Abroad (Global Studies in Growth Pattern)*, Delhi: Scientific Information Bureau, Defence Science Laboratory, 1966.

Rawdin, Eugene, "Field Survey of Information Needs of Industry Sci/ Tech Library Users", in *Proceedings of the 38th ASIS Annual Meeting*, New York: Greenwood, 1975: 12, 41-42.

Roberts, N. and Wilson, T.D., "The Development of User Studies at Sheffield University: 1963-88", *Journal of Librarianship*, 20(4), Oct. 1988: 270-90.

Robertson, S.E. and Sandy Hansman, "Journal Acquisition by Libraries: Scatter and Cost-effectiveness", *Journal of Documentation*, 31, No. 4, December 1979: 273-82.

Rosenberg, Victor, *Application of Psychometric Techniques to Determine the Attitudes of Individuals Toward Information Seeking*, MS Thesis, AD 637 713; AFOSR 724-66, Bethlehem, Pa.: Lehigh University, 1966.

Rosenberg, Victor, "Factors Affecting the Preferences of Industrial Personnel for Information Gathering Methods", *in* Tefko Saracevic Comp. & ed., *Introduction to Information Science*, New York: R.R. Bowker, 1970: 95-100.

Rosenbloom, Richard S. and Francis W. Wolek, *Technology and Information Transfer: A Survey of Practice in Industrial Organisations*, Boston: Harvard University, Graduate School of Business Administration, 1967.

Rosenbloom, Richard S. *et al.*, *Technology Transfer and the Flow of Technical Information in a Large Industrial Corporation*, 2 Vols., Cambridge, Massachusetts: Harvard University, Graduate School of Business Administration, 1965.

Rothwell, Roy and A.B. Robertson, "Contribution of Poor Communication to Innovation Failure", *Aslib Proceedings*, 27(10), October 1975: 393-400.

Rowley, J.E. and C.M.D. Turner, *Dissemination of Information*, London: Andre Deutsch/A Grafton Book, 1978.

Saha, J., "User Studies for Evaluation of Information System and Library Resources", in *Users of Documentation: Papers presented at 35th Conference and International Congress on Documentation*, Buenos Aires City, 14-24 September 1970, Paris: FID, 1970.

Sathyanarayana, R., *Categories of Users, their Information Requirements and Information Gathering Habits*, A Paper Presented at Fifth Information Officers Training Course (INFOTRAC V) 6-31 May 1985, Manila, Philippines. Organised by TECHNONET ASIA and APCTT National and International Transfer and Development, Paper II-2, N.p.n.p.

Schussel, George, "Advent of Information and Inquiry Services", *Journal of Data Management*, 7(9), September 1969: 24-31.

Scott, Christopher, "Science of Science: What Scientists Read and Why?", *Discovery*, 20(3), March 1959: 110-14.

————, "Use of Technical Literature by Industrial Technologists", in *Proceedings of the International Conference on Scientific Information*, Washington, D.C., 16-21 November 1958, Washington, D.C.: National Academy of Sciences, National Research Council, 1959, 1: 245-66 (Preprints, p. 235-56).

————, *Use of Technical Literature by Industrial Technologists: A Study of Technical Information in the Electrical Industry 1957-58* (Survey designed by Leslie T. Williams), The Social Survey Report No. 245, London: The Social Survey, 1960.

Shalini, R. and K.S. Chudamani, "Channel Selection by Indian Scientists for Communication", *in* R.N. Sharma and S. Seetharama, eds., *Proceedings of the Seminar on Primary Communications in Science and Technology in India*, 4-8 December 1978, Bangalore, New Delhi: CSIR, 1978: 103.

Shaw, Ralph R. Pilot, *Study of the Use of Scientific Literature by Scientists*, Washington, D.C./Metuchen, N.J.: NSF/Scarecrow Reprint Corporation, 1956/1971.

————, *Studies on the Use of Literature in Science and Technology*, Washington, D.C.: National Science Foundation, n.d.

Shefield, C. and Rosin, C., *Space Careers, Quill*, New York, 1984: 157-9.

Sherwin, C.W. and R.S. Inemson, *First Interim Report on Project Hindsight (Summary)*, Washington, D.C.: Office of the Director of Defence Research and Engineering, 13 October 1966. Quoted from Krishna Subramanayan, *Scientific and Technological Information Resources*, New York: Marcel Dekker Shuchman, Hedvah L., "Informal Information Networks and Woman in Engineering", *in* Benefield, A.R. and E.J. Kazlanskar, (eds.), *Communicating Information: Proceedings of the 43rd Annual Meeting*, Anaheim, California, 5-10 October 1980, Vol. 17, ASIS, New York, pp. 242-45, Inc., 1981: 14.

————, *Information Transfer in Engineering*, Rep-461-46-27, Connecticut: Futures Group Inc., 1981.

————, "Information Technology and the Technologist: A Report on a National Study of American Engineers", *International Forum on Information and Documentation*, 7(1), January 1982: 3-8.

Shuchman, Hedvah L., *Information Transfer in Engineering*, Rep-461-46-27, Connecticut: Futures Group Inc., 1981.

————, "Information Technology and the Technologist: A Report on a National Study of American Engineers", *International Forum on Information and Documentation*, 7(1), January 1982: 3-8.

Simpson, I.S., *How to Interpret Statistical Data: A Guide for Librarians and Information Scientists*, London: Library Association, 1990.

Singh, B.N., "Information Needs of Engineering Scientists", *International Library Review*, 13(2), April 1981: 167-88.

Singh, S.N., "Assessing Information Needs and Users: A State of the Art Report", *Herald of Library Science*, 18(1-2), January-April 1979: 38-45.

Singh, S.N., "Role of the Library in Communication Process and Information Flow: Seminar Proceedings", *Herald of Library Science*, 19(1-2), January-February 1980: 72-81.

Skelton, Barbara, "Scientists and Social Scientists as Information Users: A Comparison of Results of Science User Studies with the Investigation into Information Requirements of the Social Sciences", *Journal of Librarianship*, 5(2), April 1973: 138-56.

Slater, Margaret, *The Neglected Resource: Non-usage of Library Information Services in Industry and Commerce*, London: Aslib, 1981.

———, *Non-use of Library Information Resources at the Workplace: A Comparative Survey of Users and Nonusers of Onsite Industrial-Commercial Services*, London: Aslib, 1984.

———, ed., *Research Method in Library and Information Studies*, London: Library Association, 1990.

Slater, Margaret and P. Fisher, *Use Made of Technical Libraries*, Aslib Occasional Publication No. 2, London: Aslib 1969.

Sridhar, M.S., "A Mathematical Approach to Relations in Thesauri", *Journal of Library and Information Science*, 5, No. 1, January 1980: 77-79.

———, "Study of Library Visits and Inhouse Use of Library Documents by Indian Space Technologists", *Journal of Library and Information Science*, 7(2), December 1982: 146-58.

———, "User Participation in Collection Building in a Special Library: A Case Study", *IASLIC Bulletin*, 28(3), September 1983: 99-106.

———, "Document Reservation Pattern in a Special Library: A Case Study", *Library Science with a Slant to Documentation*, 20(1), March 1983: 39-48.

———, "Use of Technical Reports and Standards", *IASLIC Bulletin*, 29(3), September 1984: 99-106.

———, "Are Demand Forecasting Techniques Applicable to Libraries?" *Library Herald*, 23 (2&3), July-October 1984: 84-89.

———, "Study of Co-authorship and Collaborative Research among Indian Space Technologists", *R&D Management*, 15(3), July 1985: 243-49.

———, "Citing Pattern of Indian Space Technologists", *International Library Review*, 17(3), July 1985: 259-74.

———, "Book Procurement Delay: A Demotivator to User Participation in Collection Development", *in Building Library Collections and National Policy for Library and Information Services*, Seminar Papers of 30th All India Library Conference,

Rajasthan University, Jaipur, 28-31 January 1985, Delhi: ILA, 1985: 329-34.

Sridhar, M.S., "A Case Study of Lentout Use of a Special Library", *Library Science with a Slant to Documentation*, 22(1), March 1985: 19-34.

———, "Use of Current Journals by Indian Space Technologists", *The Serials Librarian*, 10(3), Spring 1986: 77-93.

———, "Subject and Longitudinal Use of Books by Indian Space Technologists", *Collection Management*, 8(1), Spring 1986: 101-15.

———, "Pattern of Card Catalogue Consultation in a Special Library", *IASLIC Bulletin*, 31(1), March 1986: 9-16.

———, *Study of Information Seeking Behaviour of Space Technologists with Emphasis on Correlating User Characteristics with such Behaviour*, Ph.D. Thesis, Mysore: University of Mysore, 1987.

———, "Information and Communication Behaviour of Women Space technologists", *R&D Management*, 17(4), October 1987: 301-09.

———, "Library-use Index and Library-interaction Index as Measures of Effectiveness of a Special Library: A Case Study", *in: Proceedings of XXXIV All India Library Conference on Library and Information Services: Assessment and Effectiveness*, Calcutta: ILA, 1988: 449-65.

———, "Is Cost Benefit Analysis Applicable to Journal-Use in a Special Library", *The Serials Librarian*, 15(1/2), 1988: 137-53.

———, "Sociometric Analysis of Information Communication among Indian Satellite Technologists", *Library Science with a Slant to Documentation and Information Studies*, 25(2), June 1988: 78-111.

———, "Customer-characteristics as Criteria for Market-segmentation in Libraries", *in* S.K. Kapoor and Amitabh Chatterjee, ed., *Marketing of Library and Information Services in India: Papers Presented at the 13th National Seminar of IASLIC*, Calcutta, 20-23 December 1988, IASLIC Special Publication No. 28, Calcutta: IASLIC, 1988: 43-52.

———, "Information-seeking Behaviour of the Indian Space Technologists", *Library Science with a Slant to Documentation and Information Studies*, 26(2), June 1989: 127-65.

———, "Patterns of User-visit, Movement and Length of Stay in a Special Library: A Case Study", *Annals of Library Science and Documentation*, 36(4), 1989: 134-38.

Sridhar, M.S., "Studies on Use of Library Collections by Scientists, Engineers and Technicians", *AGLIS Journal*, 7(4), December 1989: 9-17.

———, *User Research: A Review of Information Behaviour Studies in Science and Technology*, Bangalore: Biblio Infon Service, 1990.

———, "A Study of Correlation of Use, Citation and Publishing of Journal Papers by Indian Space Technologists", *Collection Management*, 12(112), 1990: 147-52.

———, "Information Requirements of the Indian Space Technologists", *Library Herald*, 29(3-4), October 1990-January 1991: 125-36.

———, "Review of Indian User Studies in Science and Technology", *in* Sharma, C.D. and Ojha, D.C., eds., *Advances in Library and Information Science v.3. Information Systems: Science and Technology*, Jodhpur: Scientific Publishers, 1992: Chapter 3, 31-55.

———, "Non-users and Non-use of Libraries", *Library Science with a Slant to Documentation and Information Studies*, 31(3), September 1994: 115-28.

———, *Information Behaviour of Scientists and Engineers*, New Delhi: Concept Publishing Company, 1995.

Srinivasan, S., "Impact of User Study in the Improvement of Documentation Services in Developing Countries", in *Users of Documentation: Papers Presented at the 35th Conference and International Congress of Documentation*, Buenos Aires City, 14-24 September 1970, Paris: FID, 1970: 1-14.

Stibic, V., *Personal Documentation for Professionals: Means and Methods*, Amsterdam: North Holland, 1980.

Stone, Sue and Harris, Colin, *Crus Guide 1, Designing a User Study: General Research Design*, Sheffield: British Library Board, 1984.

Thompson, James, *End of Libraries*, London: Clive Bingley, 1982.

Tornudd, Elin, "Study on the Use of Scientific Literature and Reference Services by Scandinavian Scientists and Engineers engaged in Research and Development", in *Proceedings of the International Conference on Scientific Information*, Washington, 16-21 November 1958, Washington, D.C.: National Academy of Sciences, National Research Council, 1959: 1, 9-65, Preprint 1.

Trueswell, Richard W. *et al.*, *Experiment in Measuring Certain Information Seeking Behaviour of X-Ray Crystallographers*, Technical Report No. 1, Illinois: Northwestern University, 1965.

University of Cambridge, Library Management Research Unit, "Factors Affecting the Use of Seats in Academic Libraries", *Journal of Librarianship*, 7(4), October 1975: 262-87.

University of Pittsburgh, The Senate Library Committee, The Study of Library Use at Pitt by Professor Allen Kent *et al.*, *A Pittsburgh Reply*, University of Pittsburgh, July 1979: 30-38.

Urquhart, D.J., "Physics Abstracting Use and Users", *Journal of Documentation*, 21(2), June 1965: 113-21.

U.S. Federal Council for Science and Technology, COSATI, *Recommendations for National Document Handling Systems in Science and Technology*, Washington, D.C.: U.S. Department of Commerce, 1965.

Van Cott, Harold P. and Robert G.A. Kincade, *Feasibility Study for Determining Requirements of Bibliographical Information Services and Systems*, Final Report AIR-F-57-11/67-TR-7, Washington, D.C.: American Institute for Research, 1967.

Vermaelen, C.H., "What About the Non-users of the Public Library?" *South African Journal for Librarianship and Information Science*, 49(1), July 1981: 10-14.

Voigt, Melvin J., "Researcher and his Sources of Scientific Information", *Libri*, 9(3), 1959: 177-93.

————, *Scientist's Approaches to Information*, Chicago: ALA, 1961.

Wade, N. "Citation Analysis: A New Tool for Science Administrations", *Science*, 188, 1975: 429-32.

Walford, A.J., "Circulation, Loan and Inter-library Loan", *in* Batten, W.E., ed., *Handbook of Special Librarianship and Information Work*, London: ASLIB, 1975: 285.

Weinberg, Alvin, "Science, Government and Information", *in* Manfred Kochen, ed., *The Growth of Knowledge: Readings on Organisation and Retrieval of Information*, New York: John Wiley, 1967: 36-59.

Wersig, Gernot, "Communication Theory and User Analysis: The Communication Theory Frame of Reference", in *Users of Documentation: Papers presented at the 35th Conference and International Congress of Documentation*, Buenos Aires City, 14-24 September 1970, Paris: FID, 1970: 1-13.

————, "Zur Systematick der Denutzerborschung", *Nachnichten fur Dokumentation*, 24(1), February 1973.

Wersig, Gernot and Gunther Windel, "Potential Basic Research on Users for New Orientation of Information Services", *International Forum on Information and Documentation*, 6(4), October 1981: 21-23.

White, Herbert S., "Cost-effectiveness and Cost-benefit Determinations in Special Libraries", *Special Libraries*, 70, No. 4, April 1979: 163-69.

Wilkin, Anne, *Information Needs of Practitioners: A Review of the Literature*, BLR & DD-5611, London: The London University, 1981.

Wills, Gordon and Christine Oldman, "An Examination of Cost Benefit Approaches to the Evaluation of Library and Information Services", *in* F.W. Lancaster and C.W. Cleverdon, ed., *Evaluation and Scientific Management of Libraries and Information Centres*, Leydon, Noordhoff, 1977: 165-84.

Wilson, Patrik, "The Catalog as Access Mechanism Background and Concepts", *Library Resources and Technical Services*, 27(1), Jan./Mar. 1983: 6-16.

————, *Public Knowledge and Private Ignorance: Toward a Library and Information Policy*, London: Greenwood Press, 1977.

Wilson, T.D., "On User Studies and Information Needs", *Journal of Documentation*, 37(1), March 1981: 3-15.

Wolek, Francis W., "Engineer: His Work and Needs for Information", *in* J.B. North, ed., *Proceedings of the 32nd Annual ASIS Meeting*, New York: Greenwood, 1969.

————, "The Complexity of Messages in Science and Engineering: An Influence on Patterns of Communication", *in* Carnot E. Nelson and Donald K. Pollock, eds., *Communication among Scientists and Engineers*, Massachusetts: D.C. Heath Lexington, 1970: 233-65.

————, "Preparation for Interpersonal Communication", *Journal of the American Society for Information Science*, 23(1), January-February 1972: 3-10.

————, "Managers and the Distribution of Scientific and Technical Information", *R&D Management*, 14(4), October 1984: 225-28.

Wood, D.N., "Where Mechanical Engineers Get their Technical Information", *The Chartered Mechanical Engineer*, 14(5), May 1967: 212-15, 220.

Wood, D.N. and D.R.L. Hamilton, *Information Requirements of Mechanical Engineers: Report of a Recent Survey*, London: The Library Association, 1967.

World Federation of Engineering Organisations, Committee on Engineering Information, *Engineer's Needs for Scientific and Technical Information* by A. David *et al.*, WFEO, 1979.

INDEX